162254

BCFTCS

£24.99

Ethics in Journalism

D1149352

Ethics in Journalism

6th Edition

Ron F. Smith

© 2008 by Ron F. Smith

BLACKWELL PUBLISHING
350 Main Street, Malden, MA 02148-5020, USA
9600 Garsington Road, Oxford OX4 2DQ, UK
550 Swanston Street, Carlton, Victoria 3053, Australia

The right of Ron F. Smith to be identified as the Author of this Work has been asserted
in accordance with the UK Copyright, Designs, and Patents Act 1988.

All rights reserved. No part of this publication may be reproduced, stored in a
retrieval system, or transmitted, in any form or by any means, electronic, mechanical,
photocopying, recording or otherwise, except as permitted by the UK Copyright,
Designs, and Patents Act 1988, without the prior permission of the publisher.

Designations used by companies to distinguish their products are often claimed as
trademarks. All brand names and product names used in this book are trade names,
service marks, trademarks, or registered trademarks of their respective owners.
The publisher is not associated with any product or vendor mentioned in this book.

This publication is designed to provide accurate and authoritative information in
regard to the subject matter covered. It is sold on the understanding that the publisher
is not engaged in rendering professional services. If professional advice or other expert
assistance is required, the services of a competent professional should be sought.

First edition published, 1983
Second edition published, 1987
Third edition published, 1994
Fourth edition published, 1999
Fifth edition published, 2003
This edition published 2008 by Blackwell Publishing Ltd

1   2008

Library of Congress Cataloging-in-Publication Data
Smith, Ron F.
[Groping for ethics in journalism]
Ethics in journalism / Ron F. Smith. – 6th ed.
   p. cm.
 Includes bibligraphical references and index.
 ISBN 978-1-4051-5934-0 (paperback)
1. Journalistic ethics–United States. I. Title.

PN4888. E8G66 2008
174′. 907–dc22

                                   2007028078

A catalogue record for this title is available from the British Library.

Set in 10.5/13 Sabon
by Newgen Imaging Systems (P) Ltd, Chennai, India
Printed and bound in Singapore
by Utopia Press Pte Ltd

The publisher's policy is to use permanent paper from mills that operate a sustainable forestry policy, and
which has been manufactured from pulp processed using acid-free and elementary chlorine-free practices.
Furthermore, the publisher ensures that the text paper and cover board used have met acceptable environmental accreditation standards.

For further information on
Blackwell Publishing, visit our website:
www.blackwellpublishing.com

To Rene

UCB

UCB

Contents

List of Illustrations

Preface

Chances are, if you're reading this book you're planning a career in TV or newspaper journalism. If you're like many of us, you chose your career because you like to write and think you're pretty good at it. Or maybe you want the excitement and prestige of being an anchor on TV. Or perhaps you want the challenge of meeting lots of people, ranging from the powerful and the famous to the powerless and forgotten.

You understand why you are required to take courses in news writing and editing. Your employers are going to expect you to perform these tasks. And you probably won't balk at taking a mass-media law course. You know you don't want to lose a million-dollar libel suit.

However, why must you read books like this one? Why must you study journalism ethics? I'm going to offer four reasons. You and your instructor are welcome to add to this list.

- You need to think about what your role is as a journalist. Journalism plays a greater role than just allowing us to satisfy our desire to write, to be on TV, or to have the proverbial front-row seats to history. Journalists give communities an opportunity to see themselves. We point out the problems in society and show its successes. We are also playing a role in America's experiment in self-government by informing voters about their government. If we lose sight of the important role the news media play in American society, our society will be the worse for it.
- Journalism is going through a tough time. Nearly every poll shows that people are losing respect for journalists and that they doubt if they can trust the news media. Their dissatisfaction is not with journalists'

technical abilities. It is with our ethics and our sense of what our role is in society. Your technical skills as a writer, editor, or producer are not going to amount to much if the public doesn't believe you.

- Some of the behavior of journalists stems from a basic lack of morality. We can at least understand the motives of a reporter who, hot in the chase of a story, bends the rules. But there is no defense for reporters at major papers who make up stories wholesale or manufacture quotes from nonexistent sources. Yet, unfortunately, reporters have done that at some of our best newspapers, including *The New York Times* and *USA Today*. You are entering the profession at a time when you will have to regain the moral high ground. Our democracy demands an informed citizenry, and your job will be to make sure that journalism fulfills that role.

- Journalism ethics continue to be challenged by problems in ownership. There is no question that good corporate owners can foster quality news organizations. The first chapter of this book highlights the quality of news projects at news organizations, two of which are owned by large corporations. But as corporate owners feel the pressure of investors, they too often take steps to boost their bottom lines by cutting staff and thus reducing the quality of their journalism. It will fall on your shoulders to try to practice ethical journalism in an environment that is filled with hindrances.

As you read this book, challenge yourself. Put yourself in each story that opens a chapter. If you were in that situation, how would you handle the problem? What responsibilities do the journalists have to their sources, their readers and viewers, and their employers? Are there other ways to handle the problem? But also ask yourself how you would react to the reporter's conduct if you were a source. And ask yourself what impact the story would have on you as a reader or viewer. Chapter 2 offers some insights on how philosophers have approached ethical problems and provide some additional factors to consider.

Many people helped me as I continued the work of Professor Eugene Goodwin, whose first edition of *Groping for Ethics in Journalism* won the Frank Luther Mott-Kappa Tau Alpha Research award in 1983. Foremost is Rene Stutzman, a reporter in the *Orlando Sentinel's* Sanford bureau. As a first-rate journalist, she provided valuable insight as we discussed many of the cases covered in this book. And as my wife, she tolerated my secluding myself in my office working on the book.

About a dozen other newspaper and TV reporters, editors, and anchors read parts of the book. Their contributions were vital in ensuring the accuracy and completeness of the material. Also, I thank the reporters and editors at *The Tampa Tribune* for helping me to a better understanding of convergence, and those at the *South Florida Sun-Sentinel* for letting me sit in on some of their meetings.

My students have also shaped this work. Many have done so directly. Michelle Martinez and Maureen Tisdale made key contributions to sections on diversity. Other students have also helped track down references and anecdotes. As anyone who has taught can attest, my students, through class discussion and written work, have broadened my understanding of the issues. They have also been candid in their critiques of early drafts of the manuscript, helping me to avoid dry passages and reduce some of the long-windedness that marked earlier editions.

Blackwell Publishing assigned a great staff to this endeavor. Production editor Lisa Eaton kept the project moving forward gracefully. As a former copy editor myself, I was most impressed with the work of Sally Landsdell. Her detailed editing of the manuscript saved me from some embarrassing mistakes.

Despite the quality of the people who read portions of the manuscript, the observations of my students, and the care taken by Blackwell Publishing staff, I am sure you will find an occasional mistake. We'll try to get it right next time. If you have comments or questions about the book, feel free to e-mail me at rsmith@mail.ucf.edu.

Ron F. Smith
Professor
University of Central Florida

Part 1 Principles and Guidelines

1   The Search for Principles

Imagine a city as big as New York suddenly grafted onto North Carolina's Coastal Plain. Double it. Now imagine that this city has no sewage treatment plants. All the wastes from 15 million inhabitants are simply flushed into open pits and sprayed onto fields.

Turn those humans into hogs, and you don't have to imagine at all. It's already here.

A vast city of swine has risen practically overnight in the counties east of Interstate 95. It's a megalopolis of 7 million animals that live in metal confinement barns and produce two to four times as much waste, per hog, as the average human.

All that manure – about 9.5 million tons a year – is stored in thousands of earthen pits called lagoons, where it is decomposed and sprayed or spread on crop lands.

That's the beginning of a series of news stories that appeared in *The News & Observer* in Raleigh, N.C. Having that much manure in your backyard can lead to problems. The paper talked to experts and reported:

- New scientific studies had determined that contaminants from hog lagoons are getting into groundwater. One North Carolina State University report estimated that as many as half of existing lagoons – perhaps hundreds – are leaking badly enough to contaminate groundwater.
- Scientists are discovering that hog farms emit large amounts of ammonia gas, which returns to earth in rain. The ammonia is believed to be contributing to an explosion of algae growth that is choking many of the state's rivers and estuaries.

- Experts said the odor is absorbed by the fatty tissues in the human body: "That's why some people say they can smell the odor on their breath long after they left the farm."
- The odor may be more than a nuisance. A Duke University researcher said that it was affecting residents' mental health. She found that people living near large hog farms experienced "more tension, more depression, more anger, less vigor, more fatigue and more confusion."

With all the concerns about the environment and health of the residents, you might imagine that government agencies were trying to do something about this dangerous situation. Guess again. According to *The News & Observer* series:

> You don't have to look hard to spot the pork industry's connections in North Carolina politics and government. Just start at the top.
>
> U.S. Sen. Lauch Faircloth, a Republican who leads a congressional subcommittee on the environment, is a wealthy hog farmer.
>
> Democratic Gov. Jim Hunt is the top recipient of political contributions from Wendell H. Murphy, whose Duplin County hog company is the biggest in the nation.
>
> The chairman of the environment committee in the state House, Republican John M. Nichols, is building a large hog operation in Craven County and will raise pigs for Murphy.
>
> The chairman of the Senate committee on environment and agriculture, Democrat Charles W. Albertson of Duplin County, is a friend of Murphy's, and – judging from contributions – the pork industry's favorite legislator...
>
> To people with grievances against big pork, the alliances look like a power bloc.
>
> "We have not found a sympathetic ear anywhere," said Robert Morgan of Lillington, a former U.S. senator who represents plaintiffs in four lawsuits against large-scale hog farms.

The ethics rules of the North Carolina Legislature do not bar representatives with a personal stake in a bill from pushing it in the Legislature. So it was considered both legal and ethical for one hog producer to be elected to the General Assembly and then to help pass laws worth millions of dollars to his company and his industry.

The "King Hog" series was a major project for *The News & Observer*. Special projects editor Melanie Sill and reporters Pat Stith and Joby Warrick spent seven months interviewing hundreds of people and searching through mounds of records. Photographers, graphic artists, and editors also worked on the project. The result was a series of stories that provided a detailed portrait of the growth of hog factories and stirred many North Carolinians to reconsider the factories' impact on the state.[1] The series won a Pulitzer Prize for public service.

In Houston, television station KHOU opened its 10 o'clock program with a report by its Defenders investigative team. Reporter Anna Werner began the segment like this:

ANNA WERNER:	It was a new marriage for Cynthia and C.J. Jackson.
CYNTHIA JACKSON:	We were just two middle-aged people trying to start over and to have fun.
WERNER:	So one June day this choir teacher and her husband packed up her Ford Explorer.
JACKSON:	He says let's just take a ride.
WERNER:	And they took off for Galveston. But as Jackson drove back north something went horribly wrong.
JACKSON:	As I went to change lanes, I heard a pop.
WERNER:	What she heard was the tread coming off a back tire, a Firestone Radial ATX that came with the car.
JACKSON:	I yelled at my husband, hey baby wake up! The truck is shaking!
WERNER:	Then the car began to roll.
JACKSON:	Next thing I remember waking up in the hospital.
WERNER:	And she was facing bad news. Both of her legs would have to be amputated below the knee. But worst of all, her husband of a year and a half was dead... leaving her with one haunting memory.
WERNER:	So the last time you remember seeing CJ was when he looked up... do you find yourself thinking about that?
JACKSON:	(whispered) Yes...
WERNER:	Now, she does the best she can with a life that's very different than the one she had planned.

Werner then reported a story about a 14-year-old cheerleader who was riding in a Ford Explorer on her way to a homecoming pep rally. One of the Explorer's Firestone tires came apart at highway speed. The vehicle flipped three times, killing the girl. Werner told viewers:

Those are just two of many similar cases the Defenders found all over Texas – as many as a dozen over the past few years. And all of them have a familiar combination: a Ford Explorer and a Firestone ATX tire with what's called tread separation, where the tread literally peels off the tire. When that happens, experts say, with some vehicles it can mean a devastating rollover crash.

Werner's report lasted for nearly 10 minutes. In gathering information for it, Werner not only talked to local accident victims, she had traveled to Washington to talk to a former head of the National Transportation Safety Board. She interviewed an expert on tire construction and a former employee of Firestone Tires who admitted that he had made bad tires. She tracked down similar accidents involving Explorers and Firestone tires in other states.

Werner also contacted Ford and the Bridgestone/Firestone tire company and asked them to give their side of the story. A Ford spokesperson told her that the Explorers were not to blame: It was "driver error" that caused the problems. Firestone would not comment on the air, but sent a letter saying the company stood by the safety of its tires.

Immediately after Werner's report was broadcast, viewers flooded the station with reports of other accidents involving Explorers with Firestone tires. Werner began to put together a follow-up story. When Firestone officials learned she was doing another report, they fired off a letter to executives at the A.H. Belo Co., the owners of the station. The letter accused Werner of "falsehoods and misrepresentations" in her reports about the tires. "This series has unmistakably delivered the false messages that Radial ATX tires are dangerous, that they threaten the safety of anyone using them, and that they should be removed from every vehicle on which they are installed," a Firestone vice president wrote in the letter. "Each of these messages is simply untrue." Furthermore, Firestone charged, KHOU was more concerned with "sensationalism and ratings" than serving its viewers. If the station really wanted to help Houston-area drivers, it would do reports on "proper tire maintenance procedures" and "proper driving methods."

Although the letter did not mention libel or directly threaten lawsuits, it was clear that Firestone meant business. Other media were slow to pick up the story. It was months before newspapers and networks started writing about the potential problems. A KHOU journalist told *The New York Times* that he thought the strongly worded letter from Firestone may help explain why other news media stayed away. Nevertheless, the letter did not scare off KHOU. The station broadcast a nine-minute segment by Werner in which she reported more accidents caused by defective tires.

Months after KHOU's first reports, the National Highway Safety Agency opened an investigation that concluded KHOU was right. Bridgestone/Firestone began to recall 6.5 million tires. As Rep. Billy Tauzin of Louisiana said, "It took a television station's publicly embarrassing the agency to get the agency off the dime." *The New York Times* editorial-ized, "Had it not been for a Houston television report on the problem that triggered a spate of complaints to the agency earlier this year, most drivers would still be unaware of their danger."[2]

The series won the station and Werner several honors, including a Sigma Delta Chi award from the Society of Professional Journalists and a prestigious Peabody Award.

In Springfield, Ill., Scott Reeder heard parents and teachers ask each other why incompetent teachers were never fired. The answer was always the same: "They can't fire him – he's got tenure." Reeder, however, isn't an ordinary parent who frets about the quality of his child's education. Reeder covers state government in Illinois for newspapers in Kankakee, Ottawa, Moline, and Rock Island. He decided to find out how difficult it was for schools to fire bad teachers.

The task was not easy. Illinois does not have particularly good public-record laws that would require government to provide reporters with the information they want. Teacher records were even harder to obtain because they were spread among the state's 876 school districts, and personnel records were often sealed. But Reeder was undaunted. He had another reporter take over the routine stories he normally would have written. In the next six months, he:

- Filed 1,500 Freedom of Information Act requests demanding that school districts show him their public records. On one occasion, his newspaper company had to file a lawsuit and get a court order before Reeder could see the records.
- Read every arbitration case involving a schoolteacher and a school district.
- Spent countless hours poring through court records and legal documents and tabulating the results.
- Interviewed hundreds of people, including parents, students, teachers, lawyers, and experts in education.
- Conducted one of the largest media document searches in the history of Cook County, which is the home of Chicago.

Reeder had set aside six months to work on this one story. He quickly learned that there was so much to do the investigation became more than a full-time job. "I worked straight through a number of weekends," Reeder said. "I didn't take vacation and even found myself inputting data on a laptop computer in a hospital maternity ward as my wife and newborn daughter slept nearby."

What did his investigation uncover? It is extremely rare for a tenured teacher in Illinois to be fired. Reeder found one small rural district that had spent more than $400,000 in attorney fees to fire one teacher – and the case was still in the courts. One district could not fire an assistant principal who fathered a child by one of the seventh-graders at his school. The courts ordered him to pay child support, but he kept his job.

Reeder also discovered:

- Illinois has about 95,000 tenured teachers, but on average only two are fired each year for incompetence.
- In the past 10 years, 94 percent of the districts had never even attempted to fire a tenured teacher.
- During that time, 84 percent had never given a tenured teacher an unsatisfactory rating on year-end evaluations. "Just about everyone gets an 'excellent' or 'superior' rating," one superintendent told him.

Reeder thinks the reason so few bad teachers are detected and fired in Illinois has to do with the clout of the state's teacher unions. On a statewide level, they are the largest contributors to the political campaigns of Illinois legislators. They have forked over more than $16 million in the past 12 years. On the local level, teachers sometimes elect their bosses. School board elections are often off year, meaning they occur when there are no highly publicized races like those for president or governor. Only a handful of people vote. Observers say the teacher unions get the voters out for those minor elections and elect candidates favorable to teachers. Most districts don't have the money for big pay raises. So when the unions ask for job security instead of pay, the boards happily agree to rules that make it difficult to identify and remove teachers who are underperforming.[3]

The above three reports are examples of thoroughly reported, well-told news stories. Nearly everyone would agree that they are first-rate journalism. We would take that a step further and say that they exemplify "ethical journalism."

They made life better for lots of people. *The News & Observer*'s King Hog informed citizens about a major development in their state and heightened voters' awareness of an important societal issue. The journalists showed compassion for people who lacked the political clout to make their concerns known. Editors and managers were willing to expose some of the state's most powerful businesspeople and politicians.

Undoubtedly, KHOU improved the safety of thousands of motorists. The series challenged the federal government to investigate these cases. KHOU went ahead with the stories even though the station was taking on two major corporations that spend lots of money on television advertising. When Scott Reeder wondered why Illinois public schools just didn't fire the bad teachers, he started on a course of action resulting in reforms that may improve the quality of public education in Illinois.

These reports illustrate another truth about the ethics of journalism. Unlike most lawyers and many doctors, most journalists do not work for themselves. These journalists worked for managements that displayed courage in shielding the news team from the pressure of powerful people in business and government. They were willing to free reporters to work for months on stories – instead of limiting them to stories that can be quickly reported in order to fill the news hole. *The News & Observer*, KHOU and Reeder's Small Newspapers Group gave the journalists the time and support they needed to create quality, ethical journalism.

Journalism and Ethics

To many, "ethical journalism" is an oxymoron in the same category as "jumbo shrimp" and "military intelligence." In an Internet discussion group for journalists, a police reporter ridiculed ethical questions as "mental masturbation for people who want to get master's degrees." He's not the only journalist who has a faulty understanding of ethics. Perhaps the most common misconceptions are these:

- Some think of ethics only as a list of rules that spell out what they can and cannot do: Do not accept freebies, do not engage in activities that may create a conflict of interest, do not plagiarize, etc.
- Others fear that if reporters get "too ethical," they will produce wishy-washy journalism: They will be so concerned about hurting someone's feelings or doing the wrong thing that they will not pursue the truth aggressively.
- And some write off the whole area as little more than a public relations ploy to make people like reporters. Reporters aren't supposed to be liked, they say. They're supposed to report the news.

But ethics is broader than these people recognize. As will be discussed in Chapter 2, most philosophers consider ethics to be the study of the distinctions between right or wrong, virtuous and vicious, beneficial and harmful. Professions place more specific ethical demands on their practitioners. Lawyers, for example, are required to give their clients the best possible defense even if they doubt their innocence. Physicians swear they will do no harm to their patients. Priests and psychologists are obliged not to repeat what they are told during confession or counseling.

Just as lawyers, doctors, and priests have special responsibilities, journalists too have obligations that define their profession. Although some might quibble with this list, most American journalists would agree that they share these goals:

- To inform the public about incidents, trends, and developments in society and government. Journalists are obliged to gather information as best they can and to tell the truth as they find it. They must be undaunted in their pursuit of truth and unhampered by conflicting interests.
- To treat people – both those in their audience and those who are making news – with fairness, respect, and even compassion. It does journalists little good to strive for the truth if a large number of people do not believe news reports because they do not trust or respect the news media.
- To nurture the democratic process. For people to govern themselves, they must be informed about the issues and the actions of their government. The news media are the chief providers of that information.

Journalism and democratic society

The expectation that journalists should explore both social and political issues has long been fundamental in the United States. Even before the American Revolution, newspapers were leading fights on religious, health, and political issues. For example, a newspaper founded by Ben Franklin's older brother, James, clashed with Puritan clergy on the issue of smallpox inoculations. As the Revolution neared, colonists used pamphlets and newspapers to rally support against England. After the British imposed the hated Stamp Act, interest in politics grew and so did the number of American newspapers. These publications were so much a part of American intellectual life that once the new country was established, the First Amendment to the Constitution guaranteed press freedom.

Although historians debate what the Founding Fathers had in mind when they wrote the First Amendment, early American editors believed they understood what their role was to be in this new democracy.

Their comments sound very modern. One South Carolina editor argued that as long as newspapers were keeping tabs on Congress, senators could not "betray their trust; convert serious matters into jokes; or transfer mountains into molehills." Another editor interpreted the First Amendment much as the Supreme Court would more than 180 years later in its ruling in *Times* v. *Sullivan*. He wrote, "Considerable Latitude must be allowed in the Discussion of Public Affairs, or the Liberty of the Press will be of no Benefit to Society."[4] To these Colonial journalists, freedom of the press was vital if the American experiment in democracy was to work.

Modern editors feel much the same way. "If you look at the history of this country . . . the thing that makes this experiment in government unique among democracies has been the continued independence of the daily newspaper serving as a critic and watchdog of government," said James D. Squires, when he was editor of the *Chicago Tribune*. "It goes hand in hand with us being the forum in which the political debate is played out."[5] Thrity Umrigar, a reporter for the *Akron Beacon Journal*, contended that "journalism is an idealistic profession. It is based on the hopeful belief that if readers know the truth, they will make intelligent, informed decisions that will change things for the better. The power of the pen, the freedom of the press, the First Amendment, are optimistic, even joyous ideals."[6]

Some worry that many journalism students today do not appreciate the role that journalism plays in democracy. Studies have found that many students gravitate to print journalism because they have been told they can write. Likewise, a recent study found that about half the students majoring in broadcast news were drawn to what was called the "actor" side of the business. They wanted to be television personalities.[7] Neither group is drawn by the core principles of journalism. When some students begin work in the news media, they develop an understanding of the importance of journalism and see the impact they can have. Unfortunately, others never catch on. They take a cynical view of their profession and that cynicism is often reflected in the quality of their work.

Journalists as watchdogs

Journalists have been talking about their "watchdog role" since the early days of the American republic. Another popular phrase used to define the role of journalists is relatively new. "The public's right to know" became a mantra of American journalists after World War II as journalists fought to expand access to information about government.

The idea that journalists are watchdogs in their communities is common in the English-speaking world. American journalists – particularly newspaper journalists – overwhelmingly embrace the watchdog role. A large-scale survey found that about two-thirds of American journalists said investigating government claims was among their top priorities.[8] British and Australian journalists are even more committed to the watchdog role, with more than 80 percent of them listing it among the most important roles for the news media.

Journalists in some other nations see their role differently. Only 12 percent of journalists in Germany and 25 percent in the Netherlands consider investigating government claims to be an important role of the news media. They – like many other European journalists – are more likely to consider analyzing and interpreting the news as a major responsibility.[9] Adam Gopnik wrote in *The New Yorker*, "French journalists tend to think that there are more interesting things to do in life than to pester some politician or official who has never said anything interesting in the first place for one more quote." The strength of France's most important paper *Le Monde* is not its exhaustive reporting but its large section of editorials and opinion pieces, Gopnik said.[10] One group of researchers decided that the differences in news cultures were so distinct they identified journalists' attitudes as either Anglo-American or European-Continental.

Many American political and news blogs combine American watchdog spirit with heavy doses of analysis. These blogs are so different from American mainstream media that many refuse to label them "journalism." Because most of them do little original reporting, veteran journalist Michael Shear told a convention of bloggers, "You are political activists. You are gossips. You are agitators. You are not journalists."[11] Others see blogs as "participatory journalism," because they convey news and invite input from so many sources including traditional media, other bloggers, and their own readers.

Whether or not their work qualifies them for the title "journalists," there can be little doubt that many bloggers take very seriously their watchdog role in their niche areas. Columnist Arrianna Huffington, whose Huffington Post is one of the largest blogs, calls bloggers "the true pit bulls of reporting." She notes that bloggers have taken big bites out of several major politicians in recent years. Powerful Republican Sen.

Trent Lott was brought down after he seemed to wax fondly about the days of racial segregation in the South. "Bloggers turned him from Senate majority leader into political chum by pursuing a story the mainstream media passed on," Huffington wrote.[12] After Sen. George Allen of Virginia used what apparently was a racist term in a speech, blogs kept the story alive and uncovered other allegations from Allen's past. He was narrowly defeated in his re-election bid. Web sites had such an impact on the 2006 elections that *The New York Times* said it was America's first blogger and YouTube election and predicted these new media outlets would play an even bigger role in national politics.[13]

Public doubts its self-proclaimed watchdogs

While mainstream journalists in Britain, Australia, and the United States may envision themselves as watchdogs protecting the public from governmental misconduct, many in the public would prefer to have protection from the media. The public has lost much of its faith in news people. In Australia, journalists were rated below used-car salespeople in one survey. In Britain only 15 percent of the public said they expected newspaper journalists to tell them the truth, while 52 percent expected to be told the truth by total strangers.[14] Another survey found that only 20 percent of people in Britain had trust in their newspapers. That was the lowest among European Union countries, even lower than Italy where, at the time of the survey, the prime minister owned many of the nation's television networks and newspapers and required them to support his policies. Trust was highest in Belgium, Luxembourg, and Finland; about 60 percent of their populations said they trusted the news media.[15]

Americans' respect for journalists is plummeting. In the 1980s, the American public had as much trust in the news media as it did in most other aspects of society and only 16 percent of the public gave low credibility ratings to their daily newspaper. Today that figure is 45 percent. "Public trust in the three broadcast networks, leading news magazines (*Time* and *Newsweek*), and CNN also fell," Carroll Doherty, associate director of the Pew Center, wrote. "The percentage saying they could trust little of what they saw on ABC News rose from 13 percent to 36 percent, CNN from 15 percent to 28 percent, and so on." The public is, at best, unsure about trusting the news media as its watchdog. "After all, more and more citizens each year don't think they can trust the press at all," Doherty concluded.[16]

Other researchers suggest that Americans have lost sight of the importance the Founding Fathers put in the news media. Only 14 percent were able to name freedom of the press as one of the freedoms protected by the First Amendment. [Americans were more likely to see freedom of religion as essential to a democracy as they were freedom of the press.] About 43 percent said they thought the news media had "too much freedom." Almost one in four believed government should be able to censor newspapers.[17] It is dumbfounding that so many Americans would rather have government bureaucrats editing the news than journalists.

And matters may be getting worse. High-school students appear to offer even less support to press freedom. More than one in three high-school students told researchers that they thought the Constitution goes "too far" in the rights it guarantees. About half the students said they would have no objection to laws that would require the news media to get government approval before reporting stories. "These results are not only disturbing; they are dangerous," Hodding Carter III, president of the foundation that funded the study, told the Associated Press. "Ignorance about the basics of this free society is a danger to our nation's future."[18]

Perhaps the most damning indictment of the press was reported in a large-scale survey by journalism professor Robert O. Wyatt a few years ago. Although Americans pride themselves on living in a free country, he found that they probably would not ratify the First Amendment if it were on the ballot today.[19]

Are things really that bad?

Here's a conundrum. Many would argue that today's news coverage is much better than that of, say, 40 years ago. Both television and newspaper reporting today provides more thorough stories on a wider variety of topics. Advances in technology allow television news programs to provide live reports on most breaking stories. Newspapers are emphasizing in-depth stories. The Internet has created hundreds of new sources of information and commentary. Today's journalists are better trained, better educated, better paid, and more professional than ever before. They may even be more ethical than most people. A study using a standard sociological test of moral and ethical reasoning found that journalists were more "sophisticated moral thinkers" than people in most professions were. They concluded: "Thinking like a journalist involves moral reflection, done at a level that in most instances equals or exceeds members of other learned professions."[20]

Researchers have compared how journalists see themselves and how the public sees them. "Journalists believe they are working in the public interest, and are trying to be fair and independent in that cause," they concluded. "The public thinks these journalists are either lying or deluding themselves. The public believes that news organizations are operating largely to make money, and that the journalists who work for these organizations are primarily motivated by professional ambition and self-interest."[21]

Many have tried to explain this mystery by pointing out that Americans' respect for all organizations, including churches, schools, and government, has declined. To some degree they are right. Yet none of these groups has lost as much respect as the news media.

It may be that a combination of factors has soured the public's view of journalists. One may be that the public is more familiar with how the news is gathered and that familiarity has bred contempt. Not long ago, if a politician or military leader held a press conference, the public would either read about it in the newspaper or watch highlights on the evening news. The public would never know whether journalists asked stupid questions or behaved brutishly. Today, the news conference is likely to be broadcast live. The public can see journalists in action. Often that isn't pretty.

The 24-hour television news networks have had an impact, too. Some of the coverage has been impressive, particularly of the 9-11 attacks. Yet, the 24-hour news cycle combined with the constant hunt for ratings has also caused cable news to overplay meaningless stories. Police chasing a stolen car in California suddenly becomes national news. A teenager missing in the Aruba, while certainly a news story, receives the same massive coverage as the outbreak of war. Also, cable news has created the "rant shows" in which guests are encouraged to have angry arguments. These programs are often hosted by news personalities who blur the roles of news anchor, talk-show host, columnist, commentator, and reporter. For example, Bill O'Reilly on Fox News objects to being called a reporter, preferring the term "analyst." Yet many Americans are unaware of the distinction and judge all journalists by his behavior.[22]

Journalists are also under attack by many politicians who have discovered that bashing the media is an effective campaign tactic. "The media is everybody's favorite whipping boy," said Matthew T. Felling, media director of a nonpartisan media research center. "When politicians attack each other, it's irritating partisan politics. But when politicians attack the media, everybody jumps on board." If a campaign hits a bad snag, candidates prefer not to acknowledge a problem. They will portray themselves as the victims of a vicious, biased press.[23] News talk shows – sometimes out of an obligation to provide balanced coverage – discuss the candidates' attacks on the media, thus amplifying the criticism and undoubtedly reinforcing negative opinions of the media in many people's minds.

Television shows also shape some perceptions of journalists. Only police officers and lawyers are shown more often than journalists are during entertainment programs on prime-time television. But these portrayals are rarely flattering. Only 14 percent of the fictional newspaper reporters and 24 percent of their television brethren are shown favorably, according to one study. Most reporters are depicted as unethical, sloppy, insensitive, and foolish.[24]

Although some recent movies have provided positive images of journalists, that is not generally the case. After viewing more than 1,000 films depicting journalists, one researcher in the early 1990s said only a few showed journalists as the least bit competent.[25] A *New York Times* story about reporters in films was headlined "Movies Blast Media, Viewers Cheer." Glenn Garelik pointed out that the image of reporters has changed. The wisecracking of earlier reporters has become arrogance, and reporters who had been shown as the working-class enemies of pretension are now seen as pretentious themselves.[26] As the public's respect for journalists continued to erode in the 2000s, another *Times* writer Caryn James contended that the movies are treating journalists even worse. James wrote: "The more that confidence plummets, the more likely movies are to portray reporters unfavorably; and, in a snowball effect, the more unsavory reporters appear on screen, the more that image takes hold." As an example, she cited what she called a "throw-away scene" in the movie *Cinderella Man* in which an insensitive journalist makes a boxer's wife cry by asking her if she thinks her husband will be killed in the ring.[27]

The American public has also become aware that the media are owned by huge, out-of-state businesses that are more concerned with the bottom line than the public good. Although journalists, particularly print journalists, may see themselves as independent seekers of truth, to many of the public they are just lackeys working for corporate America. When corporations cut the number of reporters covering the news, they are reinforcing the public's belief that the primary role of newspapers is to fill the pockets of wealthy owners – not to provide a public service.

Another factor in the decline in respect for journalists is the tendency of many people to lump all news outlets into a monolith. Phrases like "the mainstream media" (MSM) mask a dizzying variety of news media. The term lumps together cable news debate programs like "The O'Reilly Factor" with *The New York Times,* crime-riddled local television news in some markets with the network's nightly news, and Geraldo Rivera's grandstanding with Jim Lehrer's sober *News Hour* on PBS. This MSM monolith becomes one big, easy-to-attack entity. For example, after the death of Princess Diana, early news accounts erroneously suggested that freelance photographers, the paparazzi, caused the car crash that killed her. The next day, photographers working for news outlets in small-town America were cursed by passers-by as "the killers of Di." When a reporter at a news conference asked a woman who said she had an affair with President Bill Clinton if he used condoms, many people condemned the conduct of insensitive reporters. The question was asked by a "reporter" from Howard Stern's radio program, which prides itself on its tastelessness.

The British public is less likely to tar all media with the actions of some. They routinely divide their newspapers into the "red-top tabloids" and the "quality broadsheets." In the past, the terms referred to the actual size of the printed pages in these papers, with tabloids being smaller newspapers about the size of the American grocery-store tab *National Enquirer.* Although the British papers today are mostly the same size, the names and their connotations still stick. British tabloids like *The Sun, News of the World,* and *The Daily Mirror* package their news with sensationalized, sometimes exaggerated reports and pictures of scantily clad women. On the other hand, Britain's quality broadsheets like *The Guardian* and *Independent* are among the world's most respected newspapers with solid reporting and analysis. The British have great respect for the public-supported BBC, which some consider the world's pre-eminent broadcast news source.

Improving the Profession

The chapter opened with portions of *The News & Observer*'s "King Hog" series, KHOU's report on Firestone tires, and Scott Reeder's work on

Illinois education. They are excellent examples of "ethical journalism." To produce these exceptional series, the journalists:

- *Practiced the principles of ethical journalism.* They found stories that shed light on a part of society that probably had been overlooked by many people. And they were diligent in finding the facts. The King Hog series told the voters of North Carolina about some of the actions of their state government and their elected officials. The KHOU series warned consumers about a hazard and prompted government regulators to do something about it. Reeder spent months looking through public documents and filed more than 1,500 public-information requests when bureaucrats were not forthcoming.
- *Were talented at their crafts.* To be ethical and credible, journalists must be competent at what they do. If a story is incomplete or has errors, the public is misinformed. And if the story is not told well, the public may not bother to read it or watch it on television. Most of us will not wade through a sea of bad writing, dull video, and uninspired design.
- *Worked for a strong news organization.* The News & Observer, Small Newspapers, and KHOU gave them the support and time they needed to produce their stories. And management stood behind the journalists as they challenged influential political figures and powerful corporations. While first-rate journalism is produced every day in second-rate newsrooms, having enlightened owners and managers is often a major ingredient in the practice of ethical journalism.

Notes

1. The "King Hog" series was written by Melanie Sill, Pat Stith, and Joby Warrick. It ran in *The News & Observer* from February 19 to 28, 1995. It is on the Internet at www.pulitzer.org. For the aftermath, see Craig Whitlock, "NandO hog series takes top Pulitzer, Public service prize rewards stories on pork industry," *The News & Observer*, April 10, 1996, p. A-1.
2. Information about the KHOU reports came from "Defenders Investigate Accidents," aired on KHOU, August 10, 2000: "Local TV uncovered national scandal," *The New York Times*, September 13, 2000; "11 News Defenders: Firestone ATX Tires," aired October 5, 2000; Richard Connelly, "Rubber fetish: Glory days for KHOU and Anna Werner," *New Times*, September 28, 2000; "Firestone letter to Belo and KHOU executives," posted

on KHOU Web site, February 10, 2000: Alicia C. Shepard, "Local heroes," *American Journalism Review,* December 2000; "What they are saying about KHOU's groundbreaking Firestone stories," posted on KHOU Web site.

3. Scott Reeder's series on Illinois schools is online at www.thehidden-costsoftenure.com. They appeared in Small Newspapers in 2005. Also see Scott Reeder, "Teacher failures," *IRE Journal,* March/April 2006.

4. William David Sloan, James G. Stovall, and James D. Startt (eds), *The Media in America*, Worthington: Publishing Horizons, 1989, p. 104. It has an interesting section on Colonial editors, pp. 99–120.

5. Interview with Goodwin, February 10, 1986.

6. Thrity Umrigar, "A feeling of being set adrift," *Nieman Reports*, Fall 2001.

7. Lynn Corney, "Watchdogs or actors?: Student perception of television journalists, " paper presented at the annual meeting of the International Communication Association, 2006.

8. The first is reported in John W.C. Johnstone, Edward J. Slawski, and William W. Bowman, *The News People: A Sociological Profile of American Journalists and Their Work*, Urbana: University of Illinois Press, 1976. David H. Weaver and Cleveland Wilhoit have replicated and expanded on their research three times. See their books *The American Journalist: A Portrait of U.S. News People and Their Work*, Bloomington: Indiana University Press, First Edition, 1986, and Second Edition, 1991, and their report, "The American Journalist in the 1990s: A Preliminary Report of Key Findings from a 1992 National Survey of U.S. Journalists," Arlington: Freedom Forum, 1992.

9. Mark Deuze, 'National news cultures: A comparison of Dutch, German, British, Australian and U.S. Journalists," *Journalism and Mass Communication Quarterly,* Spring 2002.

10. Adam Gopnik, "The end of the world," *The New Yorker,* November 15, 2004.

11. "An MSM rebuke and admonition for bloggers," Beltway Blogroll, June 20, 2006.

12. Arianna Huffington, "Now the little guy is the true pit bull of journalism," *The Guardian*, March 14, 2006.

13. Ryan Lizza, "The YouTube election," *The New York Times,* August 20, 2006.

14. MORI poll, February 2002, cited in Karen Sanders, *Ethics and Journalism*, London: Sage Publications, 2003.

15. Ian Black, "British newspapers 'the least trusted in Europe,'" *The Guardian*, April 24, 2002.

16. Carroll Doherty, "The public isn't buying press credibility," *Nieman Reports,* Summer 2005. Also see "Media: more voices, less credibility" at http://people-press.org/commentary/.

17. "National Polls of Journalists and the American Public on First Amendment and Media," University of Connecticut, May 16, 2005.
18. "Survey finds First Amendment is being left behind in U.S. high schools," John S. and James L. Knight Foundation Web site at www.knightfdn.org, January 31, 2005.
19. George Garneau, "Press freedom in deep trouble," *Editor & Publisher*, April 20, 1991. Wyatt's report is titled "Free Expression and the American Public" and was commissioned by the American Society of Newspaper Editors.
20. Lee Wilkins and Renita Coleman, *The Moral Media: How Journalists Reason About Ethics,* Mahwah, NJ: LEA Publications, 2004.
21. Project for Excellence in Journalism, "The State of the News Media 2004," at www.journalism.org.
22. "Fair Reporting," a segment on "The O'Reilly Factor," January 31, 2006. A transcript is at www.foxnews.com/story/0,2933,183441,00.html.
23. Quoted in Nick Madigan, "Making an issue of the media," *The (Baltimore) Sun,* August 20, 2006.
24. Gerald Stone and John Less, "Portrayal of journalists on prime time television," *Journalism Quarterly*, Winter 1990, p. 707.
25. Bill Mahon's findings in his master's thesis at Penn State University are cited in Chip Rowe, "Hacks on film," *Washington Journalism Review*, November 1992, p. 27. A study of the newspaper industry's efforts in the 1930s and 1940s to have journalists shown in a more favorable light can be found in Stephen Vaughn and Bruce Evensen, "Democracy's guardians: Hollywood's portrait of reporters, 1930–1945," *Journalism Quarterly*, Winter 1991, pp. 829–837.
26. Glenn Garelik, "Stop the presses! Movies blast media. Viewers cheer," *The New York Times*, January 31, 1993, national edition, pp. H11 and H18.
27. Caryn James, "The decline and fall of journalists on film," *The New York Times,* July 19, 2005.

2 The Study of Ethics

Imagine you are sitting around with a group of friends, laughing and talking. You gossip about people who aren't there, discuss sports and even argue about politics and current events. Then one of your more thoughtful friends begins to talk quietly.

"You know," the friend says, "we spend a lot of time putting down other people. Athletes who act like the laws don't apply to them. Auto mechanics who fix things that aren't broken. Politicians who promise things they never deliver. Corporate executives who cook the company's books and get rich.

"We'd like to think that we wouldn't do those things because we think that we are 'good, moral' people. But what if you were given a ring that had the power to make you invisible? You could sneak into any home, office, or business. No one would ever see you. You could eavesdrop on any conversation. You could lie and cheat and never be found out. You could gather passwords, hack your way into computer systems, put money in your bank account, and change all your grades to A's. You could do whatever you wanted. You could steal, even kill, and know that no one would see you do it.

"How would you behave if you had such a ring? If you are honest with yourself, you know you would put the ring on and forget all about being a 'good, moral' person. You would do whatever makes you happy."

Your friend's comments may prompt a lively discussion. But his argument is not very original. Glaucon made the same challenge to Socrates about 2,500 years ago,[1] and philosophers have been dealing with similar questions ever since. What do we mean when we say some actions are good? What do we mean when we say actions are bad or unethical or immoral? And, even if we know right from wrong, why should we do the right thing? Aren't people who lie and cheat usually the ones who get ahead in life?

In this chapter, we will look at how some philosophers have tried to answer these questions. From studying these philosophers' ideas, you may be able to develop some new strategies on how you can handle ethical problems.

The Birth of the Study of Ethics

In many ways, for Western civilization the formal study of ethics began 2,500 years ago with Socrates, a teacher in Ancient Greece. His teaching style was to ask increasingly difficult questions of his students and anyone else who would submit to his grilling. "You're a man known for your high moral standards," he would say. "So you would be a good person to ask this question: What does it mean to be moral?" The person, flattered by the way the question was asked, would offer a response. Then Socrates would ask a series of follow-up questions that would expose the inconsistencies and weaknesses in the man's answers. Socrates claimed he was not being mean-spirited when he cut their arguments down. He said he believed that this continual questioning would eventually lead to basic truths. Many students apparently enjoyed his approach, which we now call the Socratic method, and he became a popular teacher. Nevertheless, people in authority were annoyed by him. They put Socrates on trial, convicted him of undermining the morals and deities of Athens, and ordered him to drink a deadly substance called hemlock.

Socrates left no writings. Much of what we know about him came from the writings of people who knew him, particularly his most famous student, Plato. Plato's books read like conversations and are on topics ranging from politics to the nature of the real world. These conversations are not dry lectures. Some are more like barroom talk; in fact, in one of Plato's dialogues the participants drink until some of them pass out. All the while, they continue to discuss philosophic topics ranging from the role of government to the nature of pleasurable sex.

Plato honored his old teacher by naming the main character in these conversations Socrates. Today, philosophy professors are faced with the problem of trying to sort out what the real Socrates believed and what Plato himself believed but had the character named Socrates say.

Plato started his own school in Athens. He also had a famous student, Aristotle, who became one of most important figures in both Western philosophy and science. These three men – Socrates, Plato, and Aristotle – have played a key role in shaping the understandings of ethics in Western culture.

Virtue and the Greeks

When Glaucon posed his question on why people should worry about ethics and morality, he clearly thought he had Socrates stumped. After all, the wearer of the magical ring could commit any act without fear of being caught. Why would anyone worry about ethics or morality if there were no penalty to pay?

To Glaucon's surprise, Socrates agreed with him. Socrates said it was obvious that people do whatever makes them happy. Sensible people never intentionally make decisions that harm themselves. To Plato, ethics and morality were not lists of laws that kept people from enjoying life. Instead, ethics provided a guide to help people live good lives.

Plato argued in a lengthy dialog called *The Republic* that people are composed of three temperaments. One consists in the base drives that cause people to seek food, sex, and other creature comforts. A second is an assertive nature that drives them to defend themselves, to compete against others and survive in the practical world. The third is reason.

Plato then asked his listeners to imagine a person who is controlled by only one of these elements. Imagine people who are constantly driven by sexual desire. Or people who are continually ready to fight and must win at all costs. These people can never satisfy their desires and there-fore can never be happy. To Plato, a person could be happy only when all three parts – the need to fulfill basic animal drives, the competitive spirit, and the power to reason – are in balance. Plato believed that once people came to this awareness, they would not knowingly choose to live an unhappy life. "Think hard," Socrates said to Glaucon. "You will always find that doing the right thing is best for you."

Developing Socrates' teachings, Aristotle provided an outline of how people can learn appropriate behavior. He called it the *doctrine of the golden mean*. Aristotle contended that the right course of acton almost always lies between two extremes. An example: Eating properly lies somewhere between starvation and gluttony. To go without eating is clearly not healthy; yet, eating 20 pieces of pizza may be equally unhealthy. From experience, reasoning, and training, we learn to eat the quantity of food that suits our needs. Keep in mind that when Aristotle uses the word "mean," he is not referring to a mathematical average. He is not saying that if 20 pieces of pizza are too much and zero is too few, then 10 pieces would be just right. People discover the right amount to eat through experience and reason. Another example: Aristotle thought that bravery lies somewhere between foolhardiness and cowardliness. Foolhardy soldiers are reckless and get killed. Cowardly soldiers run. But a brave soldier uses his training and reasoning abilities to find the right moment to attack the enemy and win the battle.

Paul Lester, a journalism professor and ethicist, applied Aristotle's golden mean to a situation in which photographers are assigned to take pictures at the funeral of a person whose death – for one reason or another – is in the news. One extreme reaction might be for a photographer to refuse to take the pictures because the presence of a photographer may increase the family's grief. Another extreme reaction would be for a photographer to decide that since the funeral is newsworthy, photographers should be allowed to move around freely, shooting whatever they like whenever they like. Lester suggests that ethical photographers would find a mean between these extremes. They would take pictures at the funeral, but they would dress appropriately and use longer lenses that allowed them to stay in the background as much as possible. By looking for the golden mean, the photographer would obtain the pictures but avoid causing the family additional pain.

To Aristotle and other Greek philosophers, living life well was the natural goal of humankind. They believed that through education, experience, and reasoning, people could learn how to live well. Because their philosophy was based on the search for a virtuous life, some modern writers classify it as "virtue-based ethics."

The Social Contract and Hobbes

Thomas Hobbes was a timid English scholar who strongly influenced British – and, later on, American – ethical and political thought. He was a controversial fellow in the 17th century: Both the Catholic Church and

Oxford University wanted to burn his books, and there was serious talk of burning Hobbes as well.[2]

To Hobbes, prehistoric humankind found itself living in a world of "continual fear and danger of violent death." To survive, early humans had to be aggressive, take what they needed, and hoard the materials necessary for life. In this original state of nature, human life was "solitary, poor, nasty, brutish and short," according to Hobbes. Yet, people sought peace, prosperity, and long life. To achieve these goals, they formed alliances. They learned that two people had a better chance of fighting off wild animals than one person alone did. They learned that they had more success overcoming starvation and other natural calamities when they agreed to work together. Hobbes called these agreements *social contracts*. People entered into them for one simple reason: self-interest. Hobbes believed that people were motivated entirely by self-interest.

But if people do only what is best for them, Hobbes's philosophy seems to have a basic contradiction: If people are motivated purely by self-interest, why should they keep their promises? It would seem to be to a person's advantage to accept help but to refuse to help others in return.

Hobbes acknowledged the problem, but he thought he had an answer. Suppose a friend trusts you enough to leave her purse at the table while she is out of the room for a few moments. Once she is gone, it is clear to you that you could steal some of her money. If you took just a few bills, she would not immediately notice their absence. By the time she figured out the money was missing, it is unlikely she would connect you to the theft. The end result of violating your friend's trust would be that you had more money and presumably could use it to increase your happiness. Yet, most people would reject the idea of stealing money, especially from a friend. Hobbes contended that the reason people don't steal is that they have decided the risk of getting caught is simply too great. Taking a chance on losing friends and having the reputation as someone who stole from a friend is not worth the money they would get.

Hobbes took that idea a step further. His belief was that everyone wants to live as a competent person in a peaceful, prosperous, orderly society. The framework of that society depends on people living up to their social contracts. If they break their promises, they risk damaging the peace of their society. Therefore, in the long run, reasonable people recognize that it is in their own interest to keep their promises, in most instances.

Much like the Greeks, Hobbes believed that most people could use reason to separate right action from wrong. He thought that living ethically would become habitual. However, he accepted that some people will break their social contracts by cheating or stealing. In small, primitive societies, people in the community will find ways to force others to abide by their social contracts or leave the community. But in larger, more complex societies, governments are required. Hobbes believed that the role of a government is to enforce laws to ensure the peace and prosperity of its citizens.

Another English philosopher, John Locke, agreed that governments are formed by social contracts. However, Locke added the idea that these contracts work both ways. A government exists to ensure peace and prosperity and has power over people. But if that government is not achieving that goal, citizens can replace it. The thinking of Hobbes and Locke was echoed in the American Declaration of Independence, and Thomas Jefferson and Thomas Paine acknowledged that they were influenced by Locke's writings.

Based on the social contract theory, journalists can learn to weigh the benefits and risks of their behavior. For instance, reporters may want to use an underhanded way of getting a great story, but if they do so, they run the risk of alienating the public and thereby undermining their own influence in the community. Journalists can draw another lesson from Hobbes. Recognizing the competitive nature of the news media, Hobbes would probably advocate tough codes of ethics and strict laws concerning libel and privacy as methods of ensuring that journalists abide by their social contracts.

A 20th-century version of social contract theory was advocated by Harvard Professor John Rawls. He believed that people are continually creating social contracts with everyone they encounter. Students form social contracts with their professors, with each of their classmates, with roommates, and so on. Rawls believed that we should try to make each of these contracts ethically right.

What is ethically right? Rawls offered a test: Before deciding what to do, people should consider their potential courses of action as if they don't know which role they will play in any encounter. Rawls referred this as being under a "veil of ignorance" and used an example to explain his idea. Suppose you have been asked to cut a birthday cake. You like cake and decide to cut one large piece for yourself and small pieces for everyone else. However, if don't know which piece will be yours, rather than risk getting a small piece you may decide that the best course of action for you is to cut the pieces equally. Rawls's idea is that people should consider the effects of their behavior from the point of view of everyone involved.

One lesson journalists can learn from Rawls is that their stories have a considerable impact on many people. Ethicists call each person affected by an action a "stakeholder." Every news story has several stakeholders. When journalists conduct interviews, they form social contracts with their sources. The source implicitly agrees to tell the truth, and the reporter agrees to quote the source accurately. As the story is being written, the number of stakeholders mushrooms. People mentioned in the story are stakeholders, as well as their families and perhaps the organizations they are associated with. People with opposing viewpoints may believe they have been harmed because their opinions were minimized or overlooked altogether. The news organization where the reporter works is a stakeholder. In a broader sense, the profession of journalism is a stakeholder. The largest stakeholder in a news story is the public. They depend on reporters to explain to them what's going on.

Rawls's theory promotes a sense of fairness by requiring journalists to consider the impact their actions may have on all of these stakeholders and thereby to judge the moral value of the story. Of course, reporters cannot avoid injuring some stakeholders: A mass murderer could argue that reporting his crimes would harm his reputation and shame his family, for example. A benefit of applying Rawls's veil of ignorance is to identify all the people who may be affected by the story and to attempt to avoid harming any of them without good reason.

John Stuart Mill and the Utilitarians

John Stuart Mill was raised in a world of philosophy. His father, John Mill, and his godfather, Jeremy Bentham, were both philosophers. Like many fathers, John Mill wanted his son to follow in his footsteps, so he devised an education plan that he thought was sure to produce a great philosopher. Mill started teaching his son Greek when John Stuart was 3 years old and Latin when he was 8. By the time he was a teenager, he was editing philosophic treatises for publication. His father hoped that his son would champion a philosophy called utilitarianism that he and Bentham had founded. But, as often happens, young John did not follow in his footsteps. In his 20s, John Stuart Mill rejected many aspects of his father's and Bentham's utilitarianism and created his own version. His books, particularly *On Liberty*, *Utilitarianism*, and *The Subjection of Women*, made major contributions to Western political philosophy and ethics.

A general principle of utilitarianism is that everyone should try to act in a way that will produce the greatest good for the greatest number. Utilitarians disagreed among themselves on how strictly to apply these principles and even on how to determine "the greatest good." Mill's father and Bentham contended that a child's game was better than an opera because games provided more contentment to more people. Mill, however, argued that there were higher and lower pleasures. The uneducated may seem content with the lower pleasures. But educated adults prefer the higher pleasures, independence and the dignity of being a reasoning human. Therefore, he would advocate societal spending for both games and opera even though opera will appeal to fewer people.

To utilitarians, the consequences of our actions are what matters most. Suppose a reporter is trying to uncover the truth about an important health issue. And suppose she decides that, in order to get the story, she needs to steal patients' health records from a hospital. Is stealing the right thing for her to do? To many strict utilitarians, the answer is determined by the results. If she writes a story that really does result in improvements in the health care system, then she has behaved well. But suppose the public outcry about reporters stealing private documents is so great that the health issue is all but forgotten? Then her actions do not produce much good and may impede future investigations. To many utilitarians, her conduct in these circumstances is not good.

Other utilitarians believe that they can produce a kind of calculus to determine right and wrong. They consider the amount of a good and the amount of harm an act may do. And they factor in the number of people who will benefit from the act or the number who will be harmed. They then choose the course of action that maximizes the good. While using a mathematics-like formula to decide right and wrong may seem strange, the use of research and, yes, mathematics does play a role in many decisions. When friends are trying to choose a movie or a restaurant, they may pick the one that most of them find acceptable; or, at least, that the lowest number find unacceptable. On a larger scale, honest political leaders weigh the benefits of opposing plans before making decisions. If they must choose when spending tax money between hiring more police officers or building new roads, they try to gather information and pick the one that provides the greater benefit to the community.

People who accept utilitarianism as an ethical model disagree among themselves on one basic question: Should the standard apply to individual actions or to general rules? The disagreement is often framed in an exaggerated case like this one: Suppose a hospital has several patients in desperate need of transplants. One will die without a new heart, another needs new kidneys, a third must have a new liver, a fourth new eyes, and so on. But the hospital can find no donors whose body parts could be successfully placed in these patients' bodies. Then they discover a patient already in the hospital who would be the perfect donor. He is a homeless person, has no friends or family, is in an irreversible coma, and is slowly dying. Is it ethical for the doctors to hasten the man's death so they can harvest his body parts? (Most utilitarians oppose killing, many arguing that it is difficult to know what a person will do with the rest of his or her life. In this manufactured example, the man is near death in a coma.)

Act utilitarians would judge the consequences of the action. Hastening the man's death would result in saving the lives of several people, therefore bringing happiness to scores of friends and family members. So, if act utilitarians follow the doctrine strictly, they may decide that hastening the homeless man's death is the right thing to do.

However, *rule utilitarians* would have second thoughts. They judge an action by what the consequences would be if the action became the rule that people lived by. In the hospital example, they would pose this question: What would be the consequences if everyone knew that doctors had a rule that they could kill some patients in order to get body parts for other patients? Chances are, many people would be hesitant to seek medical assistance for themselves and their loved ones. The end result might be that many people would not be treated for their illnesses. Rule utilitarians would say that the rule in this case would not be beneficial to society and therefore that harvesting the homeless man's body parts would not be right.

Foes of utilitarianism lob several criticisms at it. One criticism is that it is difficult to predict the consequences of our actions. Even simple decisions can have unexpected results. A reporter may believe that a story about teen suicide will cause schools and the public to understand and help depressed youths. But the story may have the unintended effect of touching off a wave of "copy cat" suicides.

Another criticism is that it is difficult to weigh questions of the greatest good objectively. In effect, the individual has to decide what is best for others. History is filled with examples of one nation or group of people making decisions that they think will improve life in other nations or groups; the result is often disastrous.

Finally, many people aren't satisfied with the basic tenet of utilitarianism. Utilitarians are concerned primarily with an action's consequences, not with the person's intentions or motives. Suppose two people win the lottery. One goes on a wild spending spree and in a few months is broke. The other decides to use all the money to build a shelter for abused children. Unfortunately, the shelter, which is not insured, is destroyed by fire before it is completed. The person is left with no money and no shelter. The consequences of these people's actions are similar: Neither of them accomplished much good with their winnings. Yet many people are included to view the actions of the second person more favorably. In effect, many shift the emphasis in deciding ethical issues from the results to the motives and intentions of the actors.

Kant and the Categorical Imperative

Immanuel Kant was a German who lived at about the same time as John Stuart Mill. Unlike the utilitarians, Kant contended that intentions – he used the word "goodwill" – should be the basis for ethical judgments. If a person acted out of goodwill, Kant considered the actions ethical, regardless of the consequences.

Kant developed a method to judge whether a person's action were the result of goodwill, which he called the *categorical imperative*. He described it like this:

> Act as if the maxim of your action were to become through your will a universal law of nature.

Kant meant that we should make ethical decisions as if we are creating laws or rules that everyone should follow. He offered some examples of how he would apply his ethics. Suppose you are broke and out of work. You have no job prospects. Should you borrow money even though you know you will never be able to repay it? Kant argued that you should not. He applied the categorical imperative like this: The idea of a loan – rather than a gift – is that the loan will be repaid. If the person's intention is not to repay the loan, the very notion of a loan is destroyed. If borrowing money with no intention of repaying it became the norm, no one would lend money.

Kant also applied his categorical imperative to breaking promises nd lying. What if you created a rule in society that people could break promises and tell lies any time they wanted? Soon people would no longer believe others or expect them to keep their promises. If a rule allowing lying became universal, the distinction between lying and truth-telling would not matter.

Unlike Mill and the Greeks, Kant did not argue that doing the right thing will necessarily be to a person's benefit. Kant believed actions should not be judged by their consequences. So whether anyone, including the person doing the action, benefits from an action is not important. Kant believed that the real test of morality is whether people do the right thing even if it is against their own self-interest. Because of this emphasis, his approach is often called *duty-based ethics.*

Many journalists see value in duty-based ethics. They argue that the news media have a duty to print all truthful, newsworthy information that they uncover. After all, informing the public is the reason we have news media (as opposed to advertising media and entertainment media). If journalists do not fulfill this duty, then the news media are not justifying the rationale for their existence. This idea is well ingrained in most journalists. When they are deciding if a story should be printed, most begin with the assumption that if it is truthful, it should be printed. They back away from this assumption only after they are convinced that there are good reasons not to report the story.

Duty-based ethics is also evident when journalists go to jail rather than reveal their sources or give government officials their notes. Even when disclosing the information may serve a public goal (to help achieve justice in a trial, for instance), they believe it is their duty to follow the rule that journalists should remain independent of government and keep their promises.

Making Ethical Decisions

Few people today would argue that any one of the philosophers discussed above has provided a perfect model for making ethical decisions. Instead, they contend that we can draw ideas from each theory and construct an outline of how ethical decisions should be made. Most of these outlines follow similar steps. We'll look at one called "Potter's box," named for Harvard Divinity School Professor Ralph Potter. Potter suggests that ethical decision making should go through four interrelated stages. He explained the steps using the model in Figure 2.1.

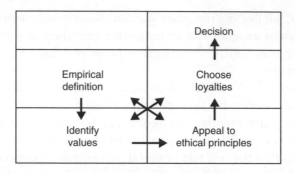

Figure 2.1   Potter's box.

The first step in Potter's box is to define the problem. Suppose a student accuses a professor of sexual misconduct and asks editors of the campus newspaper to write a story. Before they make a decision, they need more information so they can understand the situation. Potter called this seeking "empirical definition." They may ask if the source is trustworthy, whether the student has any way of proving that the event occurred, if the student has an ax to grind, if the student has approached the department chair or university about the problem. They will want to interview the professor about the accusations. As part of gathering information for this empirical definition, editors will also consider the stakeholders in the situation. Who will be affected by the story?

The second step in Potter's box is to identify the values that should play a role in making a decision. Editors will want to consider some professional values. They may believe that the role of the news media is to provide truthful information. They believe it is important for the media to be fair. They may envision the role of the media as righting wrongs. Personal values, such as honesty, trust, and fairness, may also be considered.

The next step calls for the editors to view the situation from a variety of ethical viewpoints:

- Utilitarians would want them to consider the consequences. Would society benefit from the story? Would the amount of good to society outweigh the harm that the story might cause?
- Kant would ask them to consider their intensions in running the story. He would caution them to consider what would happen if everyone behaved as they are contemplating behaving.
- Hobbes would encourage them to consider the social contracts they have with the various stakeholders.

- Rawls would ask them to apply a veil of ignorance and to consider the situation in light of all the people involved. What if they were the student involved? The professor? Other students on campus? Campus administrators? Other journalists? The managers and owners of the newspaper? Parents of students? Townspeople?
- Aristotle would counsel that they avoid extreme behavior. Perhaps the best course of action lies somewhere between publishing all the information and not writing the story. Or perhaps there are other stories that could be written that would accomplish the desired goal.

The fourth step in the Potter box is to determine your loyalties. In this situation, several loyalties come into play. Editors have the professional loyalties that come with being a journalist. They also have loyalties to the student who has been harassed, to the tipster, to the school, to their colleagues. They have loyalties to themselves, their sense of conscience, and their well-being.

Finally, taking the results of all four steps into consideration, you must make a decision. If everyone applies these four steps, will we all arrive at the same conclusion as to what is ethical? No. The goal of ethics is not necessarily to get everyone to agree on the same course of action. The value of these guidelines is that they require you to make a thoughtful, informed decision rather than shooting from the hip. Occasionally, you will discover that your initial reaction to an ethical problem changes as you consider it in greater depth.

Further reading

Almond, Brenda (1998) *Exploring Ethics: A Traveller's Tale*, Oxford: Blackwell Publishers.
Darwall, Stephen (1998) *Philosophical Ethics*, Boulder, CO: Westview Press.
Singer, Peter (ed.) (1993) *A Companion to Ethics*, Oxford: Blackwell Publishers.
Sterba, James P. (2000) *Ethics: Classical Western Texts in Feminist and Multicultural Perspectives*, Oxford: Oxford University Press.

Notes

1. Glaucon's observations about the Ring of Gyges are in Plato, *The Republic*, Book II.
2. *The Cambridge Dictionary of Philosophy* (Robert Audi, gen. ed.), Cambridge: Cambridge University Press, 1995, p. 332.

Part 2 Telling the Truth

3 Truth and Objectivity

As far back as the early 1900s, smokers had jokingly referred to cigarettes as "coffin nails" and "cancer sticks." But the joke went sour in 1952 when the *Reader's Digest* magazine ran an article titled "Cancer by the Cartoon." The article contended that the health hazards of smoking were real. In the next few years, other magazines and newspapers quoted scientists and doctors whose research suggested a link between tobacco and disease. Even in-house research done by the cigarette companies was confirming the cancer connection.

The tobacco industry executives knew they were in trouble – and they found a clever solution. They created the Tobacco Research Council. Despite the name, the organization did little real research. Instead, it fought a public relations battle trying to cast doubt on legitimate studies. If a scientist at a university reported that lab rats were much more likely to get cancer when they were exposed to smoke, the Tobacco Research Council held press conferences pointing out the flaws in comparing rats to humans and ensuring smokers that there was no documented link between smoking and disease.

When reporters wrote their stories, most of them tried to be fair and present both sides. What readers and listeners learned was something like this: Qualified researchers at a university said that smoking was bad and seemingly equally qualified scientists at a research institute said that there was nothing to worry about. Many smokers threw up their hands in confusion – and continued to smoke. Even after Congress in 1965 required labels to warn "Caution: Cigarette Smoking May be Hazardous to Your Health," the industry continued to deny the connection. As late as 1989, nearly 20 years after cigarette ads were banned from

TV, spokespeople for the industry were still appearing on the morning network news shows writing off the cancer risk as "just statistics" and insisting that smoking had not been proven to cause cancer.[1]

Were reporters right to give equal weight to researchers from the Tobacco Research Council and researchers with major universities and cancer societies? Were they right to continue to balance anti-smoking messages with denials from the people who were employed by the tobacco industry? These questions underscore the complicated interplay between two commitments that Americans expect from their news media: One commitment is to truth telling and the other to fair, balanced, and objective reporting.

The first of these two commitments seems obvious. The Society of Professional Journalists' Code of Ethics lists "Seek Truth and Report It" as the first of its four major ethical demands on journalists. CBS News anchor Walter Cronkite used to end each nightly newscast by saying "That's the way it is," suggesting to viewers that they had just learned the important truths of the day. The problem for journalists, as will be discussed in this chapter, is deciding what truth means in the context of daily journalism.

There's less agreement on the public's second expectation: Most Americans consider it important that journalists be objective. Perhaps an indicator of this is the way Fox News' slogans, such as "We report, you decide" and "Fair and balanced," resonate with Americans. Yet, journalists and academics have heated debates over whether objectivity is possible, what it means, and if it is even good for journalism.

The question of objectivity is further clouded by another demand that many place on journalists: They are encouraged to be proactive in their communities. They are supposed to "right wrongs," "be a watch-dog," "make a difference," and, as one journalist boasted, "comfort the afflicted and afflict the comfortable." That places journalists in an impossible position: They are supposed to fight the injustices in society and at the same time to be nonjudgmental and not take sides. *The Washington Post's* E. J. Dione described the reporters' plight like this:

> Be neutral yet investigative; be disengaged but have an impact; be fair-minded but have an edge. Therein lies the nut of our tortured relationship with objectivity. Few would argue that complete objectivity is possible, yet we bristle when someone suggests we aren't being objective – or fair, or balanced – as if everyone agrees on what they all mean.

This chapter will look at the origin and interplay of these three ideals: being objective, seeking the truth, and righting wrongs.

What Is Truth Anyway?

It may seem like a simple question. But, as the cliché says, the devil is in the details. Ancient Greek philosophers argued over what truth means. Some contended that people could learn the truth by using their senses of sight, smell, touch, and hearing: If you see a dog running down the lane, you know there is a dog, a lane, and an action called running. People who make this argument are called empiricists.

Others argued that it isn't that simple. They said that our eyes can be deceived by magician's tricks and even everyday occurrences. If you push a stick into water, it appears to bend. Yet, you don't believe that the stick bent as it entered the water any more than you believe that the magician pulled a rabbit from an empty hat. These philosophers, who were called rationalists, argued that our senses are fallible. The use of reason and experience is a better way to obtain the truth.

Plato and Aristotle tried to develop systems that combined the two. Their efforts resulted in two very different philosophies. Plato believed that contact with the physical word yielded only temporary truths. The real truths or permanent truths can be learned only through enlightenment by study and reason. Aristotle placed the emphasis differently. He believed that by observing and categorizing the real world, he could produce truths that he and other scientists could confirm by testing. Aristotle developed rules of logic and created an early version of the scientific method.

Early American journalists tended to see the world in terms of their own ideas and philosophies. Their papers were highly partisan, and many depended on funding from political parties. Editors assumed that their opinions were the truth, so that's what they put in the paper. Getting the other side of the argument was silly. One editor said it would be like preaching Christianity in the morning and paganism at night.

Beginning in the middle of the 19th century and continuing through much of the 20th, American society underwent profound scientific and technological developments. Cars, trains, medicines, surgical techniques, airplanes, telephones, movies, radio, refrigeration, and space travel were invented and improved on during this era. Scientists were redefining matter with their theory of atoms. Psychologists like Sigmund Freud were trying to find causes for human behavior. Einstein was proving that all things are relative. Scientists were revered, and many Americans began to equate truth with empiricism and the scientific method.

Philosophers called this embrace of empiricism and science "logical positivism," while in literature, the arts, and sociology it was often called "modernism." Some of its basic tenets were:

- The way to understand the world is to observe it closely and to classify and analyze what is seen.
- Facts and opinions are separate things, and facts are the basis of truth.
- People can objectively obtain facts. For example, a scientist can be trusted to read a thermometer and record the temperature correctly.
- Scientific developments are making the world a better place.

As American temperament was altering, high-speed printing presses were changing the finances of newspapers. Owners could print lots of papers and wanted to sell them to much larger audiences than merely people who shared their opinions. They hired reporters and assigned them to report news that would attract readers – often reports of crime and the courts. These stories required reporters to interview people and be present at events for their stories. Journalists were developing a new standard of discovering truth, one shaped by logical positivism.

Over time, journalists began to view themselves as objective searchers for truth, much like scientists. By the middle of the 20th century, they had come to accept that opinion and facts were different: News columns were for facts and editorial pages were where opinion belonged. Reporters were supposed to get the facts right and keep their own opinions out of what they wrote. In practice, this often meant that they would interview one official source and relay that person's comments as accurately as possible. If that source was wrong or the information was incomplete, journalists assumed that other sources would come forward to tell them. The reporter would then write another story based on these new facts.

Some scholars in the 1940s disagreed with the idea that journalists should do little more than collect facts. They organized the Commission on Freedom of the Press, chaired by Robert Hutchins, Chancellor of the University of Chicago. The commission argued that the duty of the press was to provide a "truthful, comprehensive and intelligent account of the day's events in a context that gives them meaning." It wrote, "It is no longer enough to report the fact truthfully. It is now necessary to report the truth about the fact." For example, that a senator made a particular statement is a fact. The press's real concern, in the mind of the commission, was not merely reporting this fact accurately. The press should provide enough context that citizens can understand the problem and judge the senator's comments.[2]

The commission's suggestions had little immediate impact on journalism. Newspapers continued to follow their own practices. Reporting became such a nonjudgmental task that a *Washington Post* editor once said he would prefer to hire reporters who didn't think at all. The press made a fetish of this kind of detachment, according to former University of Illinois Communications Dean Theodore Peterson.[3] Journalists of that era told stories of calling their newspaper offices in the middle of hurricanes and having editors order them to get sources such as fire chiefs or police officers to confirm that the wind was blowing hard. It would not have been objective for reporters to give their own opinions.

The unthinking reporter

The press received a major lesson in one flaw of this extreme kind of objectivity. Sen. Joseph McCarthy of Wisconsin won election to the Senate at a time when many Americans believed that Communists were slowly taking over America by secretly infiltrating the leadership of our government, military, political parties, and media. America had won World War II, but it seemed to be losing during the ensuing peace. McCarthy learned that in this environment, if he made a sensational charge about Communists in government, the papers would report what he said almost word for word. Even if reporters doubted what he said, their stories would repeat his accusations. He announced that he had uncovered Communists or Communist sympathizers in the State Department, the military, the Voice of America radio station, the news media, law offices, and on and on. Before his crusade began, McCarthy's main claim to fame was being voted the "worst senator" by the press corps one year. He quickly became a major player in Republican politics and one of the most feared men in Washington.

The shallowness of such reporting angered many journalists. They knew they were being used. Some asked to be taken off the McCarthy beat.

Others carried on reporting the hearings that ensued, but were totally frustrated. In *The Powers That Be*, David Halberstam described the plight of Phil Potter, a reporter for Baltimore's *The Sun*:

> During the various McCarthy hearings, [Potter] would astonish admiring colleagues by coming back to the Sun bureau and writing a first draft of a story in which all his anger, all his rage at what McCarthy was doing would come forth: "Joseph R. McCarthy, the no good lying son of a bitch from Wisconsin. . . ."
>
> Then, having vented his spleen and released his anger, he would tear up the story and sit down and go to work. Often when Potter had finished for the day he would go to the National Press Club, where he would find some of his colleagues and tell them that they had to start covering McCarthy, trying to explain what McCarthy was like, what he was doing. It was, he thought, missionary work. Most of his colleagues thought he was simply too involved. A story was a story. If Joe said something, you reported it; that was all it took.[4]

Fortunately, not all journalists of that era saw their jobs as repeating whatever charges McCarthy made. Some newspapers attacked him, and *The Washington Post* coined the term "McCarthyism" to refer to his practices. But the biggest challenge to McCarthy's credibility came from a news medium that was then in its infancy: television. CBS's highly popular newsman Edward R. Murrow exposed some of McCarthy's tactics on his program *See It Now*. Murrow's report contributed to McCarthy's downfall. After the Senate in 1954 voted 67 to 22 to censure him for his reckless and abusive conduct, many in the press took a hard look at how they had been used by this skillful abuser of truth.[5]

One outcome of the McCarthy era was that many reporters and editors recognized that truth telling meant more than simply compiling what officials said. They began to seek out additional sources for their reports. Researcher Leon Sigal documented this when he studied front-page stories in *The New York Times* and *The Washington Post*. He found that reporters in the 1950s often used only one source, usually some high official. By the 1970s they were using many more sources, including some who disagreed with the official version or provided another interpretation of the information.[6] Usually, reporters were looking for balance. If a Democratic senator made a statement, reporters would track down a leader of the Republican Party to get the GOP's (Grand Old Party's) reaction. The reporter then wrote a story quoting both sides.

One unavoidable result of this shift was that the news became, in many ways, more subjective. Instead of being neutral conduits of information, reporters began to play an active role in the formation of the news. They began to decide which statements had to be challenged and which sources needed to be contacted for balance. Even if the reporters were trying to be fair and accurate, two reporters covering the same event could produce stories that were very different.

Can balance produce lazy journalism?

Presenting both sides may provide a more complete story than the single-source stories of the past. But it may not help society get at the truth of complex issues. Instead, reporters may settle for easy-to-do, balanced stories when more detailed reporting and thought are needed. Dante Chinni, writing in *The Christian Science Monitor,* offered this hypothetical: Suppose the Boston Red Sox beat the New York Yankees, 8–0.[7] The reporter wants to find out why the game was so lopsided. She interviews a Boston fan who tells her it was because of the Red Sox's excellent hitting. Then she talks to a disappointed Yankee fan who blames it all on lousy Yankee pitching. The reporter could produce a balanced story with comments from both Yankee and Red Sox fans. But, Chinni argued, the story will not get at the real question: Why was the game so lopsided? He contends that the answer isn't to be found by balancing viewpoints but by studying the box score, carefully viewing the game, and interviewing participants who are in a position to make wise observations. Determining why the game was lopsided requires effort. He concluded:

> So it is with any number of stories. . . . When reporters don't make the effort to sort through the evidence and simply fall back on 'this side says this, and that side says that,' they are being lazy.[8]

Steven R. Weisman, the chief diplomatic correspondent for *The New York Times,* told *Columbia Journalism Review* that when reporters push to get at the heart of an issue, they produce better journalism. He noticed that when he was an editorial writer and not an objective reporter, "I pressed the reporting further because I didn't have the luxury of saying X says this and Y says this and you, dear reader, can decide who is right."[9]

All too often, a side effect of balanced stories is that they tend to make all commentators seem equally credible. By the late 1990s, climatologists overwhelmingly agreed that global warming was a real phenomenon; only a small number disagreed. Yet, researchers found that most news stories tended to give each position equal weight. *Science* magazine executive editor Donald Kennedy explained that "there are a great many thoughtful reporters in the media who believe that in order to produce a balanced story, you've got to pick one commentator from side A and one commentator from side B."[10] The result, according to researchers, is that "the American public and policymakers have been presented with the misleading scenario that there is a raging debate among climate-change scientists regarding humanity's role in climate change."[11] Because of this, the number of Americans who believed that global warming may be a problem decreased during the 1990s and 2000s as the amount of scientific evidence saying it was a problem increased.[12]

These observations do not mean that journalists should reject the importance of balance in stories altogether. Pulitzer winner Ross Gelbspan contends:

> When balance should come into play is when the content of the story revolves largely around opinion: Should society recognize gay marriage? Should abortion be legal? In such coverage a journalist is ethically obligated to provide roughly equivalent space to the most articulate presentation of major competing views. When the story focused on an issue in which various facts are known, it is the reporter's responsibility to find out what those facts are."[13]

Problems with determining balance

Through the late 20th and early 21st century, editors knew that stories about the Middle East were likely to draw lots of criticism. Some readers saw a bias in the media for Israel; some were certain that most stories favored the Palestinians. An example of this occurred in 2006, when two Israeli soldiers were kidnapped by Hezbollah, a political and military group in Lebanon. In retaliation for the kidnapping, Israelis bombed Lebanese cities, and Hezbollah answered back by firing rockets at Israeli cities. Journalists had lots of photographs and video of death and destruction. Some TV networks and newspapers deliberately tried to show equal numbers of pictures of dead Lebanese and Israelis. Others rejected that kind of mathematical balance. Bill Keller, executive editor of *The New York Times*, said his editors decided which pictures went on the front page by judging each picture's quality, originality, and relevance. "You don't say, 'Yesterday we fronted dead Lebanese innocents, so today we have to front dead Israeli innocents,'" he said. "But you aim over time to portray the full range of the war's consequences."[14]

Trying to portray the full range of the conflict's consequences was not easy. Some argued that because approximately eight times as many Lebanese were killed, there should be more pictures of their dead. Others pointed out that most of the Lebanese dead were innocent civilians and most of the Israeli dead were military. Some thought that the deaths of civilians, including children, should get more coverage. Others noted that military people were sacrificing their lives for their country. They deserved respect and extra coverage because of their bravery.[14] What is curious is that each of these arguments was made in the name of "balance." Yet each would have yielded a very different front page or newscast.

Perhaps no area of American news coverage is under more scrutiny than that of candidates running for office. Many people see political bias. They are certain that the sins of Politician A are being overlooked while Politician B's minor indiscretions are big news, that Politician C's campaign is getting all the media attention, or that reporters are putty in Politician D's hands.

Some claim that these accusations are nearly unavoidable. Longtime CBS newsman and commentator Eric Sevareid observed that there is plenty of "biased reading and hearing" – many people see bias in the media when the facts in a story do not jibe with the way they would like the world to be. This is especially true for true believers in a cause or a candidate. *Los Angeles Times* media reporter David Shaw ran into this when he reviewed two books critical of the media – one written from a liberal perspective and one from a conservative viewpoint. He stated that reading the books back to back "is a bit like listening to two people's accounts of a football game in which each rooted for the opposite side." One author saw liberal bias in the same news accounts in which the other author saw conservative bias.[15]

Media researchers have taken up the challenge of determining if media bias does in fact exist. Some determine balance by measuring the amount of newspaper space or the number of minutes in newscasts that each candidate receives. The assumption is that if the coverage is balanced, the candidates will receive approximately the same amount of space or time. This may work in some campaigns when the candidates are equally well known. But in other campaigns, incumbents have such large leads in the early polls that they choose to run safe campaigns. They speak only to groups of party loyalists on uncontroversial topics. The challenger, however, may be running an energetic campaign that is raising real issues. Many people would contend that the challenger's campaign is more newsworthy and believe that it should receive more coverage.

Recognizing that simply counting stories and minutes may not be an effective way to judge campaign coverage, researchers have tried to judge the tone of the stories. They attempt to classify "favorable" and "unfavorable" stories or "positive" and "negative" depictions. Defining these terms can be difficult. Even when people agree on the definitions of terms like "positive" and "negative," applying them can be problematic. As researcher Michael Robinson has pointed out, some critics said that when Ronald Reagan won a landslide victory in 1984, he had to overcome overwhelming negative coverage by network television. Others said that his campaign received a major boost from the TV networks because their "superficial, picture-oriented coverage fit perfectly with his masterful media management." Others noted that the words spoken about Reagan in reporters' voiceovers were largely negative, while the video gave a positive image of him as a strong, handsome leader at ease with everyday Americans.[16]

Even if researchers conclude that one candidate received considerably more bad press, the cause of the discrepancy may not be bias. The handlers of Democratic presidential candidate Michael Dukakis knew that many voters thought he was a wimp. To improve his image, they arranged a photo op in which he would engage in the manly activity of driving an army tank. Unfortunately, the handlers did not recognize until it was too late that the driver of a tank does not sit on top of the gun turret like the images of George C. Scott in the movie *Patton*. Instead, the driver stays inside the tank and must stick his head through a port or use a periscope to see outside. Instead of a macho candidate, Dukakis appeared on the news with his head bobbling wildly from side to side. The event triggered lots of media coverage about why Dukakis was running such a bad campaign. A researcher studying the campaign during this period might conclude that there was a bias against the liberal Democrat. Yet, in this case, the negative coverage may not have been a sign of any reporter bias.

The Question of Objectivity

Brent Cunningham, managing editor of *Columbia Journalism Review*, wrote that if he asked 10 journalists what objectivity means, he guessed he would get 10 different answers. Each would have been widely different. When the Society of Professional Journalists rewrote its code of ethics a few years ago, the word "objectivity" was dropped from the document entirely.

Few people would claim that decisions about what is news are objective in the sense that mathematics is. Listen to how the editor of a major southwest newspaper decided what he thought belonged on the front page: "To me, it comes down to two questions: Is this story boring or interesting? Is this story relevant or irrelevant to our readers?" He added, "Some stories may be boring but still have to be reported because they're important." Interesting, relevant, and important. Clearly, those are decisions that are shaped by editors' training, their understanding of their audiences, and their own life experiences. Anyone who has been in a newsroom knows that editors and reporters often disagree vehemently about what is newsworthy. At most newspapers, the top editors meet to decide what stories will be on Page 1. Even among these highly experienced journalists, the discussions are often contentious.

Cunningham wrote that a better definition of journalistic objectivity was offered by Michael Bugeja, now a professor at Iowa State: "Objectivity is seeing the world as it is, not how you wish it were."[17]

That's also the way Stephen Berry, who won a Pulitzer prize before becoming a professor at the University of Iowa, looks at objectivity. Berry argued in *Nieman Reports* that it is easy to reject objectivity if it is defined only as requiring reporters to grab quotes from both sides before they write their stories. Berry contended: "Objectivity is a standard that requires journalists to try to put aside emotions and prejudices, including those implanted by the spinners and manipulators." While he acknowledged that no journalist ever achieves pure objectivity, it is "an ideal, the pursuit of which never ends." He quoted Walter Lippman, the intellectual father of objective journalism, as saying that objectivity created no conflict for "aggressive analyzers and explainers." The aim, Berry wrote, was for the reporter to deal with personal biases "to help the journalist see the facts as accurately as human frailty allows."[18]

Tim McGuire, former editor of the *Star Tribune* in Minneapolis, argued that if newspapers were to continue to succeed, they must not abandon objectivity. He said that when he taught a college class, he was amazed that the students saw bias in stories that reporters would never dream anyone would fault as being biased. He said the experience convinced him that

> newspapers must continue to serve the entire community to be successful. Newspapers must be what I call the 'information general store' where everyone in the reader audience feels welcome.[19]

Do all journalists claim to be objective?

The idea that the news should be objective is so intertwined with America's perception of journalism that most people in the United States – including many journalists – are surprised to learn that this is primarily a North American ideal. European papers often allow their stories to contain a distinct political slant. In the UK, for example, readers of *The Guardian* know the paper will give a liberal interpretation to the news, while *The Telegraph* and *The Sun* provide conservative views. As its name suggests, *The Independent* is not centered in one political orientation, yet its reporters are allowed much more latitude than is common in the American media. French, Italian, and German newspapers are even more overt in their blending of news and analysis. These papers also portray a much wider spectrum of political thought than do American newspapers. David Shaw of the *Los Angeles Times* noted that in Europe, "seven different journalists might put seven different spins on a given story."[20]

A handful of American news outlets lean toward this European model. *The Washington Times* is owned by the Rev. Sung Myung Moon's Unification Church and competes with one of America's top dailies, *The Washington Post*. "We are known as a conservative paper, so our story selection is based on what conservatives might be interested in," one *Washington Times* editor said on the Society of Professional Journalists' Web site.[21] News organizations owned by Rupert Murdoch's News Corp. are also likely to be conservative. His news properties include the Fox News network and *New York Post* in America; *The Sun*, *The Times*, and Sky News in the UK; and scores of newspapers and TV news outlets in other countries.

Blogs, truth, and objectivity

The Internet is inhabited by thousands of blogs. The nature of blogs is constantly changing and what they will be a decade from now is uncertain.

Many blogs are personal ramblings much like diaries in which people share the details of their daily lives. Mainstream news media are also embracing blogs. Their Web sites feature blogs written by regular reporters who provide insights into news events and often into the newsgathering process itself. They usually include space for readers to offer their own opinions and ask questions. In recent years, another kind of news-oriented blog has acquired thousands of devoted readers. Some have staffs much like an ordinary news organization; most are one-person operations. Most take news from traditional sources, rewrite it and then analyze it, often with a clear slant. A few blogs also include original reporting. These news blogs may be craving out standards for truth different from those of mainstream American media.

Many bloggers prize immediacy. They pass along what they have heard without vetting the story through editors. This procedure has allowed them to break major stories that the mainstream media were slow to cover. It also means that bloggers must be more willing to accept the possibility of being wrong. Matt Drudge, who created one of the first news blogs although he doesn't like the term, once said he figured about 80 percent of his stories were accurate. Few in the mainstream media would accept an error rate that high. Yet Drudge has a tremendous following and was called one of the 100 "people who shape our world" by *Time* magazine in 2006.[22]

Blog readers seem to understand this notion of truth. In a survey, about 61 percent of them found blogs to be "more honest" than other media outlets. They said they trusted blogs because the best of blogs have these traits:

- Blogs often limit themselves to a niche expertise. While newspapers try to cover the whole world, bloggers often become experts on their topics. For this reason, some readers consider them more trustworthy.
- Bloggers are open about their motives. Because they let readers know their biases and subjective approach, they have greater freedom to speak from the heart and use a personal voice. Many readers find this voice more sincere than those of mainstream reporters whose belief in objectivity causes them to mask their feelings so that readers never know how they really feel about issues.
- Bloggers are transparent about sourcing. Because they link to documents, sources and supporting evidence to buttress their own authority, readers believe they have an easier time second-guessing the accuracy of bloggers than they do mainstream reporters.

- When bloggers err, the credible ones take responsibility and post the corrected information alongside their erroneous stories.To many blog readers, this willingness to admit mistakes justifies the trust they have in the blogger.[23]

Chicago Sun-Times columnist Richard Roeper sees some irony in the fact that some people place more faith in bloggers than in the mainstream media. He has pointed out that bloggers often "soak up the news via the wire services, Time.com, Newsweek.com, and about 50 other mainstream-news-organization-dot-coms, before they unleash their opinions."[24] Jeff Jarvis, a media executive who is also a blogger, would not disagree. He believes that the news should be more of a conversation than a lecture. "The news isn't done when we print it," Jarvis has said. "That's when the public can add questions, corrections, perspective. That will improve news and it will also change our relationship with the public."[25]

Many newspapers are applying an idea much like Jarvis is suggesting. They allow readers to add comments to the online versions of stories, with these often appearing on the same page. Unlike traditional letters to the editor, these comments are not edited. Whatever the reader writes is what appears. Some editors are pleased with the conversational framework this gave their online editions. Others find readers' comments objectionable and perhaps libelous. These editors are looking for what they hope are more responsible ways to allow reader input on their Web pages.

Should Journalism Abandon Objectivity?

Geneva Overholser, former editor of *The Des Moines Register* who now teaches journalism at the University of Missouri, is a longtime advocate of shifting away from objectivity. "All too often, a story free of any taint of personal opinion is a story with all the juice sucked out," she has said. "A big piece of why so much news copy today is boring as hell is this objectivity god. Keeping opinion out of the story too often means being a fancy stenographer." Although she said that she understands the concerns of editors who believe that moving away from objectivity "will open the floodgates of opinion writing," she argued that a greater danger is posed by the boredom of "wishy-washy, take-it-or-leave-it writing that is wholly objective."[26]

In an article in *Nieman Reports*, Overholser argued that three positive results might be achieved if the media were less strongly committed to pledges of objectivity. First, she contended that the news media might attract more readers and viewers. She pointed out that the "fastest-growing media sectors – alternative, ethnic, and online media – are known for having a viewpoint. Clearly, they meet a hunger – even a public need. So do more partisan 'mainstream' media, exemplified by Fox News." Second, she noted that interest in politics and voter turnouts are higher in countries where the press is more openly partisan and were higher in the United States before the era of "objective journalism." And third, she wondered if much of the criticism of the media would disappear if journalists were less likely to hide behind the flag of objectivity and more willing to acknowledge their points of reference. "Ideological leanings are not themselves harmful," she wrote. "It is deceit that is wrong – the false presentation of one's intentions." Not fulfilling the promise of objectivity is "hoodwinking the news consumer."[27]

Thomas Mitchell, editor of the *Las Vegas Review-Journal*, also wondered if objective reporting might be driving people away from interest in the political system. He pointed to surveys indicating that Americans have little appetite for political news. He wrote in a column:

> To which I reply, maybe it isn't that the public doesn't care for politics. Maybe it is that you cover politics in such a boring, middle-of-the-road, noncommittal fashion that it induces yawns instead of yelps. Why not come out swinging from an unabashed point of view? Use judgment. Take a stance. Challenge preconceptions.[28]

Gary Gilson, executive director of the Minnesota News Council, lamented that newspapers were always talking about letting reporters write with attitude, but he rarely saw it until he read a personality profile in *The New York Times* by David Carr. The story emphasized the writer's wit and insights. Gilson wrote:

> What I loved about Carr's storytelling was the fact that he convinced me that he KNEW what he was talking about and he TOLD us, instead of hiding behind the journalistic convention of having to attribute every idea to some authoritative source. The debate has gone on for years about whether news organizations should allow reporters to write what they know. Maybe this seeming relaxation of the rules at *The Times* signals a sea change for that newspaper and for the news business.[29]

The formula seems to work well in many countries. Some consider the British public the best informed in the world,[30] and unquestionably they are among the world's most avid newspaper readers. While just over half of Americans read newspapers each day, nearly 70 percent of Brits buy one of the 11 national dailies every day, and about 83 percent buy their local paper. Altogether, according to Britain's Newspaper Society, nearly two out of three buy at least two newspapers every day. Other nationalities are equally devoted to newspapers. More than 80 percent of the populations of Sweden, Singapore, Norway, Finland, and Iceland buy a paper daily, as do three out of four Germans. Their papers tend to be more serious than those in America.

Some argue that the shift away from objectivity has helped ratings of some American cable news networks. Fox News, considered a conservative voice, took the number one spot from CNN. CNN and CNN Headline News fought back by allowing their commentators to take more strident political stances.

"Journalism of attachment"

Martin Bell, a war correspondent for the BBC, advocates what he calls "journalism of attachment." Bell described himself as a traditional BBC objective journalist until he covered the war in Bosnia–Herzegovina. He wrote that in Bosnia he discovered that

> You can be fair to everybody, but you can't stand neutrally between good and evil. You can't say well, Hitler killed six million Jews, but my word he made the trains run on time, because you are not dealing with moral equivalents.[31]

CNN's Christiane Amanpour applied a similar understanding of fairness when she covered that war. She wrote in *Quill*:

> I have come to believe that objectivity means giving all sides a fair hearing, but not treating all sides equally. Once you treat all sides the same in a case such as Bosnia, you are drawing a moral equivalence between victim and aggressor.

Amanpour cited an example. When a shell landed in a market in Sarajevo killing 68 people, mostly Muslims, the Muslims said that the Serbs had fired it. But the Serbs said that the Muslims had fired the shell themselves to gain sympathy. Rather than reporting both sides equally, Amanpour tried to put the bombing in context by citing United Nations figures that the "overwhelming number of mortar shells and sniper fire into the city was from the Serb side." She called the notion that the Muslims had deliberately killed their own people "disgusting."[32]

Amanpour understood that she could be accused of not being objective in the traditional sense. She wrote:

> This increases the burden upon us journalists in the field to act responsibly, to weigh what we do or say, to understand that in these dangerous situations, words we utter matter and can have consequences.... How many times have you heard crusty old TV newsmen say, 'It ain't brain surgery, it's just TV.' But if we go back to the original premise that TV has become the most powerful medium of our time, then it is as important as brain surgery. It's about feeding minds.[33]

Cases to Discuss

These scenarios are based on the experiences of reporters and editors. They have been modified for space and impact. In most of these situations, a reporter would seek advice from an editor – and the editors would make the final decision. But the initial input would come from the reporter, and good editors would listen carefully to the reporter before deciding. On some cases, you can check to see what the real editors did. That doesn't mean they did the right thing, but you can compare your thoughts with theirs.

Truth case 1: The fudging coach

As a sportswriter, you spend a lot of time at the local state university's athletic complex. Most coaches are called "Coach" or by their names. But the current football coach is always addressed as Doctor. His secretary answers the phone that way, and his players and staff shorten it to "Doc." You ask another coach about it and she says, "If you work that hard to get a degree, you deserve the title." You agree.

The football program had been weak for years. University officials decided to take a chance on Doc, who had been an assistant coach at a smaller school for two years and was gaining a reputation as a great recruiter. The gamble paid off. Doc took over a team that had one win and 10 losses the season before he was hired. Now, two years later, the team is likely to win the conference title. Headlines call him "Dr. Victory," and alumni are already worried that other universities will try to woo him away.

You're at a party and some of your friends are joking about the courses that someone would take to get a Ph.D. in physical education. The next day, you wonder what you do study when you get a doctorate in physical education. You know that the coach attended a prestigious university. You check its Web page, but can't find information about a graduate program in physical education. Perhaps it's called something else. So you do a number of searches and can find no graduate courses in any topic related to recreation or physical education. You assume you're wrong about where the coach got his doctorate, so you check the biography issued by the sports information office. You have the right school. Maybe it has discontinued the program. You call the university's public relations office and are told that the university has never offered graduate degrees in physical education.

You get an appointment to talk to Doc. You tell him what you've learned. At first he looks surprised and then starts laughing. "It's really nothing," he says. "It all began as a kind of joke." He explains that after he graduated from college, he injured his knee while preparing for an NFL tryout. His playing career was over and he had hospital bills. So his old coach offered him a job. He listed him as a graduate assistant, paid him the highest salary he could, and made him eligible for the university health insurance. At the first team meeting, the coach introduced him and joked that he was getting a doctorate in nuclear engineering. "From then on, the players called me Doc. The name stuck. I guess later on somebody in sports information took the joke seriously and put that in my bio." He said he would have it corrected.

That sounded possible. The public records laws in your state are good. So you check his file with the university administration. You find that he listed the degree on his application and that the committee recommending him for the position considered it a plus that he had a doctorate in physical education from such a prestigious university.

You can't decide if this is a story. You know that in college sports a coach is hired or fired by his won–lost record, not his education. If he wins the big games, he could probably have flunked out of elementary school. However, you also remember reading about Notre Dame hiring a head football coach and then firing him a few days later when it turned out he had fibbed on his résumé.

When you confront Doc with the new information, he asks, "What's the deal here? I don't need a Ph.D. to coach. They didn't hire me because

I had a Ph.D. That's not even in the job description. They hired me to win football games and that's what we are doing. All you're going to do is embarrass some good people at the university – and prove that you don't have much of a sense of humor."

Apply Potter's box and decide if you will use this story.

Truth case 2: Nobody's perfect

You are a feature writer at a good-size newspaper. You have a job you really like. You write a column that features slice-of-life profiles of people struggling to get by in your community. Your stories grab at readers' compassion and have resulted in offers of cash and jobs to those you describe. The column is popular with readers who often alert you to people you might profile.

You have spent the day working on two columns that will appear in the paper in coming weeks. You received lots of tips about a lonely guy in a wheelchair who engages people in friendly conversations as they wait for buses or stroll past him on their way to work. People seem to enjoy swapping jokes with him. He isn't a beggar and doesn't accept offers of donations.

The other is a young couple who have encountered the difficulties of finding work in the city. The man has been working as a handyman but isn't getting much work. They are living in an abandoned car. Their main source of income comes from his wife, who sells her blood at a local blood bank. Without that money, they would probably starve.

Your paper requires reporters to do basic background checks on people. You discover that the man in the wheelchair has a long record of complaints on file with police, including many for harassing young women. One report dubbed him "the wheelchair pervert." The handyman also has an arrest record that includes drug delivery and burglary, and the girlfriend has been jailed twice on solicitation charges.

You wish that all the subjects of your pieces could have spotless records. But many people in these circumstances have to resort to crime. The purpose of the column is to create compassion and to tell a good story. If you include criminal backgrounds, the flow of the narrative will be broken and no one will sympathize with your subjects. You wonder if sometimes it isn't better to highlight the good in people than to dig out the dirt. So you write the profiles, emphasizing their positive efforts to deal with unfortunate circumstances.

Do you agree or disagree with the feature writer? (*The newspaper's decision is at the back of the book.*)

Notes

1. An interesting account of the news coverage of the early medical findings about cancer and tobacco can be found in Karen Miller, "Smoking up a storm," *Journalism Monographs*, December 1992. Also see Morton Mintz, "Judge says tobacco industry hid risks," *The Washington Post*, April 22, 1988; Carol Leonnig, "U.S. trial against tobacco industry opens," *The Washington Post*, September 22, 2004; John Stauber and Sheldon Rampton, "How the American tobacco industry employs PR scum to continue its murderous assault on human lives," *Tucson Weekly*, November 22, 1995; and "Science, Tobacco and You," a Web site at Florida State University,   http://scienceu.magnet.fsu.edu/content/tobaccohistory/docs/civilwarstud.html.

2. *A Free and Responsible Press: Report of the Commission on Freedom of the Press*. University of Chicago Press, 1947 (Midway Reprint, 1974), pp. 20–29. Also see Theodore Peterson, "The Social Responsibility Theory of the Press," in Fred Siebert, Theodore Peterson, and Wilbur Schramm, Four Theories of the Press, University of Illinois Press, 1956 (pb edn 1973), pp. 73–104.

3. Peterson, *op. cit.*

4. David Halberstam, *The Powers That Be*, New York: Alfred A. Knopf, 1979, p. 194.

5. McCarthy and McCarthyism have been the subject of many books, including Richard H. Rovere's *Senator Joe McCarthy*, a 1959 book reprinted by the University of California Press in 1996, and Robert Griffith, *The Politics of Fear: Joseph R McCarthy and the Senate*, Amherst: University of Massachusetts Press, 1987. A few more recent books have presented McCarthy in a more favorable light, including Ann Coulter, *Treason: Liberal Treachery from the Cold War to the War on Terrorism*, New York: Three Rivers Press, 2003. Some mistakenly confuse McCarthy's Senate committee with the House Committee on Un-American Activities, which blacklisted Hollywood writers and investigated the Ku Klux Klan and the anti-Vietnam War protests.

6. Leon Sigal, *Reporters and Officials*, Lanham, MD: Lexington Books, 1973.

7. It should be noted that *The Christian Science Monitor's* office are in Boston.

8. Dante Chinni, "When media aims for balance, some views and facts get lost," *The Christian Science Monitor,* July 11, 2006.

9. Brent Cunningham, "Re-thinking objectivity," *Columbia Journalism Review,* July/August 2003.

10. Chris Mooney, "Blinded by science," *Columbia Journalism Review,* November/December 2004.

11. Max Boykoff, "The disconnect of news reporting from scientific evidence," *Nieman Reports,* Winter 2005.

12. Cunningham, *op. cit.*

13. Ross Gelbspan, "Disinformation, financial pressures and misplaced balance," *Nieman Reports,* Winter 2005.

14. Lorne Manly, "In wars, quest for media balance is also a battlefield," *The New York Times,* August 14, 2006.

15. David Shaw, "Of isms and prisms," *Columbia Journalism Review,* January/February 1991, pp. 56–57.

16. Michael Robinson and Maura E. Clancey, "Network news, 15 years after Agnew," *Channels,* January/February 1986.

17. Cunningham, *op. cit.*

18 Stephen Berry, "Why objectivity still matters," *Nieman Reports,* Summer 2005.

19. Tim McGuire, "Two perspectives: Reporting with attitude," *Newsworthy,* Winter 2004.

20. David Shaw, "How media gives stories same 'spin,'" *Los Angeles Times,* August 25, 1989.

21. Robert Buckman, "Editors explain the ethical process they go through when determining story content and placement," Society of Professional Journalists Web site at www.spj.org, posted 2005.

22. Ana Marie Cox, "Matt Drudge: Redefining what's news," *Time,* April 30, 2006.

23. J. D. Lasica, "Transparency begets trust in the ever-expanding blogoshere," *Online Journalism Review,* August 12, 2004.

24. Richard Roeper, "What's old is news: Media finalists for online honors," *Chicago Sun-Times,* August 31, 2006.

25. Steve Outing, "What journalists can learn from bloggers," Poynter Online, December 20, 2004.

26. From her remarks in the 13th annual Otis Chandler lecture at the University of Southern California School of Journalism, quoted in M. L. Stein, "Here we go again!" *Editor & Publisher,* November 28, 1992.

27. Geneva Overholser, "The inadequacy of objectivity as a touchstone," *Nieman Reports,* Winter 2004.

28. Thomas Mitchell, "Professional introspection or radical heresy?" *Las Vegas Review-Journal,* December 1, 2002.

29. Gary Gilson, "Breaking the rule of objectivity," Minnesota News Council Web site, www.news-council.org, posted March 3, 2006.

30. Statistics from the November 2006 audit can be found at Web sites of the Newspaper Society, www.newspapersoc.org.uk, and *The Times* (London), www.timesonline.co.uk.

31. Zoe Smith, "If you ask me: Martin Bell," onlinepresgazette.co.uk, November 13, 2006.

32. Christiane Amanpour, "Television's role in foreign policy," *Quill*, April 1996. Also see Sherry Ricchiardi, "Over the line?" *American Journalism Review*, September 1996.

33. Information in this section was drawn from Christiane Amanpour, *op. cit.*, and Sherry Ricchiardi, *op. cit.*

4 Errors

Suppose you are a sexual harassment officer at a large university. Your job requires you to win the trust of the college community. Students must feel free to talk to you about very personal problems. They must believe that you will take their concerns seriously and do your best to solve them. Faculty and administrators rely on your judgment, sensitivity, and diligence in dealing with these delicate issues. Since part of your job is educating people about sexual harassment, you give speeches to campus and community groups and are interviewed by reporters frequently.

One day you are reading your local paper, and you are shocked. You see a story about efforts to reduce sexual harassment on your campus. The story cites a case you know about, an incident involving a note-taking pool in the university's medical school. Two male students took notes at a lecture on the female reproductive process and passed them along to other students in the pool. The notes included many sexist comments, leading one student in the pool to file an official complaint with the university.

Then you see your name in the article and begin to read what you supposedly said. In the article, you sound as if you don't take harassment complaints very seriously. You are quoted as saying you believe that the note-taking incident "is a situation for an apology and a night at the bar rather than a formal investigation." The article goes on to quote you as attacking professors in the university's professional schools. It claims that you expected many sexual harassment problems in those schools because "the whole construct of their reality is male and power oriented." And, although you know that the university has no double standard in the way it treats students and faculty accused of sexual harassment, you are quoted as saying that it's a lot trickier to get your university's administrators to deal with complaints against faculty members than those against students.

You know these are not your opinions. And you know you did not say these things to the reporter because the reporter never even interviewed you! What can you do?

This was the circumstance that Donna Ferrara-Kerr, a sexual harassment officer at the University of Calgary, found herself in after the *Calgary Herald* "quoted" her. When the story appeared, she said the reaction was "immediate, fierce and detrimental." The misquotations undermined her ability to win the trust of harassed people at the university and damaged her relationships with many people on campus. She said she received several calls from outraged people, many of whom doubted her when she said those were not her opinions.

After she complained to the newspaper, the reporter sent Ferrara-Kerr a note admitting she had made a mistake: She had mistakenly attributed statements to Ferrara-Kerr that someone else had made. The paper printed a correction.[1]

Unfortunately, Ferrara-Kerr's experience with the news media is not unique. Even the best and brightest journalists make mistakes. On the same day that *The New York Times* announced on Page 1 that it had won a record seven Pulitzer prizes, it ran four corrections on Page 2. Most of the mistakes are the result of reporters proving that they are human. ("Doctors bury their mistakes," some editor once said. "We print ours.") Nevertheless, on occasion, as we'll see in this chapter, journalists pass along inaccurate information for less forgivable reasons.

How Many Mistakes?

Newspaper and TV news stories are filled with errors. Professor Scott Maier reviewed years of studies and found that the percentage of stories with errors ranged from about 40 to 60 percent. When he gave copies of news stories from 14 newspapers to sources named in the articles, they found factual errors – mistakes in dates, places, titles, spellings, and so on – in about half of them. They also found lots of "subjective errors," meaning they disagreed with the emphasis or context the reporter gave to some parts of the story.[2] Other researches have found that local TV news tends to have fewer factual errors, perhaps because there is usually less detailed information in its reports. However, sources are more likely to complain about subjective errors, which may be a result of compressing the story to suit TV's time demands.[3] Magazines, even with their longer deadlines, are not much better. A fact checker for *Columbia Journalism Review,* which publishes articles written by leading journalists and journalism professors, said that in her three years with the magazine, she has found mistakes in every article she has edited.[4]

All researchers come to one conclusion: These errors are damaging people's faith in the news media. Surveys by the American Society of Newspaper Editors found that "even seemingly small errors feed public skepticism about a newspaper's credibility."[5] And readers told the researchers in one study that they saw lots of small errors:

- 35 percent see spelling or grammar mistakes in their newspaper more than once a week;
- 21 percent see them almost daily;
- 23 percent of the public find factual errors in news stories at least once a week.

Mistakes in spelling, punctuation, and basic information may seem minor. Collectively, however, they can cause the public to doubt the ability of journalists. About three-fourths of the people asked said they were losing faith in the accuracy of the news media. During a focus group, one reader asked ASNE researchers, "Do they have journalism degrees or did they just get out of kindergarten?"[6] One editor understood what the reader meant. "If you make mistakes, it taints everything you do," he said. "If you don't get the date of the daughter's wedding right, how can people believe what else you write?"

Why So Many Errors?

If journalists are better trained and better paid than ever before, why do they make so many mistakes? The answers range from lack of knowledge of the community to unyielding competitive pressures.

Not knowing the community

Many errors in news stories are caused by reporters' isolation from their communities. Ironically, some of this isolation is the result of tougher ethical guidelines that require journalists to be very careful about the organizations they join and the people with whom they socialize. This may prevent conflicts of interest, but it does little to increase journalists' sensitivity, understanding, and knowledge about the people and events they cover. The problem is worsened by the tendency of journalists to make friends primarily with other journalists.

News people often begin their careers at small newspapers and TV stations. Often they plan to live in these small communities only until their big break comes along and they land a job with a major paper or larger-market station. So they don't bother developing ties and friendships or learning much about their communities. When they leave, management hires more beginners to replace them. One veteran small-town newspaper editor said, "Most of our mistakes are caused by being a small newspaper that hires inexperienced people who generally are new to the area."[7] Former Mayor Gus Morrison of Fremont, Calif., described the reporters who have covered his city as "bright, young people who don't know anything – eager and low paid. By the time they learn anything, they go to a different newspaper. There's no history."[8]

Carelessness

Carelessness can lead to silly errors that make the paper itself look foolish, as did these two newspaper corrections:

> It isn't as though the use of nitrous oxide by dentists has just appeared on the scene. It was first used as an anesthetic gas Dec. 11, 1844. That's not a typo. Eighteen eighty-four.[9]
>
> Our newspaper carried the notice last week that Oscar Hoffnagle is a defective on the police force. This was a typographical error. Hoffnagle is, of course, a detective on the police farce.[10]

Perhaps the most common errors caused by carelessness are misspelled names and incorrect addresses and dates. Many editors consider such mistakes unforgivable. The *St. Petersburg Times* fired a veteran photographer for making errors in photo captions. The paper's photo director said its policy was that if in one year "you have three spelling errors [in names], your future on the photo team is in question." The fired photographer had misspelled a name while he was on probation for earlier errors.[11]

Sloppiness – and the related sin of making assumptions – can also create very serious errors. After some lacrosse players at Duke University were suspected of raping a dancer at a team party, the prosecutor was accused by many in the Raleigh–Durham area of grandstanding to publicize his re-election campaign. *The News & Observer* in Raleigh, N.C., ran a story indicating that the prosecutor was pursuing indictments against the men before he had even asked police to collect some key pieces of evidences. Six editors had read the story, and none of them had questioned the timeline it reported. Yet, two days later, the paper admitted that the story was wrong. While looking through investigative records that had been made public, the reporter assumed he understood the meaning of dates scribbled in the notes. He hadn't. The prosecutor had received the evidence nearly two weeks before pursuing charges. The paper's public editor feared that the mistakes would "contribute to the perception of journalistic sloppiness." He said that the reporter's error "was one of carelessness, not malice."[12]

Ignorant reporters?

Journalists are no longer the uneducated louts that the legendary editor and writer H. L. Mencken saw in the American newsrooms of the 1920s. Mencken wrote,

> It is this vast and militant ignorance, this widespread and fathomless prejudice against intelligence, that makes American journalism so pathetically feeble and vulgar, and so generally disreputable.[13]

Unfortunately, ignorance is still a problem. Only 10 percent of editors and publishers in America felt their reporters were well prepared to cover complicated governmental issues, one study found. The editors said reporters need better education in economics, political science, business, and other subject areas. Sources say the same sort of things. When researchers asked them why the sources thought the reporter made errors in stories about them, the top response was that reporters didn't understand what they were writing about. They thought that reporters had not spent enough time researching the topic to make sense of the information the sources were providing.[14]

At one time, reporters gained some of this knowledge and background on the job. At most newspapers and most large TV stations, reporters devoted most of their time to covering beats such as the police, city hall, and the courts. After six months or a year of dealing with the police, city, or judicial systems daily, the reporters got to know how things worked. Because of cutbacks and changes in news focus, reporters are spending less time on beats and more time doing general assignment work. The Minnesota News Council scolded a TV reporter and determined that her coverage of a complicated condemnation case was "unfair" and "inaccurate." The council concluded that she was a general-assignment reporter who was in over her head. One council member, a former TV reporter, said, "I would be terrified if I were a reporter [given this kind of story to cover] and I didn't know how things worked at city hall."

Reporters' ignorance also shows in the coverage of the legal system and of business. Several lawyers told David Shaw of the *Los Angeles Times* that they were "astounded by the number of reporters who accepted what they said – or did not say – without either question or challenge, either out of laziness, ignorance, or a fear of being perceived as ignorant." A judge in Florida once stopped an interview when a young reporter asked what "plaintiff" meant. And a survey of business executives found that only 27 percent of them thought business reporting was fair and accurate.[15] One business executive said he had encountered reporters who did not know the difference between stocks and bonds or recognize the significance of a company buying back its own stock, even though these issues were fundamental to the stories they planned to write.[16] In one survey, 80 percent of business editors said that graduating journalism students were unprepared to cover financial news.[17] Economists interviewed by *Business Week* paid journalists a backhanded compliment. They said they could find no political bias in news coverage of economic issues. But, the economists said, this lack of bias was not caused by the reporters' objectivity. They said that reporters simply did not understand the issues and let candidates play fast and loose when they spoke about the economy.[18]

Ignorance can also result in stories that fail to provide perspective. "Too many stories are very broad but only a quarter-inch thick" because the reporter does not know the background and significance of news events, according to Sandra Mims Rowe, editor of *The Oregonian* in Portland. She believes that reporters need expertise so they can report with authority. "You can't just grab a quote or two or stick a microphone in somebody's face. We need to know as much as our readers."[19]

Some editors are so concerned about journalists' lack of knowledge that they believe journalism education needs to be overhauled.

The ASNE continues to push for requirements that journalism majors spend most of their undergraduate days taking classes outside their major in the liberal arts and sciences so they will know more about what they cover. The editors do not want to see students overload their schedules with writing and communication courses at the expense of political science, history, sociology, and other areas that will give them better backgrounds.[20] Some newspapers turn their newsrooms into classrooms occasionally. They invite experts and college professors to teach staffers short courses in economics, computer spreadsheets, policy issues, and other topics. Unfortunately, these classes are rare. Two-thirds of the nation's journalists receive no regular skills training at all, according to an industry survey. [21]

Perhaps it is asking too much of journalists that they have at least above-average knowledge of the many subjects they deal with every working day. But journalists now have many quick sources of information, including the Internet and electronic databases. In a few minutes searching Google or Lexis-Nexis, reporters can learn enough to reduce errors in their stories and to win the confidence of expert sources, many of whom don't want to spend their time teaching the basics to every reporter who calls.

The fear of math

Mathematics is also a trouble spot for journalists. One newspaper gave a math quiz to its reporters, editor, and photographers. The quiz asked them to do things like calculate the percentage increase in a mayor's salary. They answered 68 percent of the questions correctly, which is barely passing in most schools.[22]

Unfortunately, errors involving math are found in papers ranging from *The New York Times* to small-town weeklies. Reporters confuse "percentages" with "percentage points," miscalculate averages, and misunderstand basic statistical data. *The Atlanta Journal-Constitution* ran a lead story headed "No. 1 again: Atlanta ranked most violent." Two days later, also in the lead spot, the paper ran this headline: "Wrong number: Atlanta's not No. 1 in crime." The story acknowledged that reporters had made a mistake in their mathematical calculations and analyses.[23]

Lots of mistakes are made when math-shy reporters try to interpret campaign polls. *The Kansas City Star* reported that a poll showed that one candidate had "a slim lead" of 46 percent to 43 percent. Several readers pointed out that the margin of error on the poll was plus or minus 4 percentage points. Two days later, the paper referred to the same poll, more correctly, as showing a "neck-and-neck" race.[24] Errors like this are common. Although reporters frequently discuss surveys and polls, many have never taken the time to learn what key terms like "margin of error" and "probability sampling" mean.[25]

A failure to put numbers in context can also result in very misleading stories. *The Florida Times-Union* in Jacksonville did a series of stories about a local high school that was "out of control" and had a "culture of violence." The school led the district in the number of fights and felony arrests. However, as readers pointed out, the high school was larger than most area schools. When the numbers were calculated on a per-capita basis, the school was much like other area high schools.[26]

Editors often demand that reporters find numbers that indicate the significance of an event. If one sexual predator uses the Internet to track down young girls, it's a tragic incident. But if there are 50,000 of these creeps, then it's a tragic trend. Unfortunately, reporters aren't always discriminating in the numbers they choose to use. *Dateline NBC* reported that "50,000 predators were prowling for children online." After *Dateline* used the figure, the attorney general of the United States cited it in a speech, attributing the number to *Dateline*.

Editors at *Legal Times* magazine could find no experts who had heard of the 50,000 number, so they asked *Dateline* where it had found that figure. The researcher for *Dateline* explained that he had asked an FBI expert if it could be true that there were 50,000 predators. The expert said he had no solid evidence, but, "Depending on how you define what is a predator, it could actually be very low." In a follow-up story, reporters at National Public Radio interviewed another expert who said he laughed when he heard the 50,000 number because it is so often used in off-the-cuff estimates. He said that in the 1980s when the kidnapping of children was big news, it was widely reported that 50,000 kids were taken every year. The number was later shown by FBI statistics to be highly inflated. In the 1990s when demonic cults were in the news, the cults were alleged to have killed 50,000 people a year as part of ritual sacrifices. That was more than the total number of homicides reported that year. When secondhand smoke became a villain in news reports, estimates were that it killed 50,000 people a year although no hard evidence supported the figure.

Carl Bialick, a reporter who tracks numbers for the *Wall Street Journal*, concluded, "Maybe the appeal of the number [50,000] was that it wasn't a real small number – it wasn't like 100, 200 – and it wasn't a ridiculously large number, like 10 million. It was like a Goldilocks number – not too hot, not too cold." Bialik contends that journalists do not question numbers enough. "When you find a number that backs up the thesis you've adopted for your story," he said, "it can be really hard to pass it up."[27]

The "infallibility syndrome"

A sports copy editor tells the story of a beginning sportswriter who wrote a basketball story in which he misspelled the name of one of the high schools. When the editor pointed out the error, the reporter became indignant. He said he was there and that's the way the name was spelled. Even after the editor showed the reporter a picture with the spelling clearly visible on team uniforms, the reporter continued to insist he was right.

Although this may be an extreme case, many reporters and editors suffer from a malady that can only be called "infallibility syndrome." This syndrome may be a byproduct of the pressures journalists face. Reporters, producers, and editors are expected to achieve a super-human feat: They must be right all the time. This pressure causes many to resist any suggestions that they may be wrong.

The syndrome may be responsible for many of the errors in the paper. Sometimes reporters become so sure they are right that they fail to check and double-check their information, or they assume that they understand what their sources mean. As one copy editor said, some journalists can't admit to themselves that they have made mistakes "because the idea of a mistake is so stigmatized. In a perverse turn-about, the intense fear of mistakes just makes for more mistakes."[28]

Reporters who have their egos in check and are willing to admit to being human recognize that they can make mistakes. To avoid errors, they repeat information back to sources and look things up in reference materials. They also recognize that sources can be wrong, so they call additional sources just to verify the facts.

Getting caught up in the story

CNN had a dramatic story for the debut of *NewsStand*, an investigative news program. The story claimed that the American military had used nerve gas in Southeast Asia and had hunted down and killed deserters.

Reporters said that a retired admiral who was chairman of the Joint Chiefs of Staff had confirmed the information.

The story was questioned even before it was broadcast. CNN's own Pentagon reporters had long ago stopped interviewing the admiral, who was 86 years old and lived in an assisted-care retirement home. After the story was broadcast, CNN yielded to the criticism and started its own in-house review of the story, which soon led to its retraction. CNN concluded that the reporters and producers had not been deceitful. They believed every word they wrote. "If anything, the serious flaws in the broadcast . . . may stem from the depths of those beliefs." Reporters and producers were so certain the allegations were true that they discounted any information that was contrary to what they believed. The reporters denied the accusation. They continued to say their story was accurate and accused CNN of caving in to government pressure.[29]

Maintaining the narrative

At one time, newspaper stories related the bare-bones facts and emphasized the five W's – who, when, what, where, and why. Today's newspaper writing is more complex. Writers are expected to find a narrative, a story they can tell so that their reports have more impact. Here's the opening of a story in *The Virginian-Pilot* about the murder of a security guard at Virginia Wesleyan College:

> Walter Zakrzewski didn't want to leave Chicago. His roots, his family were there.
>
> But his wife, Mary Ann, wanted to be close to her family in Hampton Roads. So this year, Zakrzewski left his job at the steel mill and headed east to find another job and another home.

Family members immediately called to complain. They pointed out minor factual errors. Zakrzewski lost his job some time ago when the steel mills closed. But more important, his mother-in-law said, was the false implication in the story. "I don't appreciate you putting down that they moved here because of my daughter," she wrote. The family thought the story placed too much of the blame for his death on his wife's insistence that they live near her parents. The reporter and his editor said that the reporter had reported what he had been told and that they were "very surprised when we recognized the story could be interpreted that way." The paper's public editor suggested that additional attribution may have solved the problem, but he noted that "such attribution is sometimes omitted to provide a narrative feel."[30]

Understaffed newsrooms

It is no secret that many news organizations have fewer people in their newsrooms than they did in previous years. Some journalists have been laid off outright. Others have been bought out, in effect given a bonus for resigning. Even at news organizations that have not taken these drastic steps, managers have decided not to replace journalists who retire or leave for other jobs. The result is fewer journalists in the newsroom being expected to do more.

Nowhere is that more evident than on the copy desks. Traditionally, stories were edited at least twice for errors: once by an assigning editor who oversaw the reporter's work, and once by a copy editor whose job was to check the stories for grammatical, factual, and ethical problems and write the headlines. Often other editors too would read the story before it was printed. Even at the smallest papers, it was rare for a story to appear in the paper without its being reviewed by at least one editor.

This line of defense against error is getting weaker and weaker at many publications. As cost-cutting measures, some newspapers have reduced the number of assigning and copy editors. The result is often a constricted copy flow. One copy editor at a large Midwestern newspaper described it like this:

> [I]f for example there are 35 stories appearing in the paper, more likely than not, 25 of the stories move to the copydesk in the last 45 minutes before the paper is slated to lock up – everything (or much of it) pops near deadline. That puts a strain on the ability to check facts, weigh fairness, check spelling and grammar, rectify inconsistencies, write a good headline and trim the story to fit the hole.[31]

Copy editors used to be called the "final guardians of journalism ethics" because they were the last editorial employees to read a story. They still play this role at quality newspapers. But at most papers, copy editors no longer merely edit copy. Although editors have always designed pages, they must also produce them on computers, a job formally done by non-journalists in the composing room. In a recent survey, a large number of them told researchers that their jobs were now primarily checking for grammar and AP Style, writing headlines and using computers to lay out pages.

They had no time to check for factual errors and libel or to raise ethical concerns. One lamented that "other departments sometimes forget that we are not trained monkeys drawing boxes on the computer."[32]

TV news directors also struggle with reviewing stories before they are broadcast. News staffs overwhelmingly favor having their scripts reviewed, but reporters admit that does not happen often. Only about 10 percent of the scripts they use for their live reports get checked by anyone. Even many investigative and sweeps-week packages are not reviewed before they are broadcast.

A Newslab survey found that local TV journalists said their stations do not provide the resources needed to make their reports to be as accurate as possible. "In an effort to save money, many of the safety nets to catch mistakes and errors have been cut," one respondent wrote. "More than ever, the quality of the newscast depends on the quality of the producer, because there is no one to catch his/her mistakes."[33]

Lack of diversity in newsrooms

Newspaper and TV station managers have long acknowledged that news coverage would better serve their communities if their newsrooms were more diverse. For years, most have had a goal of achieving "parity," meaning that the percentage of minority journalists would equal the percentage in their communities. They still are not close to meeting that goal. Although minorities make up about a third of the U.S. population, less than 14 percent of the people in newspaper newsrooms are minorities: about 6 percent are black, 5 percent Latino, 3 percent Asian American, and less than 1 percent Native American.[34] TV stations have long been required by the Federal Communications Commission to diversify their staffs. Still, they have not yet achieved parity. About 22 percent of newsroom employees are minorities: about 10 percent African-American, 10 percent Hispanic, 3 percent Asian-American, and less than 1 percent Native American. In local radio, the minority workforce is about 6.4 percent.[35] (This issue is also discussed in Chapter 14.)

Checking Facts and Quotes with Sources

An editor of *The Atlanta Journal and Constitution* once said he had been interviewed countless times through the years and had been quoted correctly only once.[36] Former ABC religion correspondent Peggy Wehmeyer said she always asks reporters who interview her if she can see the story before it's printed. "Almost always if they do let me see it, I find mistakes."[37]

Unfortunately, their experiences are not common. When researchers compare quotes in news stories about trials with the official transcripts, they often find differences. However, most journalists would refuse to let Wehmeyer or any other source read their stories before they are printed. "I don't think it's ever acceptable to show stories or read back quotes," Matthew V. Storin told *American Journalism Review* when he was editor of *The Boston Globe*. "One of the dangers of reading quotes back is that person will say, 'I didn't say this,'" he said. "You leave yourself open to being pressured to change what they said." Sources may also pressure editors to kill or change stories that are unfavorable to them.[37]

To some, showing stories to sources is "weak-kneed journalism." Frank Stansberry, a *Business Week* reporter before becoming a corporate public relations executive, said, "As a PR person, I never had the temerity to ask a reporter to see a story, and as a reporter, I would have been offended to have been asked."[38]

However, readbacks are common at magazines such as *Time, National Geographic*, and *The New Yorker*. Some newspaper reporters also make it a standard practice. Jay Matthews of *The Washington Post* said he has read or faxed copies of stories to sources for the past 10 years. "I've done it this long without any serious mishap. Every year I'm more confident about the process." He said he became a believer the first time he read back a story to a source. He had made a serious error but was able to correct it before the story was printed. Matthews added that he has found readbacks most helpful in catching "the unconscious errors, the verbal misunderstandings, the odd misspellings, the mental lapses that occur in communication between human beings. . . ."[39]

Many journalists would like to see the practice spread. They think making sure that stories are correct is worth the additional hassle. "I just have a really hard time seeing the downside," investigative reporter Rosemary Armao of the *South Florida Sun-Sentinel* said.[40]

Even opponents of readbacks agree that sometimes calling back sources to check facts is necessary. Storin said he was surprised to hear one of his reporters at *The Boston Globe* telling a source about a story before it ran in the paper. After talking with her, he decided she was doing the right thing. "When she does medical stories with medical sources, she calls them to go over the gist of what they say. I consider that not only acceptable, but . . . it makes sense."

Fred Brown, former co-chair of the Society of Professional Journalists' ethics committee, has created a set of rules that he follows when checking with sources. He makes it clear to them that he is trying to make his story completely accurate, not to accommodate them. He begins checking his accuracy during the interview. He asks questions like: "I think I understood what you said about bird flu and down pillows, but let me read it back to you to be sure I have it right." He is hesitant to change quotes unless the new quote explains the story more clearly. Also, he generally allows sources to read only parts of a story, not all of it.[41]

A Disaster Brings Out the Best – and the Worst

Some of the coverage of Hurricane Katrina that hit the Gulf Coast in 2005 was remarkably valiant. Local journalists kept working even though their homes and families were caught up in the devastation.

Journalists at *The Times-Picayune* in New Orleans had to abandon their downtown building and set up shop in makeshift newsrooms. Yet they continued to report on the paper's Web site and on blogs. Their coverage was marked by knowledge of the city and by a dogged determination to get the story right. When *Times-Picayune* reporters heard rumors of a school where scores of people had been trapped and many had drowned, they got rowboats and went to the school. There were no bodies; the rumor was false. Some less diligent news organizations simply reported the rumor and got the story wrong, further stressing families with loved ones who lived near the school. Along the Mississippi coast, *The Sun Herald* in Biloxi never stopped publishing, even on the day the hurricane hit. Papers, which were passed out at evacuation centers, contained detailed reports of the extent of the damage. The paper set up discussion boards on its Web site so that people could exchange information about missing friends and loved ones.

Both papers received Pulitzer prizes for public service, the highest award a newspaper can be given. Judges lauded *The Sun Herald* for "providing a lifeline for devastated readers, in print and online, during their time of greatest need." *The Times-Picayune* received a second Pulitzer for its breaking-news coverage of the tragedy.

Network and cable news journalists were widely praised for their ability to amass the equipment and personnel needed to show the world what was happening. Andy Smith of *The Providence Journal* noted that while some TV personalities exploited the situation (Geraldo Rivera wept as he held up a 10-month-old baby at the Convention Center), others distinguished themselves by playing hardball with federal officials who were trying to spin the failures of the rescue efforts. Typical was ABC's Ted Koppel's response when, three days after the storm hit the city, Michael Brown, the head of the Federal Emergency Management Agency, said that the federal government had just learned that there were people in the convention center. "Don't you watch television? Don't you listen to the radio?" Koppel asked.[42]

Mistakes cause hardships

Obviously, during the hurricane reporters were faced with unprecedented obstacles. Phone lines were down and cell phones were dead. There was no electricity. Gasoline was so difficult to find that the police resorted to siphoning it from stranded vehicles. Even if journalists had gas, the floodwater made auto travel impossible. The normal avenues of information had disappeared. The government was overwhelmed, and the police had lost communication. Instead of serving as sources for reporters, many emergency officials were getting their information from the news media.

Clearly, in such circumstances mistakes are bound to happen. Yet, when journalists looked back on the coverage, many were surprised by the number of stories that contained serious errors. Among the mistaken information:

- Babies were raped in the Superdome and convention center.
- A 7-year-old girl died after she was raped and her throat cut.
- Thirty to 40 dead bodies were stored in a convention center freezer.
- Hundreds of bodies were stacked in the Superdome basement.
- Snipers and armed mobs targeted victims trying to leave the Superdome.
- Shots were fired at military helicopters trying to rescue victims.

All of these reports were erroneous. Only 10 people altogether died at the Superdome and convention center, and only one of them was murdered. There were no substantiated claims that snipers fired on victims outside hospitals. Reports that military helicopters had been fired at were rejected by both the National Guard and the Coast Guard, the only two military agencies involved.[43]

These mistakes may have hindered rescue efforts. After hearing reports of shots being fired at rescue workers, police delayed and even stopped help from coming to New Orleans. The AP reported that one medevac helicopter service stopped airlifting the sick and injured from the Superdome after officials heard reports that shots had been fired at a military helicopter.[44] According to *The New York Times,* police kept teams of paramedics from entering the disaster scene for nearly 10 hours because of reports of armed mobs. While sick patients were stuck in hospitals with no air conditioning, no running water, and dwindling food and medical services, ambulances that could have rescued them stayed in "safe" areas outside the city.[45]

The news reports of murder and mayhem frightened many in neighboring communities. Some took steps to keep the victims out of their communities. The Superdome and convention center, where thousands were being held, were near on-ramps to bridges that led to dry land in the city of Gretna on the other side of the Mississippi. However, Gretna police officers, having heard reports of drug-crazed thugs and murderers, blocked the bridge and forced about 5,000 people to return to downtown New Orleans. Buses that could have carried people out of the city sat idle because drivers thought they needed police protection to drive into New Orleans.

Why so many errors?

Reporters were bombarded by reports of death and destruction. That took its toll on many of them. Brian Thevenot is the *Times-Picayune* reporter who mistakenly wrote that a freezer in the basement of the convention center contained 30 or 40 bodies, including a 7-year-old girl with her throat cut. He later explained the scene to *American Journalism Review*:

> As I walked briskly through the dimly lit area inside the food service entrance of New Orleans' Ernest N. Morial Convention Center, the thought of pulling back the sheets covering the four stinking, decomposing corpses in front of me seemed wrong, even perverse. Before I'd even thought to ask, one of the two soldiers who escorted me, Arkansas National Guardsman Mikel Brooks, nixed the prospect of looking inside the freezer he and another soldier said contained "30 or 40" bodies.

"I ain't got the stomach for it, even after what I saw in Iraq," he said.

I didn't push it. Now I wish I had, as gruesome as that may seem. The soldiers might have branded me a morbid fiend and run me the hell out of there, but my story in *The Times-Picayune* would have been right, or at least included a line saying I'd been denied the opportunity to lay eyes on the freezer.[46]

It's difficult to blame Thevenot for not looking in the freezer. Later he discovered the soldiers had not looked in the freezer either. They had heard about the bodies and the dead child from some other soldiers while standing in the food line. *The Times-Picayune* ran a correction – but not before the story was reported worldwide.

Rumors at scenes of tragedies are to be expected. Even small-city police reporters are often surprised at obviously fraudulent accounts volunteered by supposed witnesses. At major news events, reporters routinely have to discount rumors. In a *New York Times* story headlined "More horrible than truth: News reports," David Carr wrote:

I was at the World Trade Center towers site the afternoon of Sept. 11, 2001. People had seen unimaginable things, but a small percentage, many still covered in ash, told me tales that were worse than what actually happened. Mothers throwing babies out of the towers, men getting in fights on the ledges, human heads getting blown out of the buildings, all of which took place so high up in the air that it was hard to distinguish the falling humans from the falling wreckage.[47]

Few of these rumors were ever reported by the hundreds of journalists on the scene. At one point, ABC's Peter Jennings scolded his reporters on air when he thought they might be reporting unverified information. A detailed review of TV news coverage found that during 9-11, reporters spent little time repeating rumors and anchors reminded viewers when they were reporting information that had not been confirmed.[48]

Many in the media were much less cautious in New Orleans. What developed was an "echo chamber," as *Boston Globe* reporter Kevin Cullen called it. Each time people heard about an act of violence, it was assumed it was a new incident. As a deputy police chief explained, "One guy saw six bodies. Then another guy saw six bodies. And another guy saw the same six and all of a sudden, it becomes 18."

Adding to the media's difficulties, Mayor Ray Naggin and Chief of Police Eddie Compass seemed to confirm frightening tales of violence and to report others, many of which proved untrue. Some suggested that

Naggin and Compass were hoping the stories would prompt faster relief efforts by federal officials. Others, like the *Times-Picayune's* Michael Perlstein, doubted city officials were deliberately exaggerating. He said:

> I think that the mayor was caught up in the same thing that a lot of people were caught up, reporters, officials and everyone else here included, and that there was a communications blackout. He was getting reports from pretty credible sources. But, by then, it had been passed along four or five different times, the story exaggerated each time along the way.

Some contend that social class and race may have caused many in the media to lose their skepticism. Carl Smith, a professor at Northwestern University, told David Carr he was not surprised that Americans so readily believed even the worst of the rumors. "There is a timeless primordial appeal of the story of a city in chaos and people running loose," he said. The rumors offered "the fulfillment of some timely ideas and prejudices about the current social order." Kevin Cullen believes that the city's reputation as the "Big Easy" and its notorious high murder rate caused many to accept the reports of violence.

Another element may also have been at work. "While many would be loathe to admit it," Cullen wrote, "the idea of poor black folks simultaneously looting Wal-Mart of guns and widescreen TVs in some apocalyptic 'Get whitey!' frenzy seemed perfectly feasible to many reporters and editors, not to mention readers, listeners and viewers." He said class and race were "intrinsically bound up in New Orleans" and many reporters had trouble making sense of it.

Five ways the media can improve

Thevenot of the *Times-Picayune* believes that the coverage would have been better if journalists had followed basic tools of reporting, such as the following:

- *Question persistently.* Reporters should have fired persistent questions at would-be sources: "How do you know that? Did you see it? Who told you this? Are you 100 percent sure this happened? Who else can confirm it?" One journalist concluded that too many reporters began to believe a story was corroborated if they heard the same rumor twice.
- *Be upfront about verification.* Thevenot said that newspaper and TV reporters should not back away from this honest statement: "This account could not be independently verified."

- *Correct mistakes prominently and promptly*. Hub Brown, an associate professor of broadcast journalism at Syracuse University, told Thevenot that broadcast journalists need to be as "meticulous" as print journalists in correcting their mistakes. "Why not have a segment in the newscast that says, 'We've reported this through the past day, and it turned out to be wrong'?"
- *Use exact attribution*. Explain who sources are and how they came about their information – even official sources.
- *Don't rush things into print or onto the air*. Av Westin, a former vice president of ABC News, said that journalism requires thoughtful editing. "When I was at ABC, nothing got on the air without having the piece read in to us," he told Thevenot. He said the 24-7 news cycle leads to "the reporting of rumor and speculation.... Rather than saying, 'Let's wait five minutes,' they just go with it because it's in front of them. They keep learning that lesson and forgetting that lesson."[49]

Notes

1. The original story was "Dean probes sexism issue," *Calgary Herald*, November 15, 1991, p. B1. The correction was printed the next day. The newspaper's ombudsman, Jim Stott, discussed the incident in "More flexible error correction policy would serve all," *Calgary Herald*, December 8, 1991, p. A7.
2. Scott Maier, "Accuracy matters: A cross-market assessment of newspaper error and credibility," *Journalism and Mass Communication Quarterly*, Autumn 2005.
3. Gary Hanson and Stanley T. Wearden, "Measuring newscast accuracy: Applying a newspaper model to television," *Journalism and Mass Communication Quarterly*, Autumn 2004.
4. Ariel Hart, "Delusions of accuracy," *Columbia Journalism Review*, July/August 2003.
5. American Society of Newspaper Editors, *Examining Our Credibility: Perspectives of the public and the press*, 1999.
6. "Accuracy matters," in *Examining Our Credibility*, American Society of Newspaper Editors, www.asne.org.
7. Donica Mensing and Merlyn Oliver, "Editors at small newspapers say error problems serious," *Newspaper Research Journal*, Fall 2005.
8. Nancy Davis, "Views from City Hall," *Presstime*, August 1998.
9. Reprinted in "The lower case," *Columbia Journalism Review*, November/December 1990.

10. Paula LaRocque, "Corrections, however painful or funny, needed for credibility," *Quill*, April 2005.
11. "Errors in print a firing offense?" *News Photographer*, April 1998.
12. Ted Vaden, "Lacrosse error clouds story's credibility," *The News & Observer*, August 3, 2006.
13. H. L. Mencken, *Promises: Sixth Series*, New York: Knopf, 1927, p. 15.
14. Scott Maier, *op. cit.*
15. "F.Y.I." *Washington Journalism Review*, January/February 1993, p. 13.
16. Cortland Anderson, remarks to APME Convention, Toronto, October 21, 1981.
17. Mary Jane Pardue, "Most business editors find news reporters unprepared," *Newspaper Research Journal*, Summer 2004.
18. *Business Week*, November 11, 1996.
19. Sandra Mims Rowe's comments were taken from her remarks at the Asian American Journalists conference in Boston, August 15, 1997, and from "Journalism values in an era of change," a speech to a Poynter Institute Conference in New York, February 14–16, 1996.
20. Seymour Topping, "'Expert journalism' requires a broad education," *ASNE Bulletin*, November 1992, p. 2.
21. Geneva Overholser, "Careening toward extinction with salvation firmly in hand," *Columbia Journalism Review*, September/October 2002.
22. Scott R. Maier, "Journalists + math = anxiety, self-doubt," *The American Editor*, January/February 2002.
23. Geneva Overholser, "Reading into what you read," *The Washington Post*, June 2, 1996.
24. Derek Donovan, "Readers share skepticism about election polls," *The Kansas City Star*, October 29, 2006.
25. If you were curious enough to check this footnote, you might want to read journalism Professor Philip Meyer's *Precision Journalism*, Lanham, MD: Rowman and Littlefield, 4th edn (May 2002). Probability sampling is a highly precise method of making sure everyone has an equal chance of being in the sample pool. For example, selecting every 10th person entering the library is not a legitimate sampling method.
26. Wayne Ezell, "When headlines go too far," *The Florida Times-Union*, September 3, 2006.
27. "Prime number," *On the Media*, NPR, May 26, 2006.
28. Ariel Hart, "Delusions of accuracy," *Columbia Journalism Review*, July/August 2003.
29. Information taken from reports on the CNN Web site, July 2, 1998.
30. Marvin Lake, "Security guard came to area willingly," *The Virginian-Pilot*, October 22, 2006.

31. Quoted in Susan Keith, "Newspaper copy editors' perceptions of their ideal and real ethics roles," *Journalism and Mass Communications Quarterly,* Winter 2005.
32. *ibid.*
33. Deborah Potter and Amy Mitchell, "Getting It Right," study posted at www.newslab.com.
34. The American Society of Newspaper Editors surveys diversity each year and posts the results on its Web site, www.nsne.org.
35. The Radio Television News Directors Association surveys diversity each year and posts the results on its Web site, www.rtnda.org.
36. Eleanor Randolph, "The other side of the pen," *Messages: The Washington Post Media Companion,* Boston: Allyn and Bacon, 1991, p. 351.
37. Alicia C. Shepard, "Show and print," *American Journalism Review,* March 1996.
38. Information taken from reports on the CNN Web site, July 2, 1998.
39. Jay Matthews, "When in doubt, read it back," *Washington Journalism Review,* September 1985.
40. Alicia C. Shepard, "Show and print," *American Journalism Review,* March 1996.
41. Maria Trombly, "To check or not to check," *Quill,* May 2004, and Fred Brown, "Letting sources check your story can be a good thing," *Quill,* April 2006.
42. Andy Smith, "TV at its best," *The Providence Journal,* September 9, 2005.
43. Taken from Kate Parry, "A duty to separate fact from rumor; Post-hurricane coverage reviews failed to substantiate the most extreme stories. How did the Star Tribune do?" (Minneapolis) *Star Tribune,* October 9, 2005.
44. Adam Nossiter, "Superdome evacuation disrupted because of fires and gunshots; More National Guardsmen are sent in," Associated Press, September 1, 2005.
45. Jim Dwyer and Christopher Drew, "Fear exceeded crime's reality in New Orleans," *The New York Times,* September 29, 2005.
46. Brian Thevenot, "Myth-making in New Orleans," *American Journalism Review,* December 2005/January 2006.
47. David Carr, "More horrible than truth: News reports," *The New York Times,* September 19, 2005.
48. Amy Reynolds and Brooke Barnett, "This just in . . . How national TV news handled the breaking 'live' coverage of September 11," *Journalism and Mass Communication Quarterly,* Autumn 2003.
49. The media coverage of Katrina was widely studied. It should be noted that figures continued to change and that myths continued to be

exposed long after the event. The information presented is as accurate as possible. Among the articles consulted were Adam Nossiter, "Superdome evacuation disrupted because of fires and gunshots," *Associated Press*, Sept. 1, 2005; Andy Smith, "TV at its best," *The Providence Journal*, Sept. 10, 2005; David Carr, "More Horrible Than Truth: News Reports," *The New York Times*, Sept. 19, 2005; Eric Deggans, "Media outlets exaggerated some of New Orleans' woes," *St. Petersburg Times*, Sept. 28, 2005; Jim Dwyer and Christopher Drew, "Fear Exceeded Crime's Reality in New Orleans," *The New York Times*, Sept. 29, 2005; Anne Applebaum, "The Rumor Mill," *The Washington Post*, Oct. 5, 2005; Robert E. Pierre and Ann Gerhart, "News of Pandemonium May Have Slowed Aid," *The Washington Post*, Oct. 5, 2005; "Taking journalists by storm," *The News Media and The Law*, Fall 2005; Brian Thevenot, "Apocalypse in New Orleans," *American Journalism Review*, October/November 2005; Marc Fisher, "Essential Again," *American Journalism Review*, October/November 2005; Thevenot, "Myth-Making in New Orleans," *American Journalism Review*, December 2005/January 2006; Matthew Power, "Immersion Journalism," *Harper's*, December 2005; "They Shoot Helicopters, Don't They?" *Reason*, December 2005; Katie O'Keefe, "Ethical Firestorm," *Quill*, December 2005; Kevin Cullen, "Rumors, Race and Class Collide," *Nieman Reports*, winter 2005; Scott Cohn, "Journalists were fair in covering Katrina," *Quill*, January/February 2006; and James O'Byrne, "Katrina: The Power of the Press Against the Wrath of Nature," Poynteronline, www.poynter.org, posted Sept. 1, 2006.

5 Transparency

Spokane editor Steve Smith knew the story would hit many nerves. His readers had elected Jim West to the Washington state Legislature several times, and now he was the city's mayor. His popularity came in part from his pro-family stance and what some described as his "anti-gay agenda." Now, Smith's newspaper, *The Spokesman-Review*, was going to report that the popular politician had been "trolling for young men on an Internet Web site" and had recently offered benefits and a city hall internship to a teenage boy he was pursuing. The paper discovered that in the 1970s West had been accused of sexually molesting at least two boys while serving as a Boy Scout leader. He denied the charges.

Smith anticipated what would happen once the story appeared: "We knew the mayor would come after the newspaper with every tool in his considerable political arsenal." The mayor would deny the stories. The mayor's friends would say reporters must have twisted his words and taken quotes out of context. The paper would be accused of making innocent acts by the mayor seem evil and of entrapping the mayor. Even people who did not like the mayor would question the paper's outing the mayor and violating his privacy.

Normally, a newspaper staff would have to steel themselves to the criticism and hope that readers would trust the paper's reporting. But Smith had another plan. "Our defense, we decided, would be full disclosure, upfront, of the information underlying our stories," Smith explained in *Nieman Reports*. The paper would allow readers "to review all of the material with which we were dealing so that they could decide for themselves if we had been fair to the mayor, if we were contextually accurate as well as factually accurate, if, in short, we were credible."

The newspaper posted on its Web site full transcripts of conversations the mayor had with a consultant posing as a 17-year-old boy, transcripts of all reporters' interviews with the mayor and his chief accusers, copies of all official documents the paper used in its investigation, and the raw notes Smith took when the mayor called him "to tearfully explain his hellish life as a closeted, conflicted and now accused gay man."

Smith said the opening of the newspaper's files served its purpose. Although the paper's daily circulation is about 90,000, its Web site with the documentation drew 519,000 unique page visits. "Again and again readers told us how much they appreciated seeing the background material," he said.[1]

Smith acknowledged that this was an unusual circumstance and that the paper would not normally print reporters' notes or transcripts of interviews. But he said he was committed to a transparent newsroom that allowed readers to understand and in some cases participate in newsroom decisions. Among the things his paper does to be more transparent:

- Every day five bloggers critique the paper on its Web site.
- Five editors participate in an online blog answering readers' questions. Some of the questions and answers are reprinted each week on the paper's editorial pages.
- The meetings where editors make news decisions and choose what will be on Page 1 are webcast on the paper's Internet site.
- Those meetings are also open to the public, who can participate in the discussions. The time and place of the meetings are announced every day on Page 1.
- A local journalism professor serves as a part-time ombudsman for the paper, writing an occasional column and resolving readers' complaints.

Smith's actions are in stark contrast to the way journalism has traditionally been practiced. In this chapter, we look at many of the new ways the news media are engaging in self-regulation and explaining themselves to the public to make their actions more transparent. And we see how the public is holding the media accountable.

Explaining Ourselves

Smith's *Spokesman-Review* is not the only paper to try to be more transparent, and its editors are not the only ones who believe that journalism benefits from openness. When Richard Davis was convicted in a highly publicized murder trial of killing Polly Klaas, he turned toward the family and extended both middle fingers. (see Figure 5.1). It's not the kind of thing readers expect to see when they open their morning paper. Yet, the *San Jose Mercury News* ran photographs of the killer's gesture and explained its decision in a front-page letter to readers, saying that the picture illustrated the character of a child killer and the contempt he had for society. The *San Francisco Chronicle* also ran the picture – but without the editor's note.[2] The *Mercury News* received about 1,200 responses, two-to-one in favor of publication. The *Chronicle* got 130 calls, nearly all of which were critical. The paper's editor at the time was not surprised by the different results. "People love to know how and why you make decisions," Jerry Ceppos told *American Journalism Review*. "It's an easy way to get some of our credibility back."[3]

Some papers use blogs to explain themselves. At *The Dallas Morning News*, editors not only explain their decisions in blogs, they also allow readers to join in the discussions. They hope blogs will let readers understand that the editor writers do not meet "in some dark, dank, smoke-filled chamber and await orders from on high about what to say and when to say it." Reader reaction has been positive, and the blog receives thousands of visits a day.[4]

Correcting the record

Corrections are the most obvious – and most painful – way the media explain themselves to the public. Research suggests that readers respect such honesty. In a national survey, 78 percent said corrections made them "feel better" about their newspaper. About half of readers routinely check the corrections.

American newspapers are the world leaders in running corrections. Some papers pride themselves on correcting even the smallest of errors. *The Hartford Courant* even points out when a middle initial was reported incorrectly; the *Courant* averages 100 corrections a month. And the trend at most papers is toward running more corrections. Gina Lubrano, reader representative at *The San Diego Union-Tribune*, said her paper printed only seven corrections in 1960. Now it publishes over 700 a year. "I don't think today's *Union-Tribune* is making more errors than its predecessors did decades ago," she wrote. "It's just that correcting errors – both big and small – is a priority." In 2005, *The Boston Globe*

Figure 5.1   Polly Klass' murderer. The *San Jose Mercury News* took the unusual precaution of including a front-page letter explaining its decision to publish this photograph of Richard Allen Davis' obscene gesture. (*Photo courtesy of the San Jose Mercury News*).

had more than 1,000 corrections; *Oregonian*, 800; *Orlando Sentinel*, 779; *Star Tribune* in Minneapolis, 611; *The Kansas City Star*, 482; and *Akron Beacon-Journal*, 450.[5] There's even a Web site – www. regrettheerror.com – that catalogs news media corrections. Some are amazingly funny, making the site popular with both journalists and non-journalists.

Some local TV news stations treat corrections very serious. They have written guidelines that news staffs must follow. If they discover the mistake in time, they run a correction immediately. Because viewers may not watch all 90 minutes of the local newscast, producers repeat the corrections the next day. Less diligent stations will correct the air the next time the story is broadcast. Some are not completely honest and camouflage their errors by saying, "We've now been told."

Lots of local stations are even less forthcoming. Despite findings that as many as one-third of their stories contain inaccuracies, only a sixth of the stations run corrections as often as once a month, according to one study. Another found that about a third of local stations never or very rarely correct their mistakes on the air. A broadcast journalist told researchers for NewsLab that whether his station ran a correction depended on who spotted the error. "Unless a viewer points it out, usually the newsroom also overlooks it." Another station had a similar policy: "Most errors are swept under the rug hoping no viewer calls us on it." At other stations, the errors are discussed among news staff members, but are not reported publicly.[6]

Network news has been slower than newspapers in adopting systematic ways of correcting errors. Although prompt corrections are required by codes of ethics at all of the TV networks, corrections remain rare. "*The Washington Post* and *The New York Times* ran 2,000 corrections between them last year," Michael Gartner, former president of NBC News, said. "The TV networks ran fewer than a half-dozen. Corrections should not be so rare that when they are made they are big news."[7] Some individual TV programs set their own standards. ESPN's *Pardon the Interruption*, which features discussions and arguments among sportswriters, was one of the few cable-news programs in 2006 that regularly set aside time for corrections.

Acknowledging mistakes is an integral part of many serious news blogs. "They prominently post corrections to errors, publishing them quickly," Steve Outing wrote in Poynter Online. Some place corrections as the first item on a page so readers will be more likely to see them.[8] For some blogs, corrections are a necessary part of their approach to reporting. Unlike traditional media that try to verify facts before they are published, some blogs believe their role is to report rumors first and then correct them if they prove to be wrong. They hope their willingness to run corrections will help them keep the trust of their readers.

Second-guessing the coverage – publicly

Some newspaper editors are going a step further than just correcting factual errors. They tell readers when they think their own news judgments were wrong. Editors at both *The New York Times* and *The Washington Post* examined their papers' coverage during the days leading up to the U.S. invasion of Iraq. Each confessed to readers that the reporting was not as rigorous as it should have been. On its front page, the *Times* said,

> In some cases, information that was controversial then, and seems questionable now, was insufficiently qualified or allowed to stand unchallenged. Looking back, we wish we had been more aggressive in re-examining the claims as new evidence emerged – or failed to emerge.[9]

The *Post* was equally chagrined. It admitted that stories that were skeptical of whether Iraq's Saddam Hussein had weapons of mass destruction were buried deep inside the paper, while stories repeating the Bush administration's assertions that he did were placed on Page 1.[10]

Two years after the *Orlando Sentinel* editorially supported the sale of an abandoned Navy base to a Chicago developer, the paper acknowledged that it had not been critical enough of the deal that allowed the developer to buy "valuable land at a rock-bottom price" and provided too many tax incentives. The paper quoted one city hall reporter as saying he was suspicious of the deal at the time, but he did not write anything because he believed there was an informal policy at the paper of not reporting "anything critical of [then Orlando Mayor Glenda] Hood."[11] The paper received letters to the editor congratulating it on its candor.

Ombudsmen

Many newspapers have turned communicating with readers into a full-time job. They have ombudsmen, also called reader representatives or public editors. In addition to dealing with readers' concerns, most write columns explaining how news decisions were made. Occasionally, the columns are brutally honest. The ombudsman at *The Boston Globe* bashed one of the paper's columnists for making unsubstantiated charges about a political candidate.

Several newspapers experimented with ombudsmen in the 1960s; many dropped the position in the 1980s and 1990s. But as newspapers become more aware of the need for transparency, interest in ombudsmen has been rekindled. Still, the role is not common in the United States. Many editors oppose having them. They contend that ombudsmen are an unwanted barrier between readers and journalists who should "feel the wrath of readers" after they have made controversial news decisions. Other editors would rather spend limited resources on hiring more reporters instead of an in-house critic.[12] Also, many journalists are too thin- skinned to welcome criticism. An ombudsman at *The New York Times* complained in his column that editors and reporters were not forthcoming in answering his questions.

Ombudsmen are more common on Canadian newspapers and in many European countries. *The Guardian* hired Britain's first ombudsman in 1997, although other British papers have been slow to join in.[13]

Codes of ethics

As early as the 1920s, newspaper organizations adopted codes of ethics and asked their members to abide by them. Note the word "asked." The codes had no teeth and members were not punished if they broke the rules. A big push came in the 1970s when codes were adopted by the Society of Professional Journalists, Radio-Television News Directors Association, Associated Press Managing Editors Association, the ASNE, and the national organizations of travel writers, sportswriters, editorial writers, and business writers. All of these codes were entirely voluntary.

Newspapers and TV news departments gradually began to write their own codes that spell out certain kinds of conduct that will not be tolerated. Many address difficult issues like anonymous sources, privacy, and accuracy. These codes often outline the penalties for breaking the rules, ranging from verbal warnings to dismissal.

Many people who are strongly committed to improving journalism are not sure that codes of ethics will cure the media's problems. They note that often the codes address only the easiest ethical problems such as freebies, but they do little to determine rules that will lead to better journalism. Others contend that many codes don't help journalists deal with real reporting problems. For example, many codes of ethics say that the news media "must guard against invading a person's right to privacy." That admonition offers little guidance to working journalists. "Many important stories require reporters to draw the fine line between private facts and information that the public needs to know," said Laurie A. Zenner, a media lawyer.[14]

Most news organizations post their codes of ethics on their Web sites. The Society of Professional Journalists' code of ethics can be found at www.spj.org, and the Radio and Television News Directors Association's code is posted at www.rtnda.org. A collection of newspaper and TV codes is available at www.asne.org. A code of ethics patterned after the Society of Professional Journalists' code has been proposed for bloggers by the Online News Association at www.cyberjournalist.net.

Being Held Accountable

The news media have more watchdogs today than at any time in history. First, many American news organizations often are quite willing to expose each other's flaws. The transgressions of Jayson Blair of *The New York Times* and Jack Kelley of *USA Today* were reported in papers and on TV news throughout the nation. (Blair and Kelley are discussed in Chapter 6.) Newspapers like the *Los Angeles Times* and *The Washington Post* assign some of their most prolific writers to covering the news media. *Columbia Journalism Review, American Journalism Review, Online Journalism Review*, and Romenesko's blog on Poynter Online are widely read by journalists. CBS has a blog called Public Eye on cbsnews.com that includes stories about news coverage and allows readers to join in on discussions of issues in journalism. The site does not limit itself to CBS News. Often it discusses other networks, including carrying links to videos of their gaffes.

The newest source of media criticism is the variety of blogs that have sprung up in recent years. Bill Powers, media critic at *National Journal*, says:

> Suddenly, there are about 10 million more media critics than there were 10 years ago. I actually think there are a lot of bloggers who are so good at it that I sort of wish they would be picked up by mainstream outlets and do both.[15]

The blogs police the media in two ways. Sometimes they challenge the validity of media reports. Dan Rather based a *60 Minutes* story concerning President George Bush's military record on memos he had been given. Within hours of the broadcast, writers on the conservative blog *Free Republic* rejected the authenticity of the memos. One contributor using the name "Buckhead" noted that the memos appeared to have been prepared on office equipment that had not been invented in1972, when the memos were supposedly written.[16] When Israeli planes bombed Lebanon in 2006, writers on the blog *Little Green Footballs* suggested that pictures of smoke rising over Beirut after Israeli bombing had been doctored. Reuters later fired the photographer when he admitted he had digitally altered the photo to make the smoke look more intense.[17] Perhaps the most popular task for many bloggers is to find bias in what they call the MSM (mainstream media). Blogs are often politically partisan and consistently argue that the MSM is too liberal or too conservative.

News councils in the United States

One method of voluntary regulation is common in Europe and Canada but is nearly nonexistent in the United States: the news council. Only Minnesota has a well-established council. Councils have been created in Washington state and Hawaii and proposed in Southern California and New England.

News councils allow people who feel they have been wronged by the media to file complaints, often at no charge. Although each news council has its own way of handling cases, the following are generally true:

- News organizations voluntarily join the council. Often they provide the bulk of the operating funds. In Germany and some other European nations, the government funds the council.
- Anyone can file a complaint against the media without the aid of attorneys.
- Before councils will listen to a complaint, all parties must agree that they will not file suits in the case.
- Journalists and complainants must make an effort to work things out before their case is heard by the council. In Minnesota, about 95 percent of complaints are dropped or settled at this stage.
- At the hearing, each side presents its case to the council. The council listens to the case and asks questions. Because the councils are not courts of law, they do not have to follow the traditional rules of evidence of regular trial courts.

- Councils usually try to have a mix of members from the media and the public.
- News councils are not courts of law. They cannot penalize wrongdoing or award monetary damages. The only thing the media can win is the satisfaction of having the council agree with them. If the news council upholds a complaint, the news organization must carry a story reporting the finding. That's the only punishment the council can impose.
- Councils often hear cases that involve questions of fairness that would not be heard by regular courts because the issues involved are outside the bounds of libel and privacy laws.
- The Minnesota News Council has sided with the media in about half its decisions.[18]

Supporters of councils believe that they can improve journalism by punishing bad reporting and by changing the public's image of journalists. Columnist Martin Schram wrote, "A news council seems like a sane middle-ground alternative to the old standard media response to complaints: (1) Write a letter to the editor or (2) Sue us."[19] Mike Wallace of CBS's *60 Minutes* argued that news councils might lead the public to regain confidence in the news media:

> The American public might be reassured by our willingness to open ourselves up to the kind of public scrutiny that we ourselves use in evaluating the work, the accomplishment – and the failings – of others.[20]

Not everyone agrees that councils are a good idea. Stanley Hubbard of KSTP-TV in Minnesota said he saw no need for councils:

> If somebody feels we've done something wrong, they can talk to us directly, or they have recourse in the courts. I don't want to be in a situation where a panel of people is sitting in judgment on our judgment.[21]

Others are concerned that news councils may chill the pursuit of controversial stories by tying up reporters and editors with complaints that would not be allowed in a court of law. They contend that even frivolous complaints might require hours of mediation and preparation. Former WCCO-TV news director John Lansing worries that because news councils are not bound by the same rules that the courts are, they will give powerful institutions "further protection from public scrutiny and a big club to wield against the press." The council does not limit what participants can say before or after its hearings. When Northwest Airlines brought a complaint against WCCO, Lansing said that the corporation aroused public opinion against the station by using "advertising channels, labor unions and competing media in a textbook display of a corporate power play. Any media outlet in Minnesota will think twice before taking Northwest on again."[22]

Deciding who will be on these news councils is also of concern to many journalists. Former *Washington Post* editor Ben Bradlee said that the old National News Council was "taken over by kooks."[23] The *Seattle Post-Intelligencer* refused to appear at a hearing of the Washington News Council in 2006 because editors did not believe some of the members of the panel would be impartial.[24]

Councils in other countries

Americans are often shocked when they first see newspapers in the UK. Instead of the rather prudish newspapers common in most American cities, they pick up tabloids with lots of crime, titillation, and pictures of topless women. On the day this chapter was written, the front page of the most popular paper in England, *The Sun*, contained the headlines "Cannibal cats OAP alive" and "Soldier 'Beasted to Death,'" as well as a story about actresses in a British TV series. Although the cover may remind Americans of *National Enquirer*, inside the paper had short, snappy coverage of Parliament, politics, and the economy, all told with a right-wing tilt. It is a real newspaper. George Bush gave an exclusive interview to *The Sun* in August 2006. Former Conservative Prime Minister Margaret Thatcher listed an endorsement by *The Sun* as one reason for her election.

Britons buy considerably more newspapers than Americans and gobble up the tabloids. *The Sun*'s circulation is nearly twice that of *USA Today* or *The Wall Street Journal* despite serving a much smaller population. The British tabloids have long been locked into heated circulation wars, and often they veer away from what might be called the standards of responsible journalism.[25]

During the last part of the 20th century, members of the royal family, particularly Princess Diana, Prince Andrew, and Prince Charles, were often targets of the tabloids. In the early 1980s Queen Elizabeth II sued *The Sun* after it began a series of stories based on interviews with a former palace employee. One story detailed 23-year-old Prince Andrew's sex life in Windsor Castle. When the tabloid teased a story headlined "When barefoot Di buttered my toast," the queen had the series stopped and, as many joked, Britons never found out the presumably tasty details.

The tabloids grew even bolder as rumors began to swirl of the disintegration of the marriage of Charles and Diana.

Even by British standards, the tabloids were out of control. Parliament appointed a committee headed by Sir David Calcutt to create more effective controls over the press. Calcutt proposed a government commission that could levy fines and even order newspapers to pay compensation to people who the commission believed had been wronged. He proposed privacy measures that would have allowed the government to order newspapers not to print stories that it thought were offensive.

Fearing such strict censorship, newspaper editors in 1991 decided they would rather regulate themselves and agreed to establish the Press Complaints Commission, which would set standards and cajole editors to follow them. Functioning much like the Minnesota News Council, the commission receives more than 5,000 complaints a year. If it agrees the newspaper was wrong, it will ask the newspaper to print a retraction or correction. Among the first notable complaints was one filed by Prince Andrew, who thought the media were badgering his young children. He won, but the press did not leave the royal family alone. The tabloids printed pictures secretly taken while Princess Di was exercising in a gym and wrote a story based on an intercepted phone call in which Prince Charles told his lover that he would like to be reincarnated as her tampon.

Journalists in most parts of Europe have not engaged in behavior this extreme. Yet, most countries have long had councils. The Swedes, who have had freedom of the press since 1766, established the first news council in 1918. European councils tend to hold the media to stricter privacy standards than American laws. Some of the common complaints are whether the names of crime victims and suspects should be reported. A famous soccer player filed a complaint after Sweden's largest newspaper printed a picture taken by a surveillance camera of him walking into a nightclub. The newspaper decided to settle with him rather than go before the press council. In America, a celebrity on a public street entering a nightclub would generally be considered fair game.[26]

Are We Being Too Transparent?

At one time journalists saw no need to explain themselves and shrugged off questions by saying, "My work explains itself." Some worry that the pendulum has swung too far the other way. They believe that instead of self-examination, transparency is turning into self-flagellation. Rachel Smolkin, managing editor of *American Journalism Review*, asked:

> Are we trying too hard to explain ourselves, being too needy, wasting too much time on the therapist's couch, with a motley lot of bloggers, partisans and pundits as our Dr. Phil? Is more transparency always better, or are there dangers lurking within an otherwise healthy movement? In short, is the pressure for explaining spiraling out of control?[27]

New York Times public editor Byron Calame also isn't sure that being open with readers about decisions will necessarily satisfy them. He fears that media critics on both the left and the right already have their minds made up. While transparency may increase many readers' understanding of the news media, he doubts it will change the minds of many people who doubt the impartiality and quality of news coverage.

The Spokesman-Review's Smith told *American Journalism Review* that he cringes at the suggestion that transparency is simply the journalism business's craze *du jour*. "It's not a silver bullet," Smith said. "It's not a solution to our ongoing problems. It's just one little piece of a lot of things we need to be doing, and even those may not be enough."[28]

Notes

1. Steve Smith, "Sharing all that reporters knew with readers," *Nieman Reports*, Fall 2005.
2. Jerry Ceppos, "Dear reader," *San Jose Mercury News*, June 19, 1996, p. 1.
3. Susan Paterno, "I can explain," *American Journalism Review*, July/August 1998.
4. Keven Ann Willey, "Readers glimpse an editorial board's thinking," *Nieman Reports*, Fall 2003.
5. Gina Lubrano, "Errors and a newspaper's credibility," *The San Diego Union-Tribune*, February 6, 2006, and "Readers respond to corrections in print," *The San Diego Union-Tribune*, April 15, 2001, p. 7B.
6. "Making it right," *NewsLab Report*, Winter 2003.
7. "TV news: Truth? Consequences?" *Newsworthy*, Summer 1993.
8. Steve Outing, "What journalists can learn from bloggers," Poynter Online, December 20, 2004.
9. "The Times and Iraq," *The New York Times*, May 26, 2004
10. Howard Kurtz, "The Post on WMDs: An aside story," *The Washington Post*, August 12, 2004.

11. Manning Pynn, "Behind the scenes of an old story," *Orlando Sentinel*, November 11, 2001.
12. Kate McKenna, "The loneliest job in the newsroom," *American Journalism Review*, March 1993, pp. 41–44.
13. Ian Mayes, "Trust me – I'm an ombudsman," *British Journalism Review*, No. 2, 2004.
14. Laurie A. Zenner, "Code violations: Codes run afoul of First Amendment," *Newsworthy*, Spring 1995.
15. "Interview: Bill Powers," *PR Week*, August 28, 2006.
16. See Corey Pein, "Blog-Gate," *Columbia Journalism Review*, January/February 2005. The posts were on freerepublic.com and may still be in its archives.
17. Maria Aspan, "Ease of alterations creates woes for photo editors," *The New York Times*, August 14, 2006.
18. Kristin Tillotson, "Watching the watchdog," *Star Tribune*, November 2, 1996, p. A12.
19. Martin Schram, "Bring back National News Council," *The Montgomery Advertiser*, January 9, 1997, p. 15-A.
20. Mike Wallace, Remarks at the 19th Annual Frank E. Gannett Lecture at the Media Studies Center, New York, December 4, 1996.
21. Tillotson, *op. cit.*
22. John Lansing, "National News Council would lead to more timid press," *Star Tribune*, December 21, 1996, p. 21-A.
23. Troy Clarkson, "News councils: Pro and con," *Presstime*, May 1998, p. 35.
24. Craig Harris, "P-I won't participate in news council hearing," *Seattle Post-Intelligencer*, August 15, 2006.
25. A standard history of British journalism is *Power Without Responsibility* by James Curren and Jean Seaton, London: Routledge, 2003.
26. Reported on the Global Electronic Web site of the University of Stockholm, "Journalism & Ethics 2003," at www.jmk.su.se/global03/project/ethics/index.htm. Also see the Allmänhetens Pressombudsman-Pressens Opinionsnämnd Web site at www.po.se.
27. Rachel Smolkin, "Too transparent?" *American Journalism Review*, April/May 2006.
28. *Ibid.*

6 Faking the News

A foreign correspondent for an American newspaper and an Israeli government official dodged their way down a crowded Jerusalem street on their way to lunch at a popular pizzeria. When they got there, the restaurant was packed and people were jostling each other to get through the door. One would-be diner, a young man in a white T-shirt and with a black pouch attached to his waist, pushed ahead of the correspondent. Deciding the place was too busy, the correspondent and the official began to look for another restaurant.

After they had walked less than 30 yards, a blast rang out. The young man had ignited a bomb inside the restaurant, creating a ghastly scene. The correspondent wrote in his newspaper story:

> Victims' arms and legs rained down onto the street. Three men, who had been eating pizza inside, were catapulted out on the chairs they had been sitting on. When they hit the ground, their heads separated from their bodies and rolled down the street.

The correspondent saw that their eyes, much to his horror, were still blinking. The street was filled with the injured. The reporter caught sight of a man with a long shard of glass penetrating his temple. Another victim, a young man, was bleeding profusely "from where his genitals had been."

Then, as police and rescue workers began to arrive, the correspondent got a first-hand taste of daily life in such a troubled spot. He described it in his story this way:

> Suddenly, a Palestinian man ran up to an injured Israeli as if to help. An Israeli soldier butted the Palestinian in the chest with his rifle, knocking him to the ground.

"I'm a nurse! I'm a nurse!" the Palestinian yelled. As he got up, another Israeli soldier threw him against a wall, grabbed him by the neck and placed him under arrest.

Two other soldiers hauled him off, hitting him in the head as they walked.[1]

Journalists rarely witness such major breaking news stories. But for Jack Kelley of *USA Today*, it was all in a day's work.

Two years earlier in the Balkans, he had followed a small band of Kosovo Liberation Army fighters as they set out to ambush the Serbs. The soldiers herded goats ahead of them in order to set off any land mines as they climbed their way through icy mountain passages. They came upon a village under attack. Kelley said he was stunned that he could hear the sound of Serbian militia "talking and laughing in the quiet valley as they torch a village." Then, Serbian sharpshooters opened fire on the KLA fighters. Kelley hid behind a boulder as bullets buzzed around him.

Later, in an interview with *American Journalism Review,* he recounted watching shrapnel rip through the body of one of his companions. He told the interviewer that he began to pray. He had seen what happened to others who had been captured by the Serbs: Their throats were slashed, their eyes were gouged out, and the men were emasculated. "I really believed they were going to hunt us down and kills us all," he said.

Why would a man take such risks less than two weeks before his wedding day? "I didn't trust NATO," he told the interviewer. "I didn't trust the Yugoslav propaganda about the KLA. I wanted to see for myself." But gathering the story took its toll on him. He said:

> I'm not sleeping, and when I do, I have nightmares. Not a day goes by that I don't live this over and over. The worst thing was seeing that shrapnel lodged in Skala's throat. I actually saw it hit. It severed his windpipe.[2]

Kelley's ability to be at the right place at the right time allowed his writing to be filled with striking details that shaped many readers' understanding of world events. In a story from Hebron, he wrote,

> After a quick prayer, Avi Shapiro and 12 other Jewish settlers put on their religious skullcaps, grabbed their semi-automatic rifles and headed towards Highway 60.... As they crouched in a ditch beside the road, Shapiro, the leader of the group, gave the settlers orders: Surround any taxi, 'open fire' and kill as many of the 'blood-sucking Arab' passengers as possible.[3]

Kelley's vivid story made Avi Shapiro the embodiment of belligerent anti-Arab Israelis.

Shortly after 9-11, Kelley was in the right place for another great story. He found an Islamic school in Pakistan where students readied for the day they could be suicide bombers. He said one student told him, "I will get your children. I will get their playgrounds. I will get their schools, too. I will get all of you." Then another student held up a picture of the Sears Tower in Chicago and said, "This one is mine."[4] Again, Kelley's story had long legs as columnists and bloggers made reference to the "Sears kid" as an example of the mindset of Pakistani culture.[5]

Kelley wrote dozens of tremendous stories, and many considered him *USA Today's* top reporter. The paper's editors nominated him for Pulitzer prizes five times. The problem was that many of his yarns either weren't true or were greatly embellished. A suicide bomber had killed many people at a pizzeria. But no bodies were decapitated, and the bomber wasn't at all like the man Kelley described. An investigation by *USA Today* found that he had never been to the Pakistani school and the existence of Avi Shapiro could not be verified. As many have pointed out, it's unlikely that a devout Jew would have said his prayers before he put on his yarmulke. *USA Today* found several other key discrepancies in Kelley's stories dating back to 1991.[6]

Kelley's exploits illustrate a sad truth: Some journalists engage in shameful reporting abuses. They fabricate stories, plagiarize, make up quotations, or embellish the facts. These kinds of fakery are rare, but that they occur at all is disturbing to those seeking a more ethical journalism.

Fabricating News

In earlier days, newspapers enjoyed manufacturing news for their readers. Even Benjamin Franklin made up stories for his highly popular newspapers. After the American Revolution, journalists would invent stories to attack politicians their newspapers did not support. Unabashed journalistic hoaxing in America may have reached its highpoint in 1835 when the *New York Sun* discovered "man-bats" on the moon. The lengthy stories, complete with drawings of the manlike creatures with wings, helped the *Sun* achieve the largest circulation of any daily in the world. After the hoax was uncovered, the paper's editors told readers it was a slow time for news and they just wanted to brighten their readers' days.

News organizations know that today's readers are less forgiving. Fabricating stories not only undermines the truth-telling function of journalism, it also violates the trust between reporters and editors. At most news organizations, editors read copy and do as much fact checking as they can. But in daily journalism there is rarely enough time for them to check every fact. Editors must trust their reporters. Their first instinct when a story is challenged is to want to stand behind their reporters. When they discover that trust has been betrayed, some editors react immediately. A study found that about two-thirds of offenders are fired outright.[7] Others are given severe warnings. In serious cases, editors too face dismissal. The editor of *USA Today* was replaced shortly after the Kelley fiasco was uncovered.

Two top editors at *The New York Times* were brought down by the infamous doings of another wayward reporter. Jayson Blair was on the fast track at the *Times*. Although low-level editors had concerns about his work, he continued to receive plum assignments, particularly for such a young reporter. Then the truth came out. *Times* investigators compiled an amazing list of journalistic frauds that Blair had committed. In a front-page story, the paper reported that he "filed dispatches that purported to be from Maryland, Texas and other states, when often he was in New York, fabricated comments, concocted scenes and lifted material from other newspapers and wire services." Instead of going to the scene, he would look at photographs and TV news reports and then describe the scenes as if he were actually there, adding a comment or two from an imaginary source or borrowing a quote from other reporters' stories. At the time of his firing, *Times* researchers had found serious problems in 36 of the 73 stories he had written for the national desk.[8] About a month after Blair was fired, *Times'* editor Howell Raines and managing editor Gerald Boyd resigned.

Often journalists who cheat take extreme measures not to get caught. Stephan Glass, a promising young writer at *The New Republic* magazine, made up a story about a 15-year-old who hacked his way into the computer systems of major corporations. He was so good at hacking that after one company hunted him down, it chose not to punish him. Instead, it hired him to improve the security of its own computer systems.

To keep editors from recognizing that this story was a fraud, Glass created a Web site for the bogus company and got a cell phone so if any of his editors called the number listed there, they could leave voice mail. When this scam was discovered, editors determined that Glass had a history of creating phony documents to disguise his deceit. He had forged faxes and letters from nonexistent sources to prove that his stories were accurate. He even gave editors the phone numbers of friends who had agreed to pose as his sources.[9]

Janet Cooke and Jimmy's world

The Washington Post was stung by the most famous hoax of the modern era of American journalism. The story was a dramatic account of an 8-year-old heroin addict. The writer, Janet Cooke, gave him the name "Jimmy," and her Page One article was headlined "Jimmy's world: 8-year-old heroin addict lives for a fix." Cooke's article began:

> Jimmy is 8 years old and a third-generation heroin addict, a precocious little boy with sandy hair, velvety brown eyes and needle marks freckling the baby-smooth skin of his thin brown arms.

The article went on to paint a dreary and hopeless picture of Jimmy's world in southeast Washington. He lived with his mother, an ex-prostitute, and her lover, Ron, a pusher who got Jimmy hooked on heroin. At the end of the article Cooke described Jimmy being "fired up" with an injection of the drug:

> Ron comes back into the living room, syringe in hand, and calls the little boy over to his chair: "Let me see your arm."
> He grabs Jimmy's left arm just above the elbow, his massive hand tightly encircling the child's small limb. The needle slides into the boy's soft skin like a straw pushed into the center of a freshly baked cake. Liquid ebbs out of the syringe, replaced by bright red blood. The blood is then reinjected into the child.
> Jimmy has closed his eyes during the whole procedure, but now opens them, looking quickly around the room. He climbs into a rocking chair and sits, his head dipping and snapping upright again, in what addicts call "the nod."
> "Pretty soon, man," Ron says, "you got to learn how to do this for yourself."

The story of Jimmy saddened and outraged many Washingtonians, including the mayor, who ordered a search for the child. The police chief threatened to have Cooke and the *Post* editors subpoenaed if they did not reveal who Jimmy was. *Post* lawyers replied that the paper had a right under the First Amendment to protect its sources.

The *Post* entered the story in the Pulitzer prize competition, and the jurors – with only the dissenting vote of *St. Petersburg Times* editor Eugene C. Patterson, who called the story "an aberration" that should never have been printed – awarded it the Pulitzer for feature writing. Cooke, who had been on the *Post* staff for a little more than eight months, had won a Pulitzer at the age of 26.

But then her house of lies began to crumble. *The Toledo Blade*, where Cooke had worked before going to the *Post*, decided to do a local-woman-makes-good story about her, but soon found that biographical information in the AP story announcing her Pulitzer didn't jibe with the paper's records. Instead of graduating Phi Beta Kappa from Vassar, she had earned her B.A. at the University of Toledo. She had not studied at the Sorbonne in Paris and was not fluent in French, Portuguese, Italian, and Spanish, as she had written on her *Post* application. She had studied French in high school and college. Editors at the *Blade* passed along their findings to *Post* editors. By early the next morning, Cooke confessed to her editors that "Jimmy's world" was a fabrication. She had never encountered or interviewed an 8-year-old drug addict. He was a "composite" of young addicts social workers had told her about. She resigned, and the *Post* gave back the Pulitzer.

Why Do Journalists Cheat?

All professions have cheaters, of course. Lawyers bill clients for hours they never worked or steal money from clients' trust funds; doctors defraud Medicare or perform unnecessary medical procedures to fatten their bank accounts; business executives cook their books to make their own stock holdings more valuable. Author David Callahan described America in the 21st century as "the cheating culture."[10]

Researchers don't have hard numbers for how much cheating is done by people working in professional positions, partly because personnel actions are often private and partly because cheaters are likely to lie on surveys. Better numbers are available from colleges, where it is estimated that cheating is up by about 35 percent in the past decade.

Callahan believes that America's obsession with money causes people to cheat. Also, parents and schools place great pressure on young people to get and keep jobs with high salaries and/or social status. Cheating is a way of dealing with these pressures. When people who do not cheat lose out to cheaters, they feel like chumps – and may become cheaters themselves when the situation is right.

Furthermore, parents may inadvertently be teaching their children that dishonesty is an easy way to deal with problems. Research by sociologists has shown that parents who cheat (even on "little" things like pirating cable TV) are more likely to have children who cheat in school.

On first glance, it seems odd that cheaters would be attracted to journalism, a profession that puts such importance on truth and accuracy. Yet even very talented journalists have fallen for the temptation of taking shortcuts. Patricia Smith was one of the *Boston Globe's* top feature writers and columnists. She had so much talent that she was a frequent speaker at writing symposiums. After she was fired by the *Globe* for making up sources for her stories, many were stunned to learn that she had a history of less than honest behavior. *Globe* editors had been suspicious of earlier stories and had given warnings. Before joining the *Globe,* Smith was at the *Chicago Sun-Times,* where she was reprimanded for sneaking into its computer system and altering her story so a copy editor would be blamed for a mistake that Smith herself had made. She was also suspected of writing a review of an Elton John concert she had not attended. Her review misstated the songs he had performed and the clothes he had worn.[11]

Other journalists turn to cheating to handle competitive pressures. In most newsrooms, reporters compete with one another. Getting lots of stories on the front page is career enhancing. On major stories, reporters are competing directly against reporters from other news outlets. S. C. Gwynne, a *Time* magazine correspondent, wrote in *Texas Monthly* that one of his toughest assignments was covering the murder of 12 students by two classmates at Columbine High School in Colorado. More than 1,000 reporters were combing the Denver suburbs looking for new information. Gwynne's assignment was to "penetrate the so-called Trenchcoat Mafia, the loose cabal of friends to which the shooters supposedly belonged." But the teens were avoiding reporters. Gwynne said he made hundreds of calls trying to find someone who could put him in contact with one of them. "My editors were calling me, upset that, in spite of my remonstrance that I was doing all I could, they had just seen this or that [Trenchcoat] Mafia member on TV," Gwynne wrote. He drove to their homes and to the homes of their friends. At each location, he found scores of TV crews and newspaper reporters already camped on their front yards. He said:

> After a week of abject terror and fear of certain failure, I finally got a phone call returned. It led to a 2 a.m. interview with a bona fide member of the Mafia at the very last moment before my deadline. Without that call, I would have failed miserably, and it would have been brought up at my yearly job evaluation.[12]

Gwynne wrote that he understood the "breakneck pressures" that led some journalists to fudge the truth, but he was proud that so few journalists give in. "There are thousands of instances each year in which pack journalists face crushing competitive pressure and editors screaming at them to produce – and considering the incentive to stretch the truth, it is amazing how fundamentally right the media get the story," he concluded.

Others believe that some of the norms of journalistic writing make life unduly difficult for reporters. John Gushue, a reporter for the Canadian Broadcasting Corp., pointed to "our preoccupation with finding ordinary people for stories." Every journalist knows the format. If reporter is writing about a medical discovery or new laws outlining shady loan practices, the story will open with the poignant tale of a real person, preferably a local, who has been a victim. Gushue wrote in *Media* magazine that he agrees these anecdotes can make articles more readable. But the search for these real people can tempt otherwise solid reporters to fudge the facts so the story will have "a human face that adds nothing of journalistic value."[13]

Not only must journalists find this human face, often their work is judged by the number of sources they have contacted. The reason for this is obvious. Stories with more sources are likely to be more balanced, and stories with better quotes will be more readable. Yet, the search for additional secondary sourcing can create problems for reporters on a deadline. The Associated Press fired reporter Christopher Newton even though the bulk of his stories were completely accurate. After getting the facts and details he needed, he padded his stories with quotes from made-up sources. As Jack Shafer pointed out in *Slate*, while most writers make up quotes to give their writing more punch, "Newton took the opposite tack, making the stories less interesting – if that's possible – by inserting insipid invented quotations that read like blurred type." He apparently believed his editors wanted the additional sourcing.[14]

The Sacramento Bee fired Dennis Love, a 47-year-old political writer, for beefing up the number of sources in his stories by taking quotes from other papers. *American Journalism Review* observed that most of the quotes were what some journalists call "filler quotes" that are not essential to the story. When asked why he did it, Love said:

> I think several things contributed to it in my situation. No. 1, it's just a simple human fallibility of taking a shortcut where one was available, concerning some stories that maybe I didn't care as much about as some other stories. I know that sounds maybe sort of cavalier. But I really do think that it was a character weakness.[15]

Handling Quotes

While not an ethical transgression on the scale of making up 8-year-old heroin addicts, editors and reporters fret over the accuracy of what they put in quotation marks. The general rule is that what's inside quotation marks is supposed to be exactly what the person said. If the reporter wants to change what the person said, then the reporter should paraphrase.

> *Direct quote (exact words):* The mayor said, "I will fight like hell any plan to tear down our historic City Hall."
> *Paraphrase:* The mayor said he would fight any plan to tear down City Hall.

Some reporters use someone's exact words to create lively direct quotes that the person never really said. They cherry-pick from the exact words used. The person may have offered a fairly colorful expression early in the interview and a somewhat clever sentence a few minutes later. The temptation is to combine those two bits and create one great quote. Most editors disapprove of mangling the context of quotes this way.

Cleaning up inarticulate comments

People sometimes say the most interesting things during interviews and conversations. However, when their comments are written down verbatim, grammar slipups leap out at readers. Some comments are clear when you can hear the voice inflections and see the hand gestures, but become inarticulate ramblings when reduced to the printed word. The question becomes how much you can clean up these quotes and still ethically put them in quote marks. For a *Columbia Journalism Review* article, Kevin McManus asked two journalists how they deal with this problem. One told him:

> We have an informal policy which is a, uh, policy that's, uh, not uncommon in newsrooms around the country, which is, uh, that if you, uh, uh, uh, uh, put a sentence, uh, between quote marks, uh, that ought to be what the person said.

The other journalist told McManus he edited quotes in "certain inoffensive ways." When asked what they were, the journalist said:

> Well, ways that, uh, you can, for instance, uh, if the language is, um, horribly ungrammatical and, uh, makes the speaker – as spoken language sometimes is – makes the speaker look like a complete idiot, you can, quote, correct his or her grammar slightly, or make the person agree with the verb. The noun agree with the verb, something like that.[16]

These reporters are trained writers, good with words. But their spoken English is far from perfect. McManus wonders if you can ethically salvage their quotes.

A few journalists contended in a *Washington Journalism Review* article that they never cleaned up quotes. Famed Texas reporter Mollie Ivins argued that "people stand up on the floor of the Texas Legislature and make jackasses of themselves all the time. It is not my responsibility to make them look good."[17] Similarly, *Chicago Tribune* reporter Timothy McNulty told McManus he believed that changing a quote to make a person sound better is like altering a photo to change the way the person dresses.[18]

Mike Needs, former public editor at the *Akron Beacon Journal*, received complaints from readers both when the paper cleaned up quotes and when it didn't. One reader complained that Cleveland Cavalier star LeBron James spoke like an English professor when he was quoted in the newspaper but was totally ungrammatical on TV. Another reader chided the paper for quoting a business executive as saying, "There's many opportunities out there." The reader thought the grammar of the otherwise articulate businessman should have been fixed. Needs said that he didn't think the paper ought to have fixed the grammar in direct quotes in either case.[19]

Occasionally, sources ask reporters to take their nonsensical quotes and "make that proper English." Many journalists are willing to oblige. "Don't quote what I said, quote what I mean," Richard J. Daley, long-time mayor of Chicago, used to demand of reporters. Daley was famous for his fractured English. He once told reporters: "The policeman isn't there to create disorder, he's there to preserve disorder." Chicago's print journalists reported what he meant, while the electronic replayed the quote the way he said it.[20]

Cleaning up "dirty words"

Although movies, recordings, and even daytime TV shows are becoming very graphic in their use of four-letter words, newspapers remain almost prudish protectors of their readers' modesty. Often they change quotations, pictures, and sometimes even the facts to avoid offending. David Shaw, media writer for the *Los Angeles Times*, said a headline in his paper in the 1970s once called a 69-car crash on a freeway a "70-car pileup" to avoid "titillating or offending readers." At about the same time, the paper removed the genitals from a picture of a male lion at the zoo because editors were afraid children might see them.[21]

Although those cases are extreme, reporters occasionally must decide how to handle quotes by sources who sprinkle their conversations with off-color words. They and their editors consider many things when deciding how much of the language will be quoted verbatim. The prominence of the person involved is one major consideration. "If the president of the United States says 'fuck,' I'm going to quote him," observed Benjamin Bradlee, when he was executive editor of *The Washington Post* several years ago.[22] Bradlee may have meant it as a joke, but modern politicians have tested his rule. The *Post* was one of the few papers to quote Vice President Dick Cheney's words exactly when he told Democratic Sen. Patrick Leahy on the Senate floor: "Go fuck yourself." *Newsweek* and many other publications quoted it as "Go f--- yourself." Some publications were even less frank and said Cheney had told Leahy "to perform a crude act upon himself."

President George Bush was a bit milder in comments that were inadvertently taped. He told British Prime Minister Tony Blair, "See the irony is that what they need to do is get Syria to get Hezbollah to stop doing this shit and it's over." For the first time in its history, *The New York Times* printed "shit," as did several other papers, including *Los Angeles Times, Orlando Sentinel* and *Salt Lake City Tribune*.

The *Chicago Tribune* used "s----," and CNN silenced the word rather than replacing it with a bleep.[23] Some editors argued that the using the word was important because it illustrated the casual relationship Bush had with the British prime minister.

Democrats can have potty mouths too. A year after he lost the 2004 presidential election to Bush, John Kerry told *Rolling Stone* that he never expected Bush to "fuck up" the war in Iraq so much. No mainstream newspapers used the exact quote.[24]

Sports editors automatically delete locker-room language from their stories. But Chicago White Sox Manager Ozzie Guillen caused them to reconsider when he described a writer for the *Chicago Sun-Times* with these words: "What a piece of shit he is, a fucking fag." Major papers, of course, backed away from "shit" and "fucking." The *Sun-Times* subbed the word "deleted" for both of them in first-day stories but changed to "s---" and "f------" in later stories. The *St. Louis Post-Dispatch* used "expletive." The word that editors gave editors more trouble was "fag." The *Sun-Times* and many other papers used it. The *Chicago Tribune* was among the papers that considered the word too offensive. Some papers reported only that the manager had used a "vulgar homophobic" term.[25]

Using euphemisms for vulgarities can sometimes create problems. When Jimmy Carter was running for president, he agreed to be interviewed by Robert Scheer for a feature in *Playboy*. Carter, whose image was that of a straight-and-narrow Baptist from rural Georgia, used the words "screw" and "shack up" and admitted that he had "lusted" after women in his heart. Carter's comments were reported by most newspapers. However, editors at *The New York Times* considered the word "screw" too raw for a family newspaper. They substituted the phrase "a vulgarism for sexual relations." The next day editors recognized that readers might assume he had used the "f-word" instead of "screw." So they printed a clarification that Carter had used "a common but mild vulgarism for sexual relations." As Shaw pointed out, it took the *Times* "eight words to clear up the confusion originally caused by having used five words to replace one word."[26]

Occasionally newspapers substitute a more acceptable word and hope that quotation marks or brackets will alert readers to the change. After mechanical failures forced driver Tony Stewart out of an Indianapolis 500 race, a TV reporter asked him the how-do-you-feel question during a live network broadcast. Stewart responded, "All my life this is all

I've wanted to do. And every year I get shit on. How would you feel?" But *USA Today* quoted him as saying, "All my life this is all I've wanted to do. And every year I get 'dumped' on. How would you feel?"

The constantly changing meanings of slang can create problems for editors. The Minneapolis *Star Tribune* ran a story about a writer who balked when a TV network asked him to be part of a six-member script-writing team. The paper quoted him as saying, "If I ain't writing it all, I ain't writing it at all... Six people to write a sitcom. No wonder they all suck." The copy editor headlined the three-paragraph brief, "Why sitcoms suck." Readers wrote the paper complaining about the word "suck." Lou Gelfand, the paper's ombudsman at the time, agreed:

> At the fore of this discussion should be respect for readers. I'm persuaded that lots of them find the slang meaning of 'suck' offensive. Its use in the locker rooms and by youth who have heard it on television doesn't make it the common, everyday language of ordinary people.[27]

Although most papers cling to a strict no-vulgarity policy, the *Virginian-Pilot* in Norfolk has eased its standards. The paper will use "sucks" and "pissed off" if the story calls for it. Editor Denis Finley said the goal of the new policy "is not to put more profanity in the paper and lower our standards; rather, it is to see where we need to accept that certain words have become part of our vernacular and have lost their meaning as profanities."[28] How readers react may be another story. National Public Radio received many complaints from its listeners, who are generally considered more liberal than most Americans, when a reporter asked an official of the Army Corps of Engineers this question about the lack of preparation for another Katrina-sized hurricane in New Orleans: "You hear people who are really pissed at the Corps. What do you say to those people?"[29]

Staging the News

One reason people watch TV news is so they can see events as they happen. Newspaper readers also want photographs that capture the event. Sometimes, this demand for pictures pushes the media into ethical quicksand.

Newspaper photographers often engage in a benign form of staging the news. They may ask people to pretend to be talking on the telephone or engaging in some activity that seems appropriate to the story. Editors assume the public will recognize that these are posed pictures.

TV reporters sometimes practice another small-time deception. The anchor may introduce a package by saying, "Here's our Jane Doe with the story." Doe will report the story from the scene of some news event. At the end, she will say, "Back to you, Harry," and the anchor will thank Doe for her fine report. The viewer is given the impression that the report is live and that the two people are talking to each other. Often they are not. It's what some call a "look-live." The anchor is in reality introducing a taped news story. Advocates of look-lives say they satisfy the public's preference for live coverage without the reporter having to spend valuable waiting at the scene to do a live segment. But some journalists don't agree. "This has to do with deceiving the viewer," Al Tompkins, an experienced broadcast reporter, told Baltimore's *The Sun*. "If a television station would lie to you about that, then why in the world should we believe their journalism?"[30] He contends that the story would have the same value if the anchor said, "Our Jane Doe got the story," and the reporter signed off without trying to create the illusion that the piece was shot live.

At other times, when TV reporters seem to be live at the news scene, they may be live but they may not be at the scene. They are standing on the TV station's parking lot with a highway or a fence or a lake in the background, whatever would be appropriate to the story. They give their "live" reports and are interviewed through their earpieces by the anchors sitting in studios perhaps a few hundred feet away.[31]

Careful viewers of network programs may notice how similar government buildings appear on the nightly news. Reporters sometimes use a downtown church with large white pillars as a backdrop for stories about Congress, the White House, or the Supreme Court to create the illusion of their being at those buildings.[32] Some have been known not to leave the studio in the winter. They don their heavy coats and stand in front of projected images of the appropriate buildings.

Unjustifiable deceptions

In one classic case, a photographer for the *St. Petersburg Times* attempted to liven up routine coverage of a baseball game between Eckerd College and Florida Southern. He asked a barefoot student in the stands to print "Yeah, Eckerd" on the soles of his feet. When his editors found out about his ploy, he was fired. A *Times* editor explained, "One of the cardinal sins of a journalist is to tell a lie."[33] A photographer at *The Indianapolis Star* took a similar shortcut when editors wanted a picture of a child getting a vaccination shot at a county health clinic. When he arrived, no children were getting shots. So he drafted a boy who was there for another procedure and asked a nurse to pretend to be giving the shot. In a "Note to readers," the paper's editor said:

> Such distortion of the truth is a violation of our policy on ethics and of our commitment to readers to always be honest in our delivery of the news. The *Star* apologizes for the misrepresentation and the bad judgment that led to it.[34]

Some reporters have been even more creative in the name of journalism. In Minnesota, a TV reporter for KCCO wanted pictures to illustrate a story about underage drinking. When he couldn't find any teens drinking, he bought two cases of beer for six teenagers and then filmed them happily chugging away. When the ruse was uncovered, the reporter and cameraman were not only fired, they were charged with violating state liquor laws. They pleaded guilty and were fined $500, sentenced to 10 days in jail, and required to do community service.[35]

Occasionally journalists resort to more elaborate tricks. In the early 1990s several lawsuits were filed against General Motors charging that GM pickup trucks had a design defect that increased the likelihood their gas tanks would explode in crashes. *Dateline NBC* wanted to illustrate the problem. So producers bought one of the trucks, filled it with gasoline, and then crashed a car into it. The truck exploded in a sea of flames, while cameras recorded the event from both outside and inside the vehicle. After the segment ran, GM investigators tracked down the remains of the wrecked truck and bought it from a junkyard. They X-rayed the gas tank and discovered that it had not ruptured, as NBC had suggested. Instead, GM discovered that remote-control incendiary devices had been placed on the truck to make sure there would be a fire when the car and truck collided. After GM announced its findings at a press conference, NBC officials took the unusual step of having a four-and-a-half–minute apology to GM read during the program. Anchors Jane Pauley and Stone Phillips, who apparently did not know of the deception, pledged that such "unscientific demonstrations" would never again be used on the program.[36]

Unfortunately for NBC, at about the same time as GM was challenging that story, *NBC Nightly News* ran a piece about the environmental damage caused by the timber industry's clear-cutting of forests. The report showed fish floating belly-up in a river, fish that NBC said had died because of clear-cutting in the Clearwater National Forest. A few days later, NBC acknowledged that there were two problems with the report. The fish were not in a stream in Clearwater National Forest – and they were not dead. They had been stunned by forestry officials as part of a fish count in another stream. Shortly after these incidents, Michael Gartner resigned as president of NBC News.[37]

File footage can be an easy way to make TV news more visual. For a story about the decline in the number of people flying, producers can dig out pictures of planes taking off and landing. But file footage can also mislead viewers. KSTP in Minneapolis investigated what reporters considered lavish spending on meetings for state employees held at expensive resorts. During the report, the station showed pictures of families having a great time at the resorts being mentioned. Many viewers assumed these were pictures of the state employees. They weren't. A producer had found some video of the resorts shot during the summer. The employee meetings were during the winter. In Minnesota, that makes a considerable difference.[38]

No one contends that these stories are typical of TV journalism. They are aberrations. But the public doesn't seem to understand that. A few months after NBC News rigged the GM truck fire, the *Los Angeles Times* asked people how common fakery was in the news media. Surprisingly, 56 percent said they thought it was common.[39]

Manipulating Photographs

Most journalists want the public to believe that the pictures, sounds, and video they use are accurate depictions of the news. But the sad truth is that phony pictures have been around for a long time. In the rough and tumble days of the 1930s, newspaper photographers carried props like stuffed bears, broken dolls, and damaged briefcases. They tossed these props at crime scenes or traffic accidents to make their pictures more tragic. Photographers are not supposed to manipulate the scene any more, but occasionally they do. When a photographer near Seattle wanted more drama in his coverage of a memorial service for a high-school athlete, he moved one of the large pictures of the athlete at the front of the chapel so it would be behind the mourners he wanted to photograph.[40]

Early newspaper photographers not only added and rearranged props, they recreated entire scenes. For a sexy story about a trial, they had actors pose as if they were in a courtroom. The photographers pasted photographs of the real newsmakers over the faces of the actors. Often the expressions on their faces were totally inappropriate, but the poor reproduction of pictures in those days made it tough for readers to tell that the photos weren't real.

Texas Monthly revived this stunt in the 1990s, according to *Wired* magazine. The magazine twice electronically pasted the head of Gov. Ann Richards on pictures of models. One seemed to show Richards dancing with her opponent in the gubernatorial race, and the other showed her astride a Harley-Davidson motorcycle. Richards said the models had such nice bodies, she could hardly complain. But many readers did. *Texas Monthly's* editors said the covers had hurt the magazine's credibility so badly that they stopped using any manipulations that might fool readers.[41]

Computers today can so competently change photographic images that even experts cannot separate the real ones from the fakes. In one infamous incident, staff members of *National Geographic* magazine had a great picture of a camel in the foreground and a pyramid in the background. But the picture couldn't be cropped so that both the camel and the pyramid would be on the magazine's cover. So they used a photo-imaging computer to move the pyramid so it would fit. *The Orange County* (Calif.) *Register* had a more noble purpose in mind when it altered a picture of a young man whose pants were unzipped. A technician zipped them up for him using the paper's photo-imaging software. Other papers have protected the modesty of people in photos by enlarging gymnasts' costumes and softball players' uniforms. For a story about adult entertainment in the city, editors at the *Louisville Courier-Journal* remade the front page after they digitally added several inches of material to a stripper's sweater who was doing a high kick. Because she was wearing a black g-string, editors realized that many readers might think she was bottomless.[42] The paper later acknowledged that it should have substituted a different picture.

Photographers sometimes use photo-editing software to improve an image to the point that it no longer represents the actual scene. A photographer at *The Charlotte Observer* had a great shot of a firefighter silhouetted against a sunrise as he was being hoisted over a fire by an aerial ladder truck. The photographer decided to make the picture even better by turning the sky a deeper red and giving the sun a more distinct halo. A few years earlier, the same photographer had to return awards from the North Carolina Press Association because he had made similar enhancements to the pictures he had entered. Editors decided they could no longer trust his work and fired him.

Some photographers have altered pictures in such a way as to change readers' understanding of the story. During fighting between Israel and the Lebanese Hezbollah group in 2006, a freelance photographer hired by Reuters took a photo that showed smoke rising out of a Lebanese city that had been attacked by Israelis. He used Photoshop to darken the pillars of smoke and then duplicated them throughout the image. The result was a picture that suggested the damage to the city was worse than shown in the original picture. When bloggers pointed out the amateurish changes, Reuters dumped him as a freelancer and went back through his previous work. Editors found that he had added several additional "missiles" to a picture of an Israeli jet firing on targets in Lebanon. What he had identified in captions as missiles were later determined to be flares.

At *El Nuevo Herald,* published by *The Miami Herald,* photographers combined two photos to create a phony image to go along with an anti-Castro story about prostitution in Havana. Some defended the publication because such practices are more accepted in Latin American publications. But editors at *The Miami Herald* did not agree with that reasoning.[43]

Some photo manipulations do more than trick readers. They anger them. When football player O.J. Simpson was arrested in the murder of his ex-wife, both *Time* and *Newsweek* had the same cover: the mug shot police took of Simpson at police headquarters. But, sitting side by side on the nation's newsstands, the magazines looked considerably different. The Simpson on the *Time* cover appeared to be much more sinister than *Newsweek's* O.J. – *Time* had darkened his face and made subtle changes in his features. James R. Gaines, the magazine's managing editor, said his staff had turned the police-station mug shot into an image that better told the story. He pointed out that the picture was called a "photo-illustration" on the magazine's contents page. But many were offended that the magazine would tamper with reality in covering such a volatile story. Some saw racial overtones in the handling of the photo, a charge that Gaines strongly denied.[44] Many journalists pointed out that most readers would never have known it was an illustration if *Newsweek* had not used the same cover.[45]

British newspapers tend to have fewer ethical concerns about manipulating photos. The conservative newspaper *Evening Standard* in London accused a liberal candidate of hypocrisy because, according to the newspaper, he falsely billed himself as a man of the people. To illustrate the story, the paper photographed the man and his wife in a pub and then digitally substituted a bottle of champagne for the beer they were drinking.[46] Editors at *The Guardian* wanted to spare readers the gory aftermath of a terrorist bombing in Madrid, so they removed a severed limb from a picture.[47]

The ability to manipulate sound and video has caused broadcast journalists to search for new guidelines as to what's acceptable. KLAS-TV in Las Vegas had powerful footage of a shootout inside Harrah's Las Vegas casino. Viewers could watch as a gunman killed a tourist and shot a security guard. The whole event had been caught by the ubiquitous security cameras in the casino. The only problem for KLAS was that surveillance video does not include sound. So, a technician taped the distinct clanking of slot machines and found some recordings of gunshots. He added the sounds to the videotape of the shootings at the casino. Carl Gottlieb, a former TV news director and deputy director of the Project for Excellence in Journalism, told the *Las Vegas Review Journal*:

> To add that was really unnecessary. It's unfortunate that stations feel they have to do this. What did it add to the viewers' understanding of the story? When it comes to news, a story is supposed to be representing the truth. And the truth is there was no audio [on the surveillance video].[48]

Many news organizations are trying to establish policies to deal with the ethics of photo-imaging technology. Some have outlawed any manipulation of news pictures, while others require editors to explain any alterations in the captions. The *Chicago Tribune*'s policy is succinct: "We do not alter editorial photos, period." *The Dallas Morning News* takes a similar stand. The Associated Press Managing Editors organization was even blunter. In a report on electronic imaging, APME said, "This is supposed to be about electronic photo manipulation, but it's really about lying. The more we mess with pictures, the more we mess with our credibility."[49]

Some scoff at the concern over the new equipment. Lou Hodges, while a professor of professional ethics at Washington and Lee University, contended that the only reason people get upset about technology is that they believe the myth that photographs objectively portray an event. No photograph captures "what really happened." Instead, the photographers have already imposed their subjectivity into the image when they decide to take a picture or not take one. He said:

> And once the noteworthy event has been chosen and the photographer is on the scene, other crucial value judgments follow: What aspect of the scene is most important and how can I capture it? What angle, background, framing, light, distance, moment to shoot?

Hodges also pointed out that even in a traditional darkroom, photographers routinely use techniques like burning and dodging to emphasize parts of the picture, and then in the cropping process remove elements that do not contribute to the photograph's major emphasis. In his view, the real challenge of using Photoshop is to learn to use it to produce better pictures.[50]

The National Press Photographers Association revised its code in 2004 to take into account the changing technology. In the past the association had acknowledged the need for some manipulation – lightening a football player's face in a contrast photo, for example. But, the new code states,

> Editing should maintain the integrity of the photographic images' content and context. Do not manipulate images or add or alter sound in any way that can mislead viewers or misrepresent subjects.[51]

Researchers at the University of Wisconsin surveyed news photographers and found that about 29 percent of them said they would remove telephone wires from a picture if they detracted from the image, 27 percent said they would close a zipper, and 19 percent would combine two photos to produce a better image.[52] Other photographers would like to see the American media adopt a system like the one the Norwegians have. The media there agreed to put a warning logo on all altered photographs, even if the alterations are relatively minor.[53]

Plagiarism

After a sports columnist for the *San Antonio Express-News* stole several paragraphs from a column in the *Fort Worth Star-Telegram,* the paper ran an apology in its sports section and held a meeting in which sportswriters were reminded of the evils of plagiarism. The next day the columnist was reading the *Houston Chronicle* and found that the paper had lifted quotes from a story he had written.

Such dishonesty is serious enough when a college student does it, but it can be career smashing for a professional writer. Shortly after *The Boston Globe* fired columnist Patricia Smith for making up stories, it suspended popular columnist Mike Barnicle, a 25-year veteran of the newspaper, for repeating jokes without attributing them to a new book by comedian George Carlin. Barnicle at first told editors he had never read Carlin's book. However, a local TV station replayed Barnicle recommending the book during a TV appearance.[54]

The *St. Petersburg Times* obtained a resignation from a reporter after she passed off as her own about a third of an article on credit cards from *Changing Times* magazine. She put a letter on the newsroom bulletin board the day she resigned that read:

> Twelve years of dedicated journalism down the drain because of a stupid mistake. I am writing this public explanation for a selfish reason. It will be easier for me to live with myself knowing that the truth is known. But I hope my mistake will serve as a lesson to others. I have let the *Times* down. I have let myself down. But most of all, I have let the profession down. And for that I am truly sorry.[55]

Editors at *The San Jose Mercury News* were impressed with a story about poverty in San Francisco written by a young reporter who had just graduated from journalism school. They had a much different impression of the reporter when they learned that the first five paragraphs were a slightly modified version of a story that had appeared in *The Washington Post*. The reporter had made changes like turning "half-century" into "half a century" and "working men who streamed into the city" into "solitary working men who streamed into the city."[56]

These examples may represent a surprisingly widespread problem. John Seigenthaler, former publisher of the *Nashville Tennessean* and editorial director of *USA Today*, said:

> I'm confident plagiarism happens with a lot more frequency than any of us knows. Part of it is new technology, but more of it is just plain misunderstanding and absence of sensitivity. And sometimes it's a total lack of ethics.[57]

Broadcast journalists also engage in plagiarism. Stephen Isaacs, a former producer at CBS News and associate dean of the Columbia School of Journalism, told *The Boston Globe*, "Hundreds of incidents of plagiarism have taken place that I know of."[58]

Some small TV and radio stations have been known to read the news directly from local newspapers without crediting them. Reporters and editors at the Reading, Pa., *Times and Eagle* got so angry they persuaded management to sue a local station. Most radio news executives are opposed to stealing the news. Scot Witt, news director at WDCB in Glen Ellyn, Ill., said, "Any radio newsperson worth his or her salt will provide the proper credit." But, he added, understaffing and the loss of many veteran reporters to other media have "placed the editorial pen in the hands of unqualified folks."[59]

Technology has made it easier to acquire stories from other news organizations quickly. A reporter can tie into the Internet or databases like Lexis-Nexis and read the offerings of newspapers, broadcast stations, and wire services throughout the world. The *Chicago Sun-Times* dropped a columnist after he admitted that he had used information in his columns that he had not reported himself but had gathered through a computer database search. He had credited the newspaper's librarian who helped him with the search, but not the newspapers that created the material, according to *Editor & Publisher* magazine.[60]

Plagiarism does not always involve copying parts of another writer's prose. Some reporters recycle quotes. They see a good quote from a source in another newspaper or on television. They then use that quote in their own stories without acknowledging the work of the original reporter. The sports columnist at the *San Antonio Express-News*, who was caught stealing from the Fort Worth *Star-Telegram*, wrote a letter to readers pointing out that if he had given credit to the reporter who originally got the quotes, he "would have avoided any appearance of plagiarism and, in fact, would have served to compliment the work of a colleague from another Texas newspaper. Unfortunately, that did not happen."[61]

It doesn't take many words to credit another writer. Here are three examples in which the *Orlando Sentinel* took information from other news reports but gave proper credit:

"Whenever there is a suspicious death we would have an inquest to determine how the person died," Bradley Neely, chief inspector of the Coroner's Office, told Associated Press Television News.

Frankie Andreu and another former Armstrong teammate who requested anonymity because he still works in cycling told *The New York Times* that they never saw Armstrong take any banned substances.

The 25-year-old Lafave, who became a tabloid sensation after her arrest in 2004, also acknowledges that her victim might "have a hard time trusting women one day. I'm sure he has to be living with the guilt of – quote, unquote – ratting me out," according to transcripts of the interview with Matt Lauer released by NBC on Tuesday.

However, as Eleanor Randolph observed in *The Washington Post* several years ago, "The easiest way to avoid plagiarism is to give credit. But the average journalist enjoys giving credit about as much as your local 7-Eleven."[62]

Notes

1. Jack Kelley, "Explosion, then arms and legs rain down," *USA Today*, August 10, 2001. The detail about the blinking eyes was edited out of Kelley's original story.
2. Sherry Ricchiardi, "Suicide mission," *American Journalism Review*, June 1999. For other Kelley exploits, see Ricchiardi, "Assignment: Afghanistan," *American Journalism Review*, November 2001 (note: These articles were written before Kelley's deceptions were uncovered) and Jill Rosen, "Who knows Jack?" *American Journalism Review*, April 2004.
3. Jack Kelley, "Vigilantes take up arms, vow to expel 'Muslim filth,'" *USA Today*, Sept. 4, 2001.
4. Jack Kelley, "Trainees eager to join 'jihad' against America," *USA Today*, Sept. 27, 2001.
5. See John Gorenfeld, "Blood-thirsty Arabs, vigilante Jews," *Salon*, March 23, 2004, and Tim Spira, "Unbelievable!" *The Guardian*, July 18, 2006.
6. Details of the *USA Today* investigation are from Bill Hillard, Bill Kovach, and John Seigenthaler, "The problems of Jack Kelley and *USA Today*," available on the *USA Today* Web site; Blake Morrison, "Ex-USA TODAY reporter faked major stories," *USA Today*, March 19, 2004; and Julie Schmit and Blake Morrison, "Unbelievable timing, incredible account," *USA Today*, March 19, 2004.
7. Norman Lewis, "Newspaper plagiarism trends since Jayson Blair," a paper presented to the AEJMC Convention in San Francisco, 2006.
8. Dan Barry, David Barstow, Jonathan D. Glater, Adam Liptak, and Jacques Steinberg, "Times reporter who resigned leaves long trail of deception," *The New York Times*, May 11, 2003. For an account of the Blair episode and its role in the removal of Harold Raines as *Times* managing editor, see Seth Mnookin, *Hard News: The Scandals at The New York Times and the Future of American Media*, New York: Random House, 2004.
9. Glass's fabrications were widely reported, including Ann Reily Dodd, "How a writer fooled his readers," *Columbia Journalism Review*, July/August 1998, pp. 14–15; Howard Kurtz, "*New Republic* fires writer over 'hoax,'"

The Washington Post, May 11, 1998, p. D-1; "At *New Republic,* the agony of deceit," *The Washington Post,* June 12, 1998, p. B-1; and *"George's* sorry statement of affairs," *The Washington Post,* June 8, 1998, p. D-1.

10. David Callahan, *The Cheating Culture,* New York: Harcourt, 2004.

11. Ellen Warren, "The poetic columnist who fell from grace," *Chicago Tribune,* August 12, 1998; and Lamar B. Graham, "An unbelievably good story," *Boston Magazine,* August 1991.

12. S. C. Gwynne, "Media culpa," *Texas Monthly,* June 2004.

13. Joe Gushue, "Rethinking the human element," *Media,* Fall 2004.

14. "Reporter's sources dubious," *Orlando Sentinel,* October 22, 2002; and Jack Shafer, "Fib Newton: The lesson behind the AP's sacking of reporter Christopher Newton," *Salon* (www.salon.com), October 23, 2002.

15. Lori Robertson, "Ethically challenged," *American Journalism Review,* March 2001.

16. Kevin McManus, "The, uh, quotation quandary," *Columbia Journalism Review,* May/June 1990, pp. 54–56.

17. Jacques Leslie, "The pros and cons of cleaning up quotes," *Washington Journalism Review,* May 1986, pp. 44–46.

18. Quoted by McManus, *op. cit.,* p. 54.

19. Mike Needs, "Final column sums up columns not yet written," *Akron Beacon Journal,* June 25, 2006.

20. John Drury, "Should reporters quote what they say, or what they mean? *Solutions Today for Ethics Problems Tomorrow.* Chicago: Society of Professional Journalists, October 1989, pp. 11 and 21.

21. David Shaw, "The press and sex: Why editors lean to dots, dashes, euphemisms," *Los Angeles Times,* August 19, 1991, p. A-19.

22. Mitchell Stephens and Eliot Frankel, "All the obscenity that's fit to print," *Washington Journalism Review,* April 1981, pp. 15–19.

23. See Phil Rosenthal, "Even if it's news, is it fit to print?" *Chicago Tribune,* July 18, 2006, and "'Shit' happens, as most news outlets report Bush profanity," *Editor & Publisher,* July 17, 2006.

24. See Helen Dewar and Dana Milbank, "Cheney dismisses critic with obscenity," *The Washington Post,* June 25, 2004; William F. Buckley Jr., "On the right," *National Review,* March 13, 2006; Jonathan Alter, "The imperial (vice) presidency, *Newsweek,* February 27, 2006; Kim Eisler, "Do conservatives swear more?" *Washingtonian,* September 2005; and Associated Press, "There he goes: Reagan's mike tattles on him," *The Orlando Sentinel,* March 1, 1986.

25. See Greg Couch, "Guillen crosses line with latest slur," *Chicago Sun-Times,* June 21, 2006; and Neil Steinberg, "Our products move globally, our freedoms should too," *Chicago Sun-Times,* June 23, 2006.

26. Shaw, *op. cit.*

27. Lou Gelfand, "Photo, headline gave some readers offense," *The Minneapolis Star-Tribune*, October 29, 1995.
28. Marvin Lake, "Profanity standards relaxed just slightly," *Virginian-Pilot*, July 6, 2006.
29. Jeffrey Dvorkin, "Are NPR reporters too involved in their stories?," posted on www.npr.org, June 5, 2006.
30. David Folkenflik, "Tricks of the trade," *The Sun*, May 15, 2001.
31. Ginger Casey, "Beyond total immersion," *American Journalism Review*, July/August 1999.
32. Tal Sanit, "Stand and deliver," *Columbia Journalism Review*, July/August 1992, pp. 15–16.
33. Thomas Collins of *Newsday*, "News photographers under fire," *Orlando Sentinel*, December 12, 1981.
34. "Note to readers," *The Indianapolis Star*, August 7, 2002.
35. "2 plead guilty to buying beer for teens for TV story," *Orlando Sentinel*, February 24, 1993, p. A-6, and "TV news pair get jail time for buying beer for teens," *Orlando Sentinel*, March 24, 1993, p A-10.
36. "Dateline NBC," February 9, 1993. A detailed account of NBC's story can be found in "TV's credibility crunch," *The Washington Post National Weekly Edition*, March 8–14, 1993, p. 6.
37. Jonathan Adler, "On the ropes at NBC News," *Newsweek*, March 8, 1993.
38. Determination 121, Minnesota News Council, www.mtn.org/~newscncl/complaints/determinations/det_121.html.
39. David Shaw, "Poll delivers bad news to the media," *Los Angeles Times*, March 31, 1993, p. A-16.
40. Tod Stricker, "Photo manipulation: How far is too far?," *PhotoMedia*, Fall 2003.
41. Jacques Leslie, "Digital photopros and Photo(shop) realism," *Wired*, July 22, 1998.
42. "Darts and laurels," *Columbia Journalism Review*, March/April 1997, p 22. Also see Robert King, "The amazing growing sweater," on the Poynter Institute Web site, www.poynter.org. King was presentations editor at the time.
43. Donald R. Winslow, "Reuters apologizes over altered Lebanon war photos, suspends photographer" and "A question of truth," posted on the Web site of the National Press Photographers Association, www.nppa.org, on August 7, 2006 and August 2, 2006.
44. James R. Gaines, "To our readers," *Time*, July 4, 1994.
45. "*Time* manipulates photograph," *The Washington Post*, June 22, 1994, p. 2.
46. Taken from information on the British Complaints Commission Web site, www.pcc.org.uk.

47. Ian Mayes, "Trust me – I'm an ombudsman," *British Journalism Review*, Vol. 15, No. 2, 2004.
48. Ken White, "KLAS-TV reporter adds sound to silent casino security video," *Las Vegas Review-Journal*, February 23, 2002.
49. Nancy M. Davis, "Electronic photo manipulation: Many are doing it, and editors, photojournalists urge strict guidelines to protect credibility," *Presstime*, February 1992, pp. 22–23.
50. Lou Hodges, "The moral imperative for photojournalists," in *Protocol*, Washington: National Press Photographs Association, 1991, pp. 7–8.
51. The new code of ethics is on the NPPA Web site, www.nppa.org.
52. Sheila Reeves, "What's wrong with this picture? Daily newspaper photo editors' attitudes and their tolerance toward digital manipulation," *Newspaper Research Journal*, Fall 1992/Winter 1993, pp. 131–155.
53. Patrick Boyle, "Standards for photography's cutting edge," *Washington Journalism Review*, November 1992, p. 12.
54. Leslie Miller, "Globe columnist asked to resign," *The Boston Globe*, August 5, 1998.
55. Roy Peter Clark, "The unoriginal sin: How plagiarism poisons the press," *Washington Journalism Review*, March 1983, pp. 43–47.
56. Cynthia Gorney, "Getting it right," *American Journalism Review*, March 2001.
57. Larry Tye, "Plagiarism seen as common but little discussed," *The Boston Globe*, July 16, 1991, metro section, p. 1.
58. *Ibid*.
59. Alicia C. Shepard, "Does radio news rip off newspapers," *American Journalism Review*, September 1994, pp. 15–16.
60. Mark Fitzgerald, "*Sun-Times* drops columnist over plagiarism," *Editor & Publisher*, June 27, 1990, p. 17.
61. Robert Rivard, "A commitment and a confession," *San Antonio Express-News*, July 15, 2000.
62. Eleanor Randolph, "Plagiarism and news," in *Messages: The Washington Post Media Companion*, Boston: Allyn and Bacon, 1991, p. 345.

Part 3   Reporting the News

7 Working with Sources

Caroline Lowe, the police beat reporter for WCCO-TV in Minneapolis, had just returned from vacation. While she was calling her usual sources looking for stories, a police officer gave her a tip. He said the public would be shocked to see what happens on Hennepin Avenue at night. He said drug dealing, urinating in the streets, and fighting were every-night occurrences.

Lowe and photojournalist Nancy Soo Hoo placed a camera in the area and soon discovered the tipster was right. But, instead of doing a story about the lawlessness, she wondered why the cops had not done something to stop it. She checked with other sources, including some police officers. They told her the problem was with the police officers assigned to the area. So Lowe and Soo Hoo expanded their probe. Soon they discovered officers sleeping in a movie theater while an assault was happening in the lobby. They videotaped patrolmen hanging out in strip joints and a supervising officer working an off-duty job in the middle of a regular shift.

Clearly, it was a great story. But Lowe faced a problem. If her report was broadcast, she might lose many of her police contacts. Those relation-ships had allowed her to beat the competition on some highly publicized murder cases and to break major stories, including one about drunken pilots on a Northwest Airlines passenger jet. She explained:

> Sources are a beat reporter's bread and butter. I spent 15 years developing sources in the criminal justice system and I've worked hard to earn the trust and loyalty of my police sources. And I knew the story on the downtown foot patrol could threaten some of those relationships.

Her news director told her that she could give the story to other report-ers if she wanted. That way, the story would be broadcast, but she could avoid being blamed for it. Nevertheless, Lowe decided to do the story herself for three reasons. "The first was my strong belief that the story should be told," she said. Second, she felt "ownership" of the story; she wanted to play a role in how it was reported. Also, she wrote, "I knew that I would have to live with the story no matter who did it." If sources are angry enough at a particular news outlet, they often refuse to talk to any of its reporters.

Lowe and Soo Hoo's report was aired over two nights. City leaders reacted immediately. The police unit was reorganized, four veteran officers and the head of the unit were fired or suspended, and the City Council called for extensive reforms. Police reactions to Lowe came just as quickly. Many officers gave Lowe dirty looks and hassled other cops because they were friendly to her. "I expected such reactions, but they still hurt," she recalled. "At least one encounter left me in tears."

But most of her best sources stood by her. She said:

> Many voiced a similar sentiment: They were embarrassed by the story and frustrated that the department hadn't cleaned its own house. But they understood why I had done the story and didn't hold it against me. Some even thanked us.

Lowe wrote that to her surprise, after the story aired she was called by new sources offering tips and information.[1]

Lowe's experience highlights the human and ethical problems that reporters frequently encounter. Reporters and their sources have "an inextricable interdependence," according to Jeremy Iggers, a reporter of the Minneapolis *Star Tribune*. He wrote that reporters "are keenly aware that future access to information depends on how they handle today's story." At the same time, sources are also trying to cultivate reporters so they can present their ideas and spins to the public.[2]

Selecting Sources

As discussed in Chapter 3, reporters had it easier in earlier days. They tended to talk to people in authority and then repeat what they said in their stories. Single-source stories were common. If that source was wrong, reporters figured another source would come forward and they would write another story based on what the second source had to say.

Today, newspapers and TV network journalists no longer write many single-source stories, although they are more common on local TV news.[3] Reporters now gather comments from official sources and then go to other sources to ensure that their stories are balanced. When journalists select sources, their choices can make a major impact on the stories they write and can shape the information that the public receive.

When United Airlines and U.S. Airways were considering a merger, reporters from *The Washington Post* and the *New York Post* talked to different sources. These headlines appeared in those papers on the same morning:[4]

"Fares won't take off, say experts" – *The Washington Post*
"Experts say air fares to soar after big merger" – *New York Post*

Sometimes reporters and TV producers select fiery advocates so their stories and broadcasts will be packed with conflict in hopes of attracting readers or viewers. Yet, in seeking conflict, they may be sacrificing the honesty of their stories. One critic of this tactic is Jon Stewart, a comedian whose "The Daily Show" on the Comedy Channel has become a source of news for many people. Stewart criticized what he called the "argument programs" on cable news channels. He contended that such programs were "hurting America" because they present the issues in extremes of black and white. They provide little "intelligent discourse." Instead, they tend to make problems seem unsolvable and compromise impossible.[5]

The criticism is not limited to the cable talk shows. Cole Campbell, editor of *The Virginian-Pilot* in Norfolk, said:

Journalists keep trying to find people who are at 1 and at 9 on a scale of 1 to 10, rather than people at 3 to 7 where most people really are. Journalism should say that the people from 3 to 7 are just as newsworthy and quotable as those at either end of the spectrum lobbing bombs toward the middle.[6]

Another tempting deviation from truth-telling is for reporters to go for the easy sources rather than track down people who can provide context for their stories. They may be drawn to groups that are media savvy with active public-relations programs. Or they may rely on "quote machines," sources who they know will say things in pithy ways that make perfect quotes. TV journalists have an even tougher time because they need to find sources who can speak well on the air and present their views quickly, preferably in 20-second sound bites. The decision to use these reliable sources may affect negatively the variety of information the public receives.

Often when the public accuse the media of bias, they point to the selection and treatment of sources. The argument is that often reporters select sources they agree with and ask them softball questions. The tough questions are reserved for sources they disagree with. Editors, too, can be afflicted with this ethical shortcoming. Ombudsmen at *The Washington Post* and *The New York Times* acknowledged that editors tended to bury deep inside the paper any stories that quoted people who were opposed to President Bush's plans to invade Iraq in 2003.

Ideally, editors serve as a guard on reporters, sometimes asking for stories to be rewritten to make them more complete and fair. Newsroom education can also help. When a newspaper in the Southwest was gearing up for protests by Operation Rescue, a militant anti-abortion group, editors noticed that many of the journalists involved in the coverage were pro-choice. So they asked a well-respected staff member who opposed abortion to explain his position. Editors thought the ongoing discussions led to better coverage.

Balancing personal attacks

When stories include attacks on people or businesses, journalistic practice requires that the people under fire be allowed to defend themselves, preferably in the same article. The public editor of *The New York Times* chastised some of his paper's reporters for not giving that opportunity to people criticized in their stories. He contended that balance was important even if the attack is oblique. In one case, a reporter quoted a man as saying that an abandoned boat near his business was being used for wild parties and that he had seen young teens drunk on it. After the story appeared, the owners of the boat denied the charge and wanted to know why they weren't given a chance to reply. The public editor agreed that the reporter should have contacted them before running the story.

In another case, a politician accused his opponent of having said "stay the course" several times, a phrase being used during the 2006 elections to indicate support for Bush's handling of the war in Iraq. A reporter checked *Times* databases and wrote that the candidate had in fact never used the phrase. After the story appeared, readers wrote that they had heard him say it. A second check found at least five stories in the *Times* with the quotation. The public editor said that before accusing the politician of making a false campaign charge, the paper should have given him a chance to rebut the criticism. In this case, he believed it may have prevented the *Times* from getting the story wrong.[7]

Sometimes it is difficult to get the other side. With stories about law and order, reporters often find it almost impossible to avoid single-source, one-sided stories. Sometimes the only sources available on crime news are the police and prosecutors. In most states, arrest records and indictments are public record, but jailhouse interviews with suspects are limited or even not allowed. Also, defense attorneys may advise their clients not to the talk to the media, preferring not to give away their strategy before the trial or to give the case more publicity. Just as often, prosecutors and attorneys in civil suits may actively seek media coverage by contacting reporters and even staging press conferences to announce major suits.

Some people make it difficult for reporters to get their side of the story. They hang up on them or have relatives shoo them away from their homes. Then, after the story appears in the paper or on the news, they call to complain that the story said only bad things about them. Apparently, they were under the mistaken opinion that if they do not comment to reporters, reporters will not write the story. To avoid the appearance of bias, reporters often take additional steps to get interviews and then outline in their stories the efforts they made to contact everyone involved.

The Care and Feeding of Sources

Reporters know that they must have good sources. Good sources take care of reporters, feed them news tips, point them toward other sources, and provide background information that makes their stories more authentic. That's why good reporters, especially when they are first assigned a beat, spend lots of time getting to know as many people on their beats as possible. Those minutes spent schmoozing with a source can pay off later in solid information and leads to stories.

Reporters' relationships with sources will vary widely. With some, reporters will develop purely businesslike relationships. The reporter goes to the source with questions within the person's expertise; the source comes to the reporter when the source has information for a story or wants to influence the direction the story will take.

With other sources, reporters may have much friendlier relationships. Mary Murphy, a veteran police reporter, said she tries to maintain friendly relations with police officers. She shoots guns with them at the police department's pistol range, shares jokes and gossip, and doesn't back away when she encounters them in social situations. She believes that this camaraderie helps her on the job. "It's a lot easier when you arrive at the scene and you already know some of the cops," she said. Other reporters have had similar experiences. A reporter assigned to cover courts baked cookies and pies for the bailiffs and clerk's staff. When a heated confrontation flared in a courtroom, one of the bailiffs alerted her. She turned the tip into a solid story. A business writer in football-mad Florida knew nothing about sports when she took the job. But she learned that she had an easier time striking up conversations with businessmen if she could discuss Gator and Seminole football intelligently. So, for the first time in her life, she became an ardent reader of the sports section.

Becoming too dependent

A young reporter outlined in a journalism discussion group the problems she was having covering local police. She admitted she had not printed some newsworthy stories if the police told her they would prefer she didn't – or if the police didn't want to give her the information she knew she was entitled to. She was afraid to do anything that might cross them because she feared they would shut her out entirely. To make matters worse, her state had weak public-records laws.

Even veterans, like Carolyn Lowe in the opening of this chapter, worry that if they push too hard for information or report something negative, they may lose sources. In Lowe's case, although her stories about run-amok police officers did cost her some sources, they also netted her new sources who believed they had a found a reporter they could trust with their information. That's not as unusual as inexperienced reporters might believe.

Steve Brill, a veteran investigative reporter, was once sued for libel by a lawyer-turned-government-official. After Brill won the suit, the man continued to be one of his sources. Brill wrote in a Poynter discussion group:

> I always found that sources would still cooperate after a "bad" story – and respect you more – if you didn't suck up to them or compromise for them, as long as you also made sure to treat them fairly, which includes giving them a real, explicit shot to rebut anything negative you might be writing.

Brill explained that people become sources because they want to ensure that their points of view are represented. They need reporters to do that.

A reporter in a small New England town learned that lesson after the local school superintendent stopped talking to her because she wrote a tough story about him. For two weeks, he refused to talk to her. Each time, she included a sentence explaining, "The superintendent, who has said he will no longer speak to [this paper], did not return calls for comment." Finally, the superintendent returned one of the reporter's phone calls. As a colleague explained later:

> But only after trying to get in one more dig. "You're probably wondering why I'm calling you back," he said near the end of the call. "Well, I think I've made my point." Of course, he had made a point: He needed the reporter (and her paper) more than she needed him.[8]

Beginning reporters can become overly dependent on sources. They are assigned to cover governmental bodies, courts, or law enforcement, and often they have very little background in these areas. It can be difficult to understand the jargon and procedures of such bureaucracies. Reporters may begin to rely on a friendly mayor, police officer, sheriff, or county official to understand the issues and to avoid making errors in their stories. These friendly relationships can create problems. The helpful officials may assume that since they helped the reporters, the reporters will naturally reciprocate and write stories that serve the officials' interests. Write a story that serves her interests. Occasionally reporters do that, although most are leery of getting into mutual back-scratching pacts. A reporter in the Midwest found himself ensnared in such a misunderstanding when a police officer who had been very helpful to him was named in a formal citizen complaint. The officer made it very clear that he was upset when the reporter – his "friend" – treated the complaint as he would any other news story.

Murphy believes reporters can avoid this trap. "You always remember that you are a reporter and they really aren't your friends," she said. She has managed to convey this relationship to her sources. Stoney Lubins, a sergeant in a police department that Murphy covered, said: "We like Mary, but we know she's a reporter and she has a job to do and we have a job to do." The key to developing this kind of relationship, Murphy said, is to treat the officers fairly every time. "You burn them one time and they will never help you again."[9]

When sources become friends

Reporters occasionally do become friends with their news sources, seeing them socially as well as professionally. After all, reporters and their sources often share common interests and backgrounds. It is no wonder that friendships develop between coaches and sportswriters, politicians and political reporters, and police and police reporters. In smaller towns, reporters and their sources are more apt to meet after work because the social network offers fewer opportunities for them to avoid one another.

When reporters and sources are friends, the friendship can cause both of them problems. Sometimes it's easy for the source to forget that the "friend" is also a reporter. Ellen R. Findley, a reporter for *The Advocate* in Baton Rouge, L.A., called an attorney "who was a very good friend" to ask him about the mayor's race. She was interviewing him for a story, but he thought they were just talking. When her story appeared, she said, "we both got a lot of flak – me from him, him from the politicians he offended."[10]

Editors and news directors try to keep an eye on these things. The *Sarasota Herald-Tribune* moved two reporters off their beats because the managing editor said they were "too close and too chummy" with sources. She explained, "It's difficult because you want a warm, friendly relationship, but not too friendly."[11]

Reporters have also been known to identify too closely with the people they cover. At one newspaper, the police reporter began to carry a phony badge and applied for a permit to carry a gun. A more common concern is when sportswriters begin to talk of "we" when they refer to the teams they cover. To get around these problems, some editors and news directors regularly rotate reporters on beats. Or, as the WCCO news director suggested in the opening of this chapter, they assign another reporter to do the negative stories to keep the beat reporter from risking the loss of prize sources.

Some reporters have trouble dealing with sources because they believe an adversarial relationship is necessary if the press is to be a true watchdog of government and other important institutions. They keep their distance from officials and their subordinates. Worse, they may discount every word officials say as being self-serving. The result is often shallow stories that reflect the reporters' biases.

Beyond friendship

Occasionally, reporters are drawn to their sources in ways that go beyond journalistic enterprise. In the past, male reporters would brag that they "scored more than a story" by developing friendships with female employees in government offices. Given the sexism of the day, women reporters who used the same tactic would be accused of sleeping their way to their insider information.

Perhaps one of the more notorious source–reporter relationships involved Laura Foreman and Henry "Buddy" Cianfrani. Foreman at the time was a 34-year-old political reporter for *The Philadelphia Inquirer*, and Cianfrani was a 54-year-old state senator and south Philadelphia political kingpin. Cianfrani was one of Foreman's sources, and she covered his political campaigns. They were also lovers. During their affair, he gave her a fur coat, a sports car, and other expensive gifts. They shared an apartment. When her supervising editors at the *Inquirer* heard rumors about the relationship and questioned her, she feigned innocence and said she was the victim of idle gossip by reporters who were envious of the stories she was breaking. Foreman moved on to *The New York Times* in its Washington bureau, where her secret life was exposed when FBI agents and reporters from the *Inquirer* began investigating Cianfrani. *Times* editors took a hard line when they learned about Foreman's past. After only eight months on the job, they forced her to resign.[12]

Other reporters have had intimate relationships with sources and still enjoyed successful careers. In the 1980s Judith Miller, a controversial reporter at *The New York Times*, lived with Les Aspin, a Democratic congressman from Wisconsin, and frequently quoted him in her stories about national security.[13] In Atlanta, Marion Brooks was a reporter and anchor at WSB-TV while she was having an affair with the city's married mayor, Bill Campbell. To many in the WSB newsroom, the affair was an "open secret." Then she was called to testify at the mayor's trial on corruption charges. She told the jury that the mayor had given her expensive gifts and always paid cash when he took her on more than 20 trips including getaways to San Francisco, Mexico, the Bahamas, and Paris, always staying in five-star hotels. At the time of her testimony, she had left the Atlanta station and was an anchor at WMAQ-TV in Chicago, where her bosses called her a "valued employee" but said they had discussed the case with her. Brooks's friends told the *Chicago Sun-Times* that she recognized she had made a mistake and that she was working hard to regain her credibility in Chicago.[14]

Because source–reporter romances can create severe problems for the people involved and their coworkers, most news organizations try to lessen the problem by moving the reporter to another beat. But that doesn't always work. A reporter at a Midwestern paper told *American Journalism Review* that after she left the police beat to cover city politics, her friendship with one of her police sources became more serious. She told her editor, who said she could never write anything about the police department. That was fine with her. But when another police officer filed a lawsuit against the department, lawyers argued the newspaper had printed details about the case that it should not have known. They accused the reporter of getting information from her policeman boyfriend and passing it along to other reporters. The reporter denied the charge, but admitted it was a painful experience to have her credibility challenged so openly. TV camera crews followed her for a few days after the suit was first filed. She told *AJR* that she will still have an occasional beer with a source, but she is more cautious:

> I don't really want people to know personal things about me anymore, and I don't want to know personal things about them. And I guess that's the way it should be.[15]

Not only can source–reporter relationships be hard on the reporter's professional life, they can create tensions for the couple. The reporter may recognize that the person on the next pillow could provide key information needed to break a story, but ethical or legal considerations may interfere. Ybeth Bruzual, a news anchor at Channel 13 in Orlando, contends that reporter–source relationships are often doomed from the start. "Someone will get hurt," Bruzual said. "It is inevitable that one will want more from the other professionally because of the intimacy."[16]

The After-the-Interview Request

Occasionally, at the end of an interview, reporters are hit with a tricky request. The source will ask, "You're not going to quote me, are you?" Before reporters answer that question, many take into consideration how media smart the person is. If the source deals with the media regularly and if the reporters made it clear they were working on a story, most reporters – but not all – feel justified in using the information and the person's name. Reporters Daniel Schorr of CBS and Abe Rosenthal of *The New York Times* were questioning President Gerald Ford when Ford blurted out that the CIA had been plotting to kill foreign leaders. In Cold War America, that was an admission that would shock many

Americans who did not believe their country would engage in such practices. Ford immediately asked the journalists not to report what he had
said. The *Times* did not use the story, but CBS did. Other news organizations followed with their own investigations.[17]

Many reporters agree with Schorr and take the position that anything
said to them during an interview can be used in their stories. Gordon
McKibben, ombudsman at *The Boston Globe*, received complaints from
two people who were quoted in the *Globe* but did not expect to be. One
was an elderly woman who had revealed some personal information to
a reporter. The other was an employee of a company that was facing
legal action. When a *Globe* reporter called him, he said he had been
told not to talk about the case and directed the reporter to the company
lawyer. However, the reporter continued to ask questions and the man
responded to them "to be friendly," he said. When the man's comments
appeared in the paper, he was fired. McKibben cautioned his readers:

> It is a fact of life: Reporters are after news and specifics and names. If you
> don't want to see yourself quoted, or talk about sensitive issues, say so and
> hang up or walk away. Get the ground rules straight at once. Don't talk
> first, and then decide to go "off the record."[18]

In Raleigh, N.C., Ted Vaden, public editor of *The News & Observer*,
received a similar complaint but offered a different response. A mother
called a reporter to ask for additional information about a story in the
paper. She and the reporter chatted for a few moments and some of
what the mother said appeared in a follow-up story. The mother said she
didn't recognize she was being interviewed. Vaden said he agreed with
the general principle that anything said to a reporter is fair game. He
said that works well with people who understand the unwritten rules,
but he argued that people who are not used to dealing the media should
be given "broad leeway" and that reporters should ask people if they
mean for a statement to go in the paper. He wrote:

> When we're seeking information from private citizens, they are free to
> share that information or not. They, not we, own the information. And if
> we take it without asking, we're taking something that's not ours. [19]

Many reporters already abide by this practice. Mike Feinsilber, who was
Washington news editor for the AP, said that he did not want to take
advantage of inexperienced interviewees, so he would remind them, "Don't
tell me anything you don't want in the newspaper."[20] Other reporters take

steps throughout the interview to make sure that sources know they may be quoted. Barry Michael Cooper, who wrote for *The Village Voice* in New York, said he would stop an interview "when I think subjects could be hurting themselves inadvertently." He would remind them that the interview is on the record and ask them if they wanted to continue.[21]

This practice can create serious problems for reporters. Alex Klein of *The Washington Post* was investigating strange bookkeeping practices before the merger of AOL and Time Warner, the largest in history at that time. After long days of hard work, he thought he had the sources he needed to break the story. Then he ran into an unexpected snag: His sources changed their minds about being quoted. He said:

> When some of my sources were afraid to take on the biggest media company in the world and wanted to withdraw their comments before publication, I let them go. My thought was that it just meant that I needed to work a little harder to report my story.[22]

Some newspapers have formal policies that if inexperienced sources decide later that they do not want to be quoted, the reporter must honor that request. The Freedom Forum has made a similar recommendation.[23]

Paying for News

Edward Fine was high in one of the towers of the World Trade Center when the buildings were rammed by airplanes on September 11. He was one of the fortunate ones who escaped the building uninjured. As Fine walked from the devastation, his clothes coated in the grayish debris, a photographer took his picture. The remarkable image ran on the cover of *Fortune* magazine and appeared in other publications throughout the world. It was a small bright spot amid the horror of the day.

As the first-year anniversary of 9-11 neared, many journalists looked Fine up and asked to interview him. He said he would be glad to be interviewed, but only if he was paid $500 for an hour-long interview or $911 for two hours. "Giving interviews takes time out of running my business. I think it's justified," he told the *New York Post*, which said it did not pay to interview him about his charging to be interviewed.

In many parts of the world, journalists might have forked out the money without batting an eye. British media have a long history of checkbook journalism. Neville Thurlbeck of the UK's popular tabloid

Figure 7.1   Pay the source? A businessman walks from the World Trade Center after the 9/11 terrorist attack. A year later, he wanted $911 to be interviewed and photographed. (Photo by Stan Honda, Agence France-Presse)

News of the World, said, "We've done it for 160 years."[24] About two-thirds of British journalists see nothing wrong with shelling out money for stories.[25] Often these payments are huge. Sky News, the British sister network of Fox News, and the tabloid *News of the World* paid $200,000 and $350,000 respectively to a woman for the story of her affair with soccer player David Beckham. And eight years after her affair with President Bill Clinton became a media sensation, Monica Lewinsky was still able to get more than $700,000 for an interview with Britain's Channel 4, according to news reports.[26]

Checkbook journalism in Britain is not limited to celebrity news. *The Sun* and other British media have covered crime stories by paying witnesses, victims, and even police officers for exclusive information. *The Sun* once paid the son of a murder victim $20,000 for an exclusive report on his reactions when authorities reopened the murder case several years after the crime.[27] Even the venerable BBC paid about $40,000 for the story of a convicted burglar.[28]

Throughout Britain and Europe, government officials often demand "honorariums" before they grant interviews. Tennis and soccer stars frequently receive large amounts of money to talk with European reporters after their games.[29] In Russia, some officials even have written lists of fees based on the length and nature of the interview. In other eastern European nations, government officials rarely tip reporters off to stories – unless there is payment involved.

American news media traditionally have had policies against checkbook journalism. However, as competition between the cable news and network news has grown more intense, some believe that news executives are finding ways around the rules. When a Georgia woman disappeared shortly before her wedding, the search became a national story and thousands of dollars were contributed to a fund to help find her. When she reappeared, she initially told police she had been kidnapped and taken to Arizona by a man who repeatedly raped her. Then she admitted the truth: She had become overwhelmed by the wedding preparations and had run away. That made her a must-have story for the morning TV news programs and nearly all of them were trying to book her. But she picked Katie Couric, then on NBC's morning program, after NBC paid her for the rights to a made-for-TV movie about her. NBC denied the money was to buy the interview.[30]

Why not pay for interviews?

One reason American media hesitate to engage in checkbook journalism is the fear that people will lie or exaggerate if it puts bucks in their pockets. It was reported during the 1992 presidential campaign that *Star*, a grocery-store tabloid, had paid Gennifer Flowers (reportedly $150,000) for her account of an affair she said she had with Bill Clinton. Immediately, other reporters were told of women who were willing to invent stories of Clinton affairs if the price was right.[31]

The perception that people will lie or exaggerate for money is so strong that some criminal trials have been tainted by checkbook journalism. Prosecutors did not ask some people to testify in the O.J. Simpson trial because they had sold their stories. In Britain, many thought schoolteacher Amy Gehring was found not guilty of having sex with underage students because jurors doubted the testimony of students who had received cash from a tabloid.[32] In another case, the UK's *News of the World* promised a young girl a $25,000 bonus if the man accused of sexually molesting her was convicted.[33] Her testimony was the key evidence in the trial.

A second argument against checkbook journalism is that many people will withhold information unless they are paid for it. Stan Honda, the photographer who took the picture of the man leaving the World Trade Center, said that people demanding money is becoming more common.[34] "I am surprised that so many people think that we do pay for news coverage." Marci Burdick, news director at KYTV in Springfield, Mo., said, "Even at this level, around the 80th [largest] market, it is an increasing trend. People are shopping their home video and trying to get us into a bidding war."[35]

60 Minutes executive producer Don Hewitt pointed out that money isn't the only inducement that some producers offer to get people to appear on TV programs. They promise that they will ask only soft questions. Or they will negotiate what will and will not be asked during an interview. Hewitt said it was not healthy for journalism.[36] The British magazine *OK!* not only pays celebrities for interviews, it gives them approval of all pictures and stories.[37] Some American magazines negotiate similar deals with celebrities in exchange for exclusive interviews.

A third argument against checkbook journalism is financial. News organizations fear that if they begin to pay for interviews they will be required to shell out a constant stream of cash. Robert Greene, a legendary *Newsday* investigative reporter and college journalism professor, suspects that it will be costs – not ethics – that stop bidding wars between the news media for stories. That apparently is what happened in Australia. Executives at one news program said they saved about $1.3 million a year when it stopped paying sources.[38]

Kenny Irby of the Poynter Institute has a more idealistic objection:

> Fundamentally, when people are paid for their stories it threatens the journalistic process. A purposeful, fair enterprise needs be vested in voluntary sharing, not the wishes of the highest bidder.[39]

Is information a commodity?

Some reporters see contradictions in outright bans on checkbook journalism. John Tierney, a reporter for *The New York Times* who wrote a series of stories about street people in New York, said many of them asked him for payment in exchange for being interviewed. He wrote:

> Sometimes I explained that I couldn't pay them, but that I could buy them a meal during the interview. Things would go well until we sat down in a restaurant and the person announced: "I'm not hungry now. Just give me the money and I'll eat later."

He said it is difficult to explain why it is "ethically superior to buy a homeless man a $30 dinner than it was to give him $10 in cash."

Tierney contends some interviews would be easier if there was a cash transaction between source and reporter because it would clarify the relationship. Then sources would understand that he was neither a friend nor an advocate. They would know he was a reporter who had paid them for information for his stories. But Tierney cautioned that he did not believe all sources should be paid. When they are paid, he believes readers should be given details of the deal.[40]

But American journalists remain overwhelmingly opposed to checkbook journalism. In one poll only 17 percent of journalists said they thought paying for an interview would ever be justified.[41] Polls have found that the public, too, opposes the practice. Fewer than a third of them believe that checkbook journalism is ethically acceptable.[42]

Notes

1. Caroline Lowe, "Heat on the beat," *Newsworthy*, Winter 1994.
2. Jeremy Iggers, "Journalism ethics: Right name. Wrong game?" *Newsworthy*, Spring 1995.
3. For example, a study in the San Francisco area found that 35 percent of TV stories and 9 percent of newspaper stories had one source. See "Quality gap between newspapers and television newscasts widens in Bay Area, researchers find," news release by Stanford University, September 23, 2003. For a fuller version of the report, see John McManus, "Quality gap between newspapers and television newscasts widens in Bay Area," www. gradethenews.org.
4. Headlines appeared in May 25, 2002 editions of the papers.

5. Jon Stewart's comments were made during an appearance on Fox News's "Crossfire" on October 15, 2004. A transcript is available at www.mediamatters.org.

6. Quoted in James Fallows, *Breaking the News: How the Media Undermine American Democracy*, New York: Pantheon Books, p. 246.

7. Byron Calame, "Listening to both sides, in the pursuit of fairness," *The New York Times*, November 5, 2006.

8. Brill's and Casselman's remarks were on a discussion group at www.poynter.org during January 2007.

9. Interviews by Smith, March 21, 1997.

10. Interview by Goodwin, February 15, 1981.

11. Lori Robertson, "Romancing the source," *American Journalism Review*, May 2002.

12. Details of the Foreman story are taken from "Inquirer conflict in Cianfrani case," *The Philadelphia Inquirer*, August 27, 1977; "Reporter linked to a senator's gifts," *The New York Times*, August 28, 1977; and Donald L. Barlett and James B. Steele, "The full story of Cianfrani and the reporter," *The Philadelphia Inquirer*, October 16, 1977.

13. Seth Mnookin, "Unreliable sources," *Vanity Fair*, January 2006, and Franklin Foer, "The source of the trouble," *New York*, June 4, 2004.

14. Robert Feder, "Atlanta trial dredges up anchor's past 'mistake,'" *Chicago Sun-Times*, January 27, 2006.

15. Robertson, *op. cit.*

16. Interview by Smith, Spring 2006.

17. Daniel Schorr, "Remembering Abe Rosenthal," National Public Radio, May 14, 2006.

18. Gordon McKibben, "A 'friendly' talk that cost a man his job," *The Boston Globe*, July 27, 1992.

19. Ted Vaden, "Private citizens who get into the news," *The News & Observer*, Feb. 6, 2005.

20. Interview by Goodwin, September 23, 1981.

21. Quoted from David Halberstam in his essay in "Dangerous liaisons," *Columbia Journalism Review*, July/August 1989.

22. Alex Klein, "Investigative reporting: Journalism of compassion," posted at www.businessjournalism.org, March 20, 2006.

23. Ted Vaden, "Private citizens who get into the news," *The News & Observer*, February 6, 2005, revised October 23, 2005.

24. Matt Wells, "Sun editor admits paying police officers for stories: Tabloids tell MPs that self-regulation works, *The Guardian* (London), March 12, 2003.

25. Amanda Ball, Mark Hanna, and Karen Sanders, "What British journalism students think about ethics and journalism," *Journalism and Mass Communication Educator*, Spring 2006.

26. Stephanie Gaskell, "It's OK to cash in on a scandal: Lewinsky," *The New York Post*, August 29, 2004.

27. Jon Henley, *The Guardian* (London), April 21, 2006.

28. Ciar Byrne, "BBC pays £4,500 to Tony Martin burglar for interview," *The Independent*, March 4, 2005.

29. Tamara Jones, "Reporters in Germany open wallets for stories," *Los Angeles Times*, March 26, 1991.

30. Walt Belcher, "Couric lands runaway bride for 'Dateline.' How Convenient," *The Tampa Tribune*, June 20, 2005.

31. Michael Hedges, "Media mull the ethics of buying tawdry tales," *The Washington Times*, January 29, 1992.

32. "Bang to rights," *The Economist*, March 22, 2003.

33. Reuters, "'Checkbook journalism' penalty proposed," *The New York Times*, March 5, 2002.

34. Lou Prato, "Tabloids force all to pay for news," American Journalism Review, September 1994.

35. Kenny Irby, "Paying for the story," Poynteronline, www.poynter.org, Sept. 10, 2002.

36. Josef Adalian, "'Minutes' man Hewitt blasts NBC's 'Dateline,'" *New York Post*, January 14 1998.

37. Peter Johnson, "'OK!' entry puts spotlight on checkbook journalism," *USA Today,* July 27, 2005.

38. Mark Day, "Current affairs shows move towards chequebook truce," *The Australian,* November 24, 2005.

39. Bridget Harrison, "Blood money," *New York Post*, September 9, 2002, and Kenny Irby, "Paying for the story," Poynter Institute Web site, www.poynter.org, September 10, 2002.

40. John Tierney, "Cash on delivery," *The New York Times*, April 18, 1993.

41. ASNE poll cited in Julie Dodd and Leonard Tipton, "Shifting views of high school students about journalism careers," *Newspaper Research Journal*, Fall 1992/Winter 1993.

42. David Weaver and LeAnne Davis, "Public opinion on investigative reporting in the 1980s," *Journalism Quarterly*, Spring 1992.

8 The Government Watch

When Geralyn Graham went to visit her granddaughter, she found the child living in "subhuman" conditions. She told *The Miami Herald* that the 5-year-old was "sitting in the middle of the floor, next to human feces, trying to eat a piece of bread. She knew swear words, not normal talking."

The grandmother called the Florida Department of Children and Families (DCF), the state agency in charge of rescuing children from abusive homes. Caseworkers immediately took the girl away from her mother, who was described as a chronic drug abuser, and placed her in her grandmother's care. Soon, however, the grandmother began to have problems with her granddaughter. She told caseworkers that the child "acted weird" and needed a psychological evaluation. One day, a woman who said she was from the DCF came to Graham's home and took the child away. That was the last time, Graham told police, that she saw the little girl.

Graham contacted the DCF and caseworkers assured her that the child was being well cared for, but told her that she could not visit the child. Whenever she asked about the child, she got the same response.

Fifteen months after the girl was taken from her grandmother, an adoption caseworker came to the grandmother's house and asked to see the child. It became clear to Graham that the agency did not know where her grandchild was. According its records, she was still living with her grandmother. The files even included reports from caseworkers who said they had visited the child at the grandmother's house and that she was "healthy and happy."

When asked by the *Herald*, the head of the local DCF office called it the "most troubling situation that I've seen." A state official assured the public it was an "isolated incident." A judge called the handling of the case "absolutely despicable" and accused the department of lying to the court repeatedly.

Several newspapers wanted to see the records of this incident, but the agency refused. The newspapers petitioned the court and received permission to see the files. However, when they were delivered, reporters discovered that the DCF had so heavily edited the records that the newspapers had to go back to court.

As pressure from the media and political leaders grew, the agency was ordered to account for all the children under its care. It admitted that it did not know where 532 children were. The agency said most were teens who had run away from foster homes, had been placed in out-of-state homes, or had been abducted by their parents who did not have custody.

Reporters at the *South Florida Sun-Sentinel* decided to try to see if they could find some of the missing children. They selected 24, all under the age of 14, who were listed on a state-sponsored missing children Web site. Even though the paper did not have the detailed files that DCF caseworkers had, reporters were able to find two of the children in less than three hours. Within a month, the paper had located a third of the children, often just by using directory assistance and calling relatives. They found one child who the agency had placed on its "endangered" list because his parents had long criminal records for drugs and other charges. He had been put in a foster home in Georgia after his parents were arrested on prostitution charges there.

Sun-Sentinel reporters discovered another startling fact. Although the DCF's guidelines require caseworkers to notify police when a child goes missing, many were in no rush to admit that they had lost a child under their care. They sometimes would wait months, even as long as seven years, before reporting to police that a child was missing. It is possible that some children may have disappeared without police ever being told. (Later, newspapers reported that caseworkers in one Central Florida office had hidden files in a ceiling so no one would know that cases weren't being investigated.)

The *Sun-Sentinel*'s discoveries prompted change. Two days after the stories appeared, the head of the DCF resigned. Within weeks, the Legislature changed the laws concerning how the agency reports missing children. Legislators decided that too much of the agency's work was secret. Jeb Bush, then the governor of Florida, said,

It is not acceptable to have kids that have absconded in some cases allegedly for more than a year be found by a newspaper. It does suggest that we need a new approach.

Then events took a different turn.

The agency said it was still unable to find some of the children that the *Sun-Sentinel* had reported locating. Department officials asked the paper to turn over all of its files about the kids. "They ought to be partners in this because if children are imperiled they have a duty to provide the information," Gov. Bush said. "We have asked for it, and I hope they will give it up."

However, the *Sun-Sentinel* was not willing to do that. Earl Maucker, the paper's editor, said:

Our concern is also for the children. However, we are not going to turn over all of our investigative and reporters' files to any agency. As an independent press, it's critical that we do not become, or are not perceived as, an investigative arm of any agency.

Instead, he said the paper would assist the agency on a case-by-case basis.

Later, even more saddening details of the DCF's bungling of this case became known. The woman was not the paternal grandmother, as agency employees had indicated, and was not even related to the girl. The agency's background check had also failed to discover that she had been diagnosed as psychotic and had a long record of fraud arrests. As this was written, she was awaiting trial on charges that she killed the child. Police had not found the body.

The relationship of the news media and the government is marked by constant tensions. The case of the missing children illustrates at least two of them. One is the clash between the need for government secrecy and the obligation to openness in a democracy. No one questions the requirement for government to keep private some of the information that its agencies collect about citizens, particularly abused or abandoned children. Yet, the public must know what its government is doing. When government agencies conduct their business in secret, things can go terribly wrong.

In this case, *Orlando Sentinel* editorialized, the agency's secrecy did not help the children, it "mainly kept hidden incompetence within the agency."[1]

A second tension comes from defining what role the news media should play in the running of the government. Gov. Bush thought the media should be an arm of the government helping it achieve its goals, especially since children were involved. *Sun-Sentinel's* Maucker, however, believed the media should be independent of government. It was the government's job to watch over the children in its custody; it was the media's job to watch over government.

Government Secrecy

Journalists report about most areas of American life, including business, sports, and entertainment. But it is the city, county, state, and national governments that have traditionally gotten the most intense and vigorous surveillance. Three key reasons for this are:

- Government controls many aspects of life. It can take away freedoms, imprison people, regulate businesses, impose taxes and tariffs, and even send citizens to die on battlefields.
- Government runs on tax dollars. When the government wastes money, it is wasting money collected from citizens. When it adopts new programs, those programs are paid for with money it takes from citizens in taxes.
- In a democracy, citizens can make a difference. They can influence government by voting, attending public hearings, and voicing their opinions. But first the media must alert them to what's going on.

Most elected officials understand why reporters scrutinize the government so closely. But many do not like it when that scrutiny is directed toward them. Occasionally, that's because they are engaged in wrongdoing. But more frequently, they want to avoid feeling the sting of criticism and controversy. Almost all their decisions may anger some citizens. Few people like it when their taxes are raised or their local schools are closed. Sometimes government agencies' best plans don't turn out the way they hoped, and they have failed programs and wasted expenditures. Often they would prefer to deal with these issues out of sight of the public.

"Every government has an interest in concealment; every public, in greater access to information," philosopher Sissela Bok wrote. She said many leaders "have not come into office determined to work for more open government, only to end by fretting over new, safer ways" to keep information about government actions from the public.[2]

Many journalists point to the First Amendment and believe it requires that government officials provide them with the information they want. However, the courts and legal scholars tend not to see it that way. Generally speaking, the First Amendment allows the news media to report truthful information they have discovered, but it doesn't necessarily give them any special rights while gathering information. Fortunately, most states and the federal government have passed laws requiring that governmental meetings be open and that public records be made available to the public.

Public records

In a democratic society, citizens must know how the government is functioning if they are to cast intelligent votes. Public records are one way that they can keep track of government. The very words "public records" suggest that they are open to the public.

But often that's not the case. Reporters from seven newspapers in Indiana went to local government offices and asked to see documents that were open to the public under Indiana law. Instead of helpful civic servants who gladly provided them with the information, many of the reporters were met with hostility. In some cases, the officials tried to intimidate reporters by running criminal and financial checks on them. One reporter, legally asking for public records, was taken aback when a county sheriff asked her, "Why aren't you driving your own car?" In more than half the counties, reporters were unable to get police incident reports and crime logs. In many counties they were denied minutes of school board meetings, death certificates, and the salary figures of high-school basketball coaches – all of which are public record in Indiana. When one official was shown the Indiana statute, the response was, "Go get a court order, and then you can have your public record."[3] When students at California State University in Chino tried a similar experiment, they found that only about half the agencies they contacted were willing to abide by California's public-records law.

Unfortunately, these experiences are not rare. Christopher Wills, an Associated Press reporter in Springfield, Ill., told *American Journalism Review*:

> Ask for public documents in Illinois and you may get hostile questions, bureaucratic delays, even threats from a sheriff or two. What you won't get, in many cases, is the information you wanted.

When an Iowa reporter asked for public documents, a sheriff sent a bulletin to other law enforcement agencies warning them about the nosy reporter. The bulletin included his name, address, and driver's license number.

Even basic records have been withheld. When a reporter in Fond du Lac County, Wis., asked to see an arrest record, he was told: "If you were arrested, you wouldn't want your name released, would you?" In Texas, a reporter was denied information about a sheriff who pleaded guilty to having more than a ton of cocaine in his horse trailer. Officials told the reporter that releasing the information would violate the sheriff's privacy.

Some government agencies don't flatly deny requests for public records, but they take their time in filling them. Charles Layton, a reporter at *The Philadelphia Inquirer*, requested documents using the federal Freedom of Information Act (FOIA). He received them – 17 years later.[4] His experience is not unique. A survey found that 35 federal agencies had such large backlogs of files that many unanswered requests were more than a decade old. Although the FOIA requires federal agencies to respond to written requests within 20 working days, courts often grant agencies delays. "I understand the federal government is deluged with requests, but what good is the law if basically nobody has to react to it?" asked Timothy Bunn, deputy executive editor of *The Post-Standard* in Syracuse, N.Y. He told the Associated Press his paper had waited 15 years to get CIA records on the bombing of a PanAm jet over Scotland, which killed 35 Syracuse University students.[5]

Occasionally, the results are not only slow in coming, so much material has been redacted (blacked out) that the records are nearly worthless. After the Bush administration announced that it would not release pictures of the coffins of American troops returning from Iraq, several organizations used the FOIA to request the pictures. The request was initially rejected. After a lawsuit was filed, Pentagon officials released the pictures but obscured the faces of military color guards carrying the coffins.

Figure 8.1   Military color guards carrying the coffins. This photo was released by the Bush administration responding to an FOIA request and a lawsuit for pictures of American military dead returning from Iraq. The Pentagon said it obscured the faces out of concern for the privacy of the honor guard units.

They said they wanted to protect their privacy. Most newspapers decided not to use the altered photos.[6] Some photos without the black boxes were released later to a blog, www.thememoryhole.com.

Most of the time FOIA requests are successful and have resulted in important stories for local as well as national publications. Here are some cited by *The News Media and The Law* and other magazines:

- The *Marine Corps Times* forced the recall of more than 5,000 ballistic vests purchased for use in Iraq despite their failure on performance tests.
- Using 10,000 pages of records, reporters at the *Seattle Post-Intelligencer* examined hundreds of permit exemptions to the Endangered Species Act that allow developers, miners, loggers, and others to harm, injure, or kill nearly extinct creatures.
- The Associated Press learned that the U.S. Department of Education had spent $9.4 million on public relations over the last few years.[7]

- Iowa newspapers documented that the state had used money from the federal Homeland Security Agency to increase security at things like a windmill museum but not at county courthouses and other public buildings.

In states with good public-records laws, the cost of public records is controlled. But in areas where that is not the case, government agencies may charge high fees to limit reporters' access. The police department charged *The Dayton (Ohio) Daily News* $5 per page for copies of electronic records, while other city departments asked for only a nickel a page.[8] A small-town newspaper was told that its request for public records would cost more than $30,000. To a small paper, that's a prohibitive sum. Even a large paper like *The Atlanta Journal and Constitution* balked when county officials said a database that reporters wanted would cost $3,000 to provide. After discussions with the paper, officials determined that their actual cost for retrieving the files was $143.69, which is what the paper paid.[9]

State laws may indirectly discourage government employees from releasing public records. Larry Lough, editor of Muncie (Ind.) *Star Press*, said that Indiana has no criminal penalties for not releasing public records. "But if you release a record that you're not supposed to, you can be charged with a crime," Lough said. Many government employees do "the safest thing" and refuse to release public records.[10]

Journalists fight continually for access to information that legitimately should be open. Among the tactics are:

- Throughout the nation, some reporters routinely carry public-records request forms and copies of their state public-records laws.
- Some newspapers report all efforts by officials to hide public records and explain to readers why access to those records is important.
- When Florida's public-records laws were under scrutiny, several newspapers in Florida held a "Sunshine Sunday." They put special logos on every story that used public records. Many readers – and even some journalists – were surprised that most stories in the news sections carried the logos.
- The *Pittsburgh Post-Gazette* did a year-long study of public-records and open-meetings laws in Pennsylvania, reporting the problems residents of that state have had in dealing with their government.

Increasingly, news organizations are going to court to access records. The *Milwaukee Journal Sentinel* estimated that newspapers and television stations in Wisconsin have spent thousands of dollars on attorney fees in their efforts to obtain government records, many of which previously had been available to the public.[11] In Wilmington, Del., *The News Journal* fought a four-year court battle to get records that would allow reporters to analyze how Delaware's courts handled repeat offenders. Not all news organizations would have had the money or the backbone to continue the fight that long.[12]

In Pennsylvania, the *Post-Gazette* discovered that even when citizens win court orders to obtain public records, officials sometimes drag their feet. A public-information request was made in an effort to find out why a local high school was going to cost twice as much as similar schools in the area. Officials balked at giving out the specifications until the courts ruled that the records must be released. By the time the documents were made public, construction on the school had already started.

Open meetings

A popular image of reporters has them sitting in on governmental meetings and trials and jotting down notes that they will use in their stories. But many city councils and school boards do everything they can to keep reporters out of their meetings. On some occasions, politicians want secrecy to hide wrongdoing. In Pensacola, Fla., county commissioners held secret meetings to arrange land deals that benefited their friends and campaign contributors.

Most of the time, though, political leaders want to close their meetings for less devious reasons: They want to meet in private so they can avoid the heat that often comes with some of their decisions. Often they have unofficial meetings during which they debate the issues and vote. Then, at the official meeting, they go through the formality of passing measures unanimously with no discussion and no dissent. The public is not allowed to hear the reasoning of their elected officials.

The *Los Angeles Times* estimated that 90 percent of the decisions of the Los Angeles county commission – including spending millions of taxpayer dollars on contracts, settling major lawsuits, and making policy changes – were made behind closed doors or without discussion. County Administrator David Janssen acknowledged that "by the time [the matters] come to the board the problems have been resolved."[13]

The classic ploy employed by boards intent on discussing issues among themselves without nosy reporters and the public is to meet for dinner before the official meeting. Florida law enforcement investigated allegations that Cooper City government leaders had private dinners at area bars before City Commission meetings. According to television news reports, six officials ordered 20 drinks at taxpayers' expense during one of the 45-minute dinners.[14]

Another way governmental boards avoid the public is to label their meetings "executive sessions." Good open-meeting laws spell out what can and cannot be discussed at these meetings. Councils and school boards sometimes find loopholes in open-meetings laws. In Lorain, Ohio, members of the school board tried to avoid some of the controversy involved in closing one of the city's three high schools. "The school board had several meetings behind closed doors. They kept arguing they didn't have a quorum and that it wasn't an official meeting, but serious discussions took place," Kevin F. Walsh, publisher of *The Morning Journal* in Lorain, said. Ohio has open-meeting laws, but Walsh said they "have no teeth. Very little, if anything, happens if laws are violated and officials know that."[15]

Some tech-savvy boards have "electronic meetings" by e-mail or instant messaging. Many states haven't updated their laws to take into account changes in technology. A more recent development is "rolling meetings." The government bodies properly announce and conduct a meeting but they do not adjourn it. That way, board members can reopen the meeting days later without notifying the public or the news media.[16]

Elected officials in some areas of Kentucky and New Mexico have tried a more direct way of keeping the press and public away. They refuse to release agendas of upcoming meetings. The public cannot learn what matters will be discussed at the meetings. In some instances they can't even find out the time and place of the meetings.[17] In states with weak open-meetings laws, it's left to journalists to keep officials honest. Often that means costly lawsuits. Fortunately, in states with strong government-in-the-sunshine laws, district attorneys are required to ensure that meetings are open. But even then, journalists have to know their state laws and keep track of the government bodies on their beats. All too often, they bear the responsibility of making sure that the public's business is conducted in public.

Government spin control

As governments grew in size and complexity during and after World War II, government leaders recognized that they needed to communicate more effectively with citizens. American business had already discovered this and had turned for help to a new breed of specialist: the public relations expert. Government soon followed suit, adding scores, then hundreds, and finally thousands of such specialists to the public payroll.

Today, in both government and the private sector, no major enterprise is without public relations counsel. From the largest federal commissions to the local school system, public relations experts play a key role. Often their expertise has proved helpful. Government agencies began to find better ways to assemble and package information that the public needed. And reporters often ask these public-information officers to help them find facts inside the bureaucratic mazes. But occasionally, their expertise is used to manipulate information. Image making and spin control are instruments of government strategy.

The American people and most American journalists were slow to catch on to this development. In 1960 in the midst of the Cold War, the Soviet Union accused the United States of flying sophisticated spy planes over Moscow and other Soviet territory. President Eisenhower denied it, and the American people – and many in the press – believed the accusation was just another Soviet lie. Then the Soviets announced that an American spy planes had crashed deep inside Russian borders. The U.S. government leaders responded by denying that they even had spy planes. They said that if an American plane had crashed in Russia, it was on a training mission and may have mistakenly entered Soviet airspace. By and large, Americans believed that was what happened. Then the Soviets produced CIA agent Francis Gary Powers, who admitted that he was piloting the U-2 spy plane that crashed deep inside Russia. Eisenhower's lie was exposed. As strange as it may seem today, Americans were stunned that the government would deceive them.

On the national level, officials often justify deception and concealment in the name of national security. Howard Simons, former managing editor of *The Washington Post*, said that government officials were so quick to make documents secret that he was amazed that government officials "can remember what is secret and what is not secret."

Sometimes they can't. A National Security Agency deputy was arguing to a judge that the U.S. government was justified in stopping *The Washington Post* from publishing the Pentagon Papers, the U.S. military's then-secret history of the Vietnam War. The deputy brought along a top-secret document that he said was contained in the Pentagon Papers. To drive home how secret the document was, he had sealed it in several envelopes in a double-locked briefcase. He said if the *Post* printed this information, the lives of American soldiers would be jeopardized. The judge ordered him to open the document. Fortunately for the *Post*, the lawyers had brought along George Wilson, respected Pentagon reporter for the paper, who remembered that the material had been read before an open hearing of the Senate Foreign Relations Committee. And Wilson had the transcript to prove it. As Simons added in telling this story, "That clinched that for the *Post*."[18]

The courts allowed the *Post, The New York Times*, and other papers to print the Pentagon Papers. Philosopher Bok believed they made the right decision. The papers contained information about the war that "should never have been secret in the first place," she stated. "This information was owed to the people, at home and abroad, who were bearing the costs and suffering of the war; keeping them in the dark about the reasons for fighting the war was an abuse of secrecy."[19]

Secrecy in War

During World War II, American journalists routinely wore military uniforms, and many accepted the honorary rank of captain. They hitched rides on military planes and roamed about the fronts unabated. Often military leaders would brief them in advance about military troop movements and overall strategies. In many ways, they were part of the military establishment. Their stories were subject to military approval.

The censors were particularly concerned about pictures. John Morris, a photographer and picture editor for *Life* magazine during the war, said, "The rule was: We can show enemy dead but not our own people." Morris said the breakthrough occurred in 1943:

> *Life* ran a photo from Buna Beach in New Guinea. That picture was held up in censorship in Washington for about eight months before it was released. It showed two or three American bodies face down in the sand.[20]

Despite the censorship during World War II, "the nation's news organizations eventually provided the American public with comprehensive coverage of the war," concluded Frank Aukofer and William Lawrence in a study of military–media relations.

Relations were somewhat less friendly during the Korean conflict, which did not have the same level of support from Americans as did

World War II. Censorship in Korea extended well beyond security concerns. Aukofer and Lawrence wrote:

> A story could be released only if it was accurate, did not disclose military information, would "not deteriorate morale" and would not "cause embarrassment to the United States or its allies."

> Gen. Douglas MacArthur broadened the provisions to rule out any criticism of American military commanders or soldiers.[21]

Relationships between reporters and military leaders were friendlier at the start of the Vietnam War, but they slowly soured as the American military was drawn deeper and deeper into the quagmire of Indochina. The rift between the news media and the military was not caused by reporters giving away military secrets. As a matter of fact, there were no reported cases during the Vietnam War of the news media revealing secret plans or troop movements.

The problem between the press and the brass was more basic. The military expected the media to support the war effort as had been done during World War II, while reporters believed they should send back truthful reports even if they were negative. Soon government officials and reporters in Vietnam "settled into a more or less permanent state of confrontation," according to Malcolm W. Browne of *The New York Times*.[22]

Since Vietnam, the military has tried to control the flow of information. In October 1983, the United States launched a surprise invasion of Grenada in the Caribbean. Within hours of the announcement, more than 400 American journalists had flown to Barbados, about 160 miles northeast of Grenada. But many of their journeys ended there. For the first time since the Civil War, the government denied frontline access to journalists. Some reporters and photographers rented boats or planes and tried to reach Grenada on their own. At least two boats and a plane were turned back by American warships and aircraft.

Two days after the invasion, the military agreed to fly a pool of 15 journalists to Grenada, but the pool was delayed in returning to Barbados. Television news crews sent filmed reports back to their networks, but the film did not get back to the states in time for the evening newscasts. However, films taken by military camera crews made it back in time. This prompted *The Washington Post* to describe the invasion as "the first official war in the history of the United States, produced, filmed and reported by the Pentagon, under the sanctions of the president."

By the time journalists were allowed to travel to the island, it became clear that the president and Pentagon had issued a lot of misinformation. To make the raid seem more justified, the Pentagon had reported there were at least 1,100 Cubans there, all "well-trained professional soldiers." These Cubans were supposedly planning a military takeover of the island. But the State Department later confirmed that only about 100 of the Cubans were soldiers. The rest were construction workers building an airport.

Protests from nearly all major news organizations and journalistic associations apparently pushed the Pentagon to agree to a press-pool arrangement for future Grenada-type military operations. When military aircraft bombed Libya in retaliation for terrorism in 1986, a pool of eight journalists was allowed aboard the USS *America*, an aircraft carrier from which attacking planes were flown.[23]

In press-pool coverage, the pool journalists cover the story for the entire press corps by sharing their reports and photos. Very few news organizations like press or media pools. They prefer to have their own reporters and photographers present during military operations. However, most agree that pool coverage is better than no coverage at all.

Pools become tools

Unfortunately for journalists and the public as well, the media pools after the Libyan operation did not work well. When U.S. troops invaded Panama in late 1989, a pool of reporters and photographers was flown to Panama by the Pentagon but was prevented from getting anywhere near the military action. The military said it had to protect the journalists. Instead of covering the invasion by American troops, the pool journalists were kept in windowless rooms at the airport. Once the fighting was over, they were led by their military handlers on tours of deposed dictator Manuel Noriega's various hideaways. They were shown cocaine, firearms, girly magazines, and a Hitler portrait, which were found in Noriega's lairs.

The military handlers apparently hoped that if reporters wrote about these things, Americans would be more likely to support the invasion, which ended with the arrest of the dictator on drug charges. The pool journalists rightly felt they were being used as propagandists.[24] The pool never got near the major stories that came out about six months later: More than a dozen U.S. soldiers were killed or wounded by friendly fire, and the number of casualties among civilian residents of Panama was much higher than originally suggested.[25]

Pool reporting was similarly abused by the military in the 1991 Persian Gulf War. Stanley W. Cloud, Washington bureau chief of *Time* magazine at the time and former Vietnam War correspondent, called it the "worst-covered major U.S. conflict in this century."

Not only did the Pentagon restrict Gulf War coverage to rigidly controlled pools, the pool reporters had to agree to submit their reports to military censors for "security review," Cloud noted. Some of the censorship seemed to have little to do with security. When a newspaper story quoted a jubilant bomber pilot as saying "we kicked ass," the military censors changed the quote to "our mission achieved its goal." Photographs again were also heavily censored. *Detroit Free Press* photographer David Turnley had to argue and cajole the military censors to approve a photograph of a soldier crying next to a body bag, according to *The New York Times*.[26]

Censorship is not the only control the military uses. Christiane Amanpour of CNN said in an interview on PBS's *NewsHour* that the military decided who would be in the reporting pools. "You either have to join what some of my colleagues have called the 'propaganda machine,' or you don't go and cover it at all," she said.[27]

Patrick Sloyan, a *Newsday* reporter who won a Pulitzer for his coverage of the Gulf War, told *The Seattle Times*, "I've never seen such an invasive control of the press." But what angered him more was the way the news media portrayed the war. He said it became a "bloodless war in which video was tightly controlled to where it appeared nobody died." Because there was little original video coverage of the war, television newscasts repeatedly showed video-game-like footage of U.S. missiles blasting away Iraqi strongholds. Newspapers too featured elaborate graphics showing how America was waging a clean war with pinpoint-accurate missiles hitting only military targets. The military later admitted that the accuracy of the missiles was considerably less than that had been portrayed.[28]

A few Gulf War correspondents like Chris Hedges of *The New York Times* broke out of the sole reliance on pool reports and official military briefings. Hedges, who speaks Arabic, wrote later about how he did it:

> For two months several colleagues and I bluffed our way through roadblocks, slept in Arab homes, and cajoled ourselves into (military) units. Eventually, following armored battalions in our jeeps through breached minefields to the outskirts of Kuwait City, we raced across the last stretch

of open desert and into the capital before it was liberated. Our success was due in part to an understanding of many soldiers and officers of what the role of a free press is in a democracy. These men and women violated orders to allow us to do our job.[29]

That Hedges received help from soldiers in the field is not unusual. The disagreements between the military and the media are often not between reporters and soldiers, but between reporters and military and political officials. In a survey taken after the Gulf War, more than half of the military said they thought the media should be able to report without censorship, and 82 percent agreed that the "news media are just as necessary to maintaining the freedom of the United States as the military." Among members of the news media, 76 percent opposed censorship but acknowledged the need for guidelines.[30]

Reporters embedded with troops

When the United States invaded Iraq in 2003, journalists were embedded. In some ways, it was a throwback to the days of World War II when reporters traveled with troops on the front lines. Embedded reporters lived with a group of soldiers or Marines and even went on missions with them. Walt Rodgers, the veteran CNN correspondent, traveled with the Army in an Abrams tank. "Being inside the beast isn't so bad," he told viewers. "We're getting unbelievable access. I don't believe I've ever had such access over 36 years of reporting." Even people who at first were skeptical saw merit in embedding. Deborah Potter, executive director of a nonprofit organization that trains local television news people, told *The Boston Globe* that she had early "suspicions that the military would not allow the kind of reporting we saw. It was more worthwhile than I expected it to be."[31]

Others found flaws in the coverage. One problem was the "soda straw" effect. While acknowledging that the coverage "was vastly better than anything we've had for 20 years," Alex Jones, director of a Harvard center that studies the press and public policy, told *The Boston Globe* that embedded reporters saw the war through a very limited perspective.[32] Many thought that cable news in particular relied so heavily on the video from the embedded reporters that viewers could not know whether they were watching an important battle or a skirmish. *The Denver Post* suggested the coverage was "more eye-catching than eye-opening." According to Ben Bagdikian, former dean of the Graduate School of Journalism at the University of California at Berkeley:

> The public was given a very carefully prepared script from the Pentagon, and they got a microscopic view of the reality for the individual troops. But they did not get a kind of overall look they should have as to what this all meant.

He thought reporters who were not embedded provided the more significant coverage.[33]

The early days of the coverage of fighting in Afghanistan and Iraq were marked by extensive flag waving. According to *The Washington Post,* CNN executives required all reports of civilian casualties in the Afghan War to mention the attack on the World Trade Center. During the first two weeks of the invasion of Iraq, three out of four sources quoted on network news were either current or former U.S. officials. American military successes were emphasized. It was widely reported that camera angles showing the toppling of a major statue of Saddam Hussein in Baghdad gave an exaggerated impression of the number of Iraqis who were in the plaza.

Some contend that pictures in the American news media also gave a sanitized version of the war. Michel duCille, picture editor at *The Washington Post,* told *American Journalism Review* that he thought all the media, including his paper, "went with the wave of trying to tell the story, but we weren't going against the American authorities." Many thought the photo coverage changed when bodies of four American contractors were mutilated, burned, and hanged on a bridge in Fallujah. "It is as though, rather suddenly, the gloves have come off, and the war seems less sanitized, more personally intrusive," wrote Michael Getler, ombudsman at the *Post.*[34]

Photographers during the war were carefully controlled. Only one in eight photographers believed they were given sufficient access to cover the Afghan War, according to research.[35] As mentioned earlier, the Bush Administration prohibited news pictures of coffins returning from Iraq at Dover Air Force Base. *The News Media and The Law* magazine suggested the Pentagon had determined "that public acceptance of its actions is directly related to images of flag-draped coffins." Even families of the dead were not allowed to greet their coffins or to be given pictures of coffins arriving at Dover. "They say it's for privacy, but it's really because they don't want the country to see how many people are coming back in caskets," one mother said. Burial ceremonies at Arlington National Cemetery were also off-limits to news photographers.[36]

Regular news photographers did not take some of the key pictures of the war. Because modern military makes heavy use of computers and satellite technology, troops were able to use the Internet to transmit their thoughts and photos back home. Some contributed to blogs that pointed out weaknesses in the American preparation for the war (not enough armor on Humvees and too few flak jackets, for instance). Others reported on successes by American ground troops. The military tried to limit the nature of the reports on these blogs and punished some for sending back to the states cell-phone pictures of the injured and dead Iraqis and Americans. Soldiers, perhaps inadvertently, took some of the most important images of the war. These pictures showed the inhuman treatment of prisoners in Abu Ghraib and opened an international debate about the role of American troops in Iraq.

Whether because of the tone of the coverage or because of desire to support their troops, Americans' support for the invasion increased during the early weeks of the war: Before the invasion, 58 percent of Americans favored going to war. A few weeks later, 79 percent supported it.[37] However, the early U.S. coverage drove many Americans to seek their war news on blogs and the Web sites of British newspapers like *The Guardian*, which reported greatly increased readership from the United States.

Working with Police

The relationship between reporters and the police is a complicated one. Police reporters often need lots of detailed information quickly, and the police are their best – and sometimes only – sources. To make the relationship work, many journalists believe that some cooperation between police and reporters is appropriate. Robert Greene, retired managing editor of *Newsday*, noted: "All the cops are required to give a police reporter are the basic skeleton details on the blotter report. But they give him more, plenty of background. They volunteer that information." To keep the information flowing, police reporters need to keep them happy. The ethical question is how much cooperation between the news media and law enforcement is acceptable.

At one time, reporters had few problems getting what they needed. Often police and reporters had similar backgrounds, grew up in the same neighborhoods, made similar wages, and even became drinking buddies. Reporters often roamed freely through the halls of the police station talking to patrol officers and detectives. Many equipped their cars with police-band radios and strolled around crime scenes as if they were officers.

Those days have passed. Today, most police buildings are sealed. Regular police officers in many agencies must get approval before they can talk to the news media. And police departments buy scramblers to mask their radio messages because, as an ad in a police magazine says, "No one wants the media showing up to an accident or crime scene before emergency personnel arrive."[38] The Wichita Falls, Texas, news media had to threaten a lawsuit before the police there would allow them to unscramble the police radio bands.

The role of police-beat reporters has changed too. No longer is it their prime job to report on crimes and fires. Both journalists and police agree that another part of the job is policing the police. The media have uncovered police brutality, bribery, and thievery among people who are supposed to enforce the law. On a journalism blog, one person wrote:

> If a reporter just seeks to be a buddy to law enforcement to get better access and quotes for stories, he stands to lose sight of some very troublesome social issues that lurk slightly behind the ordinary veneer of rap sheet "crime and punishment" stories.

Likewise, a police chief urged other officers to recognize that "media scrutiny helps us all by making sure law enforcement stays on the correct side of the law."

Most departments now have public information officers, PIOs, who deal with the media. By having all information funneled through PIOs, departments keep officers from having to deal with reporters and make sure that they have control over the messages being sent to the public. Reporters complain, however, that when news breaks, PIOs are not always available. When reporters do manage to track them down, they sometimes know little about the situation. Often veteran police officers are just as slow to respond to calls from PIOs as they are calls from reporters.

The void in information sometimes causes reporters to look for creative ways to get the information. Roy Peter Clark, a senior scholar at the

Poynter Institute, said he thinks that bad behavior by police reporters "is sometimes caused by a lack of access to information from official sources." Recognizing the media's need for immediate, sound information, some police departments are loosening the rules. In Baltimore, lead detectives and arresting officers can now talk directly to reporters.

However, in many areas of the country, police officials have not only stopped officers from giving interviews, they also urge victims and witnesses not to talk to reporters. In Fairfax County, Va., near Washington D.C., police gave them cards that suggested they call police before they talk to the press. Many people who received the cards assumed that meant they had to get police approval to talk to reporters. Police said they were trying to keep victims from being further traumatized. Dave Statter, a reporter at WUSA-TV in Washington, said it was an effort by police "to limit what we can do as reporters." Sandra Jontz, a *Fairfax Journal* reporter, said:

> You just feel that sometimes you bang your head against the wall in trying to present information to the public. And you've already tied our hands, and here's yet again something else that feels just a bit binding.[39]

Many editors and police officials would like to develop more relaxed relationships. Editors often urge reporters to ride along with police on their rounds, although some departments have banned the practice because of a Supreme Court decision.[40] The aim of going on ride-alongs was not to get video appropriate for the *Cops* television show, but to allow the reporters and officers to develop a better understanding of each other's jobs. One veteran reporter urges newcomers to the police beat to

> be visible, put the time in, constantly be there, show that you actually care, go on ride-alongs, go through reports... I would go to the officer-of-the-month luncheons, law enforcement awards banquets... just to make yourself visible and to understand more what working as a cop entails.[41]

New police officers are also encouraged to get to know reporters, although the advice is offered a little more begrudgingly. One guide for new cops says, "If the idea of being cooped up in a squad car with a reporter has you reaching for the Tylenol, consider rethinking your reaction." It said that ride-alongs with reporters can "foster a mutual understanding of the challenges of each other's jobs. They might even help form, dare we say it, friendships that will serve both of you well in the future."[42]

How close can reporters and police be?

The ethical question for reporters is to balance the need to develop relationships, cooperate with law enforcement, and yet maintain their independence. Some journalists take a hard line: no cooperation. They believe that any cooperation blurs the line between police and journalists.

Even helping police with seemingly minor things can create a debate in many journalism circles. Matthew Waite, then a young reporter at Little Rock's *Arkansas Democrat-Gazette*, received a tip that the drug unit was planning a large-scale crackdown on cocaine. Waite arranged to ride along with the police jump teams as they stormed into crack houses ahead of other officers. "Great fun," he said. "High speed chases, deadly force situations, resisting arrests, all within feet of my eyes."

The raids were so successful that police rounded up more suspects than they could handle. They asked Waite to help by moving a truck. He agreed, "Probably because my parents raised me to always be helpful." When he returned to his newsroom, his editors weren't happy. "My bosses weren't against being helpful, but they were concerned about crossing that line between observer and participant and about liability issues." They told him not to do it again, or he would face formal reprimand.

Veteran police-beat reporters were divided on the ethics of his conduct. Robert Short, police reporter at *The Wichita Eagle*, believed Waite was behaving as any citizen might.

> If the cop needed you to call 911 or hand him his shotgun to save or defend someone's life, would you do that? Of course you would.

However, other beat reporters thought it was important to maintain the line between being a reporter and a participant – even in cases like moving a truck. Kathryn Sosbe of *The Colorado Springs Gazette* asked:

> What happens when you take a step away from your standards, get caught in the middle, then suddenly try to become a reporter again? You really can't waffle back and forth without causing harder feelings.

Sosbe said that when reporters maintain a consistent pattern of integrity, police officers will respect them for their professionalism.[43]

Many thought a photographer in Nacogdoches, Texas, stepped over the line. A man had killed two people and was holding police at bay with a shotgun when a photographer from the local *Daily Sentinel* arrived.

The crazed man told police he wanted to talk to a reporter. So, the photographer handed an officer his camera and reporter's notebook. Posing as a journalist, the officer approached the man and took him into custody. The immediate outcome was what everyone wanted: The bad guy was arrested.

However, the longer-term consequences bothered many in the journalistic community. "Such actions compromise the perceived independence of all journalists and increase the risk they face daily in covering dangerous news stories," Ann Cooper, executive director of the Committee to Protect Journalists, told *News Media and the Law* magazine. A photographer wrote on a Poynter discussion group, "I've been hit by demonstrators who think my credentials are fake. Now I possibly may face somebody with a shotgun who decides I may not be 'real' media." He also worried that if journalists are seen as an arm of law enforcement, "the credibility of journalists could be eroded."

Holding stories, reporting untruths

Police in Hattiesburg, Miss., made a very unusual request of the local newspaper and TV station. To track down people who were trying to hire a hitman to kill a local businessman, the police planned to stage the discovery of the businessman's bloody body in a car parked on a rural road. Police wanted the media to play along with the hoax and report the story as if it were true. They hoped to catch the would-be professional killers when they tried to collect their fee.

Frank Sutherland, who was managing editor of the *Hattiesburg American* and president of the Society of Professional Journalists at the time, did not want to hinder law enforcement. But he did not want to play along. His paper printed one sentence: "Police are seeking information concerning suspected foul play directed toward Oscar Black III." The TV station, on the other hand, showed faked pictures of the bloody scene and reported that Black was probably murdered.

Sutherland defended his paper's handling of the situation. He said he had approved of the reporter's cooperating with police when she told them about the murder plot. "You can't hide behind a journalistic shield" when crimes are about to be committed. "But an important principle was at stake—you just don't lie to your readers." Cliff Brown, the manager of the TV station, said he too abided by journalism's commitment to truth. But when a person's life was on the line, "I realized there are few absolutes in the world."[44] (In the end the plot to kill the businessman never materialized.)

Police agencies sometimes anticipate that the news media will not play along in broadcasting untruths. In Orlando, Fla., a murder suspect was fleeing police. He had robbed two convenience stores to fuel what police called "a cocaine binge." Then he broke into a home and held two small children hostage. Police surrounded the home, beginning a three-day standoff. At press briefings, police said the man was treating the children well, playing with them and keeping them calm. However, after a SWAT team broke into the house and killed the man while he was asleep, police told a different story. They said the man was a violent sociopath who had shown no kindness toward the children. In negotiations with them, he had coldly threatened to kill them. Why the different stories? Police knew the man watched TV news continuously. "We were trying to help build a bond between him and the children," the chief negotiator said. "Sometimes the press uses us, sometimes we have to use the press."[45]

Bargaining for information

While many police departments may not plant bogus information this blatantly, many will ask journalists not to report information they have gathered. Occasionally, news organizations have agreed to delay reporting stories, even exclusive, high-profile ones. Under pressure from American leaders, CBS News delayed airing the photographs of the abuse of Iraqi prisoners at Abu Ghraib for two weeks so the military could prepare for the expected impact the report would have.[46] *Newsweek* reporter Michael Isikoff was ready to break the story that Monica Lewinsky had said she had sex with President Clinton. Special prosecutor Kenneth Starr begged the magazine to hold the story until he had gathered more information by having Lewinsky wear a hidden microphone. "You want to report what you know," Isikoff told *Brill's Content* magazine. "But you don't want to influence what happens."[47]

Many times the police request to withhold information is perfectly valid. A poorly timed news story might lead to a witness being harmed or to bad guys panicking and hurting innocent people. The FBI asked the news media in El Paso, Texas, for a news embargo after two small boys were abducted from their townhouse. Two and half days after the kidnapping, the embargo was lifted when the kidnappers told the family they could find the boys in an abandoned car across the river in Juarez, Mexico.

They were safe. Paula Moore, then co–managing editor of the *El Paso Times*, told readers in an article about the media blackout:

> With the FBI telling us that two lives were at stake, it was an easy decision not to run the story. We're not accustomed to withholding news from the community for any reason, but people's lives are certainly more important than an immediate story. We knew we could tell the full story later.[48]

The media have gone along with police requests only to wonder in hindsight if they did the right thing. The infamous BTK killer who abused and then murdered women in Wichita sent local news outlets lots of messages including "a doll with a bag over its head and its hands tied behind its back, postcards that seemed to refer to packages from the killer and a puzzle filled with clues to his identity." The media passed the material along to police without reporting it – at the request of police. Eventually, police were able to track the killer down after analyzing the material and solving the killer's puzzles. Later, many speculated that if the public had had more details about the case, they could have provided police with better leads. They might even have solved the killer's puzzles more quickly than police did. The result may have been a quicker arrest.[49]

Often the request to withhold information leads to a "form of bargaining that is a daily game for cops and courts reporters," wrote Kelly McBride, a veteran police reporter who now answers ethical questions at the Poynter Institute. She wrote that it happens at both large and small police departments. "It happens on stories as small as serial car burglaries and as big as serial killers."

McBride said there were times when police request holding back information because they haven't been working the case sufficiently. "And sometimes," she wrote, "they have no reasons, as least none that they'll articulate." Reporters are tempted to go along with even weak requests, McBride said, in hopes that "If I hold this out today, maybe you'll give me an exclusive tomorrow." She said from her experience that rarely works. "The detective might call you first, but two hours later the competition has the story anyway." She offered these tips:

- First figure out where the information came from. Anything that can be found in a public record, anything that is voluntarily revealed by witnesses or is observed first-hand by a journalist should be considered fair game. The case for withholding would need to be very strong.
- Lawyers and police officers should know better than try to go off the record retroactively.

- When a cop, lawyer, or an officer of the court asks you to hold back information, ask why. If he or she can't give you a good reason, publish the information.
- In the cases where investigators have a plausible request, don't agree to withhold information indefinitely. Ask: At what point will it be OK to publish this? Initially agree to only a short period of time, say 24– 48 hours or maybe a week. Then review your decision.
- Let your service to the public be your guide. Don't withhold information that misleads or creates a false impression with the audience. Instead, agree to hold back if you think doing so serves the public good. But recognize that most of the time, revealing information serves that public good as much as concealing it.[50]

Cases to Discuss

These scenarios are based on the experiences of reporters and editors. They have been modified for space and impact. In most of these situations, a reporter would seek advice from an editor – and the editors would make the final decision. But the initial input would come from the reporter, and good editors would listen carefully to the reporter before deciding. On some cases, you will see a note that indicates you can check to see what the real editors did. That doesn't mean they did the right thing, but you can compare your thoughts with theirs.

Government Watch case 1: Sons die of drugs

Two brothers, a 15- and a 10-year-old, died within days of each other of overdoses of their mother's prescription drugs. Other drugs were also found in their bodies.

A few months later, you decided to follow up with a story about the abuse of prescription drugs by younger children. However, school officials, teachers, and even police narcotics officers told you that it is not a major problem among youngsters locally. The older girl's classmates said she hated drugs because of what they had done to her mother and they were shocked that she died from an overdose. A check of criminal records showed that the mother had two arrests for possession of crack cocaine. Neighbors believe that she went through court-ordered drug rehabilitation a few years before but that it had not helped. They also told you that the mother left the children home alone while she went out partying. The state children's welfare agency had five complaints against the mom and on one occasion when paramedics had been called to the house because of a reported overdose of one of the boys, she refused medical treatment.

You decided to tell detectives what you have learned, which of course was not news to them. However, they asked you not to write the story. Off the record, they told you that they believed the mother knew considerably more about the deaths. They hoped that by keeping their investigation quiet, she might become overconfident and make a mistake that would provide them with enough evidence to arrest her and perhaps arrest a meth and prescription drug supplier. Not wanting to handicap their investigation, you decide to go along.

That was eight months ago. You go back today, four months later and nearly a year after the deaths, and get the same story. The prosecutor will only say that the case is "complicated."

Do you write the story anyway? Do you give all the details about the problems in the home and the mom's history of drug abuse and drug charges? Do you include the comments from law enforcement about the ongoing investigation and the "complicated" case? *(The newspaper's decisions are at the back of the book.)*

Government Watch Case 2: Talking to the mayor

You've got your first job as a newspaper reporter. For a month, you've been covering City Hall. One day when you report to work, the managing editor wants to see you. The mayor has called to complain. You had written a story in the morning's paper, and she claims you misquoted her and got other facts wrong. She even secretly recorded the interview and can prove your mistakes. You check your notes and decide that you did make some mistakes. The paper runs a correction.

A few days later, you call the mayor for another interview. The mayor says she will talk to you only if you allow her to read the story before it goes into the paper. She says she doesn't trust you and points out that not as many people read corrections as those who read front-page stories. She's fine with you attending her press conferences, but before she'll grant you a one-on-one interview, you have to agree to her terms.

What do you do?

Government Watch case 3: Self-defense expert

The city police have a public-service officer who is a former Marine and has a black belt in martial arts. His duties include teaching self-defense classes and speaking to neighborhood groups about crime prevention. He is in a London airport returning from vacation when he senses someone is pulling his billfold from his back pocket. He spins and grabs the hand of a young female pickpocket. The 5-foot-4-inch woman knees him in the groin, knocks him to the ground with a karate move, and kicks him in the face before fleeing. Police give him first aid, and he is able to catch his flight back home. He still has the bruises when he reports to work.

You are a reporter and hear the gossip. You call security at London's Gatwick airport. The person who answers the phone laughs when you ask about the incident. Witnesses said the woman was half his size and fashion-model thin, the guard volunteers. He reads the name from the report kept by airport security, but points out that the official report was taken by the Metropolitan Police.

You decide to get the city police officer's side. He refuses to comment and says there is absolutely no reason for you to be asking him questions about it. He says, "It's nobody's business. If it did happen, it was thousands of miles away." He points out that when he asks you to start putting home burglary reports in the paper to warn people, you won't do it. "But you will call London for something like this?" He suggests that you will "lose the few friends you have on the police force."

He, of course, is the victim, was off-duty, and did nothing wrong.

Would you use the story, identify him, and point out that his job is to teach officers how to protect themselves?

Notes

1. Information about the DCF was taken from Tere Figueras And Elaine De Valle, "Missing girl, 5, was on DCF's case list," *The Miami Herald*, April 30, 2002; Charles Rabin And De Valle, "Child welfare agency repeatedly uncooperative, grandmother says," *The Miami Herald*, May 2, 2002; Shana Gruskin and Sally Kestin, "Missing Girl's Case Not Unique," *Sun-Sentinel*, May 27, 2002; Vickie Chachere, "DCF accused of concealing files," *Tallahassee Democrat*, June 5, 2002; Kestin, Diana Marrero and

Megan O'Matz, "Lost kids easily found: *Sun-Sentinel* turns up nine of DCF's missing children," *South Florida Sun-Sentinel*, Aug. 11, 2002; Kestin, Marrero and O'Matz, "Gov. Bush calls for 'new approach' to protecting children," *South Florida Sun-Sentinel*, Aug. 13, 2002; Jim Ashe, "DCF Wants Newspaper To Submit Info About Missing Kids," *The Palm Beach Post*, Aug. 13, 2002; Associated Press, "Beleaguered DCF chief Kearney quits," *Sun-Sentinel*, Aug 13, 2002; Kestin and Marrero, "DCF Doesn't Seek Public's Help In Finding Children," *South Florida Sun-Sentinel*, Aug. 19, 2002; and "A Lack Of Credibility," *Orlando Sentinel*, Aug. 21, 2002.

2. Sissela Bok, *Secrets: On the Ethics of Concealment and Revelation*, New York: Vintage, 1984, p. 177.

3. Donald Asher, "The state of secrecy," *Quill*, April 1998, pp. 17–23.

4. Charles Layton, "The information squeeze," *American Journalism Review*, September 2002.

5. "Backlog of FOIA requests extends into the 1980s," Associated Press, November 18, 2003.

6. Rebecca Daugherty, "Even when you get it, it's not all there," *The News Media and The Law*, Spring 2005, and Rebecca Carr, "Pentagon releases hundreds of photos showing fallen soldiers in caskets," Cox News Service, April 28, 2005. See "Return of the Fallen" on the National Security Archive Website, posted April 28, 2005.

7. Daugherty, *op. cit.*

8. Rosalind C. Truitt, "Citizen concerns augment government officials' increased efforts to curtail press privileges," *Presstime*, May 1996.

9. Elizabeth Whalen, "High tech info – and high tech costs," *The Quill*, September 2001.

10. Layton, *op. cit.*

11. Amy Rinard, "Open-records ruling enforced as revision is under way," *Milwaukee Journal Sentinel*, December 9, 2001.

12. Mary Allen, "Access to court records allowed," *The* (Wilmington, Del.) *News Journal*, October 3, 2002.

13. Evelyn Larrubia, "Supervisors' decisions made mostly behind closed doors," *Los Angeles Times*, March 26, 2002, p. A1.

14. Breanne Gilpatrick, "FDLE to probe Copper City dinner allegations," *The Miami Herald*, November 9, 2006.

15. Truitt, *op. cit.*

16. Mike McWilliams, "Press-Citizen sues Board of Regents," *Iowa City Press-Citizen*, December 22, 2006.

17. Greg McDonald, "State sunshine laws under attack," Stateline.org, May 24, 2001.

18. Howard Simons, "Government and national security," excerpt from talk to ASNE Convention in *Editor & Publisher*, April 26, 1986, pp. 80–89.

19. Bok, *op. cit.*, p. 208.
20. Felicity Barringer, "Breaking a taboo," *The New York Times*, October 26, 1998.
21. Frank Aukofer and William Lawrence, *The Odd Couple: A Report on the Relationship between the Media and the Military*, Arlington, VA: Freedom Forum, 1995.
22. Malcolm W. Browne, "The fighting words of Homer Bigart: A war correspondent is never a cheerleader," *New York Times Book Review*, April 11, 1993, p. 13.
23. "Pentagon activates press pool to cover Libya bombing," *Presstime*, May 1986, p. 69.
24. William Boot, "Wading around in the Panama pool," *Columbia Journalism Review*, March/April 1990, pp. 18–20.
25. Pete Yost, "U.S. sharply distorts war news, study says," *Chicago Tribune*, January 19, 1992.
26. Barringer, *op. cit.*
27. "Covering the war," PBS's NewsHour, April 20, 2000.
28. Eric Sorensen, "The information war," *The Seattle Times*, October 6, 2001, p. A3.
29. Chris Hedges, "The Unilaterals," *Columbia Journalism Review*, March/April 1990.
30. Aukofer and Lawrence, *op. cit.*
31. Mark Jurkowitz, "The media's conflict experts say access to troops helped more than hurt," *The Boston Globe*, April 22, 2003.
32. *Ibid.*
33. Joanne Ostrow, "Iraq war coverage more eye-catching than eye-opening," *The Denver Post*, April 27, 2003.
34. Lori Robertson, "Images of war," *American Journalism Review*, October/November 2004.
35. Shahira Fahmy, "U.S. photojournalists' and photo editors' attitudes and perceptions," *Visual Communications Quarterly*, Summer/Fall, 2005.
36. Lucy Dalglish, "Censoring the truth about war," *The News Media and The Law*, Summer 2004, and John Wilkens, "Graphic images of war and its costs stir emotions," *The San Diego Union-Tribune*, April 27, 2004.
37. Julie Mason, Mike McDaniel, Andy Netzel, and L.M. Sixel, "Newest in reality TV really brings war home," *The Houston Chronicle*, March 22, 2003.
38. Jenny Christensen, "Scrambling solutions for police and first responders," www.policeone.com, undated.
39. "Will 'Victim/Witness Media Information Cards' leave crime victims better informed of their rights or biased against the press?", PBS's *Newshour*, July 20, 2000.

40. The Supreme Court ruled in 1999 that if reporters follow police into a person's home, the person's Fourth Amendment rights might be violated. Although the court's ruling was limited to entering private homes, lawyers have advised many police departments not to risk losing a conviction because of the presence of a reporter in a patrol car regardless of location.

41. David Ovalle of *The Miami Herald* quoted by Meg Martin, "Leaving fingerprints: Inside the police beat," www.poynteronline.org, November 22, 2005.

42. Scott Buhrmaster, "Six tips for improving police/media relations," www.policeone.com, undated.

43. Interview by author, September 1998.

44. Details are from Cliff Brown, "The Public's Right to Know Can Kill You," unpublished paper; Janet Braswell, "Police Stage Hoax to Stop Contract 'Hit,'" *Hattiesburg (Miss.) American*, Dec. 10, 1984; "The *American* Did Not Take Part in Hoax," *Hattiesburg (Miss.) American*, Dec. 11, 1984; Duane McAllister, "Publisher Goes on Donahue Show to Defend a Tough Ethics Decision," *Gannetter* March 1985, pp. 6-7; Frank Sutherland, "A Man Threatens Murder in Hattiesburg--And Debate Rages on Using False Stories," *Gannetter*, August 1986, pp. 4-8.

45. Roger Roy, "He's using her as a shield," *The Orlando Sentinel*, December 13, 1997, pp. A1 and A18.

46. Floyd McKay, "The images of war," *The Seattle Times,* May 12, 2004.

47. Steve Brill, "Pressgate," *Brill's Content,* August 1998, pp. 128–129.

48. Paula Moore, "Two boys are kidnapped in El Paso – and the media weigh withholding the story," Editorially speaking section of *Gannetteer*, August 1986, pp. 2–3.

49. P. J. Huffstuttee and Stephanie Simon, "Media's role in BTK case scrutinized," *The Los Angeles Times,* March 3, 2005.

50. Kelly McBride, "On the dangers of holding back," Poynter Online, posted March 5, 2005.

9 The Shady World of Unnamed Sources

President George W. Bush's attempt to bring democracy to Iraq was not going well in 2005. The United States had just acknowledged that American soldiers had mistreated prisoners in an Iraqi prison and had attacked and killed civilians who may not have had anything to do with terrorism. Polls reported that Americans' support for the war was dropping and that Bush's approval ratings were hitting record lows.

It was at this time that a "longtime reliable source, a senior U.S. government official who was knowledgeable about the matter" told *Newsweek* reporter Michael Isikoff a disturbing story. The source said that an official report by U.S. military investigators would charge that American guards at the detention center in Guantanamo Bay, Cuba, had flushed a Qur'an down a toilet in an effort to get Muslim detainees to talk. Isikoff wrote a 12-sentence brief for the *Newsweek*'s "Periscope" section. In an effort to check the accuracy of the report, another *Newsweek* reporter, John Barry, ran the brief by one of his Pentagon sources. The source suggested a minor correction, but made no comments about the gist of the article.

After the report appeared in the magazine, the reaction, as reported by *Newsweek,* was immediate:

> By the end of the week, the rioting had spread from Afghanistan throughout much of the Muslim world, from Gaza to Indonesia. Mobs shouting "Protect our Holy Book!" burned down government buildings and ransacked the offices of relief organizations in several Afghan provinces. The violence cost at least 15 lives, injured scores of people and sent a shudder through Washington, where officials worried about the stability of moderate regimes in the region.[1]

Shortly after the brief appeared, Pentagon officials told *Newsweek* that none of the reports by its investigators had included any reference to what *Newsweek* had reported. Isikoff decided to check again with the person who had given him the original story. This time, the source was less sure of the information. The source was sure that the information was on government records, but perhaps was not part of the official report by the military investigative team. When the other *Newsweek* reporter contacted the source he had used to confirm the story, he was told that the official had not meant to mislead him, but the official admitted he had no direct knowledge of anything in the military report. The magazine, which at first indicated it would not retract the story, was forced to acknowledge that it could no longer stand behind it.[2]

The announcement was met with angry denunciations. Pentagon spokesman Lawrence DiRita exploded, "People are dead because of what this son of a bitch said. How could he be credible now?" Journalists were equally critical. The *Reading Eagle* said there was "no excuse" for *Newsweek's* mistake. Media blogger Tim Porter summed up the incident as "*Newsweek* flushes credibility down the toilet."[3]

Newsweek's blunder came less than a year after Dan Rather's reports on CBS's *60 Minutes* that a source had given CBS several documents concerning President George W. Bush's service – or lack there of – in the National Guard during the Vietnam War. After at first denying that the documents were fake, CBS News admitted it could not authenticate the information. CBS News called the story "a mistake," and Rather apologized.[4]

These instances in which unnamed sources gave faulty information appeared amid a public argument over news credibility. Although Jayson Blair of *The New York Times* and Jack Kelley of *USA Today* were not the victims of unreliable sources, they had used anonymous sources to hide the fact they were fabricating the news.[5] Blair and Kelley's dishonesty was enough for Al Neuharth, founder of *USA Today*, to repeat his opposition to anonymous sources. "The only way to win the war against this evil is for journalists at all levels to ban all anonymous sources," he wrote.[6] He argued that unless anonymous sources were banned, "the public won't trust us, and we put the First Amendment in jeopardy."[7] (Blair and Kelley are discussed in Chapter 6.)

Some journalists defend the use of anonymous sources. Philip Taubman, Washington bureau chief of *The New York Times*, told *Editor & Publisher* that he considered unnamed sources an "indispensable" tool for reporters.[8] A national survey of journalists found that only about 26 percent of reporters and editors considered the use of anonymous sources as "probably not acceptable."[9]

A Love–Hate Relationship

The most celebrated use of an anonymous source was undoubtedly *The Washington Post*'s exposé of the dirty tricks and cover-ups of the Nixon administration. Reporters Bob Woodward and Carl Bernstein described their investigation in a best-selling book, *All the President's Men,* and gave their source the memorable nickname Deep Throat. Almost overnight, the prestige of reporters soared. Students flocked to journalism schools in record numbers. Many, no doubt, were looking forward to a career of clandestine meetings with secret sources late at night in parking garages, as they had seen actor Robert Redford rendez-vous with Deep Throat in the movie based on the book.

After Watergate, the use of unnamed sources not only soared, it became almost *de rigueur* to have them at some news organizations.[10] John Cochran, ABC Washington bureau chief during this period, said reporters would use unnamed sources even when they knew they could find sources willing to be named. "You could go on the air or get in the paper easier if you had an anonymous source," he said.[11]

Not long after Watergate made unnamed sources a part of everyday journalism, another *Washington Post* reporter very publicly exposed the downside to secret sources. In 1981, as we saw in Chapter 6, Janet Cooke made up a yarn about child who was hooked on heroin. Much of her Pulitzer prize-winning story relied on anonymous sources and uni-dentified people. When her deceptions were uncovered, editors and news directors began to wonder if they were giving reporters too much lati-tude in secret sourcing. The number of anonymous sources in American journalism declined for a while.

Then came the media overkill that marked the coverage of the 1994 murder trial of O.J. Simpson, a retired football player and actor. The frantic competition between cable news networks, the tabloids, and mainstream media sent some reporters in a desperate search for fresh angles. Many turned to anonymous sources. Unfortunately, some of the resulting stories were filled with inaccuracies and exaggerations that angered the judge and embarrassed many in the journalism community.

One prominent professor predicted that the mistakes made during the O.J. coverage would spell the end of anonymous sourcing. In 10 years, he claimed, journalists would look back on anonymous sources as the "bad old days in our ethical evolution."[12] That didn't happen, of course. After a short-lived decline in their use, anonymous sourcing returned. Researchers looked at award-winning stories from 1995 to 2002 and found that they contained many anonymous sources.[13]

However, the widely publicized mistakes at CBS News and *Newsweek* in the mid-2000s caused the number of unnamed sources in the American news media to drop dramatically. In 2004, researchers examined 16 papers of varying sizes and found that 29 percent of stories had at least one unnamed source. In 2005, only 7 percent did.[14] When the Associated Press surveyed editors, about a fourth of those who responded said they had banned the use of anonymous sources. Most of those papers were in small and midsize markets, which have traditionally used fewer unnamed sources.[15] However, researchers also found a significant drop in their use by "elite newspapers."[16] *USA Today*, *The Washington Post*, and the Associated Press all put new limits on secret sourcing, and *The New York Times* reworded its policies.[17] The number of unnamed sources in *USA Today* was down 75 percent after the changes.[18]

The public isn't sure how it feels about anonymous sources.[19] In a Pew poll, 76 percent agreed that there are occasions when anonymous sources are justified – particularly if there is no other way to get the information. Yet slightly more than half said anonymous sources increase their concerns about the accuracy of stories.[20] A survey by the APME found a similar conundrum. Newspaper readers consistently invoked one descriptive phrase: "the double-edged sword."[21] They recognized that the use of secret sources allowed reporters to uncover Watergate and that scores of local stories might not have come to light if governmental whistle-blowers had not trusted reporters with their information. Yet, both readers and editors know that the use of unnamed sources is risky.

Use Secret Sources or Miss Big Stories?

If President Nixon's burglars had broken into Democratic Party headquarters a few weeks earlier, it is entirely possible that the word "Watergate" would be known only as the name of a Washington hotel complex, and that Bernstein and Woodward would be just two more general assignment reporters. For a short time, *The Washington Post* had banned the use of anonymous sources. Ben Bradlee, then the paper's executive editor, had gotten tired of Nixon administration sources leaking stories only later to deny them. So he decided to ban unnamed sources altogether. *Post* reporters were instructed to walk out on politicians who wanted to go off the record and to talk on a not-for-attribution basis. Bradlee urged all news media to join in. However, other reporters continued to use unnamed sources, and they got important stories that the *Post* did not have. Bradlee dumped the policy after two days.[22]

Unlike Bradlee, some editors have not backed down on banning anonymous sources, no matter how important the story was. When anonymous reports began to swirl out of Iraq that no weapons of mass destruction had been found there, most news media jumped on the story. After all, the Bush administration had argued for the invasion of Iraq in order to destroy those weapons. But it was not a story at *The News & Observer* in Raleigh, N.C. Editors there refused to run the stories because they were based on anonymous sources. Ted Vaden, the paper's public editor, said it had been beaten before on major stories – including important North Carolina stories – by newspapers with more lenient policies on sourcing. Nevertheless, he said editors there had not considered softening their stand.[23]

Editors like those at *The News & Observer* who refuse to allow the use of secret sources worry about the following:

- Too many reporters use unnamed sources just because they are too lazy to find on-the-record sources.
- The risk is too great a risk that reporters are making up things and passing them off as comments by unnamed sources.
- Information from unnamed sources is often either inaccurate or self-serving.

Some editors have had firsthand experience with lazy reporters who do not press to get information on the record. William J. Small, former president of NBC News, said he wished he had a dollar for every time a reporter had called him and said, "'Look, why don't we do this off the record?' They're always shocked when I said I never talk off the record."[24] Nancy Woodhull recalled that when she was editor of the Rochester, N.Y., *Democrat and Chronicle*, one of her reporters turned in a story without any specific identification of his sources. Asked about this, the reporter said, "Well, gee, I didn't think they'd want their names used."[25]

Other editors fear that some of the material attributed to anonymous sources may have been the product of reporters' creativity. Several major publications, including *The Boston Globe*, *The New Republic*, and *Chicago Tribune*, have had reporters quote sources who didn't exist. Although deception on that level is rare, Robert Greene, who was a top investigative reporter and editor at *Newsday*, said he knew reporters who tried to pass off their own ideas by attributing them to anonymous sources.[26] The "source close to the campaign" may in fact be a reporter who is too lazy or too dishonest to search out real sources. Mark Washburn, an editor at *The Miami Herald*, said he reacted to anonymous sources even more strongly. He commented, "Anytime I see 'sources said,' the hairs go up on the back of my neck and I want to say 'Oh, bullshit, you made it up.'"[27]

Sinister Leakers and Secret Sources

When most people think of anonymous sources, they envision disgruntled employees who want to tell about the shenanigans of their bosses or public-minded individuals who are fed up with waste and wrongdoing. But not all anonymous sources are even that pure of heart. Often their motives are merely self-serving and aimed at obscuring the truth.

Eleanor Randolph wrote in *The Washington Post* that "a leak from a high-level official is more often a strategic move to help formulate or further a policy."[28] *The New York Times* acknowledged that it may have been used by the Bush administration in the days leading up to the U.S. invasion of Iraq. The paper's public editor wrote:

> To anyone who read the paper between September 2002 and June 2003, the impression that Saddam Hussein possessed, or was acquiring, a frightening arsenal of WMD [weapons of mass destruction] seemed unmistakable. Except, of course, it appears to have been mistaken.

The paper based many of the stories on anonymous sources who turned out to be White House officials committed to the invasion or Iraqi exiles who were friendly to the Bush administration. After talking with these people, reporters would try to substantiate their comments. The information was "eagerly confirmed by United States officials convinced of the need to intervene." The *Times* concluded in a letter to readers published nearly two years after the invasion of Iraq: "Looking back, we wish we had been more aggressive in re-examining the claims as new evidence emerged – or failed to emerge."[29]

Other times, politicians leak information so that if things go wrong, they won't be blamed. *Washington Post* writer Howard Kurtz said that when James Baker took over President George H. W. Bush's re-election campaign, he started leaking stories to key reporters that the campaign was "in shambles." As Baker had hoped, their stories reported the mess and suggested that if Bush lost, it would not be Baker's fault.

Insiders may leak information when they disagree with a decision. Several people in the Reagan White House leaked their concerns about a controversial budget proposal because they did not think their objections were getting a fair hearing by Reagan's top advisers. After almost daily leaks reporting information contrary to Reagan's economic assessments, the budget proposal was modified.[30]

Stephen Hess, who studies press–government relations, adds another variety of leakers to the list. He said that some people will leak stories to get on the good side of a reporter they think can be helpful to them in the future.[31] Government PR people are becoming masters of a related ploy. They will leak information to just one reporter because they know news outlets tend to play up stories that they have exclusively. Shortly before a State of the Union address by President Clinton, his press secretary leaked different portions of the speech to reporters from *USA Today*, *The New York Times*, and ABC's *World News Tonight*. The result? "Marginal stories that would barely rate a mention on television were pumped up by virtue of being exclusive," Kurtz wrote in his book *Spin Cycle* about Clinton's use of the media.[32]

Occasionally, even seasoned Washington observers can't figure out the motives of people in what Kurtz called the "shadowy world of unnamed sources." In 2006, the leaders of Iran made the frightening announcement that their country was on the verge of building nuclear weapons. A few days later, *The Washington Post* and *New Yorker* magazine reported that anonymous sources were saying that Bush was considering using American nuclear weapons to destroy Iran's fledging bomb program. Kurtz was curious about the motives of the leakers. He said he saw two possibilities:

- The White House wants this out because it's very effective saber rattling aimed at getting Tehran to the bargaining table.
- Military or administration sources who believe Bush might actually bomb Iran want to torpedo the program through leaks.[33]

The Trial Balloon

Reporters covering even the smallest communities and most obscure agencies quickly learn to be on guard for another perversion of the use of anonymous sources: "trial balloons." Political leaders float a bogus story so they can test which way the wind of public opinion is blowing. For example, a city official might tell a reporter, on a not-for-attribution basis, about one of the mayor's plans. Once the story appears in the paper or is broadcast, the official listens for reactions from the public. If there are no complaints, the city might go ahead with the plan. But if the plan is attacked, the mayor might announce that there was no truth whatsoever to the news report and assure voters that such an awful idea would never even be considered.

Prosecutors and defense attorneys sometimes use similar tactics. They may leak details of an investigation even when they do not have enough evidence to bring charges. They hope that the news accounts will put pressure on the people under investigation or encourage more witnesses to come forward.[34] A prosecutor in California acknowledged that people in his office "vastly overstated" when they told reporters about alleged child abuse at a day-care center. For instance, reporters were told that the children had been used in millions of child pornography pictures and films. When the case came to trial, it became clear that police had found no pictures or films at all.[35]

When police report that someone has confessed to a crime, many assume that the case is closed and the guilty party is in jail. However, Christopher Hanson, a former reporter who teaches journalism ethics at the University of Maryland, cautioned journalists that prosecutors may leak confessions "as a form of insurance: if the judge refuses to admit the confession into evidence, there is still a chance that members of the jury will have been exposed to it through the back door." [36]

Many highly publicized confessions have proven to be untrue. The media in Chicago jumped on a particularly lurid story. Police and prosecutors claimed that two boys, aged 7 and 8, had confessed to raping and beating to death an 11-year-old girl and then stealing her bike. Months later, charges against the boys were dropped. The case began to fall apart when lab analyses found semen in the girl's underpants, indicating that she was attacked by an older assailant, not by prepubescent boys. Why did they confess? They had been interviewed nonstop by teams of detectives without their parents or lawyers being present.

In another case, the *Chicago Tribune* used DNA evidence to disprove the state's first videotaped murder confession. The story was part of a series that examined thousands of murder cases over a 10-year period and found a number of dubious confessions. The videotape confession was made after more than two days of questioning during which police beat the suspect, lied to him, and yelled at him.[37]

If reporters know that using unnamed sources can lead to questionable stories, why don't they refuse to play along? One reason is the competitive urge of reporters to score good stories. The late R. W. Apple Jr. of *The New York Times* told Kurtz:

> Ours is a competitive business, and if someone with an authoritative voice says to us a decision has been made to do X, and we check it a couple of other places, we run it. So does *The Washington Post*. So does the *Los Angeles Times*. You're going to be used on occasion. You do your best to get around being used by figuring out motivation and checking the story out from a number of angles.[38]

Deciding When to Grant Anonymity

Reporters much prefer to have interviews that are completely on the record, meaning that they can use the information and the source's name. Reporters have found that many people who approach them with information really want to get things off their chests and will decide to talk on the record. But if they refuse to go on the record, some reporters must make a difficult decision, particularly if the reporter is in the middle of an interview when the request is made. Journalists consider several factors before cloaking a source's identity, including the following.

The importance of the story

Even editors who would rather not use anonymous sources recognize that some major stories would never have been reported without them. "Deep Throat" and Watergate are the most often cited. Around the country, several news organizations have uncovered corruption and wrongdoing because insiders were willing to alert reporters if they knew their names would not be used.

The motives of the source

Sometimes editors have to sort out the reasons a source wants to remain anonymous. Some sources might lose their jobs if they are identified. In a few cases, sources might be physically harmed or even killed. On the other hand, some sources may be evening old scores or advancing their own careers while hiding behind anonymity. Tom Rosenstiel, director of the Project for Excellence in Journalism, contended that reporters are "cheating readers" when they do not report that the source may be biased or have conflicts of interest.[39]

Many news organizations have revised their codes of ethics to require explanation of why secret sources were used. When the *Orlando Sentinel* reported that U.S. Rep. Katherine Harris ordered her staff to support a military contractor's bid for a defense contract after she was lavishly entertained by the contractor, the paper used two paragraphs to explain how it sourced the story:

> The former employees, both senior members of Harris' staff at the time, spoke on the condition that they not be named. Both still do political work in Washington and worry that speaking to the media will hurt their careers.
>
> Their accounts were supported by Ed Rollins, Harris' former chief strategist...[40]

Lack of other sources

Editors are also more likely to bend the rules if regular sources are being unreasonably closemouthed. During the Gulf War, the U.S. military tried to limit press coverage. As a consequence, the number of stories using anonymous sources increased in many newspapers.[41] Other times reporters say they don't have time to find sources who will talk on the record. "You're operating on deadline and you need the information," so the sources are able to demand that their names not be used, Nina Totenberg of National Public Radio said.[42]

What the competition has

For better or worse, some newspapers soften their ethical policies when they're competing with other news organizations on major stories. Editors at the *St. Petersburg Times,* a paper strongly committed to ethics, said that competition combined with tight-lipped officials led them to break their explicit written guidelines about unnamed sources during their coverage of the mutilation murders of five female students at the University of Florida. *The Florida Times-Union* in Jacksonville maintained its policy of requiring reporters to confirm all information that came from unnamed sources, and editors acknowledged that their coverage wasn't as good as papers with fewer restrictions.[43]

Forms of Confidentiality

Occasionally, reporters enter into other agreements with sources, including "off the record" and "on background." One problem is that not all reporters mean the same things when they use these terms. Many confuse what is generally called "not for attribution" with "off the record." Careful reporters will make sure that they and their sources understand the agreement before continuing.

Reporters and sources sometimes agree that an interview is "not for attribution," meaning the reporter can report the information but cannot use the source's name. Instead, the reporter writes "according to a government official" or "according to a source close to the investigation."

"Off the record" usually means that reporters will listen to the information but promise never to use it. Some reporters never go off the record because they can see little reason to collect information they can't report. Others, however, believe that talking off the record sometimes gives them better understandings of the stories they are reporting. And sometimes the off-the-record information keeps them from making bad mistakes.

An old journalism trick is to go off the record with one source and then try to find another source who will confirm the information on the record. The drawback of this tactic is that if the reporter seems to know too much about what's going on, other officials may recognize that someone has leaked information and they may guess who it was. Thoughtful reporters alert their sources that they may try to verify off-the-record information with other sources. Alec Klein, a top investigative reporter at *The Washington Post*, said he has left good material out of stories – material he got from other sources – because he thought officials might begin to suspect who his anonymous sources might be.[44]

Sometimes reporters may have a source who is not willing to tell them anything directly. However, the source will confirm information they have received from other sources. Woodward and Bernstein coined the term "deep background sources" for these people. "Deep Throat" was a deep background source.[45]

Journalists use the phrase "on background" in two ways. Sometimes sources offer reporters background information that will give them a better understanding of complicated news events. One reporter said if he were assigned a story on the "intricacies of floor and ceiling guarantees on the London Interbank Offering Rate," he would call a banking source for a "fast course" on "how it works and what are the pitfalls." He could then begin reporting the story with more expertise.[46] The reporter does not attribute the information to a source because much of it would be common knowledge in the industry.

Other times, background sessions are meetings between reporters and government leaders – sometimes at breakfast – for free-form discussion of the issues. The participants agree in advance whether the information will be on or off the record. Journalists are divided on the usefulness of such meetings when they are off the record. Some say it is a good opportunity to get an understanding of the thinking of key officials.

However, others argue that backgrounders simply give politicians opportunities to plant stories without being accountable. A *New York Times* reporter, along with five other reporters, attended a backgrounder with President Clinton in the White House Map Room. If the meeting had been on the record, he said, the reporters would have asked Clinton tough questions about some of the things he was saying and would have written front-page stories. However, "there was no point in asking tough questions, since it would just piss off the president and you couldn't use it anyway."[47]

The backgrounder has evolved its own style of attribution in Washington. Often the understanding is that the information and opinions expressed can be used, but they must be attributed to "a senior White House official," a "State Department adviser," a "key congressional aide" or some other designation. When Henry Kissinger was Richard Nixon's secretary of state, he often gave interviews in which he was to be identified as "a high State Department official traveling on the secretary of state's plane." Most readers soon figured out who the source was.[48]

Press aides for other political leaders have created another way of masking attribution. Reporters are told that the information can be used but must be attributed like this: "The president has told friends." Or they can report the comments of the politician but must write them as if they are guessing what the president must be thinking.[49]

Secret Sources, Reporters, and Jail

Two *San Francisco Chronicle* reporters used anonymous sources to report grand-jury testimony that linked the use of steroids to star baseball players Jason Giambi of the New York Yankees and Barry Bonds of the Giants. Following their reports, baseball officials revised their drug policies and Congress began an investigation. Even President George W. Bush, a former executive of the Texas Rangers baseball team, congratulated the reporters, saying they had done a "service." However, federal prosecutors wanted the names of the reporters' sources. When they refused, a federal judge sentenced them to 18 months in jail, a longer sentence than any of the people involved in the criminal case were likely to receive.

Although the case against them was dropped when an attorney admitted he leaked the documents, they would not have been the first reporters to go to jail to protect their sources. Tim Roche, a 24-year-old reporter, was sentenced to 30 days in jail in 1993 for refusing to reveal sources he used in stories he wrote about a child-custody battle he covered for *The Stuart (Fla.) News*. The child's foster mother said his initial stories on the case may have helped save the life of the child, who was going to be returned to an abusive home.[50] And Timothy Phelps of *Newsday* and Nina Totenberg of National Public Radio were threatened with contempt of Congress when they refused to identify sources they used to reveal Anita Hill's claims of sexual harassment by Supreme Court Justice nominee Clarence Thomas.[51]

As in the steroid case, reporters are sometimes saved from jail when their sources identify themselves to authorities. Susan Wornick, a reporter for WCVB-TV in Boston, had been ordered to three months in jail by a judge after she defied his order to name the sole eyewitness to a drugstore burglary. Wornick told the judge that she had promised confidentiality to the eyewitness because he feared retaliation by police. The burglary was allegedly committed by members of the Revere, Mass., police force. After the man came forward and testified before a grand jury, the judge withdrew his contempt ruling against the reporter.[52]

Not all stories that can land reporters in jail save children from abuse, protect people from corrupt police officers, or question the integrity of a Supreme Court nominee. The first reporter in modern times to go to jail to protect a source was Marie Torre, radio-TV critic of the old *New York Herald Tribune*. In 1958, she refused to identify the CBS executive she had quoted in her column to the effect that Judy Garland, the actress who played Dorothy in *The Wizard of Oz*, was being dropped from a television program because she was too fat.

Many news organizations believe anonymous sources are so basic to journalism that they have sought laws to shield reporters from having to identify their sources. About half the states have shield laws, which vary greatly in effectiveness. In states without shield laws, judges have applied either common law or provisions in state constitutions to give some protection to journalists.[53]

Using secret sources can create other legal problems, too. News organizations may have trouble winning libel suits if the sources will not testify in court. At some newspapers, editors consult with libel attorneys before using sensitive stories based on anonymous sources. Many want reporters to have sources agree that the paper can name them if the paper gets embroiled in a libel suit.[54]

Cases to Discuss

These scenarios are based on the experiences of reporters and editors. They have been modified for space and impact. In most of these situations, a reporter would seek advice from an editor—and the editors would make the final decision. But the initial input would come from the reporter, and good editors would listen carefully to the reporter before deciding. On some cases, you will see a note that indicates you can check to see what the real editors did. That doesn't mean they did the right thing, but you can compare your thoughts with theirs.

Secret Sources case 1: Senator as rapist

A member of the U.S. Congress is running for re-election and is likely to win. For a couple of years, you have known that at least eight women have accused him of sexual abuse, including one who says he raped her. You and other reporters have checked their stories as much as you can, but you can't confirm the key charges themselves since they happened in private.

The problem was that the women did not want to be identified. They were all Democrats who earned their livings as lobbyists and full-time employees of the Democratic Party. Their careers would be over if it were known that they caused the downfall of one of the party's elected officials.

Your newspaper has a strict policy against using accusations made by anonymous sources or sources who will not confront the people they are accusing. But you are considering approaching the managing editor and asking if this case could be an exception to the rule. **What factors would you consider before deciding? Would you do it?**

Suppose, whether you agree or not, the managing editor decides he wants to run the stories with anonymous sources. **Would you advocate running the stories before the election or wait until after the election?** Either way, you will anger people who will accuse your paper of influencing the outcome of the election or who will say you withheld pertinent information they could have used in deciding how to vote. *(The newspaper's decisions are at the back of the book.)*

Secret Sources case 2: Musical inmates

The county jail is an old facility not designed to handle the needs of a growing community. The jail has been criticized in official reports as overcrowded for at least two years, and a state agency has threatened to decertify it. County commissioners have not given jail improvements a high priority in county budgets.

Two veteran guards approach you. They would like to tell you about conditions in the jail and the ways the jail authorities are masking the overcrowding. But they can't be identified. It would cause problems for them at the jail. And besides, they've worked with jail officials for many years and believe they are good people dealing with an impossible task. One guard volunteers that if you agree to go off the record, they will describe the "musical inmate game." When regulators check to see if the jail is overcrowded, guards are required to move excess prisoners from cellblock to cellblock so they will be out of sight of the regulators.

It's an intriguing story. **Would you go off the record? Is it an appropriate use of anonymous sourcing?** *(The newspaper's decisions are at the back of the book.)*

Secret Sources case 3: Copyright violators

The local state university decides to close all the student computer labs on campus because they are so expensive. Instead, it requires students to own laptop computers. To make sharing files easier, the school requires everyone to use the same software for word processing, spreadsheets, etc.

Unfortunately, most computers come with a much more basic version of the program. So, thousands of students need to buy the expensive programs.

The manufacturer has designed the software so that it can be copied only once. However, a group of enterprising computer science students has found a way to get around the manufacturer's system. They have managed to do the same thing with other university-required software such as programs for drawing, page making, statistics, etc. The students do not charge for their work. Instead, they created dozens of CDs that students are eagerly passing around on campus.

Part One: Through friends, you discover the identity of the students and arrange to interview them. You think it's a great story. However, they don't want their names used. If you take pictures, they want you to make sure their faces aren't visible. **Do you agree?**

Part Two: Once the story appears, campus police contact you and want to see the pictures you took and to get the names of the students. The students are breaking the law. All citizens should help police enforce the law. An attorney for the manufacturer also calls. She wants to find the young men and stop them from violating the company's copyright. Assume that your state's shield laws are not the best. **Would you identify the students? Would you change your mind when lawyers begin to talk about how long your stay in the county jail might be?**

Secret Sources case 4: Silent students and administrators

It was a major bureaucratic blunder. The large state university you cover was updating its software to combine grade records, financial aid, student background, and other information into one database. The new system would ensure that financial aid and grant checks would be on time and that student transcripts would be updated promptly. When the university put the new system online, it seemed to be working wonderfully. Grades were quickly recorded, and student financial aid was not delayed, as had happened in the past. A few days later, however, the complaints started to pour in.

For some reason, the software confused students who were supposed to be notified that they were on the dean's list with students who had flunked out. Nearly a thousand students and in some cases their parents received letters informing them that they could not register for classes.

The problem was compounded because the system also notified financial aid and student grant agencies and some scholarship donors. The university representative acknowledged the problem and the university was trying to notify everyone about the errors, but getting the notices out was going to take some time.

You want to discover the impact the mix-up has had. Interns at your news organization knew some of the students affected. When the aid and grant checks didn't arrive, they were faced with bounced checks, late payment fees, and other financial problems. One student has already lost more than $1,000 because of the mix-up. Other students have not suffered financially, but they were not allowed to register and now some of the classes they wanted are filled.

Part One. You decide to call some of the students. The woman who had suffered greatly says she will talk, but she doesn't want her name used. Another student says his graduation will be delayed by a semester, meaning that he will have to re-apply to medical school. "I was lucky to get in this year," he says. "Who knows what will happen next year?" He too asks you not to use his name.

What things do you consider before deciding if you will quote these students anonymously?

Part Two. The assistant registrar who is in charge of computer records says he'll explain exactly what happened and why the system failed. But he doesn't want his name used. **What things do you consider before deciding if you will quote him anonymously?**

Notes

1. Evan Thomas, "How a fire broke out," *Newsweek*, May 23, 2005.
2. *Ibid.*
3. Tim Porter, "First draft," posted at www.timporter.com, May 16, 2005.
4. "CBS names memo probe panel," CBSnews.com, posted September 22, 2004, and "CBS statement on Bush memos," CBSnews.com, posted September 20, 2004.
5. Dan Barry, David Barstow, Jonathan D. Glater, Adam Liptak, and Jacques Steinberg, "Correcting the record: *Times* reporter who resigned leaves long trail of deception," *The New York Times*, May 11, 2003, and Blake Morrison, "Ex-USA TODAY reporter faked major stories," *USA Today*, March 19, 2004.

6. Al Neuharth, "The evil of journalism: Anonymous sources," *USA Today*, January 16, 2004.
7. *Ibid.*
8. Joe Strupp, "Losing confidence," *Editor and Publisher*, July 1, 2005.
9. Scott Reinardy and Stephanie Craft, "How journalists view the prevalence and acceptability of problematic practices," a paper presented at the AEJMC convention in Toronto, 2004.
10. B. P. Hussel, "Before Watergate, beyond Jimmy's world," paper presented to the AEJMC convention, 1996.
11. See "Reporting in an ear of heightened concern about anonymous sources," *Nieman Reports*, Summer 2005.
12. Alicia Shepard, "Anonymous sources," *American Journalism Review*, December 1994.
13. Miglena Sternadori, "Use of anonymous, government and other types of sources in newspaper investigative stories," paper presented at the AEJMC convention in San Antonio, 2005.
14. Tom Rosenstiel, State of the News Media Report 2006, Project for Excellence in Journalism, posted on its Web site at http://www.stateofthe-newsmedia.com.
15. David Crary, "Survey shows many newspapers never permit use of anonymous sources," AP story posted on the APME Web site and on the AP State and Local Wire, June 17, 2005.
16. Martin Renee and Esther Thorson, "Says who? Examining the use of anonymous sourcing in news stories," paper presented at the AEJMC convention in San Antonio, 2005.
17. Joe Strupp, "Wash. Post changes guidelines on quotes," *Editor & Publisher*, Feb. 19, 2004; Crary, *op. cit.*; and "Reporting in an ear of heightened concern about anonymous sources," *Nieman Reports*, Summer 2005.
18. Randy Dotinga, "Off the record, newspapers have a problem," *Christian Science Monitor*, May 25, 2005.
19. Rachel Smoklin, "69% A source of encouragement," *American Journalism Review*, August–September 2005, pp. 30–32.
20. Pew Research Center for the People and the Press, "Split over anonymous sources," part of "Public more critical of press, but goodwill persists," www.people-press.org, June 2005.
21. Ryan Pitts, "Readers describe use of anonymous sources as 'double-edge' sword," APME National Credibility Roundtables Project, www.apme-credibility.org, posted June 17, 2005.
22. Ben H. Bagdikian, "When the Post banned anonymous sources," *American Journalism Review*, August 2005.
23. Ted Vaden, "'Anonymice' menace papers' credibility," *The News & Observer*, March 6, 2005, revised October 24, 2005.

24. Interview by Goodwin, October 5, 1981.

25. Interview by Goodwin, October 16, 1981.

26. Interview by Goodwin, October 6, 1981.

27. Jean C. Chance and Connie Bouchard, "The Gainesville slayings: A study in media responsibility and unnamed sources," paper presented at the AEJMC Southeast Colloquium at the University of Alabama, March 25–27, 1993, p. 14.

28. Eleanor Randolph, "Journalists face troubling questions about leaks from criminal probes," *The Washington Post*, August 12, 1989.

29. "The Times and Iraq," *The New York Times*, May 26, 2004, and Daniel Okrent, "The public editor: Weapons of mass destruction? Or mass distraction," *The New York Times*, May 30, 2004.

30. Doris Graber, *Mass Media and American Politics*, Washington: CQ Press, 1989, p. 254.

31. "Lesson on flacking for government," *The New York Times*, August 30, 1984.

32. Howard Kurtz, *Spin Cycle: Inside the Clinton Propaganda Machine*, Glencoe, IL: The Free Press, 1998.

33. Quoted in "The tangled webs we weave," CBS PublicEye, April 18, 2006.

34. For an example of this, see Rosenstiel, *op. cit.* or Randolph, *op. cit.*

35. David Heckler, "Danger ahead: Sex abuse cases," *Washington Journalism Review*, September 1991.

36 Christopher Hanson, "Weighing The Costs Of A Scoop," *Columbia Journalism Review*, January/February, 2003.

37· Kirsten Scharnberg and Steve Mills, "DNA voids murder confession," *Chicago Tribune*, January 5, 2002

38. Quoted by Howard Kurtz, "Sez who?" *The Washington Post*, March 7, 1993.

39. Howard Kurtz, "The stream of anonymous sources," *The Washington Post*, August 8, 1998.

40. Jim Stratton, "Contractor's deal was Harris priority, former staffers say," *Orlando Sentinel*, May 4, 2006.

41. William Blankenburg, "The utility of anonymous attribution," *Newspaper Research Journal*, Winter/Spring 1992.

42. Quoted by Kurtz, "Sez who?".

43. Chance and Bouchard, *op. cit.*

44. Alex Klein, "Investigative reporting: Journalism of compassion," posted at www.businessjournalism.org, March 20, 2006.

45. Carl Bernstein and Bob Woodward, *All the President's Men*, New York: Simon and Schuster, 1974, p. 71.

46. Gary Ruderman, "Off-the-record comments should be just that," Solutions Today for tomorrow's Ethical Problems, Chicago: Society of Professional Journalists, October 1989, p. 8.

47. Kurtz, *Spin Cycle*, pp. 40–41.
48. Walter Isaacson, "The 'senior official,'" *Washington Journalism Review*, November 1992.
49. Kurtz, *Spin Cycle*.
50. "Reporter decides to serve jail time," *St. Petersburg Times*, March 11, 1993, and "Protecting a principle," *St. Petersburg Times*, March 11, 1993. Background to the case is in Bruce Sanford and Anne Noble, "Threats escalate to strip confidential sources from the reporter's tool kit," *Quill*, April 1992.
51. "I'll shield sources, reporter vows," *Newsday*, February 14, 1992, and "NPR reporter won't reveal sources," *The Washington Post*, February 25, 1992.
52. "Source saves reporter from jail term," *News Media and the Law*, Summer 1985.
53. Ralph Holsinger, *Media Law*, New York: Random House, 1987.
54. "Confidential sources," *Freedom of Information Annual Report 1979*, APME, pp. 4–5.

10 Deception

Imagine that you are executive editor of a metropolitan daily newspaper. A veteran reporter on your staff has been doing an exhaustive study of the prison system in the United States. He has spent months investigating American prisons and jails, inspecting dozens of them, and interviewing scores of prisoners and experts on the penal system. Still, he does not believe he could truly describe the psychological effect of being inside, just from talking to prisoners. He wants to pass himself off as a criminal and spend a few days in some big state penitentiary to find out what it's like from the inside. This, of course, will mean that he will have to deceive some people, because if the warden knows who he is he will get special treatment, and if the other inmates know who he is his life may not be worth a nickel. Nevertheless, the reporter believes he can arrange to get himself incarcerated without the people at the prison knowing he is really a journalist.

Do you approve of your reporter posing as a criminal for a few days, assuming that his security can be assured? Are you concerned that he will not identify himself as a reporter? Does it bother you that the people will assume they are having private conversations with a fellow inmate when in reality they are being interviewed for a newspaper story? Will the information he will learn in jail justify all the deception needed to pull off his scheme?

Those are the kinds of problems that confronted the editors of *The Washington Post* in 1971 when Ben H. Bagdikian wanted to get inside the Huntingdon State Correctional Institution in Pennsylvania as an inmate. His editor decided to allow him to do it. Bagdikian arranged his incarceration through the state attorney general's office and assumed a false identification, a false name, and a false history. The warden and Bagdikian's fellow inmates did not learn his true identity until five weeks after his release when they read about his experiences inside Huntingdon in the second of an eight-part series called "The Shame of the Prisons."[1]

When Bagdikian ran into the warden at a conference on prisons several months later, the warden accused him "of unethical behavior, of coming into his prison under false pretenses." Bagdikian said he tried to explain, but the warden was too angry. "No warden or administrator likes to think he was spied upon for public use," Bagdikian said.[2]

Ironically, the editor who approved Bagdikian's posing as a convict later began to reconsider his paper's use of deception and came to a conclusion much like the warden's: He no longer could justify using "false pretenses" to get a story. Bagdikian's editor was Benjamin Bradlee, who played a key role in the *Post*'s Watergate probe. Bradlee began to believe that if the news media were going to criticize other people for lying and using dirty tricks, reporters should not lie and trick people either.[3] Bradlee's change of heart coincided with the growing belief among newspaper journalists that honest reporting rarely needed to begin with dishonesty.

However, as newspapers began a full-scale retreat from the use of deception in the 1980s, television news began to adopt it with gusto. The ethics of deception can still stir heated debate among serious-minded journalists and among the public. In one survey, the public was evenly divided on the use of hidden cameras and using long-distance camera lenses to get photos without the subject's knowledge. But 71 percent said they disapproved of reporters not identifying themselves as reporters, as Bagdikian did in the prison.[4]

The Two Faces of Deception

What Bagdikian did in passing himself off as an inmate is often called "undercover" reporting. That term creates an exciting picture in people's minds of reporters pretending to be Klansmen and criminals. However, not all undercover reporting fits this image. Even when journalists merely pose as members of the public, their motive is still to get a story. They are misrepresenting their intentions. All undercover reporting involves deception. This deception takes two forms: active and passive.

Passive deception

No staging or setting up of sting operations is required for passive deception. Reporters using this approach simply do not identify themselves as reporters. They let others assume they are just members of the public. Perhaps the most benign use of passive deception is when restaurant critics fail to inform their waiters that they are dealing with a journalist, or when reporters doing consumer stories pose as customers to check the honesty of repair shops and other businesses.

A more elaborate example of passive deception was provided by Neil Henry, a reporter from *The Washington Post*. He was working on a story in 1983 about the exploitation of jobless and often homeless men in Washington. He stood on a street corner with a group of them until a man in a truck offered them jobs picking vegetables in the South with promises of good pay and good living conditions. He got on the truck with the others and gave his real name but did not mention he worked for the *Post*. What they encountered after they were hauled to the fields was backbreaking work, filthy bunkhouses, and overpriced meals featuring delicacies like pig ears. Sometimes, after a day's work, they had earned only enough to pay for their meals and a night in the bunkhouse.

For many journalists, passive deception is a harder call than active deception. James Squires, when he was editor of the *Chicago Tribune*, acknowledged that passive deception can be as "deceptive as lying." Nevertheless, he said, "I'm more comfortable if I can be deceptive by silence and not deliberately lie and misrepresent myself."[5] Editors at *The New York Times* apparently take a similar position. They approved reporter Jane Lii's request to go undercover for a story. However, they reminded her that she "was under express instructions to do nothing misleading." This order presented no problems for her. When the managers of a garment sweatshop saw a young woman who looked Asian, they immediately offered her a job that required brutal 15-hour days with only 15-minute lunch breaks.[6]

Most reporters are uncomfortable with passive deception. Veteran police reporter Mary Murphy of *The Portland Press Herald* in Maine has found that many people shy away from reporters. So when she goes to the scene of a crime, she will often strike up conversations with people without telling them who she is. "But not a word they say before I identify myself will be used in my story," she explains. "If they don't want to talk to a reporter, I find someone else."[7]

Active deception

Tales are often told about Harry Romanoff of the old *Chicago American* who would pose as a police officer, a coroner, or even a governor to get a story.[8] He once got the mother of mass murderer Richard Speck to talk to him by telling her he was her son's attorney.[9] Romanoff died in 1970, but his techniques have lived on.

Many older journalists have known reporters who made calls from the pressroom in police headquarters and introduced themselves this way: "Hi, I'm Mike Jones. I'm calling from police headquarters." The ploy often worked: People assumed they were talking to a police official.

That trick still resurfaces occasionally. When charges against an accused killer were reduced from murder to first-degree assault in a plea–bargain agreement, a reporter for the *Faribault Daily News* in Minnesota wanted to get the reactions of family members of the murdered man. However, she was afraid they would not talk to a reporter, so she introduced herself as an employee of the court. A family member assumed it was OK to talk openly to her and told her the agreement was "nuts." After the story appeared in the paper, family members filed a protest with the Minnesota News Council.[10]

Other reporters have used more elaborate measures. A *Newsday* reporter once printed business cards, had another reporter pretend to be his secretary, and even prepared legal documents in order to pose as a lawyer so he could gain information about a drug ring on Long Island. A *Los Angeles Times* reporter wanted to talk to a man who lived in a gated community with an equestrian theme. So he rented a horse and a riding outfit and passed by the gate attendant unchallenged.

In Britain, some soccer fans engage in so much violence and property destruction that they are known throughout Europe as "football hooligans" and "lager louts." (Lager is a popular style of beer.) To gain entry into this world, a BBC reporter claimed to be a drug dealer and got a fresh tattoo indicating he was a fan of the Chelsea football team. He was able to gain entry into one of the higher echelons of one "headhunter" group known for brutal attacks on fans of opposing teams. His undercover report resulted in several arrests, including one man, a stockbroker with a family, getting a six-year prison sentence.

Other journalists have used equally successful disguises. When Lester Piggott, the great English jockey, was riding in a race in Florida in 1992, his horse fell, throwing him to the ground and shattering several of his bones. Although hospital employees had been told to keep visitors away from the jockey because he needed rest, they allowed a priest, a mortician, and a laboratory technician to enter his room. But they weren't the people they appeared to be. They were reporters for British tabloids, wanting to get pictures of the jockey and maybe even a quote or two.[11]

American journalists have also posed as hospital employees to eavesdrop on conversations they were not supposed to hear. When Eugene Roberts, former editor of *The Philadelphia Inquirer*, was covering a murder case as a reporter for *The News & Observer* in Raleigh, N.C., he picked up a stethoscope from a desk in a hospital and walked nonchalantly into the emergency room where police were interrogating a suspect who confessed. Years after the trick, Roberts still believed he was justified. "I didn't lie to anyone," Roberts said. "We're not obligated to wear a neon sign."[12]

But some reporters believe that telling people who you are is important, even to the point of wearing signs. David Halberstam, who won a Pulitzer prize for his reporting from Vietnam for *The New York Times*, said that when he was in Vietnam, he and Horst Faas of the AP

> got these little tags that we sewed on our fatigue jackets that said "Halberstam, New York Times" and "Faas, AP." Most of the reporters began to do this. We didn't want anyone to speak to us with any misimpression of who we were.[13]

Surveys suggest that most journalists today agree with Halberstam: 70 percent of those polled said that claiming to be someone else could never be justified. Almost the same percentage of the public has told pollsters they feel the same way.[14]

From Nellie Bly to Diane Sawyer

For nearly 100 years journalists used variations of these two kinds of deception and rarely gave the ethics of them a second thought. When Bagdikian asked Bradlee if he could pose as a prisoner, Bradlee's "chief concern was security not the ethics of it," Bagdikian said.[15]

Undercover reporting goes back at least to the 1890s when Nellie Bly (her real name was Elizabeth Cochrane) pretended to be insane to find out how patients were treated in Blackwell's Island Insane Asylum. Her three articles for the old *New York World* were headlined "Ten Days in a Mad-house."[16]

The heyday for undercover reporting by newspapers was in the 1930s, perhaps because most cities had two or more papers battling for dwindling depression dollars. Nellie Bly's inside report on a mental institution was repeated by the old *Chicago Times* in 1933, this time with the headline "Seven Days in a Madhouse."[17] When journalism historian Frank Luther Mott started publishing collections of the best news stories in the 1930s, undercover reports were mainstays.[18]

Undercover reporting by newspapers continued into the 1960s and 1970s. Even Nellie Bly's madhouse story had a copier in the 1975 when an Annapolis *Capital* reporter conned his way into the mental hospital in Maryland and wrote about his six days there.[19] Pulitzer prizes were given to the *Chicago Tribune* and *New York Daily News* for undercover stories in the 1970s.

Turnaround on the Mirage

To find out about reported shakedowns of small businesses by government inspectors, the *Chicago Sun-Times* went into the tavern business. Reporters Pamela Zekman and Zay N. Smith posed as a couple from out of town and bought a tavern they called the "Mirage." They rigged the tavern with obvious plumbing and electrical problems. They also built little hideaways where photographers could snap pictures as dozens of electrical and building inspectors solicited bribes to overlook the deficiencies. Zekman and Smith allowed state officials to set up a special auditing team in the bar to uncover tax fraud by accountants who specialized in taverns, restaurants, and other cash businesses.

The *Sun-Times* exposé provided four weeks of exciting, dramatic stories and pictures. Scores of electrical and building inspectors were indicted for soliciting bribes. Ralph Otwell, who was then editor of the *Sun-Times*, called the series the most successful undercover investigation the paper had done for 40 years. Otwell said that "it documented something that had always been a truism in Chicago but yet had never been documented by anybody to the extent that we did it."[20] Journalism schools sought out Zekman and Smith as guest speakers.

Although the series attracted attention around the nation, it did not attract another Pulitzer prize to the *Sun-Times'* display case. Why no Pulitzer for such an enterprising piece of reporting? Like *The Washington Post's* Bradlee, many editors were growing concerned about the ethics of using deception. Eugene C. Patterson, a member of the Pulitzer advisory board in 1979 and 1982, said that the Mirage series caused a debate on the board. Patterson, then chief executive officer of the *St. Petersburg Times*, said he was among those opposed to giving the Mirage series a Pulitzer. He called undercover reporting "a fashionable trend I don't like to see encouraged." He said he believed "that the press as a whole pays a price in credibility when a newspaper that editorially calls for government in the sunshine and candor in business shows itself disposed to shade the truth or mask its motives..." Patterson said that undercover reporting should be limited to "extraordinary circumstance that would require a policy decision by the editor."[21]

When the Pulitzer board did not give the *Sun-Times* the prize for the Mirage in 1979 and then rejected another undercover story in 1982, most newspaper journalists began to reconsider the ethics of undercover reporting. Many editors decided to limit the use of deception by reporters. The *Sun-Times* has since stopped the practice.[22]

Undercover reporting rebounds on TV

By the early 1990s, most newspaper editors were showing disdain for deception and misrepresentation. However, hidden cameras and phony identities were becoming standard tactics of many TV news programs. Tabloid TV shows like *A Current Affair*, *Hard Copy*, and *Inside Edition* were getting large ratings with their mixture of hidden-camera exposés, re-enacted news events, and frequent stories on topless dancers and sexy murders. Meanwhile, network news magazine programs like ABC's *20/20* and *PrimeTime Live*, CBS's *60 Minutes*, and similar programs on NBC were using hidden cameras to uncover insurance fraud, auto repair rip-offs, and poor treatment of children in day-care centers. *Dateline NBC* got good ratings in 2006 and 2007 with a series of sting investigations titled "To Catch a Predator," which exposed men who pursue young girls in Internet chat rooms.

The number of undercover reports on American television has declined along with the popularity of the news magazines. That's not the case in the UK, where both Channel Five and the BBC feature major and not-so-major undercover operations. Five's popular *The Big Sting* opened one season with an exposé of people who sell designer handbags and watches on street corners. In what was probably not a shock to most Londoners, those Prada bags and Rolex watches were not authentic.

Perhaps the biggest flap over an undercover story by an American network was created by Diane Sawyer's report on ABC's *PrimeTime Live* about Food Lion supermarkets.[23] A labor union that was trying to organize Food Lion workers tipped off the show's producers about unsanitary practices in some of the chain's stores. They decided to have a researcher get a job at a Food Lion store and take along a hidden camera. At first the researcher couldn't get hired. So producers had to step up the level of deception. Union members gave her a crash course in how to wrap meat, created a phony work history for her, and supplied her with a glowing recommendation from her "previous boss" at an out-of-state grocery. She wrote on her application: "I really miss working in a grocery story, and I love meat wrapping." She said she hoped to have a career with Food Lion.

Once on the payroll, she began videotaping her fellow employees as they gave her advice on how to do her job, including ways to sell old meat and deli products as if they were fresh. They sometimes would douse old meat in barbecue sauce and sell it at a premium price since it was ready to grill. She did not witness the most striking claim made by employees. They said that some meat-counter employees would soak outdated meat in bleach and then repackage it. ABC invited Food Lion to answer the charges, but officials rejected the offer.

Public response to the segment was dramatic. Food Lion sales dropped immediately, and the value of the company's stock fell. Officials delayed expansion plans and closed some stores, causing layoffs. The company fought back with TV ads emphasizing the cleanliness of its stores and pointing out that the chain had an "above average" rating from state health inspectors.

The chain sued ABC. It did not accuse ABC of libel, nor did it claim the story was false. Instead, Food Lion accused ABC of committing fraud when the researcher lied on her application. A jury agreed and awarded Food Lion $5.5 million in 1997. A judge reduced the award to $315,000. An appeals court later threw out the punitive damages, leaving ABC having to pay Food Lion $2.[24]

A Controversial Method

For at least 30 years, people both in and out of journalism have been debating whether the news media's use of undercover reporting is justified.

Broadcast journalists are its biggest supporters, with about 70 percent of news directors approving of its use when the story warrants. According to polls by the Radio–Television News Directors Association, about 66 percent of the public would like the use of hidden cameras and microphones to be banned.[25]

The debate often centers on these questions:

- Are the hidden cameras being used purely to hype the story?
- Do the ends (uncovering wrongdoing) justify the means (using deception and possibly violating laws)?
- Are there privacy concerns?
- Are hidden cameras the best way to get the story?
- How significant and widespread is the issue under investigation?

Hype or news?

Undercover reporting with hidden cameras can yield legitimate news stories. Producer Michele Rubenstein and reporter Dave Savini of Channel 5 in Chicago investigated reports that schools were misusing "time-out" rooms. Instead of isolating misbehaving students, they found children locked in cramped, windowless closets for hours at a time. The video of the children made the story much more compelling than merely quoting students complaining about their teachers. The Legislature soon adopted tougher laws on the use of time-out rooms. "We use hidden camera here and there, when there is no other way to visualize the story," Frank Whittaker, vice president of news for Channel 5, told the *Chicago Tribune*. His station had also allowed a reporter to pose as a college student on the University of Wisconsin campus to show how easy it was for students to buy the drug Ritalin from other students.[26]

Other television stations have caught government employees wasting taxpayers' money. Shortly after the public-transportation company in Orlando, Fla., reduced service because of lack of funding, it sent 21 employees to a conference in Las Vegas. TV station WKMG followed along with a hidden camera. Employees were caught at the gambling tables and slot machines while the conference was under way. The grainy video showed one of them sitting at a card table wearing a gold watch and bracelet, smoking a big cigar, and telling Lady Luck, "Show me some love, baby." Under intense political pressure, the bus company revised its travel rules and began an audit of its spending.

Although some hidden-camera reporting can serve a public service, many worry that the technique is often used only for the hype. Reuven Frank, former president of NBC News, told a *Chicago Tribune* reporter:

> Nothing matters anymore, except the competition for audience. Everybody in the spectrum is fighting everybody else for audience, so you're getting a mushing up of [ethical] standards. Standards are fine, if they don't lose audience.[27]

There's little question that some stations have used hidden-camera reports to create drama and boost ratings. During one sweeps period, KENS-TV in San Antonio broadcast a report on homosexual activity at a public park, promoted as "Perverts in the Park." According to *Columbia Journalism Review*, the station showed hidden-camera video of "men explicitly, graphically, unmistakably engaged in oral sex" twice during the report. The anchor later apologized to viewers, explaining, "I think it's probably the result of a continued attempt to get ratings."[28]

Some undercover reports are more like pranks. A British TV program armed a luxury car with bulletproof glass and doors and parked it in a high-crime area. Hidden cameras videoed people trying to break in and steal an expensive laptop sitting on the front seat. "I think a lesson has been learnt here," the reporter said at the end of the segment. Apparently the lesson was that owners of fancy cars should be careful where they park. Police tracked down six would-be thieves; one was fined about $120 and the others were given warnings.[29]

Ends versus means

When journalists discuss the ethics of deception, they often get embroiled in a controversy that has been debated for centuries: Do the ends justify the means? Or, as Valerie Hyman, a former TV journalist and ethics teacher at the Poynter Institute, phrased it:

> If truth-telling is one of the values we hold dear as journalists, then we have to think awfully hard before we decide to be deceptive in our pursuit of telling the truth.[30]

Don Hewitt, *60 Minutes* producer, believes the ends often justify the means. "It's the small crime versus the greater good," he argued. "If you catch someone violating 'thou shall not steal' by your 'thou shall not lie,' that's a pretty good trade-off."[31] However, former *Washington Post* executive editor Benjamin Bradlee concluded:

> In a day in which we are spending thousands of man hours uncovering deception, we simply cannot deceive. How can newspapers fight for honesty and integrity when they themselves are less than honest in getting a story? When cops pose as newspapermen, we get goddamn sore. Quite properly so. So how can we pose as something we're not?[32]

Others point out that when journalists go undercover, they often break the law. People are not allowed to sneak onto restricted military bases, lie to school officials, or apply for passports under phony names. Yet undercover journalists have done each of these. Jurors in the Food Lion case sent a clear message that they did not think ABC's researchers were above the law. They thought the journalists had committed fraud by lying on job applications and should be treated like everyone else.[33]

Privacy issues

Reporters working undercover also face the charge that they are violating people's privacy. The argument is not that undercover reporters are necessarily breaking any privacy laws. Most news organizations have attorneys who guide them through the maze of state laws and court rulings. For example, Chicago TV stations sometimes do their hidden-camera investigations in Wisconsin because Illinois requires them to get a person's permission for audio recording.[34]

The concern is that reporters invade privacy in an ethical sense: People think they are talking privately to fellow employees or new acquaintances. In reality, what they are saying may be repeated to thousands of readers or broadcast to millions of people watching television. "I just think it's wrong," Tom Goldstein, dean of the journalism school at the University of California at Berkeley, told *The Washington Post*. "Journalists should announce who they are. I'm uncomfortable living in a world where you don't know whom you're talking to."[35]

The Wall Street Journal was criticized when it allowed reporter Beth Nissen to get a job in a Texas Instruments plant to see how that company tried to keep its workers from forming a labor union. The reporter deliberately talked about the union to her fellow employees.[36] Critics pointed out by openly engaging fellow employees in talk about anti-union activities, she may have jeopardized their jobs. "People don't know who you really are when they bare their souls to you, and then you smear them by invading their privacy," Lawrence O'Donnell, *Journal* associate editor at the time, said.

Editors at the *San Francisco Chronicle* set strict ground rules before they allowed a reporter to pose as a high-school student to write features about school life in the 1990s. Not only was she required to get permission from school officials before beginning the project, she had to check with every student and teacher mentioned in her stories and delete anyone who did not want to be included.[37] Editors at the *Star Tribune* in Minneapolis made a similar requirement when one of their reporters enrolled in a college course for a story questioning the academic rigor in women's studies programs.

Best way to the truth?

Perhaps the most fundamental question is whether deception is the best way to get the story. Zekman, one of the Mirage bar reporters, thinks it always is. She said undercover reporting is "a much more valid way to get at the truth of things than any other technique there is."[38] Others contend that deception should be a last resort. Undercover reporting can be "a terrific way to get stories when no other way is possible," said Hyman, a former TV journalist who now teaches ethics:

> When the more straightforward, more conventional alternatives have been considered and dismissed for legitimate reasons, and when the story itself is of such import that it must be told, deception is warranted. Our job – as journalists – is to inform, not to conceal.[39]

The problem, of course, is trying to decide when conventional techniques won't work. Zekman contended that having the *Sun-Times* buy the Mirage bar was the only way to uncover corruption in Chicago. She rejected using traditional methods or working undercover in someone else's bar. "You had to own the bar to find out whether businessmen were being extorted by building inspectors," she said. But Eugene Patterson, a respected journalist, argued that the *Sun-Times* could have exposed corruption in Chicago without the theatrics of buying the bar. He said that "hard work and shoe leather could have unearthed the sources necessary to do the Mirage story."[40]

Undercover reporting has also been used to test the effectiveness of post 9-11 airport security. In Prague, a Czech journalist climbed an airport fence to see if he could get access to planes. He was quickly arrested. "We judge this as stupid," a policeman said.[41] In Montreal, a Canadian journalist met with more success. Wearing jeans and a T-shirt, he found he could get access to most areas of the airport – including the tarmacs where jets sit – by telling people he was a workman and carrying a tape measure. "It was so easy to get in, it's scary," he said later.[42]

Many American papers have found that they could get great stories about airport security without using undercover methods. When security banned passengers from carrying liquids onto planes, *The Washington Post* talked to travelers and discovered that enforcement was hit or miss at best. In Denver, 7News interviewed air marshals and found serious problems that made it easy to detect which planes they were on. After the report, changes were made in procedures.[43]

A villain or a widespread problem?

Nearly everyone who advocates undercover reporting agrees that safeguards need to be built into the technique and that it should be only one part of the investigation. Without adequate research before the undercover project begins, reporters cannot provide enough background. The public has no way of knowing whether the story has uncovered a few bad apples or a widespread, ongoing problem. That's why Bagdikian, the reporter who wanted to go inside a prison in the example at the beginning of this chapter, had already spent a long time researching the problem before he asked if he could go undercover. He had talked to experts, visited prisons, and studied the public records that were available. Armed with this information, he knew what he was likely to encounter and knew he could judge whether his experiences in prison were typical of most inmates'. His undercover work was only one story in an eight-part series. Similarly, before *60 Minutes* opened the storefront clinic, the producer knew that illegal kickbacks at medical clinics were a growing problem costing taxpayers millions of dollars and that it was common in Chicago.

Some worry that not all stories are this carefully researched before the undercover work begins. But people both in and out of television journalism have some concerns about the *PrimeTime* Food Lion report. "I cannot believe that such a story would be done that way on any CBS program," Joe Peyronnin, CBS's senior vice president for news magazines, told the *Chicago Tribune*.[44]

Russ W. Baker wrote in *Columbia Journalism Review* that *PrimeTime* may have fallen "into a typical trap – focusing in on a villain when the problem is systemic."[45] The episode showed a few workers at a handful of stores in one chain. Viewers were left with no clue as to how widespread the problem was. Were these practices followed in all Food Lions? In all supermarkets? By focusing on only one supermarket chain, the *PrimeTime* report may have caused some people to stop shopping at Food Lion and switch to a market with even worse practices.

A way to avoid this criticism is to broaden the research. Baker noted that at the same time *PrimeTime* was preparing its Food Lion story, a local station in Atlanta, WAGA-TV, was doing a larger-scale investigation of food safety on its own. The Atlanta station found that each of the 20 supermarkets it tested was repackaging old meat. The stores included both national and local chains.[46] Similarly, when *Dateline NBC* did a story on adulterated ground beef, reporters collected samples from different stores in several parts of the country. They then sent more than 100 samples to an independent lab whose tests showed that what the label calls "100 percent ground beef" may contain as much as 20 percent pork or poultry. For a *Dateline NBC* report on supermarkets that relabeled the expiration date on meat products, reporters took a variety of samples from the nation's seven largest chains and found the practice to be widespread.

Improving the Profession

In its handbook *Doing Ethics in Journalism*, the Society of Professional Journalists suggests these guidelines for deciding when deception by a journalist is justified:

- When the information obtained is of profound importance. It must be of vital public interest, such as revealing great "system failure" at the top levels, or it must prevent profound harm to individuals.
- When all other alternatives for obtaining the same information have been exhausted.
- When the journalists involved are willing to disclose the nature of the deception and the reason for it.
- When the individuals involved and their news organizations apply excellence, through outstanding craftsmanship as well as the commitment of time and funding needed to pursue the story fully.

- When the harm prevented by the information revealed through deception outweighs any harm caused by the act of deception.
- When the journalists involved have conducted a meaningful, collaborative, and deliberate decision-making process in which they weigh:
  - the consequences (short and long term) of the deception on those being deceived;
  - the impact on journalistic credibility;
  - the motivations for their actions;
  - the deceptive act in relation to their editorial mission;
  - the legal implications of the action;
  - the consistency of their reasoning and their action.

The SPJ handbook also suggested some criteria that *cannot* be used to justify deception:

- Winning a prize.
- Getting the story with less expense of time and resources.
- Doing it because "others already did it."
- The subjects of the story are themselves unethical.[47]

Cases to Discuss

These scenarios are based on the experiences of reporters and editors. They have been modified for space and impact. In most of these situations, a reporter would seek advice from an editor – and the editors would make the final decision. But the initial input would come from the reporter, and good editors would listen carefully to the reporter before deciding. On some cases, you can check to see what the real editors did. That doesn't mean they did the right thing, but you can compare your thoughts with theirs.

Deceptions case 1: Nuclear terrorists on campus

You've read lots of news reports about terrorists trying to get materials for nuclear weapons. They wouldn't need enough for a regular nuclear bomb, according to reports. With a small amount of nuclear material they could build so-called dirty bombs, which are often sticks of dynamite surrounded by nuclear waste. The blast then disperses radioactive material over a large area.

You're rather surprised to learn that a large state university in your area has a nuclear reactor. You do a little checking and discover that the university offers tours of its reactor facility to students. When you drive by the building that houses the reactor, you see a guard sitting on a folding chair sound asleep.

So, how hard would it be for a gang of terrorists to get access to the reactor and steal enough nuclear material for one of these devices? Or perhaps they could enter the facility with bombs in their backpacks, blew up the reactor, and contaminate the university area.

This could be an important story.

Your first thought is to pack a camera, call for a tour, and see if you can document how easy it would be for terrorists to get into the facility and learn enough so they could compromise its security. Tours are usually for science students. You figure you could Google "nuclear reactors" and learn enough to bluff your way in. You won't do anything illegal or expose yourself or anyone else to any danger.

Would you do the story that way? If so, what steps might you want to take before your day as an undercover reporter? Should you worry that you might be giving terrorists a roadmap to nuclear materials? *(The decision is at the back of the book.)*

Deceptions case 2: Undercover dead police officer

An undercover police officer is found dead in a dingy bar in a tough part of town. You show up at the scene and ask to talk to the detectives working the case. The police allow you to pass through the crime-scene tape. You talk to the detectives outside the bar. They say there isn't much they can tell you at this time, and then they are called to a side alley. You take the opportunity to write down a couple of observations in your notebook. A police officer steps out of the bar and signals you to follow her. You do. She begins to point out some evidence she has found and to explain how it relates to the crime. It is clear to you that she thinks you are a detective. Her comments suggest that police believe the undercover officer may have been running his own drug business.

Do you continue to listen or do you tell her who you are? *(The decision is at the back of the book.)*

Deceptions case study 3: Flowers in the nursing home

She was a gutsy old woman who said what she believed. Voters loved her and elected her to the city council three times and the Legislature twice. She was also a hard-headed businesswoman who had inherited her husband's auto dealership and turned it into a chain of new and used car facilities. Two years ago, a magazine listed her as one of the state's 10 most wealthy women.

Last year she announced that she was going to celebrate her 70th birthday by getting married again. Her fiancé was a 25-year-old salesman at one of her used-car lots. The jokes didn't seem to faze her. "They're just jealous," she would say. Her daughters did not find it humorous. Under state law, the husband would be in line to inherit her fortune. She refused her daughter's request to make the husband sign a pre-nuptial agreement.

A couple of weeks before the wedding, the woman is admitted to a hospital. After a two-day stay, she is transferred to a residential treatment center for the elderly. Rumors are flying. The only thing you really know for sure is that the daughters will not allow the fiancé to visit her. You want to talk to her. You figure that if you walk into the center and announce yourself as a reporter, you will be asked to leave. You decide to buy a large collection of flowers. You walk up to the reception desk. A security guard is standing nearby. You ask for the woman's room number. The receptionist looks at the flowers and then gives you the room number. You ask the security guard for directions.

Once you get to her room, you identify yourself and your job. She seems coherent but very angry at her children. She says she's quite willing to talk. **Do you interview her? Do you use the material in your story?**

Deceptions case study 4: Bluto's revenge

The movie *Bluto's Revenge*, a kind of sequel to *Animal House*, is a box-office hit. It's the story of a young man who goes to the college his father attended and starts a fraternity patterned after the one his grandfather belonged to before the college shut it down. The fraternity claims to have the wildest parties, most elaborate practical jokes, and least amount of studying on campus.

You decide to do a story about partying at fraternity houses. Are fraternities really like the one in the movie? With a hidden camera, you go to the local college's fraternity row. You and the photographer have just graduated from college, so it's easy for you to crash several parties. Some of these parties make the ones in the movie seem tame. You have great video.

Back at the studio, you are busy editing the scenes that would otherwise be too raw for local TV. A colleague sees some of the video and wonders aloud if that's a good use of hidden cameras.

Use Potter's box and decide if this is an appropriate use of deception and hidden cameras. If you decide to use, are there any steps you might take before it is used? Are there any parts of the video that you would not use?

Notes

1. Ben H. Bagdikian, "No. 50061, Inside maximum security," *The Washington Post*, January 31, 1972.
2. Letter to Goodwin, November 14, 1981.
3. David Shaw, "Deception – Honest tool of reporting?" *Los Angeles Times*, September 20, 1979.
4. "Different news values," *Examining Our Credibility*, August 04, 1999, www.asne.org.
5. Interview by Goodwin, February 19, 1986.
6. Russ Baker, "Damning undercover tactics as 'fraud,'" *Columbia Journalism Review*, March/April 1997, p. 32.
7. Interview by Smith, March 17, 1997.
8. Michael Salwen, "Getting the story by hook or crook," *Quill*, January 1981, pp. 12–14.
9. Daniel Anderson and Peter Benjaminson, *Investigative Reporting*, Bloomington: Indiana University Press, 1976, p. 109.
10. "Determination 119," Minnesota News Council, www.news-council.org.
11. Tony Case, "In disguise," *Editor & Publisher*, November 14, 1992, and Richard Harwood, "Knights of the Fourth Estate," *The Washington Post*, December 5, 1992.
12. Interview by Goodwin, November 4, 1981.
13. David Halberstam in his essay in "Dangerous liaisons," *Columbia Journalism Review*, July/August 1989.
14. David Weaver and LeAnne Daniels, "Public opinion on investigative reporting in the 1980s," *Journalism Quarterly*, Spring 1992.
15. Letter to Goodwin, November 14, 1981.
16. Linda Mainiero, ed., *American Women Writers from Colonial Times to the Present: A Critical Reference Guide*, New York: Frederick Ungar, 1979, pp. 381–383.
17. Silas Bent, *Newspaper Crusaders: A Neglected Story*, New York: Whittlesey House, 1939, p. 198.
18. Frank Luther Mott, *News Stories of 1934*, Iowa City: Clio Press, 1935, pp. 258–260, 264–271.
19. Doug Struck, "Inside Crownsville," Annapolis *Evening Capital*, October 6–25, 1975.

20. Interview by Goodwin, September 9, 1981.
21. "Undercover," research report of the Times Publishing Co., St. Petersburg, Fla., and the Department of Mass Communication, University of South Florida, Summer 1981.
22. Howard Kurtz, "Hidden network cameras: A troubling trend," *The Washington Post*, November 30, 1992.
23. Details are taken from *ibid*.; "Another missing union label at ABC," *The Washington Times*, April 27, 1993; and Diane Kunde, "Food Lion roars back at critics in ad blitz," *The Dallas Morning News*, November 5, 1992.
24. "First Amendment decisions; The press wins," *The New York Times*, October 23, 1999.
25. RTNDF Journalism Ethics and Integrity Project, 1999, p. 21.
26. "TV stations' investigative units open up on hidden camera use," *Chicago Tribune*, July 2, 2000.
27. Kenneth Clark, "Hidden meanings: Increasing use of secret cameras and microphones raises ethical questions about TV journalists," *Chicago Tribune*, June 30, 1992.
28. "Darts and laurels," *Columbia Journalism Review*, March/April 1997, p. 22.
29. Tim Howard, "Donal MacIntyre's new series trivialises crime," *Time Out*, August 23, 2006.
30. Clark, *op. cit.*
31. Quoted by Colman McCarthy, "Getting the truth untruthfully," *The Washington Post*, December 22, 1992.
32. Shaw, *op. cit.*
33. Associated Press, "ABC must pay Food Lion $5.5 million," *Orlando Sentinel*, January 23, 1997.
34. "TV stations' investigative units open up on hidden camera use," *Chicago Tribune*, July 2, 2000.
35. Kurtz, *op. cit.*
36. Details are taken from Beth Nissen, "An inside view," *The Wall Street Journal*, July 28, 1978; interview with Lawrence O'Donnell, *Journal* associate editor, by author, February 22, 1982; and a letter to Goodwin from Ed Cony, then publisher of the *Journal*, June 10, 1984.
37. Kurtz, *op. cit.*
38. Interview by Goodwin, September 8, 1981.
39. Clark, *op. cit.*
40. "Undercover," *op. cit.*
41. "Czech police detain journalist testing airport security," Agence France Presse, August 11, 2006.
42. Fabrice de Pierrebourg, "It's so easy to get in, it's scary," *The Toronto Sun*, September 11, 2006.

43. "Air marshals across country warn passengers aren't safe," thedenver-channel.com, July 20, 2006.
44. Pat Widder, "Playing with fire: Blur of fact and fiction costs NBC," *Chicago Tribune*, February 11, 1993.
45. Russ W. Baker, "Truth, lies and videotape," *Columbia Journalism Review*, July/August 1993.
46. *Ibid.*
47. These criteria came from participants in an ethical decision-making seminar at the Poynter Institute for Media Studies, reported in Jay Black, Bob Steele, and Ralph Barney, *Doing Ethics in Journalism*, Greencastle, Ind.: Sigma Delta Chi Foundation, Society of Professional Journalists, 1993, pp. 112–113.

Part 4 Compassion and the Journalist

11   Compassion, Privacy, and Ordinary Citizens

A Marine from Colorado was among those taken hostage when Iranians seized the U.S. Embassy in Tehran. Months later, his family received word that their son might soon be freed. The release of the 52 hostages, coming after months of tense negotiations and even a failed rescue attempt by American military forces, was big news. Reporters from throughout the state scrambled to be there when the family received word their son was coming home.

Ramon Coronado, a reporter for *The Coloradoan* in Fort Collins, described what happened while the mob of journalists was waiting to capture the joy of Billy Gallegos' parents:

> The media camped in the sloped front yard, an area no bigger than two spaces in a parking lot. Electrical cords, telephones, television sets, radios, tape recorders, microphones, cigarette butts, coffee cups and paper from fast-food restaurants blanketed the ground. In the back, the alley was filled with television news trucks manned with technicians.
>
> About three dozen reporters and photographers were allowed inside the small home, while the rest had to stay outside. As those inside jostled for better positions, one journalist knocked a ceramic plate off a wall, Coronado reported. Photographers stood on furniture, breaking one table. A reporter from Colorado Springs was caught looking in the family's mail.[1]

In summing up his experience, Coronado wrote that "the press lost sight of the fact the Gallegoses were not just a story but are people. People with feelings and the need for privacy."

In California, a teenager was killed in a freak accident during track practice at school. Friends and officials warned his family to be prepared for the media. The "tough questions and persistence [of the reporters] may be intrusive and uncomfortable," they were told. It wasn't long before a TV reporter called. The family decided reluctantly to meet with her. "We really wanted to share our story with our city, so we braced ourselves and waited for the reporter to arrive," they explained.

But instead of the unfeeling ogre they had expected, they discovered a reporter who was "gentle and loving." Soon a newspaper reporter visited them. "What a special lady," the family said later. "Yes, she got the story, but with love in her heart. She never pushed or intruded or tried to develop a bigger story than it was. She reported the news." During the next few days, TV and print reporters from both large and small news organizations interviewed the family. "The media often take a bad hit from the public, but I must say that during our time of grief it was wonderful to be with such caring people," the family wrote in a letter to the editor printed in the *Los Angeles Times*.[2]

It's hard not to be appalled by the reporters in the Colorado incident. When journalists misbehave that badly, it leaves a foul taste in people's mouths and lessens their respect for all journalists. The family in California had a much different experience, one that is probably more common than many people realize. These two incidents highlight the basic questions of this chapter: How do you handle the privacy of ordinary people who get drawn into the news? What is the role of compassion in the demands of daily journalism?

Curiously, this discussion of compassion in journalism would surprise both members of the press and members of the public – but for very different reasons. Many journalists would be surprised to see the need for compassion considered an important issue facing journalism. And, according to polls, a majority of the public would be surprised to find out that journalists even know the meaning of the word.

Room for Humaneness?

Many journalists, especially newspaper reporters, shun the notion of compassion. They believe compassion runs counter to objective reporting, which most reporters try to practice despite widespread doubts as to whether it's achievable or even desirable. A tenet of objective reporting is that reporters are spectators and not participants in what they cover. Reporters are not supposed to get involved with the people in their stories; they are supposed to be neutral observers.

Another concern is that compassion will cause reporters to become weak-willed and forget their obligations to keep the public informed. Louis Boccardi, president of the Associated Press, recalled that when he was a young reporter covering courts, he was asked many times not to put certain things in the paper. He feared that if compassion became too prevalent in journalism, reporters would agree to these requests and legitimate news stories would not be printed.

Competitive pressures are another reason some journalists believe they must suppress compassion. Ginger Casey, when she was a reporter for KQED-TV in San Francisco, was covering a shooting at a playground. She did not want to interview any of the children who might have seen the tragedy and make them revisit its horror. Yet, she knew that dozens of reporters were swarming around the neighborhood, looking for angles for their stories. If one reporter interviewed a child, she would have to. She wrote:

> You don't want your competition to have any angle you don't have, and crying kids on camera were powerful images. If having your voice heard at a news conference scored points, so did interviewing a child. Your boss would tell you that you "kicked ass." Your resume tape would look terrific.[3]

Casey's observation suggests another reason some journalists feel they must shed feelings of compassion: They don't want compassion to get in the way of a big story that will impress their editors or news directors. This search for a career-making story may be why so many younger reporters are more likely to advocate questionable tactics including badgering sources for information and deceiving people than were their more seasoned colleagues.[4]

Does compassion improve journalism?

Many editors do not think that compassion lessens the quality of the work a journalist does. They believe that compassion makes for better reporting. Journalists often want to write stories that go beyond the bare facts. They want to humanize social problems and even provoke a sympathetic response in their readers. To do this, they must become involved with people who are experiencing the problem, interview them with sensitivity, and describe their conditions with care and compassion.

Geneva Overholser, former editor of *The Des Moines Register*, argued that the notion of journalist-as-machine has made so much newspaper writing boring, dull, and meaningless. In her view, journalists should write stories that make readers "laugh, weep, sing, hope and wonder how people can go on." That kind of writing can be achieved only if journalists have feelings and are concerned about the people and issues they write about.[5]

Jacqui Banaszynski wrote a series of stories called "AIDS in the Heartland" for the *St. Paul Pioneer Press*. The stories portrayed the final months of the life of a man with AIDS. She visited the man and his partner frequently and interviewed friends and family. Sensing that the relationship was going beyond a traditional reporter–source one, she started reminding the men that she was a reporter and told her editors to be extra diligent in editing her copy. Because friends and family members were so open with her, she read the quotes she planned to use back to them to make sure they were accurate. Her honest and compassionate reporting led to sensitive stories that gave readers a deeper understanding of the AIDS crisis. Her efforts were rewarded with both a Pulitzer prize and a Distinguished Service Award from the Society of Professional Journalists.

Feature writers are not the only ones who believe that good journalism requires compassion. Alec Klein, a top investigator reporter for the business section of *The Washington Post*, wrote that he grew up watching the piercing glare of Mike Wallace on CBS's *60 Minutes* as he put sources on the hot seat. But as he did more investigative pieces, he developed his own style. "Nice is better," he concluded. He said he knew many of the best investigative reporters in America and said most of them practiced what he called "nice-guy journalism." He explained:

> I've long come to the conclusion that the best investigative reporters are compassionate. That it takes compassion to do the job well. It doesn't mean that you're soft. It doesn't mean that you look the other way. It means that you treat people respectfully.[6]

Reporters as Vultures

In many people's minds, reporters are like foul vultures swooping around disasters and tragedies. Even adamant supporters of the news media agree that sometimes the behavior of reporters makes that analogy unfair to the bird.

Donald Nibert lost his 16-year-old daughter when a jetliner crashed off Long Island. At a journalism conference months later, he described reporters who stalked grieving families, yelled questions at surviving relatives, and lied to gain access to restricted areas. He said:

> The national news media and the local coverage were terrible. They magnified the sorrow we had to endure. For what purpose? To increase ratings? To sell newspapers? To sell magazines? To increase personal status? I don't know. But I wonder if this can be justified considering the pain they caused the families – maybe permanent pain.[7]

A few journalists are probably oblivious to how these antics look to the public. At major disasters with lots of media competition, some are under so much pressure to produce that they don't care. But most journalists don't work in such highly competitive environments. Yet they too are looked upon as vultures to many in the public. The reason may be a fundamental difference between the public and journalists in how tragedies should be covered.

Researchers posed this hypothetical: What they would do if the parents asked that the paper not print a story about their child drowning in a gravel pit? The gap between the public's answer and journalists' was huge. About 75 percent of the public said they would respect the family's request and not print the story. Of those who would print the story, hardly anyone said they would use the child's name. One person said, "It wasn't a crime and it (the name) does not add anything to the story." Another said using the name would be "cold, tacky, insensitive."

Journalists had a very different view. Only 1 percent of journalists said they'd withhold publication. About a third said they would not only publish the story, but would include the fact that the mother had pleaded with the paper not to use the story. One editor explained, "Well, that's all she wanted to tell us." Another couldn't understand the parent's request. "What's the harm [in publishing the name]?" he asked. Researchers concluded in their report to the American Society of Newspaper Editors that:

> It's essential for journalists to understand the compassion that readers feel for distraught survivors is far greater than their desire to know relevant or irrelevant details.[8]

What journalists see as reporting the news, the public sees as intruding on the tragedy of others.

Reporting or intruding

Journalists recognize the inevitable conflict between a community that is shocked by a tragedy and the reporters who are covering it. "News coverage is intrusive, and grief demands privacy," Jack R. Hart, a senior editor at *The Oregonian* in Portland, told a journalism seminar on covering tragedy. "Just the fact that [reporters and photographers] are there is offensive to the community."

Still, serious crimes, plane crashes, and the like are news. Journalists must cover them and their aftermaths; readers and viewers expect to find these stories. The key, many experienced reporters say, is to treat victims as fellow human beings. Reporter George Esper, who has covered wars and mass suicides for the Associated Press, told the seminar, "We should frame our questions with respect and research. We must be sensitive, but not timid."

TV journalists are faced with the added problems of having to fuss with equipment, which sometimes requires more than one take and tends to require staging because of lighting conditions. Because of this, TV news crews can appear callous to both their sources and the public, as did this crew described by Matthew Power in *Harper's* magazine:

> Consider the following scene, which I witnessed after the tsunami in Thailand, in the crushed remains of the Emerald Beach Resort in Khao Lak. Stuart Breisch, a doctor from Salt Lake City whose fifteen-year-old daughter had been missing since the waves had wiped out the resort, stood in the tropical sun being interviewed by a crew from *Good Morning America*.
>
> They stood with the man whose daughter was missing and had him do multiple takes of his story. They asked him to switch angles for the light. They told him, Thank you, I think we have enough narrative. How does this all make you feel? The producer stopped the shot for a moment, hoping aloud amid the destroyed landscape that whatever he had in his eye was only sunblock.
>
> They followed Dr. Breisch and his surviving daughter from temple to temple (which had all become way stations for thousands of bodies) as he searched for his daughter. There were boards set up with snapshots of the dead to aid in identification.
>
> Breisch's daughter spotted her sister's photograph among the hundreds of mangled bodies, and *Good Morning America* was there to capture the family's moment of private horror for all the world to see. Money shot. Mission accomplished. Our work here is done. And now a word from our sponsors.[9]

Of course the news crew ought to be there. It was an important story about an incredible natural disaster. News reports worldwide helped bring in more than $2 billion of relief. And, in this specific case, the Breisches apparently wanted their story told. Yet, the code of ethics of the Radio–Television News Directors Association urges reporters to respect the dignity of people in the news, particularly in situations like these. The question is whether the story could be gathered with more civility and compassion.

Approaching people about tragedies

If one truth seems to emerge from the dozens of articles that have been written about how people behave immediately after a tragedy, it is that they handle crises in very different ways. Research suggests that even trained emergency workers have trouble determining how trauma is affecting people. Trauma experts warn journalists "not to assume a person is 'taking it well' just because he or she does not appear to be affected by a tragic event." The person may be in shock or withdrawal, which "may be helping the person to survive the unthinkable horror that has just occurred." Many are in a very delicate frame of mind. An expert in the psychology of trauma has cautioned that "Whenever a reporter meets a survivor of traumatic events, there is a chance that the journalist will witness – and may even precipitate – posttraumatic stress disorder."

That does not mean that journalists should always back away. But it does mean that reporters must be sincerely compassionate. The Dart Center for Journalism and Trauma contends:

> Journalists who are sensitive to the suffering of others and understand the complexity of emotional trauma are often able to write about traumatic experiences in a way that is informative, engaging and often helpful to readers.[10]

Clearly, many people in such a situation want to be left alone. It is important that journalists honor that request. Anger is a frequent reaction to trauma, and a nosy reporter can become a good target for that anger. However, when the interview is carried out at the right time and with sensitivity, it may even be beneficial to the person. Robin Finegan, an experienced trauma counselor, said that when the interview "goes right, a victim can feel that they've taken control back; they've had that opportunity to tell their story, or talk about a loved one."[11]

Some people undergoing tragic situations want to be interviewed. The mother at the start of this chapter wanted to tell her story even though it meant dealing with dreaded reporters. Some family members become angry when reporters did not contact them but instead rely on neighbors who may not have known the person well. When a woman was murdered, her daughter complained that reporters relied on neighbors and did not talk to anyone who really knew her mother. The result was a story that painted an incomplete picture of the woman.

A police reporter at the *Orlando Sentinel* many times has had the unwelcome assignment of interviewing families who had lost sons and daughters in accidents and wars. She described one visit like this:

> As I climbed the front steps of the Winter Park home, my heart was in my throat.
>
> The woman inside had just lost her son in the war, and I was there to collect his picture for the newspaper.
>
> "What will she think of this intrusion?" I wondered. "Is there anything I can say to comfort her? What kind of business am I in?"
>
> To my great relief, the grieving woman actually seemed pleased that I was there. She told me about her son, how proud she was of him, how glad she was that his death would not go unnoticed. Then she sent me on my way with her son's picture, asking me to promise that it would be returned.

That's not always the way things go, of course. On another occasion, she called a family on the phone. "The conversation was sympathetic and polite – and also short," she said. "The emotional wound was too fresh; the family, quite understandably, did not want to talk." She understood and did not push the point.

No matter how truly sympathetic reporters are, they cannot overcome the image in some people's minds that they are vultures. After the *Sentinel* police reporter called the family, she received an angry letter from a police officer who called her efforts "a new low that members of the local media will stoop to just to get a story."[12]

Other reporters have had similar experiences. Reporter Rene Stutzman, then with United Press International, was covering the collapse of a walkway in a Kansas City hotel that killed more than 100 people. She approached a victim's family sitting in the lobby of a nearby hotel and asked if she could interview them. "If they had made the slightest indication they did not want to be interviewed, I would have stopped," she said. But family members asked her to sit down and began to talk.

"Then people in the lobby came up and started calling me names, and I had to leave."[13]

Interviewing victims and their families

Many journalists simply do not know what to say when they interview people involved in tragedies, and they end up blurting out the wrong thing. William Coté and Bonnie Bucqueroux of the Victims and Media Center at Michigan State University tell of an unfortunate encounter between a young reporter and a man who had just lost his daughter. "I know how you feel," the reporter said. "I remember when my dog died." The remark added immensely to that father's pain, according to Coté and Bucqueroux.[14]

Editor Sandra Rowe of *The Oregonian* in Portland agrees that reporters need to draw on their own life experiences when they cover tragedies:

> There are too many reporters and editors who haven't been there to have the empathy they need. Perhaps they haven't lost anyone. They need to think it through enough to say, "If I were in this person's place, how would I feel? What questions would I be able to handle? What would be offensive?"[15]

After studying the treatment of victims by journalists, the Victims and Media Center put together the following tips for reporters:

- *Grant victims and their families a sense of power and control.* They are suffering from horrific stress that has robbed them of their sense of mastery. Ask them to tell you when they say something that they do not want in the paper. Give them your phone number and tell them that they can call you to discuss the story or just to talk.
- *Discuss issues of privacy and confidentiality at the beginning of the interview.* This can prevent misunderstandings and establish trust. Explain what you need, with whom you plan to talk, and for how long. Make sure to encourage the victim to ask questions.
- *Prepare for the possibility that you will be the first to deliver the bad news.* Often reporters telephone or appear on a family's porch looking for quotes about a victim, only to find that the family has not been told yet. Organize your thoughts before you call or ring the doorbell.

- *Ask permission.* This is particularly important whenever you approach the victim's physical "zone of intimacy." Even caring gestures can be misinterpreted or seen as threatening or out of bounds. Approach them without your notebook in hand and then ask if you can take notes. Ask if you can use a tape recover. It is better to say "Would you like a tissue?" than to thrust the box at them.
- *Keep your remarks simple.* Fans of the TV shows *NYPD Blue* and *Law and Order* know that the detectives always say "Sorry for your loss." To our ears, the phrase may begin to sound trite and artificial, but using a canned phrase that strikes the right note is far better than using the wrong words. A former New York police commissioner who became a therapist suggests that at least one of these sentiments will always be appropriate: "I'm sorry this happened to you," "I'm glad you weren't killed," and, because people in tragedies often blame themselves, "It's not your fault."
- *Don't say, "I know how you feel."* Even if you think you may have suffered a similar victimization, no one can really understand what's going through a person's mind during and after a tragedy.
- *Be accurate.* Accuracy is the overarching goal in all reporting, but the stakes are much higher when dealing with victims and the family of victims. A newspaper ran a correction when it misquoted a minister at a funeral as saying the man "put himself before others" instead of "put others before himself." The mistake was not minor to the friends and families involved.
- *Be especially sensitive in placing blame.* If you mention that the victim had been drinking, does it imply that he or she was drunk? Reporting requires more than emptying your notebook, and editors should always fix their antennae to spot any inadvertent suggestion that the victim was at fault.
- *Be alert to the special impact of photos, graphics, and overall presentation.* Occasionally, a sensitive and respectful story is undercut by a tasteless picture or a headline that misses the nuances the reporter put in the story.

Patsy Day, director of Victims Outreach in Dallas, adds a couple of other points, according to Phil Record, ombudsman of the Fort Worth *Star-Telegram*. She reminds reporters that people react differently to tragedy. Journalists should be careful not to guess how people feel based on their external appearance or behavior. Some may be suffering from shock or posttraumatic stress disorder, yet on the surface they may appear very "businesslike" as they go about dealing with their loss. Some become stoic. Others cry a lot.[16]

Names in the News

For decades, journalists have worked on the assumption that names are news. In most communities, reporters want to know who was injured or killed in car accidents, shootings, house fires, and so on. Names, young journalists are told, are a standard part of news stories. Yet, people involved in the news, particularly those who have done nothing wrong, often loathe seeing their names in print.

Journalists too complain when they inadvertently became part of the news. Thomas Oliphant, a columnist for *The Boston Globe*, wrote:

> I got mugged the night before last, a humiliating opportunity to be reminded that the allies of crime victims are the cops, not the press. Any crime, of course, is humiliating. Most cops understand this and treat crime victims as people. Most journalists don't understand this and treat us as subjects.

Oliphant said that after the crime he was pulled in two directions. He wanted to call the police in hopes the mugger would be caught. Yet, he knew that by dialing 911 he would give up his privacy. He knew that some people would wonder what he was doing walking where he was that late at night. And others would chuckle that a liberal columnist had been the target of street crime. "What infuriates me as a crime victim," he said, "is that the press would insist that it alone can decide when I lose my privacy, and that my recourse to contest that decision is virtually nonexistent."[17]

Nevertheless, naming names remains a foundation of journalism. Stories with names are more believable. Readers and viewers want to know what's going on in their communities and who is involved.

Only in exceptional circumstances do journalists bend the rules on using names. When a recently widowed woman in her 70s was bilked out of $300,000 by a psychic, TV stations in Orlando agreed to use only her first name and to blur her face so she could not be recognized. The local newspaper, however, printed her full name and the community in which she lived. On the other hand, in a story about dishonest repairmen who prey on the elderly, *The Washington Post* decided to avoid embarrassing the victims and used only their first names.[18]

Naming people suspected of crimes

Police sometimes release the names of people they suspect have committed a crime but have not yet been arrested or charged. That creates a dilemma for many journalists. Reporting the names of suspects may help the cops catch the bad guys, and it is probably the newest development in the story. But many journalists also worry about the fairness of accusing someone of a crime before the police and prosecutors have officially charged them with anything. They know that once a person has been named as a suspect, many will believe that person was guilty even if police and prosecutors never find enough evidence to bring charges.

In high-profile cases, just being named as a suspect can be a massive jolt to one's privacy. Police were convinced that a bombing during the Atlanta Olympic Games was committed by security guard Richard Jewell. After extensive coverage that put Jewell's face on the front of nearly every newspaper and television broadcast in the nation, police charged another man. But Jewell remained an easily recognizable figure in Central Georgia.

Occasionally, editors are glad they did not jump when the police leaked the name of a suspect. *The Denver Post* learned that a well-known Baptist minister was being investigated for allegedly sexually harassing a parishioner. The paper decided to wait until police filed charges, which they never did. "We knew that if we named him, it would be all over for him," Frank Scandale, assistant managing editor for news, said. "Police are not infallible. Just because they are looking at someone does not mean they are guilty."[19]

Police made just such a mistake in Indiana. They provided the media with pictures from an ATM that supposedly showed a man who had committed several felonies. After his picture was shown on television and in newspapers, police acknowledged that he was not the criminal after all. One can imagine, though, the reactions the man received when he entered a bank or convenience store and reached into his pocket for his billfold.

Incidents like that have caused editors at *The Richmond Times-Dispatch* to think twice before running pictures and names of supposed suspects. After an abandoned baby was found at a Richmond mall, police gave the media a surveillance tape that showed a woman pushing a shopping cart with an empty baby carrier. They believed she might be the baby's mom. Editors at the *Times-Dispatch* thought there were too many other explanations for the empty baby carrier. The woman may be letting her child run ahead of her in the mall, or maybe the child is in another part of the mall with dad. They decided not to risk a mistaken identity and didn't use the picture.[20]

According to a survey, only about 20 percent of newspaper editors do not name suspects before they have been arrested or charged.[21] David Yarnold, editor of the *San Jose Mercury News*, said in *Editor & Publisher* that he disagreed with the common sentiment. He argued that holding off on naming suspects is one way newspapers can regain credibility. "It's more important than ever that newspapers be beacons of fairness," he said. "Situations arise all the time that challenge [the policy], but we stick by it."[22]

Naming juvenile offenders

Joe Kollin, a reporter at the *South Florida Sun-Sentinel*, observed that the roles of reporters and law-enforcement officials are occasionally reversed when it comes to the issue of naming juvenile offenders. Normally, reporters are trying to get information like names and details and police and officials are trying to limit their access to this information. In the case of juveniles, however, law enforcement officials often have pushed for the news media to use the names for the news media to name names, and the media have been reluctant to do it.[23]

In the past, when people under 18 were arrested they were tried in juvenile courts, which were closed to the public and the media. Usually the punishment handed out by these courts was less severe than adults would receive for similar crimes. Some hoped that if juvenile offenders' names were kept secret, the youths would have a better chance of turning their lives around and becoming law-abiding citizens. Also, some thought that naming them might lead to a psychological phenomenon called "labeling," which purports that people often behave the way they think they are expected to behave. If a youth is labeled as a juvenile delinquent, he will likely act like one. For those reasons, editors at *The Fresno Bee* are reluctant to use the names of teenagers. Executive editor Keith Moyer explained:

> You never know when a kid might still lead an honorable, productive life but would have a much tougher time doing so if his or her name were publicized.[24]

However, as the seriousness of teen crime grew, many prosecutors and judges became more willing to try juveniles in adult courts, which are open to the public and can be fully reported in the media. In Iowa, judges – not journalists – wanted the Legislature to change the law so that young offenders could be named. In one area of Tennessee, juvenile authorities convinced local papers to use the names of all juveniles detained. The number of crimes dropped. When Florida rewrote its juvenile code in the 1970s to allow the naming of juveniles, legislators and law officials encouraged the news media to name names, but editors balked.[25]

Many news outlets routinely use names. Managing editor Joseph T. Stinnett of *The News and Advance* in Lynchburg, Va., argues that people in the community have "a right to know that a kid has been charged with murder even if he is just 16, or even 14." Dan Kelly, a reporter at the *Reading (Pa.) Eagle*, said his paper names all suspects as soon as they are charged. "We're not coddlers and they're not victims," he explained.[26]

More commonly, editors and news directors prefer to use names of juveniles only after their cases have been moved into adult court. Whenever prosecutors decide to try young people in adult courts, reporters usually have the same access to their files and court hearings as they would in any other criminal case. The arrests and trials of two teens in Florida got media attention nationwide. A boy who killed a 6-year-old girl when he was 12 was sentenced to life without chance of parole.[27] A 13-year-old was charged with murdering his English teacher and received a 28-year sentence without chance of parole.

Details of Crimes

As recently as the 1970s, many newspapers thought the word "rape" was too explicit a description of the crime and banned its use. A reporter could write that a woman may have been "criminally assaulted" or "molested," but not "raped." One Houston paper even changed a woman's direct quote. Instead of yelling "Help! I'm being raped!" she was quoted as yelling "Help! I'm being criminally assaulted!"

Journalists disagree on how graphic these accounts should be. When a jogger was gang-raped in New York's Central Park, the gruesome details of the crime and intimate information about her previous sex life were part of the court record and were available to reporters. Many papers printed much of this information. John Corporon, vice president for news at New York's WPIX-TV, said, "It's a tragedy on top of a tragedy she already suffered, but I don't think the media can turn their backs on a story to protect her privacy."

But other journalists were bothered. When *Newsday* managing editor Howard Schneider read his own paper one morning, he found a verbatim account of the rape as contained in a videotaped confession. "I was stunned," he said. "It really troubled me. I thought, 'My God, this is incredibly explicit.'" He learned at work that day that the story had been approved by the paper's editor. Veteran reporter Gabe Pressman of WNBC-TV in New York said he too believed the media coverage of the rape of the jogger was an "outrageous violation" of her privacy. He said:

> I think there's a kind of prurient or scatological tendency in the press and television these days. Unconsciously, we like to use those little morsels. We know we're titillating people by giving them some of the raw details of the crime.[28]

Fort Worth *Star-Telegram* editors decided to give readers the choice of how much of the graphic detail they wanted after the execution-style murder of an employee of a miniature golf course. Reporters got copies of the police files. The news story reported, "The two are accused of robbing the Hurst entertainment center and fatally shooting Jonas Cherry, 28, as he pleaded for his life." The online version of the story carried a link to police records, which gave a much more vivid account and included portions of the autopsy report.

The paper's managing editor said he considered that showing the public the additional information was important. He told the paper's public editor:

> I want to know how my police operate. I want to know that the police are operating ethically and efficiently, based on the evidence and good judgment. That's the sort of insight that publication of arrest warrant affidavits gives to the public. The information may be disturbing, but the transparency is worth it.[29]

Similarly, Matthew Buckland, editor of South Africa's *Mail and Guardian*, decided to place links on his paper's Web site to video of the beheading of an American in Iraq. He contended that the Web allows readers to decide what they consider worthwhile information. "By actively clicking on the link we provide to the video stream," he said, "the user is making more of a conscious choice to view what is behind the link and therefore, we feel is taking a greater responsibility."[30]

Robert Berkman, who has written a book on digital ethics, told Poynter's Steve Outing that he was not convinced. "I don't think anything goes – that just because it's out there you can link or point to it," he said. "You should always keep your higher mission in mind." The bottom line he suggested was: Is this useful and informative? Is it meaningful?[31]

Reporting Sex Crimes

After children in San Diego, Utah, and Oregon were kidnapped within weeks of each other, the news media turned the crime of kidnapping into a major story. Talk shows featured experts on kidnapping while the evening news offered tips on "keeping your children safe." Reports hammered home that the country was experiencing what one cable network called an "epidemic of kidnapping."

So, when two teenage girls in California were abducted at gunpoint, their plight was big news. Police in California had just instituted an innovative system that alerted every police agency and much of the media and provided them with names and pictures of abductees. Police encouraged the media to run the pictures so the public could help in their search. Nearly every news outlet did its part, including national media like *USA Today* and the television networks.

Shortly after the evening newscasts, a police representative held a press conference and said that the girls had been found and that they had been raped. Turmoil erupted in many newsrooms. Most TV stations and newspapers have policies against naming rape victims, particularly when the victims are not adults. At KRON in San Francisco, the news director sent an e-mail telling her staff not to name the girls again or use their pictures. She told the *San Francisco Chronicle*:

> For me, it was a very quick decision because it is our long-standing policy not to reveal names and faces of victims of sexual assault. You can't put the genie back in the bottle, but you do what you can to protect the victims.[32]

ABC News also banned any further use of their names.

Some newspapers were right on deadline when they heard about the rapes. In Spokane, editors at the *Spokesman-Review* pulled the page before the paper was printed and removed the girls' names and pictures. *San Francisco Chronicle* and *The Florida Times-Union* in Jacksonville had already started their press runs. As soon as they could, they changed out stories so the names did not appear in later editions.

Sheila Gibbons, editor of *Media Report to Women*, said that the media's handling of this situation caused her to change her mind and advocate "including the identity of sexual assault victims in news reporters, just as reporters do in their accounts of beatings, stabbings and shootings." She wrote:

> To me, to cease referring to a rescued kidnapping survivor by name once this information becomes public merely reinforces the stigma of rape and other crimes in which sex is used as a weapon. It takes what should be out-loud outrage and reduces it to a whisper.[33]

Others have taken a similar position. Isabelle Katz Pinzler, a civil-rights attorney who was working for the National Organization for Women and the American Civil Liberties Union, said: "There are feminist arguments why it might not be a bad idea to name the victims. It might be a step toward destigmatizing rape and, by making it less of a faceless crime, it brings home the horror."[34] A young woman in Nebraska allowed the *Omaha World-Herald* to identify her after she was shot and raped by an attacker. She asked, "Why is it more shameful to be a rape victim than a gunshot victim? Surely, it is not. But there is shame in rape, and it rests squarely with the attacker, not the victim."[35]

A handful of newspapers name adult victims of sex crimes. Charles Houser was executive editor of the Providence, R.I., papers when they named a woman who was gang-raped on a pool table in a New Bedford, Mass., tavern. "Any time we are suppressing public information, we are deciding what is good for society, for the public, for an individual," he said.[36]

In a series of feature stories, editors at *The Des Moines Register* wanted to put a face on a rape victim and the aftermath of the crime. With approval of the victim, reporter Jane Schorer followed the case of a woman who was raped in a rural Iowa town. The paper gave explicit details of the crime and interviewed her about her feelings during the police investigation and subsequent trial. Many Iowans were appalled by the series. But many readers expressed appreciation that the veil of secrecy had been lifted from the crime. Schorer, who won a Pulitzer prize for the stories, said she hopes the series will "mark the point where society at large first showed itself as ready and willing to listen" to rape victims and their problems.[37]

The consensus among journalists is that names are important in news stories. Geneva Overholser, a former editor and now journalism professor, wrote on the Poynter Web site:

> Naming names is an essential part of the commitment to accuracy, credibility, and fairness. This practice frequently brings pain to individuals; truth-telling does have its victims. My own view is that recovery from difficult times is, like journalism, abetted by openness and hampered by secrecy. But the larger point is this: Openness serves society as a whole. It serves enlightenment and understanding and progress. And it serves the criminal justice system. When journalists depart from the commitment to telling the whole story, to naming names, to getting at painful truths, we tread on dangerous ground... The best journalistic principle is to tell the public what we know.[38]

The case against naming rape victims

These arguments do not wash with the more than 90 percent of editors and news directors who rarely use victims' names.[39] Rape, they say, is different from other crimes. As Robin Benedict, a Columbia University journalism professor, wrote:

> As long as people have any sense of privacy about sexual acts and the human body, rape will, therefore, carry a stigma – not necessarily a stigma that blames the victim for what happened to her, but a stigma that links her name irrevocably with an act of intimate humiliation.[40]

Some contend that it is the fear of being further humiliated that causes some rape victims not to report the crime. They cite an opinion poll that found more than two-thirds of women surveyed said they would be more likely to report sexual assaults if there were laws against disclosure of their names.[41] In Winston-Salem, N.C., where the *Journal* had a policy of naming all rape victims, the women told researchers from Iowa State University that they were angry at the paper and said having their names printed worsened the feelings of embarrassment and shame. A few said being named in a rape case had made them targets of offensive comments and insensitive phone calls.[42]

The ban against naming rape and domestic-abuse victims is not absolute. Nearly all the news media use names if the victim was also murdered, according to a study by professors at Texas Christian University. Also, most will name victims who decide to go public about the crime and agree to have their names used. Nearly half will name the victim if the person was well-known nationally, but only 7 percent if she was well-known locally. Many editors bend the rules if other media name the victim, if a wife charges her husband with rape, or if the victim was abducted.[43]

Is it fair to name the accused?

If the news media name the accused man (who is presumed innocent until proven guilty), Alan Dershowitz, a professor at Harvard Law School, believes they should also name the accuser. "In this country there is no such thing as anonymous accusation," he argued.[44] Many note that it is difficult for a man to overcome the stigma of having been accused of rape. Even if he is found not guilty, many will still suspect him. Michael Gartner, former editor of *The Daily Tribune* in Ames, Iowa, cited a case in which a local basketball player was accused of rape. After lots of media coverage naming the man but not the alleged victim, the charges were dropped. "So is that fairness?" Gartner asked.[45]

The Rocky Mountain News in Denver decided to name the woman who accused NBA star Kobe Bryant of rape when she filed a civil suit against him (but not during the criminal trial). Editor John Temple explained the rationale:

> As a general rule, the *News* names plaintiffs in civil lawsuits. Here, both sides' personal integrity and credibility are at issue and the *News* believes fairness requires that both parties be named in reporting on this civil lawsuit.[46]

After two high-profile rape cases that did not end in convictions, *San Diego Union-Tribune* editor Karin Winner began to reconsider that paper's policies. In one case, rape charges were dropped against a prominent businessman accused of assaulting an employee. In another case, a man accused of date rape was acquitted by jurors who said the woman's story was not credible. The *Union-Tribune* reported both these cases extensively, identifying the men but protecting the identity of the women. "I think we need to consider protecting the accused as well until it reaches the trial stage, and even then, I'm not sure what would be the most fair," Winner said.[47]

Nationally, about half the rape cases do not end in convictions. About one in eight editors said their papers will use the accuser's name when the suspect is found not guilty. Many people think that is a bad idea. Rape cases are difficult to prove, they point out. In some cases, it is the man's word against the woman's. If the man is found not guilty, the jury may be saying only that the evidence was not strong enough to convict.

Cases to Discuss

These scenarios are based on the experiences of reporters and editors. They have been modified for space and impact. In most of these situations, a reporter would seek advice from an editor – and the editors would make the final decision. But the initial input would come from the reporter, and good editors would listen carefully to the reporter before deciding. On some cases, you will see a note that indicates you can check to see what the real editors did. That doesn't mean they did the right thing, but you can compare your thoughts with theirs.

Privacy case 1: Intimate blogs

A 46-year-old Navy Reservist in the Middle East during the war in Iraq is fortunate enough to get a holiday leave to spend Christmas with 26-year-old wife and two children from a previous marriage, an 18-year-old son and a 16-year-old daughter. Two days after he gets home, he is murdered. His wife, her teenage lover, and another teen are charged.

Clearly, it's a major news story and you are part of the team that will cover it.

You discover that all four members of the family had blogs on the Internet. They were very open about their lives. Before she met her husband, the wife had lived with a woman and they had a wedding ceremony, not recognized in the state where they lived. She ended the relationship after she met her soon-to-be husband. She wrote on her blog that after their marriage, she had sex with her 16-year-old stepdaughter's boyfriend and was having an ongoing affair with another teenage boy. On her blog, she described with some pride how she managed to keep her affairs secret from her husband.

The husband discussed on his blog his online love affair with a cousin. When he came home on leave, he confided on his blog that he sensed his wife was cheating and had told his daughter that he was considering a divorce. The daughter said on her blog that she had told the stepmom about his plans. He was murdered the next day.

The 16-year-old daughter's blog also include details of her feud with her stepmother, her warmer relationship with her father, and her first French kiss. The 18-year-old son's Web site had a collection of songs he had written about rape, murder, and sex with dead bodies. His band performed some of his songs. He said his stepmother was a big fan and attended many practice sessions.

The blogs recount how the children had introduced the stepmom to her teen lover and the other boy accused of the murder. The daughter admitted she had a crush on one of them.

No one would dispute that details from the blogs illustrate the dysfunction in the family before the murder, and they provide detail that would certainly dominate lots of water-cooler conversations.

How much of this material should you use? Should you quote from the husband's and wife's blogs? What about quoting from his children's blogs? Is it OK to quote from a 16-year-old on material like this? Should the paper provide a link to the blogs from its Web site? *(The newspaper's decisions are at the back of the book.)*

Privacy case 2: Naming the professor

You're the police reporter in a small city. The son of a university professor was charged with four armed robberies over a Veteran's Day weekend. He allegedly held up a grocery, a bookstore, a pharmacy, and a woman using an ATM, and made off with $640 altogether. As a matter of routine, you call the home and confirm that the 26-year-old son lived in his parent's home and that the father was in fact a professor at the local university. Knowing the importance of getting the other side, you ask if the father had any comments. He pauses for a couple of seconds and then mumbles, "I guess not." You also learn that the man's mother is an Episcopal priest.

Part One: Robberies are news in a city this size, so you know you will be expected to write the story. Besides, it's little bit of a one-man crime spree. **Will you include that he lives at home? Will you mention the occupations of the man's parents? Will you write that the father had no comment on his boy's actions?**

Part Two: The father is a journalism professor. While not an employee, he occasionally writes op-ed pieces about media issues for your paper. **Does that change in any way how you would deal with the story?**

The newspaper's decisions are at the back of the book.

Privacy case 3: Riding the Raptor

A 16-year-old high-school sophomore decides to ride the Raptor at an amusement park. The ride combines the features of a bungee jump and a large swing. Riders wear harnesses that hold them in a horizontal, belly-down position. They are released from a platform approximately 80 feet high and swing rapidly toward the ground.

The young man is harnessed into the ride and released. As he accelerates toward the ground, the cable snags. He is flipped violently. Theme-park employees hustle him off to a medical facility that is owned by the amusement park. The boy is diagnosed as suffering a concussion. His parents are called, and they take him home. Because no police or emergency workers were involved, the incident goes unreported.

Six months later, his parents sue the amusement park for several million dollars. The suit alleges that the boy suffered brain damage in the incident. According to the suit, he was an honor-roll student who was already thinking about college. Now he has short-term memory loss and problems concentrating. He is in special-education classes. Teachers suspect he will have trouble getting his high-school diploma. His temperament has also changed, and he has few friends.

You decide to report the suit. But the parents beg you not to mention their son's problems. It would embarrass him and hurt his self-esteem if the whole world knew his problems. They would prefer you not to write about the suit at all. "Why bring attention to this and cause him any more pain?" they ask.

Would you write the story over their objections? Could you write the story but not name the boy? *(The newspaper's decisions are at the back of the book.)*

Privacy case 4: Should these juveniles be named?

Two boys, aged 14 and 16, were charged with felonies after they allegedly threatened to blow up a local high school and to kill any police officers who respond to the scene. "These kids were saying they were snipers, that they were going to shoot teachers," police said. The school took the unusual step of evacuating teachers and students to a nearby church as deputies searched for the boys. The youths will be charged as adults.

Do you write about the event? Do you name the boys? (The TV station's decisions are at the back of the book.)

Privacy case 5: Do you out this teen?

When a 15-year-old boy was reported missing from his job at a grocery store in an upscale suburban city, the community reacted with alarm.

Only a few days earlier, another child had been abducted. Residents put fliers about the missing teen on trees and in storefronts. They tied white ribbons to remind themselves of the disappearance. The news media joined in, running pictures of the youth and video of the white ribbons and fliers in trees.

You're a well-connected police reporter. The same day the boy disappeared, you see that police received another missing-person report. A 30-year-old man who lived across the street from the teen also was reported missing.

Part One: You wonder what to do. **Should you include the second report as part of your story about the missing 15 year old? Should you write it as a second story?** It's unlikely that the paper would use a missing-person report of a 30-year-old that soon unless there were other circumstances. If you do write it as a second story, would you want editors to package the two, meaning running them together on the same page? What inference might readers draw?

Part Two: At a tearful news conference, the boy's father did not want to talk about any possible connection between his son and the missing neighbor. "We just want to focus on getting [our son] home, that's all we're thinking about," he said. It seems a little surprising that the man is so uncaring about the missing neighbor. **Should you mention the missing neighbor in this story?**

Part Three: A police officer slips you a copy of a police report. A week earlier, the man had confessed to the boy's parents that he had sexually molested their son. The man said he was going to kill himself. Police arrived in time to take him into protective custody. According to police reports, he said he "could not understand why he would hurt someone whom he cared about so deeply." Police charged him with criminal sexual conduct. A judge released him on a $5,000 bond and ordered him to stay away from the boy. **Do you write this story?** You don't know how it relates to the disappearance. You don't know if the boy is alive. You don't normally report the names of minors who have been raped by adults. So, do you out a teenage boy who may have run off with his lover? Do you lead people to assume a pedophile has abducted the boy?

Part Four: Your paper receives the transcripts of the man's confession. He details how on a camping trip, he had tied the boy's hands and feet, then loosened the ties and sexually assaulted him. **Do you include this vivid detail in your story?**

Part Five: You receive a tip and are able to confirm that the boy had gone for help to a center that deals with teens' questions about their sexuality. **Do you write that story?**

Part Six: The bodies of the man and teen are found in car in a wildlife preserve, where the man had killed the boy and himself. Editors know you have been covering the story and want your input on deciding which pictures to use. One is an aerial photo through the windshield of the car. The legs of the man and the teen could be seen. Between the man's legs is the rifle. Neither their faces nor any blood is visible. **What do you tell them?**

(The newspapers' decisions are at the back of the book.)

Privacy case 6: Suicide downtown

On a sunny afternoon, a man stands on the ledge of a 16-story apartment building in a city of about 40,000 inhabitants. He indicates that he is going to kill himself. Police arrive and he begins to speculate on serious things like his background and motives for killing himself and on not so serious things like the predicament of going to the bathroom when you're on a ledge. For 3 ½ hours he stands there. Traffic on the downtown street is detoured and some minor traffic tie-ups are reported. People could not enter the apartment building, the largest in the city.

A crowd gathers. Some shout for him to come down. One couple tries to float balloons to him with encouraging messages. After they release one balloon, police chase them off. Many are praying. And at least one young man is recording the event on video camera because, he said, he was it was "the most dramatic thing" he's ever seen. He said he might produce a documentary that would convince people not to attempt suicide.

Finally, at about 3:30 p.m., police negotiators escorted the man off the ledge. A police spokesman said it is unlikely the man would face criminal charges and that he was "clearly despondent" over a pending divorce and financial problems. Police would get him the help he needed.

Part One: Assume you work for the primary newspaper that serves this community. **Do you want to pitch this story to your editors? If not, why not?** Assume you are asked to write it. **What would you include?** The man's name would be public record, and you certainly witnessed lots of things going on in the crowd.

Part Two: Suppose you work in a bureau of a major newspaper about 40 miles away. Your job is to cover a two-county area. In addition to the main paper, you have a special section targeted for this area with a news section. **Do you pitch the story to the editors at your main office for the main paper? Do you put it in the zoned section? What details would you include?**

(The newspaper's decisions are at the back of the book.)

Notes

1. Ramon Coronado, "Broken goblet, broken table: The media cover a hostage family," and "How far should the media go to get a story?" in Editorially Speaking section, *Gannetteer*, May 1981, pp. 2, 4.
2. Craig Kelford family, "Compassion from reporters, " *Los Angeles Times*, April 29, 1997.
3. Ginger Casey, "Playground vultures," *Quill*, November/December 1992, p. 27. The *Quill* piece is an excerpt from an article she wrote for the *San Francisco Examiner*.
4. David Pritchard, "The impact of newspaper ombudsmen on journalists' attitudes," *Journalism Quarterly*, Spring 1993, pp. 77–86.
5. Remarks made by her in the 13th annual Otis Chandler lecture at the University of Southern California School of Journalism, quoted in M. L. Stein, "Here we go again!" *Editor & Publisher*, November 28, 1992, p. 11.
6. Alex Klein, "Investigative reporting: Journalism of compassion," posted at www.businessjournalism.org, March 20, 2006.
7. Elise S. Burroughs and Barbara Z. Gyles, "When a tragedy wounds your town, coverage often adds to the pain," *Presstime*, October 1997.
8. "Prospectives of the public and the press," *Examining Our Credibility*, posted at www.asne.org, August 4, 1999.
9. Power, Matthew, "Immersion journalism," *Harper's*, December 2005.
10. A great resource in this area is the Web site of the Dart Center for Journalism and Trauma, www.dartcenter.org.
11. Dan Trigoboff, "Lessons of Columbine," *Broadcasting & Cable*, April 3, 2000.
12. Manning Pynn, "Reporters tread in sorrow's shadow," *Orlando Sentinel*, September 25, 2005.
13. Interviewed by Smith.
14. Richard P. Cunningham, "Aside from that, how was the play, Mrs. Lincoln?" *Quill*, April 1988, pp. 8–9. Details and quotes about this incident are taken from this article.
15. William Coté and Bonnie Bucqueroux, "Covering crime without re-victimizing the victim," paper presented to the National Newspaper Association's Annual Convention, Nashville, Tenn., September 25, 1996.

16. Fawn Germer, "How do you feel?" *American Journalism Review*, June 1995.
17. Thomas Oliphant, "Invaded – by the press," *The Boston Globe*, April 19, 1991.
18. Toni Locy, "Handymen did job on elderly D.C. woman," *The Washington Post*, August 10, 1997.
19. Joe Strupp, "Should newspapers name suspects?" *Editor & Publisher*, December 19, 2000.
20. Jerry Finch, "Photo of 'criminal suspect' may tell the wrong story," *The Richmond Times-Dispatch*, May 19, 2002.
21. Frank Thayer and Steve Pasternack, "Policies on identification of people in crime stories," *Newspaper Research Journal*, Spring 1994, pp. 56-64.
22. Strupp, *op. cit.*
23. Joe Kollin, "Why don't we name juveniles?" *Quill*, April 2003.
24. Rosalind C. Truitt, "Juvenile justice," *Presstime*, July/August 1996, and Thayer and Pasternack, *op. cit.*
25. Kollin, *op. cit.*
26. Constance K. Davis, "How Iowa editors are using law expanding access to names of juveniles," *Newspaper Research Journal*, Fall 2000, p. 38.
27. An appeals court ruled that the judge had probably not ensured that the boy understood a plea deal he had been offered. He was allowed to accept the deal and served three years in prison.
28. Thomas Collins, "When news gets explicit," *Newsday*, August 13, 1991, sec. II, p. 2.
29. David House, "A grim insight into the justice process," *Star-Telegram*, October 29, 2006. See "Second man now a suspect in Putt-Putt slaying," *Star-Telegram*, October 24, 2006.
30. Steve Outing, "The thorny question of linking," Poynteronline, www. poynter.org, posted Oct. 21, 2004.
31. Steve Outing, "The thorny question of linking," Poynter Online, posted October 21, 2004.
32. Julian Guthrie, "Media dilemma on identifying rape victims," San Francisco Chronicle, Aug. 3, 2002
33. Sheila Gibbons, "Sex-assault survivors deserve names, not stigma," *Women's E-News*, August 19, 2003.
34. Robin Benedict, *Virgin or Vamp: How the Press Covers Sex Crimes*, New York: Oxford University Press, 1992, pp. 252–253.
35. Michael Kelly, "A plea for more openness on rape," *The Omaha World Herald*, July 25, 2002.
36. Bruce DeSilva, "Views of newspaper gatekeepers on rape and rape coverage," unpublished paper presented at Association for Education in Journalism and Mass Communication Convention, Corvallis, Oregon, 1983.

37. Jane Schorer, "The story behind a landmark story of rape," *Washington Journalism Review*, June 1991.
38. Geneva Overholser, "Name the accuser and the accused," Poynter Online, July 23, 2003.
39. Rita Ciolli, "Naming rape accusers: A policy under review," *Newsday*, May 5, 1991.
40. Benedict, *op. cit.*, p. 254.
41. Cited by Elizabeth Culotta, "Naming alleged rape victims: Two policies within 30 miles," *Washington Journalism Review*, July/August 1992.
42. Dick Haws, "Rape victims: Papers shouldn't name us," *American Journalism Review*, September 1996.
43. Tommy Thomason, Paul LaRocque and Maggie Thomas, "Editors still reluctant to name rape victims," *Newspaper Research Journal* 16, no. 3 (1995): 42-51.
44. Dershowitz made similar observations about both the New Bedford and William Smith trials. His comments are widely quoted, including in Benedict, *op. cit*, p. 253, and Ciolli, *op. cit.*
45. Paul R. LaRocque, "Naming rape victims," *APME News*, Summer 1996.
46. Jon Sarche, "Bryant accuser publicly identifies herself in civil lawsuit," *Associated Press*, Oct. 15, 2004.
47. Gina Lubrano, "Fairness an issue in rape cases," *San Diego Union-Tribune*, August 20, 2001.

12 Privacy for Political Leaders

An outgoing president is unhappy with the way he was treated by the media. In his early drafts of his farewell address, he attacks the news media and calls them "savage." Perhaps he is reacting to rumors reported in some newspapers that he is sexually impotent. Or maybe he is reacting to the media's treatment of his secretary of the treasury, an accomplished politician who some had hoped might succeed him.

Many papers had reported juicy details about a love affair this man had with a married woman. According to the reports, the woman was down on her luck when she had asked the wealthy politician for help, and he had obliged her by giving her some money – that night, in her bedroom. The affair continued until the woman's husband found out. The husband tried to blackmail the politician, who then ended the affair. The distraught wife was left heartbroken and suicidal.

On hearing of the sordid affair, the man's political foes paid a newspaper editor to embellish his reports with the untrue accusation that the husband had been paid with government funds to keep quiet.

The man's likely opponent in the presidential race was not being given a free ride in the media, however. His moral standards were under attack too. Newspapers were reporting that he was having an affair with a woman and that he was the father of some of her children. The politician was so angry that he told the press he would not dignify their stories with a response.

When many Americans hear stories like these about the media invading the private lives of political leaders and writing stories to satisfy the hand that feeds them, they wonder if the Founding Fathers wouldn't roll over in their graves if they saw what the press was doing. But the Founding

Fathers didn't have graves when those stories were printed. Those stories were about the Founding Fathers. It was George Washington who thought press coverage was "savage,"[1] Washington's secretary of the treasury, Alexander Hamilton, who eventually admitted to the affair with the married woman,[2] and Thomas Jefferson who was reported to have fathered the children of one of his slaves.[3]

The American press has traditionally seen its role in our democracy as the Fourth Estate, an unelected but active player in the life of the republic. Some, however, would accuse the media of being too active of a player: writing stories from their own biases and mercilessly intruding on the privacy of political figures.

The Partisan Press

Some newspapers during the early days of our republic received the bulk of their money from political factions, and they were quite willing to print rumors and gossip about the private lives of opposition candidates. Often they weren't too concerned about the truth – or even the consistency – of the rumors. Washington was accused by some papers of being impotent and by others of fathering dozens of illegitimate children, including one who grew up to be a member of his own cabinet.[4]

Few political leaders escaped the newspaper rumor mill, according to John Seigenthaler, former publisher of *The Tennessean* in Nashville. Andrew Jackson was accused of convincing Rachel Robards to leave her husband and move in with him. Martin Van Buren was said to wear women's corsets that made it "difficult to say whether he is a man or woman." William Henry Harrison was depicted as senile and mentally failing. Henry Clay was reported to spend his days gambling and his nights in brothels. Franklin Pierce and John Fremont were alleged to be heavy drinkers.[5] Abraham Lincoln's wife was called a Confederate spy,[6] and Lincoln was reported to be a "Negro."

The partisan press began to fade from the scene in the mid-1800s, but papers continued to have a field day exploring the private lives of political candidates. For example, in 1884 most observers thought that Democrat candidate Grover Cleveland had little chance of winning the presidency. His hopes were further dimmed when the newspapers reported that Cleveland had fathered a child out of wedlock while he was the sheriff of Buffalo, N.Y. The woman reportedly had other lovers too, but Cleveland, the only bachelor she was seeing, accepted responsibility and had faithfully paid child support. When these payments were disclosed during the campaign, the *New York Sun* called him "a course debauchee who might bring his harlots to Washington... a man leprous with immorality."[7]

Most Republicans thought those stories would clinch the election for their man. But then another scandal made the front pages. Papers reported that the first child of Republican candidate James Blaine was born only three months after Blaine and his wife were married. Blaine announced that it was all a misunderstanding. He contended that he and his wife were actually married twice, six months apart. His message apparently failed to convince many voters, and Cleveland became the only Democrat to be elected president between 1861 and 1912.[8]

The Era of the "Lapdog"

In the 20th century, the press went from being a watchdog of candidates' morals to a lapdog, according to Professor Larry Sabato in his book *Feeding Frenzy*. The press looked the other way as candidates and political leaders engaged in drunkenness and carousing. Some of them were so drunk that they had to be carried off the floors of the House and Senate, but the voters back home would never read about it.[9]

These reporters were adhering to a gentleman's agreement that political leaders' private lives were off limits. Sabato, a professor of government at the University of Virginia, contended that this informal agreement intensified during Franklin Roosevelt's presidency in the 1930s and 1940s. The press took the position that if Roosevelt's polio did not affect the way he handled his duties, it would not be reported. The news media deliberately avoided doing anything that might show that the president was physically disabled. Of the 35,000 photos taken of FDR, only two showed his wheelchair. When Roosevelt was seeking his fourth term as president in 1944, he was desperately ill, yet many publishers – even those who supported Roosevelt's opponent – chose not to run pictures that hinted at how sick he was.[10]

But the press did not limit its discretion to Roosevelt's health problems. Roosevelt was all but estranged from his wife and had a long-term relationship with his secretary, none of which was ever reported.[11] The lack of interest in such stories was not limited to Roosevelt.

His Republican opponent in 1940, Wendell Willkie, openly kept a mistress both before and during his bid for the presidency, but that was not a story to the press of that era.[12]

Even if a politician's public image bore little relation to the truth, reporters would not write about it. President Dwight Eisenhower's quick temper and salty language were never mentioned. Instead, the media in the 1950s portrayed him as a kindly, soft-spoken grandfather figure. Albert Hunt, a *Wall Street Journal* reporter, told Sabato about a married congressman who left his family in his home district and lived with another woman while he was in Washington. Yet every two years the man would run for re-election, and his campaign would feature pictures showing him as an upstanding family man with a wife and four kids. "I never wrote about it, though today... I surely would," Hunt said.[13]

The heaviest criticism of the news media's willingness to look the other way came when the public learned of President John F. Kennedy's many affairs. Kennedy was linked romantically with actresses, an airline attendant, one of his secretaries, even the girlfriend of a Mafia chieftain – all while he was serving as president. Even before he became president, many journalists were aware of his amorous adventures. They were so legendary that the press corps covering his presidential bid joked that his campaign slogan ought to be changed from "Let's back Jack" to "Let's sack with Jack." However, not one newspaper or TV reporter did a story during the campaign or Kennedy's term in office that hinted at his extramarital exploits. Sabato wrote:

> Not only did the media not want to dig for the unpleasant truth, they willingly communicated a lie, becoming part and parcel of the Kennedy public relations team. In the press reports, Jack Kennedy, champion philanderer, became the perfect husband and family man.[14]

President Kennedy's affairs may have affected his job performance. Sabato noted that occasionally his trysts required him to be out of touch with the military command at a time when the Cold War demanded that the president always be accessible in case of a Russian sneak attack. Seymour Hersh, a Pulitzer prize-winning reporter, wrote that top military officials with urgent requests would not interrupt Kennedy when they suspected he was with a woman. Hersh said that even confirmation that the Russians had missiles in Cuba was delayed until the next morning.[15] Kennedy also opened himself to blackmail, and some argue that then

FBI director J. Edgar Hoover used his knowledge of Kennedy's affairs to gain more power for himself and autonomy for his department.[16]

Some contend that Kennedy got such special treatment because he was well liked by the press. But history suggests that explanation may be inadequate. The press also overlooked indiscretions in the personal lives of at least three presidents who preceded Kennedy and the one who followed.[17] Seigenthaler pointed out that it was historians and biographers, not journalists, who revealed the relationships between Warren Harding and Nan Britton, Franklin Roosevelt and Lucy Mercer, Dwight Eisenhower and Kay Summersby, and Lyndon Johnson and Alice March.[18] Associated Press reporter James Bacon told Hersh that actress Marilyn Monroe had given him a firsthand account of her relationship with Kennedy. "She was very open about her affair with JFK," he said. But he didn't write the story. "Before Watergate, reporters just didn't go into that sort of thing." Bacon said there was no conspiracy to hide Kennedy's philandering. "It was just a matter of judgment on the part of the reporters."[19]

This see-no-evil agreement probably was one reason people had more respect both for politicians and for reporters than they do now, according to Ellen Hume, executive director of a center that studies press and politics at Harvard University. "The news was much more upbeat in the 1940s and 1950s when [the] nation's political leaders were treated by the journalists with deference and respect," she told the *Los Angeles Times*.[20]

Growing concerns

Reporters began to wonder if their coverage shouldn't include more honest reporting of candidates' personalities. Some say the event that triggered the change was Watergate, the name given to the investigation of President Nixon's role in a break-in at Democratic offices during the 1972 campaign. The probe ultimately cost Nixon many of his supporters and led to his resignation. The criticisms of Nixon had more to do with character issues (suspicions that he lied and was mean-spirited and foulmouthed) than with his political policies.

Sabato argues that the move away from a lapdog press began earlier. He contends that by the time of Watergate, reporters had already begun to reconsider their responsibilities. In 1969 Sen. Edward Kennedy, who had a considerable reputation for drinking and womanizing, waited until the next day to report an auto accident at Chappaquiddick in which a young woman riding in his car was killed. Sabato wrote:

> Kennedy had been too flagrant, his actions too costly for one young woman, and his excuses too flimsy and insulting to the many perceptive minds in the press corps. Good reporters were ashamed of, and the press as a whole was severely criticized for, the process of concealing Kennedy's manifest vices that had preceded the senator's own cover-up of the facts surrounding the accident.[21]

Other reporters believe that it was neither Chappaquiddick nor Watergate that led to journalism's new candor in reporting politicians' private lives. Seymour Topping, who was assistant managing editor of *The New York Times* during the 1970s, argued that it was changes in society like the sexual revolution of the 1960s that allowed newspapers "to explore things that we wouldn't explore in the past." And Richard Wald, the president of NBC News at the time, noted that politicians themselves were more open in the 1970s, admitting to alcoholism and talking publicly about their divorces.[22]

For whatever reason, news coverage of the private lives of political leaders became even more intense in the mid-1970s. Stories of abuses by congressmen began to appear. But none of those stories made a bigger splash than the ones about the carryings-on of Wilbur Mills, the Democratic congressman from Arkansas who headed the powerful Ways and Means Committee. Reporters who had covered Mills knew he was a heavy drinker and appeared to be drunk at some committee meetings, but they would not pursue the story because they did not think they should invade his private life.

Then one night in 1974, Mills was stopped by police for speeding and driving with his headlights off. A young woman climbed out of Mills' car and jumped into the Tidal Basin, a body of water near the monuments in Washington. The passenger was Fanne Foxe, a striptease dancer who billed herself as the Argentine Bombshell.

Now Mills was named in a police report, and his drinking was no longer a private matter. Stories about Mills' problems began to appear in the media. A few days later, a drunken Mills climbed on stage while Foxe was performing at a Washington strip joint. This action prompted many more reporters to shed their adherence to the boys-will-be-boys notion of privacy for public officials. "The guy was falling down drunk, but the press in general portrayed him as one of the great legislative leaders in

American politics," David R. Jones, then national editor of *The New York Times,* said later. "Now, he himself says that his drinking affected his job."[23] After undergoing treatment for his drinking, Mills admitted that sometimes he had to ask aides what had happened and what he had said at committee meetings he had chaired.

Neither the Watergate controversy nor the Mills affair led to an "anything goes" mentality among reporters. The old gentleman's agreement may have been weakened, but it was still the rule of the day, as *Newsweek* reported in 1975:

> There is hardly a journalist in Washington who cannot identify at least one alcoholic or philandering congressman. Such behavior only becomes news when it either interferes with the congressman's duties – say, by preventing him from voting on an important measure – or lands him in trouble with the law, as happened in the Mills case.[24]

However, more and more journalists were wondering if they should not write about these "character issues." As Ben Bagdikian, a journalist and media critic who would later become dean of the journalism school at Berkeley, said in 1975, "Since Richard Nixon, there has been a growing feeling that the character of leading politicians is important – and that you've got to know something about their private lives to understand their real character."[25]

"Piranha press"

Just as the privacy pendulum began to swing from the gentleman's agreement of earlier years to a more probing kind of reporting, Gary Hart stumbled into the media spotlight. Hart, a Democrat, attempted to run for president in 1984, but lost support when he gave inconsistent explanations as to why he had changed his last name (from Hartpence), subtracted a year from his age, and changed facts in his official biography.

When Hart decided to try again for the presidency in 1988, rumors about his womanizing were already rampant. Even his campaign workers and big campaign contributors were concerned, and he promised them that he would mind his manners and make sure his sex life was not a campaign issue. In meetings with reporters and political columnists, he assured them he was doing nothing wrong. Hart was so insistent in his denials that he may have invited his own downfall. In an interview with a *New York Times* reporter, he said: "Follow me around. I don't care.

I'm serious, if anybody wants to put a tail on me, go ahead. They'd be very bored."

Not surprisingly, someone took up his challenge. Two *Miami Herald* reporters staked out his home in Washington that weekend. Instead of being bored, they watched as a young woman entered the townhouse and apparently spent the night. Hart at first tried to explain away the story. (The reporters, he said, had missed seeing her leave, and the reporters admitted that they had not kept a constant watch on both doors, making it possible that she had left unseen through the back door.)

A few weeks earlier, Hart and a model named Donna Rice had taken an overnight cruise to Bimini on a yacht called, of all things, *Monkey Business*. When one of Rice's friends sold the *National Enquirer* snapshots of Rice sitting on Hart's lap, Hart's efforts to explain away the reports became more difficult. The final straw came when *Washington Post* reporters told him they had evidence of other affairs. Hart decided to drop out of the race.[26]

Although many journalists were uncomfortable with the idea of reporters acting like two-bit private eyes, many justified the story on the grounds that it raised questions about Hart's honesty and his willingness to engage in risky behavior. The *Herald* reporters were honored by the Society of Professional Journalists.

The public has had trouble making up its mind about how far the press should go. Polls conducted during the Hart–Rice controversy found that about 70 percent of the public thought the reporters had gone too far.[27] Only a few years earlier, news organizations had been criticized for covering up President Kennedy's affairs.

The news media's transformation from lapdog to attack dog may have had one unintended side effect. Harvard's Ellen Hume argued that the news media's coverage "doubtlessly feeds the public's cynicism and distrust of its political leader – and of the piranha press corps which seems willing to devour anyone, at any time, for frivolous infractions as well as serious ones."[28]

Are Politicians Still Fair Game?

When Bill Clinton ran for president in 1992, he faced a barrage of news reports about sexual exploits while he was governor of Arkansas. To quell the criticism, he appeared on CBS's *60 Minutes* with his wife,

Hillary, at his side and confessed that there had been problems in his marriage. He went on to defeat incumbent George H. W. Bush. Clinton's personal life became an issue again during the 1996 elections, but had little impact on the outcome. Many voters admitted to pollsters they did not trust Clinton and doubted his honesty and morality – but they said they planned to vote for him. Even as rumors of an affair with a White House intern were filling the newspapers and newscasts, Clinton received some of the highest popularity ratings for a non-war president. Similarly, the presidential campaigns of Bob Dole in 1996 and George W. Bush in 2000 were barely affected by reports that several years earlier Dole had had an affair and Bush had been arrested for drunken driving.

Even voters in socially conservative Mississippi looked the other way when it appeared their governor did not live up to the strong family values he preached. During the Clinton–Dole race, Republican Gov. Kirk Fordice called Clinton a "philanderer" and a "congenital liar." Then, one November day, while his wife was in France, Fordice told his security guards to take the day off. That afternoon he was seen holding hands with a woman during an intimate lunch in a quiet restaurant. Later that night, as Fordice was driving alone on a Mississippi interstate, his car flipped and he was seriously injured.

The events of the day became big news in Mississippi. The waitresses were interviewed, positively identifying the governor and describing his rendezvous. Fordice's staff gave conflicting accounts of his day. Fordice himself had nothing to say for nearly two months. Then, he held a press conference and announced that the accident had caused him to suffer memory loss. He could not recall anything that happened, beginning shortly before he had lunch that day. He couldn't remember where he had gone, whom he had seen, what he had done, or how the accident occurred. Besides, he said, "even a governor is entitled to some private time." Despite these developments, public support for Fordice remained steady, but the rumored affair contributed to his wife seeking a divorce.

"Before Clinton, that kind of personal stuff just killed you," a Democratic political consultant told *U.S. News and World Report.* "Now, it's been relegated to a factor in the political equation. The attitude is, 'Yeah, sure, but I like what he did on welfare.'"[29]

Relatives of politicians

A pharmacist in Tallahassee, Fla., received a phone call from a doctor authorizing a Xanax prescription for a patient. Because it was late at night, the pharmacist decided to check back with the doctor and discovered that he had not made the call and no longer practiced medicine. The pharmacist contacted police, who arrested the 24-year-old woman when she came to pick up the drugs. Noelle Bush, the daughter of the governor of Florida and the niece of President George W. Bush, was charged with prescription fraud, a felony.

Many reporters who covered the governor knew his oldest daughter had drug problems. During the campaign, Bush had even made passing reference to the fact. Journalists also knew, but did not report, that she had entered an Atlanta rehab clinic at least once while her father was governor. But with her arrest, things changed quickly. Nearly every paper and television station in Florida carried the story, as did a large number of papers nationally, some European papers, and all of the network and cable newscasts.

Under Florida's diversion law that allows some offenders to seek treatment rather than jail, Bush was committed to a residential treatment center. Once there, she was twice caught with drugs and sent back to drug court. Attorneys for the Bush family tried to get the hearings closed "to avoid a media circus." The request was denied. When she was sentenced to 10 days in jail, some cable TV news networks covered it as breaking news.[30]

Many journalists and members of the public wondered if this woman's losing battle with drug addiction really deserved to be national news. A columnist for the *St. Petersburg Times* pointed out:

> Noelle Bush didn't choose to make her father the governor of Florida and her uncle the president of the United States. But their prominence is why an otherwise everyday occurrence is in the national news... You don't choose your family. You just have it.

Other journalists suggested that the story was relevant. When Bush was running for governor, he promised to make the fight against drugs one of his major priorities. But as governor, Bush "has taken a dim view of efforts to require treatment over prison for drug offenders," *The Tampa Tribune* noted. He had cut funding to Florida's system of special drug courts and supervised drug treatment. After his daughter was arrested, she elected to enter one of those programs and was spared jail time.[31] Many journalists saw irony in these events, and some wondered if the personal experiences might cause Bush to change his positions.

Noelle Bush, of course, is not the first family member of a prominent political family to get into trouble. The media reported the arrests of

President Bush's daughters, Jenna and Barbara, on underage drinking charges in 2001. Weeks later, *The New York Times* reported that Barbara had been seen in Manhattan "doubled over and spitting on the sidewalk."[32] Drug problems among many of the Kennedy children – including a fatal overdose – were also fodder for the press.

Most politicians know that public scrutiny is "among the prices politicians' kids pay for their parent's ballot-box success," said Frank Wooten of *The Post and Courier* in Charleston, S.C. He contended that their parents drag them into the public spotlight. They have them pose in the "obligatory family photo" to show voters what a happy family they have. They have them appear at conventions and other campaign functions. South Carolina Gov. Jim Hodges told Wooten that he was trying to provide his three children with as normal a childhood as possible. But the children were aware of their role as the children of a politician. "They've come to recognize that it comes with the territory," the governor said.[33] The news media have treated some politicians' children with respect. For the most part, they let President Clinton's daughter, Chelsea, attend college in California and grad school in England without much media attention. She received heavy coverage only when she attended a Versace fashion show with actress Gwyneth Paltrow and singer Madonna.

The bigger problem, as in the case of Noelle Bush, is when laws are broken or the relatives do other things to bring attention to themselves. There is no consensus among editors. Within a few months of each other, four newspapers were faced with covering the events involving relatives of local politicians, and each handled the story differently.

In Jacksonville, Fla., police arrested a man whose mother was a city councilwoman and whose father was running for mayor. The 35-year old was charged with child pornography and lewd behavior. Editors at *The Florida Times-Union* decided to identify his parents and interviewed his mother, the councilwoman. They ran the story and a picture of the accused man in the paper's crime column with quotes from his parents.

When the brother of the mayor-elect of Dayton, Ohio, was charged with cocaine position, the *Dayton Daily News* also placed a short story about the arrest in its local news roundup column and identified him as the brother of the politician. The paper did not print his picture or interview the accused man's brother.

The News-Journal in Wilmington, Del., was even more reserved in its coverage when the mayor's 35-year-old son was charged with rape. The paper handled the story exactly as it would any other rape. Because the

paper does not normally report the names of the parents of adult criminals, it did not mention that the accused was the son of the mayor.[34]
Mike Clark, the reader advocate at *The Times-Union*, called several ethicists and asked how they thought stories such as these should be covered.
Ken Starck, a professor at the University of Iowa and then the ombudsman for the *Cedar Rapids (Iowa) Gazette*, thought *The News-Journal*
handled the story correctly. If the paper does not normally interview the
parents of adult children charged with crimes, it should not make an
exception in the case of a political figure.

In Portland, editors at *The Oregonian* recently debated coverage
of the suicide of the son of Oregon Sen. Gordon Smith. They decided
against playing the story on Page 1. Instead, they published a short article inside the Metro section that described his son's long struggle with
clinical depression and specifically carried no details of how he died,
according to the paper's public editor. But even that was too invasive
for a few readers. "This was a troubled young man, not a public figure,"
one wrote. "He did not ask to have his struggle revealed because his
father ran for office. How does it benefit us to know that this young man
lost his struggle?"[35]

Outing politicians

At one time, outing gays was a popular activity in American society.
In Florida in the 1950s and 1960s, the state Legislature established a
committee whose job was to fight the "homosexual menace" on state
university campuses. The Johns Committee resulted in more than
100 professors being fired and dozens of students expelled. Many left
Florida universities when they were questioned by police about their
sexual orientation. Governmental agencies in other states also tracked
down and exposed gays.

The news media were involved too. Brit Hume of Fox News said that
when he was working for columnist Jack Anderson in the early 1970s,
he tracked down the son of then Vice President Spiro Agnew and confirmed that he had broken up with his wife and moved in with a male
hairdresser in Baltimore. Hume said he is "more ashamed of that story
than anything I've done in journalism. I'm sorry about it to this day."

The mainstream media no longer want to be associated with outing.
Charlie Crist, who became governor of Florida in 2007, has been the
target of claimed outings by talk shows, gay-oriented magazines, and

alternative weeklies. His sexuality was discussed whenever politicians and political reporters got together, according to *Miami New Times*. Then, "reporters head back to their newsrooms and there won't be anything about the whispers in your morning newspaper the next day."[36] Crist did receive media attention in the final days of the Republican primary after newspapers received copies of sealed court documents concerning a paternity case involving Crist. At a news conference, Crist repeated his denials that he had fathered a child.[37]

Most news outlets take a position much like *The New York Times* spells out in its code of ethics, namely that the paper only "identifies public figures as gay when it is relevant to the reporting." When *The Spokesman-Review* in Spokane reported that Mayor Jim West had used his position to offer jobs to teenage boys that he was interested in sexually, the paper contended it was not outing. In a note to readers, the paper's editor wrote, "This is not a story about sexual orientation. This is a story about alleged sexual abuse of children and misuse of power and authority."[38]

Other times, the mainstream media argue that they are not outing gays as much as they are exposing hypocrites. When newspapers reported the accusations against the Spokane mayor, most pointed out that he had "championed an anti-gay agenda during his tenure as one of the most powerful Republicans in the Legislature." A Seattle paper reminded readers that West had "supported a bill that would have barred gays and lesbians from working for schools, day-care centers and some state agencies [and] voted to define marriage as a union between a man and a woman." (The West case is discussed at length in Chapter 5.)

Scott Maxwell, a political writer for the *Orlando Sentinel*, wrote that he believes there are many occasions when exposing a hypocritical politician is justified. An example might be a candidate who claims to be a friend of the farmer and then votes against farmers' interests once he is elected. However, he suggested that there is irony in the way journalists apply the hypocrisy standard to gays. What the media seem to be saying to closeted gays is this: "We'll out you only if you have anti-gay positions. If you support gay rights, your secret's safe."[39]

Openly gay politicians remain rare. Although Rep. Barney Frank of Massachusetts has become an established national leader, only one other of Congress' 535 members was openly gay in 2006. It was estimated that there are 300 open gays among the nation's 511,000 state and local elected officials. A gay rights group says that 67 were elected to national or state office in 2006. Many were the first open gays ever elected to statewide or national office in their states.[40]

News organizations have occasionally been accused of "inning," purposefully hiding the fact that people are homosexual. A gay publication in Minnesota contended that the Twin Cities media did just that when a police officer in Minneapolis was killed in the line of duty. The magazine reported that the officer "represented the Minneapolis Police Department at Gay Pride festivals and was proud of being a gay cop in uniform."

But in the coverage of her murder, neither the newspapers nor the TV newscasts mentioned that she was gay. Some believed that by identifying the officer as gay, the media would "have forced people who espouse anti-gay beliefs to acknowledge that a cop who died protecting them from danger, whose death was being mourned across Minnesota, was a person they regularly condemn."[41]

Cases to Discuss

These scenarios are based on the experiences of reporters and editors. They have been modified for space and impact. In many of these situations, a reporter would seek advice from an editor – and the editors would make the final decision. But the initial input would come from the reporter, and good editors would listen to the reporter before deciding. On some cases, you will see a note that indicates you can check to see what the real editors did. That doesn't mean they did the right thing, but you can compare your thoughts with theirs.

Privacy of Public People case 1: The wayward president

Part One: The local state university has a young president who has brought new life to the school. Students like him. He and his wife frequently dine with students in dorms, fraternities, and sororities. Faculty like him. Alumni gifts are at an all-time high. His frequent visits with legislators in the state capital have paid off with more new programs and state funding than the university has ever received.

You work for a news organization and routinely cover the university. You receive a tip that police in the capital city are investigating an upscale prostitution ring there and that the university president's name was on a list of frequent clients. You call police in the capital, which is about 100 miles away, and they will say only that they do not comment about ongoing investigations. You check Lexis-Nexis and find reports in the newspapers that capital city police have been using undercover officers to arrest men soliciting women in certain areas of the city. "Arresting the johns is the best way to stop the trafficking in sex," the head of the vice unit is quoted as saying.

In your state, expense records of public officials are public record. So you ask to see the expense records from the past few visits the president has made to the capital. His hotel bill shows several phone calls that have black lines through them. University officials say that they were apparently personal calls and that the president had reimbursed the university for them.

You can make out the phone numbers. Checks indicate that two of them are to the Delightful Touch massage service. You do a Web search and find the Delightful Touch home page. It says it has an "all-girl" staff and has pictures of scantily clad women. In small type, a message says, "Our masseuses are independent contractors. The fee you pay us covers a basic massage. Any other therapeutic services may be negotiated with the masseuse."

You get expense accounts from other trips the president has taken on university business. Most of them have calls – all reimbursed – to massage agencies with names like Devine Relaxation and Total Pleasure Massage.

You confront the university president with what you have learned. He says that he has a bad back and that it hurts after a long drive or plane ride. He says he gets a massage in his room so that he can sleep. "All I get his a massage," he said. "I found the number in the local phone book and called for a massage. If any of those agencies engage in other kinds of things, I wouldn't know."

You call the president of the Faculty Senate. She says she is shocked. "That's not the way for a president to represent the university," she said. "Prostitution is a violation of the law, common decency, and his marital vows. I hope your information is wrong. If you are right, I'm sure the senate would pass a 'no confidence' resolution. We expect better from our university president."

The president of the Student Senate becomes angry at you when you tell him about it. "He's a great guy, a great president," he said. "I don't believe he did anything wrong. And even if he did, what he does on his own time is his own business. Why do you want to embarrass the man and his family?"

Apply Potter's box and decide if you would continue to report this story and if you would use it.

Part Two: A reporter for your paper tracks down the masseuse who visited his room on one occasion. She says, under condition of anonymity, that many women did not want to service him because he wants "kinky sex," which she describes in graphic terms.

If you didn't use the story before, would you use it now? If you did use the story, would you do a follow-up story about interviewing the prostitute? Would you include the references to kinky sex? *(The newspaper's decisions are at the back of the book.)*

Privacy of Public People case 2: Politicians' pasts

You're working on two stories as a general-assignment reporter. A 43-year-old attorney is found dead with some prescription pain pills in her purse. The medical examiner is investigating. While gathering background for your story, you learn where she went to law school and the nature of her private practice. You also discover that until 12 years ago, she was a prominent prosecutor. She was fired after she was arrested on drunken driving charges and refused to take the breath test, according to a story in your paper at the time.

The other story seemed routine. The City Council had approved the mayor's appointment of two members to the library board. But a quick check of your newspaper files discovered that eight years ago one pleaded no contest (meaning neither guilty nor not guilty) to a charge of soliciting for prostitution. He did whatever community service was expected of him and his record was expunged.

Do you include these details from the people's pasts in your stories? *(The newspaper's decisions are at the back of the book.)*

Privacy of Public People case 3: School board president runs personal ad

A single man who owns an antique shop is elected to the local school board in a midsized Old South city. He develops a reputation as a consensus builder on the board and leads many initiatives to improve the quality of the schools.

When he runs for election, a local car dealer donates $10,000, a large amount in a school board race, to his opponent. Much of the money is used to raise questions about whether the man is gay. However, he is re-elected to the school board by a slim margin. Many observers believe that the opposition campaign backfired and swayed voters to his side.

Given his ability to get school board members to work together, the man is elected chairman of the school board. He runs the meetings and plays a large role in setting the agenda. He also becomes very visible in the community. Whenever the television stations or newspaper run a story about the schools, he is the man who presents the school board's positions. The position is part-time, paying $11,000 a year.

You are a reporter and cover the school board. You receive a couple of tips that the man has placed a personal ad with a risqué picture on www.manhunt.net, a Web site for gay men. You go the site, pay the $5 fee for a week's membership, and check out the personals. Sure enough, his picture is there. He is bare-chested. His self-portrait describes in rather clear terms the kinds of sexual activities he enjoys.

Fearing that a political opponent may be setting him up by placing his picture there, you call the man. He admits that he placed the ad a couple of days ago. "It was a really stupid thing to do," he concedes. Moments later, you go back to the Web site to make sure you have the details correct, and find his page has already been removed. Fortunately for your story, you had saved a copy on your first visit.

You call another school board member. When told of the picture and the details, he fumbled to find words and then said, "This is a shame. He and I have been colleagues and friends since he's been on the board. A person is free to do whatever they want to do, but when you're a public official that's all open to the public... This just floors me."

It's 9:30 p.m. You are going to have to decide whether to pitch the story to your editor or news director. And you will need to decide how hard you want to fight to get the story told.

Think about the steps in Potter's box and the SPJ code of ethics and prepare to defend your decisions. *(The newspaper's decisions are at the back of the book.)*

Privacy of Public People case 4: A racist remark

You are a reporter in a Southern city. Your city is embroiled in a heated race to elect a new mayor. One candidate is in his late 60s, is closely tied with the city's traditional power base, and owns a well-known local business. He barely won his party's primary. The other candidate is an attorney who wants to bring the community together and to "start a new day."

Less than a week before the election, a woman says that she was at a party several months earlier with the older candidate. She says he told her that "women shouldn't hold public office." He then used the n-word in discussing problems in one large African-American area in the city. You know a story like that would have a tremendous impact on voters. When you ask the candidate, he says he hasn't used that term since he was in first grade and the family's maid scolded him. He says it's clear from the timing that this is a "dirty political trick" to destroy his candidacy.

Part One: The person who tells you about the conversation does not want you to use his name. Although he lost in the primary to the older man, he believes he has a bright political future. If the party knows he is the source for your story, he can kiss his future goodbye. But, he's worried that his party will help elect a bigot.

You have two issues to decide: **Will you use the story? Will you promise not to reveal who your source is?**

Part Two: The announcement is made at a press conference by a current member of the city council. She is an active support of the older man's opponent. She is an open lesbian and feminist who said she was shocked when the older man attacked both women and African-Americans. It was the first time she had spoken to him. He had not yet announced his candidacy for mayor. She said she came forward now because the race was so close that she believed voters needed to know that one candidate was racist and sexist.

You have a she said/he said account. He remembers meeting her at the party but adamantly denies making the remarks. She said they were talking privately so no one can confirm the conversation. You make several calls, but can find no one who says they have heard him use racial slurs.

Will you use the story? *(The newspaper's decisions are at the back of the book.)*

Notes

1.   Larry J. Sabato, *Feeding Frenzy: How Attack Journalism Has Transformed American Politics*, New York: The Free Press, 1991, p. 27.

2. John Seigenthaler, "The First Amendment: The first 200 years," *Presstime*, February 1991, pp. 24–30.
3. *Ibid*. Although historians discounted this news report, DNA testing later indicated that the story may have been true.
4. Michael Wines, "Supreme leader, pigeon in chief," *The New York Times*, March 23, 1997, p. A-4.
5. Seigenthaler, *op. cit.*, p. 29.
6. Wines, *op. cit.*
7. Details taken from David Shaw, "Stumbling over sex in the press," *Los Angeles Times*, August 18, 1991, p. A-1, Seigenthaler, *op. cit.*, and Sabato, *op. cit.*
8. Details of the 1884 campaigns are reported both by Sabato, *op. cit.*, pp. 25–51, and Seigenthaler, *op. cit.*, p. 30.
9. See Gloria Borger, "Private lives, public figures," *U.S. News and World Report*, May 18, 1987, p. 20, and Sabato, *op. cit.*, pp. 25–52.
10. Sabato, *op. cit.*, p. 30.
11. That FDR had this relationship is widely reported. See Borger, *op. cit.*, Seigenthaler, *op. cit.*, or Sabato, *op. cit.*
12. Sabato, *op. cit.*, p. 30.
13. *Ibid.*, p. 31.
14. *Ibid.*, p. 40.
15. Seymour Hersh, *The Dark Side of Camelot*, Boston: Little, Brown, 1997, pp. 238–246.
16. Sabato, *op. cit.*, p. 36.
17. See Sabato, *op. cit.*, or Borger, *op. cit.*
18. Seigenthaler, *op. cit.*, p. 24.
19. Hersh, *op. cit.*, p. 106.
20. Shaw, "Trust in media is on decline," *Los Angeles Times*, March 31, 1993, p. A-1.
21. Sabato, *op. cit.*, p. 46.
22. Harry F. Waters, "Public or private lives?" *Newsweek*, February 17, 1975, p. 83.
23. Interview with Goodwin, October 7, 1981.
24. Waters, *op. cit.*
25. *Ibid.*
26. The Hart–Rice story is widely told. For instance, Borger, *op. cit.*, has a good discussion.
27. Shaw, *op. cit.*
28. *Ibid.*
29. Douglas Stanglin, "The new politics of forgive and forget," *U.S. News and World Report*, March 3, 1997, pp. 37–40.

30. Information about the Noelle Bush case came from David Wasson, "'Saddened' Bush turns to helping daughter," *The Tampa Tribune*, January 30, 2002; Lucy Morgan, "Gov.'s daughter charged with fraud," *St. Petersburg Times*, January 30, 2002; Ronald L. Littlepage, "Perhaps daughter's arrest will trigger new thinking," *The Florida Times-Union*, January 31, 2002; Daniel Ruth, "Isn't it a bit late to worry about Noelle's privacy?" *The Tampa Tribune*, October 11, 2002; and John-Thor Dahlburg, "President's niece sentenced," *Los Angeles Times*, October 18, 2002.

31. Howard Troxler, "Take Bush to task on issues – not misfortune," *St. Petersburg Times*, January 30, 2002.

32. Jean Scheidnes, "Bush twins take full stride into glare of the public eye," *The Austin American Statesman*, July 14, 2004.

33. Frank Wooten, "Proud pops Hodges, Sanford agree: Let their little boys be little boys," *The Post and Courier*, September 15, 2002.

34. "Regional headlines," *Dayton Daily News*, November 9, 2001.

35. Michael Arrieta-Walden, "Private details and public figures make for tough decisions," *Oregonian*, September 20, 2003.

36. Julia Reischel, "Charlie Crist is NOT gay and other things the Republican Party wants you to believe on Election Day," *Miami New Times*, October 19, 2006.

37. For example, see Adam C. Smith, "Crist confronts paternity claim," *St. Petersburg Times*, Sept. 4, 2006.

38. Steven A. Smith, "Stories result of 3-year investigation," *Spokesman Review*, May 5, 2005, p. A1.

39. Scott Maxwell, "The not-so-secret Crist rumors," *Orlando Sentinel*, November 4, 2006.

40. The Web site www.victoryfund.org tracks and supports gay politicians. Also see Curtis Bull, "Governing 101: gay politicians are going back to school to learn how to be more effective public officials," *The Advocate*, October 28, 2003.

41. Ken Darling, "And she was gay," *Lavender*, October 18, 2002.

13 Compassion and Photographers

When a critic for *The Denver Post* reviewed an exhibition of news photos that had won Pulitzer Prizes, she cautioned readers, "Don't expect many Kodak moments. Olympic victories and joyous reunions do figure into the mix, but Pulitzer Prize-winning photographs, generally speaking, are not pretty pictures."

She described the array of photographs:

> Here, in black and white and color, are gritty moments of national and global tragedy: war, famine, fire, natural disaster, drug addiction, crisis, crime... Here is a Zulu man on fire, a machete driven through his blazing skull... Here is the young woman in Nairobi after a forced circumcision. Here is the Andrea Doria sinking, the drug-addicted mother cradling her daughter, the husband and wife on a beach just after their toddler has been swept out to sea. Here is the famished Sudanese girl with a vulture lurking over her shoulder.

Larry Price, *Post* assistant managing editor for photography, agreed: "These pictures hit you square between the eyes." He should know. He won Pulitzers for pictures of 13 Liberian cabinet members being executed and of a human skeleton lying in a lava field in El Salvador.[1]

Pictures – particularly shocking pictures – taken by press photographers and television news crews have had a tremendous impact on society. Americans' attitudes toward wars have been affected. A picture of the flag being hoisted on a mountaintop on Iwo Jima during World War II raised American spirits at home. During the war in Vietnam, Americans were stunned by images of a small girl running from a village, her clothes burned off by napalm; a Vietnamese officer shooting a civilian in the side of the head at point-blank range; and Buddhist monks setting themselves on fire. A photo of an Army Ranger being dragged through the streets of Mogadishu, Somalia, caused Americans to reconsider the role the United States in world affairs. Photos of the brutal civil wars in Bosnia and Liberia, of those killed by the tsunami in South Asia, and of the massive famines in Africa have struck the conscience of the world.

American life has been affected by news photos and TV video. Some contend that a picture of lynching victim Emmett Till was the first media event of the civil-rights movement. The 14-year-old's head – bloated and missing an eye – was published in *Jet*, one of the most popular African-American magazines at the time. Chris Metress, the editor of a book about the lynching, said that countless blacks told him "that the *Jet* photo had this transformative effect on them, altering the way they felt about themselves and their vulnerabilities and the dangers they would be facing in the civil-rights movement."[2] In the 1960s and 1970s, the complacency of the nation was smashed as TV and press photographers captured the images of civil-rights marchers in the South being bitten by police dogs, of young people being knocked down by blasts of water from fire hoses, and of police manhandling students, ministers, and community leaders whose offense was wanting to buy a sandwich at a lunch counter. Pictures of the despair in hurricane-wracked New Orleans and Mississippi captivated Americans and led to record giving to relief charities.

Peg Finucane, a former *Newsday* editor, argues that, as distasteful as they are, brutal pictures may be needed to reach the hearts and engage the emotions of Americans. She wrote:

> Newspapers should never have to publish photographs of dead people in a natural disaster; these photographs carry no extra information that can't be provided in a story, and sometimes they block our understanding of widespread devastation by emphasizing one victim or even several. As distasteful as it seems, however, a shot of this kind may be necessary to get the attention of jaded American audiences.[3]

Shocking pictures can also prompt many people to accuse the news media of sensationalism, insensitivity, and exploitation. Pulitzer prize-winning photographer James Dickman described the power of photography. "It's 1/500th of a second frozen, a slice of time. Readers can really look at that silver-and-paper image and make their own conclusions." But he added, "A camera is an intrusive tool. You're pointing it at something. You're taking away a moment. You're taking away privacy."[4]

Pictures of War and Death

The Associated Press Managing Editors compared the reactions of about 2,500 readers and more than 400 editors and reporters when they were shown five sensitive photos. They included a picture of a mother mourning infants who were killed by the tsunami in Asia and four from the Iraqi war: flag-draped coffins of military personnel returning from Iraq, election workers being shot in the streets of Iraq, a wounded American soldier being cared for by other soldiers, and a captured American sitting at the feet of men who were planning to behead him.

The results were surprising. "In each case, more journalists than readers wanted to run photos on the front page, and a higher percentage of readers would have not run images at all," *Editor & Publisher* magazine reported. For example, the picture of a flag-draped coffin would have been used on Page 1 by 92 percent of journalists and 66 percent of readers. About 1 percent of journalists and 12 percent of readers thought the picture did not belong in the paper.[5]

Ryan Pitts, who oversaw the study, wrote that many people said some of the pictures made them feel as if they were intruding on a sacred moment. The picture of the mother in mourning brought this response: "If your child were killed in some horrific manner, would you rush a reporter to get a picture of your wife's reaction? If not, why does this woman deserve less dignity?"

Others put themselves into the shoes of the families who might see the pictures of their loved ones. One reader rejected the picture of the wounded soldier. She said:

> I feel really strongly about this picture as I have a military son. I do not want to see his dead body in the newspaper and have it run for years and years to catch me unawares any time there is a "retrospective" about the war.

Several offered that the harm the picture might do to loved ones outweighed any good it might do; 30 percent of readers and 21 percent of journalists would have avoided it altogether.

Some were hesitant to show the bodies of dead children. The journalists pointed out that many papers have policies against using pictures of the dead, although they would have used it if they were in charge. About two-thirds of journalists and 56 percent of readers agreed that the photo belonged in the paper.

Another concern raised was the so-called cereal question: "Would I want my family to see this photo at the breakfast table tomorrow morning?" Both journalists and the public saw that as an important consideration. Some newspapers deal with this question by putting notes with stories that link to the pictures on their Web sites. Other papers, like *The Salt Lake Tribune,* print a "reader alert" on the front page warning about the nature of the photo and the page on which it appears.

Kelly McBride, a media ethicist at the Poynter Institute, was not surprised that journalists were more likely to publish the pictures. She believes journalists probably have different philosophic orientations. McBride said:

> It's probably safe to say that journalists as a group are more likely to ground their moral decisions in duty. They believe it is their duty to inform. In the wider public arena, a greater portion of people are going to ground their moral decisions in care. That means they would be concerned about harming the people in the photos, as well as the audience who might view the photo.

Ethical and emotional issues were not the only considerations cited by the public and journalists in the survey. Many said they thought decisions should also be based on what the political impact of the pictures might be. They rejected the picture of the captive American because it seemed to serve the propaganda needs of the terrorists. One journalist noted the video was given to the media by the terrorists. "In the same way that running a slick PR photo provided by a corporation undermines your journalistic independence, so does running photos provided by terrorists," she said. "You further their agenda." Concerns about political impact sometimes led to different conclusions. The pictures of the flag-draped coffins were rejected by some because they said it raised questions about the need for the war in Iraq. Others contended that it honored soldiers who had given their lives to their nation and therefore strengthened the nation's patriotism.

Pictures of Grief

Pictures of grieving relatives have become a common fixture at many news outlets. They probably receive the most criticism from the public – and stir up heated debates among journalists.

The argument for using these pictures is that they help explain an event to readers. After *The San Diego Union-Tribune* ran a picture of a weeping father alongside a casket with his teenage son's body, many accused the paper of sensationalism and invasion of the family's privacy. Gina Lubrano, the paper's reader representative, defended the picture: "The images of the mourning father told the story visually and helped readers better understand the events." She contended that it was the father's grief that "reached out of the page and into your hearts that some readers were so upset by it."[6]

A similar argument was made after a freelance photographer for *The Orange County Register* in California snapped a picture of a woman just as a police officer confirmed that her husband had died. Pat Riley, the *Register's* ombudsman at the time, said:

> It mirrored emotional reality in a powerful way and aroused our empathy. It did not, in my view, hold the woman up to ridicule. It showed her expressing natural understandable suffering, and we could all feel it.[7]

A second argument for using these shocking pictures is that the pictures can teach readers lessons about life. The managing editor of *The Californian* in Bakersfield defended a picture of the lifeless body of a 5-year-old boy surrounded by his distraught family on the ground that it might remind parents to be more careful when their kids are swimming (see Figure 13.1).[8] Some journalists push this argument to its limits. The editors of the *New York Post* ran a front-page picture of the crushed body, uncovered and face up, of the 4-year-old son of guitarist Eric Clapton after he fell from a 53rd-floor window of an apartment building. The paper claimed that it used the picture not because the victim was Clapton's son, but because it wanted to warn people of the dangers of children playing near open windows in high-rise apartments.[9]

Are the photos needed to tell the story?

However, others contend that readers and viewers don't need to see pictures to understand the grief that people suffer when they lose loved ones. That was the decision of editors at the *Star-Telegram* in Fort Worth in covering the funeral of a 6-year-old who police believed was killed by his older sister and brother. His family wanted his funeral to be private. Photographers did not go to the funeral, but gathered across the street from the cemetery and took pictures of graveside services

Figure 13.1 A family's anguish. As the weeping father kneels over the body of his young son, a rescue worker (*left*) tries to console the drowning victim's brother and other family members. The editor who ran this picture said he wished he hadn't. (*Photo courtesy of* The Californian, *Bakersfield, Calif.*)

with long lenses. The photos were "powerful, capturing a sense of the depth of grief at the service." But editors decided that "picturing those parents in that private moment would be intrusive." One editor at the *Star-Telegram* saw no reason to run pictures like these at all. He argued, "I didn't see how the photos would advance the public's knowledge of the event in any significant way." [10]

Other editors have made similar comments. *Boston Globe* ombudsman Mark Jurkowitz called a picture of a man grieving over his slain brother "gratuitous." Minneapolis *Star Tribune* ombudsman Lou Gelfand criticized his paper for running a picture of a man falling to his knees and crying after he had learned his daughter had died and another of a young man weeping after hearing that a friend had been killed in a car crash. He contended, "Denying the readers this view of someone's grief would not have shortchanged the news report."[11]

Occasionally, editors weigh the needs of telling the story against the impact the photo will have on readers' sensibilities and decide that running the picture is the right thing to do. In Hartford, Conn., a 7-year-old girl was celebrating the Fourth of July at a peaceful family picnic. As she was riding her scooter on a sidewalk, a group of people got into an argument and began shooting. One of the bullets went astray and hit the little girl in the face.

It was not the first case of violence in the area, and editors at *The Hartford Courant* were already "struggling with how to report what they thought was an epidemic of shootings" that may have been drug-related, according to Elissa Papirno, the paper's ombudsman. When editors heard of the shooting of the little girl, they thought they could use this tragedy as the first step in bringing attention to the problem.

Editors sent a reporter and photographer to the hospital to talk to the girl's family. The reporter found several of her relatives and began to interview them. Meanwhile, the photographer stayed in the background and left his cameras in their cases. When he believed the family was comfortable with the reporter, he asked if he could take some pictures of the girl. They agreed.

Looking at his film later that night, editors were drawn to the close-up image of the girl with her breathing tube and swollen eyes and lips. Editor Brian Toolan told Papirno that editors asked themselves, "Is this exploitative or is this the jarring evidence that we all need to fix the problems in the neighborhood?" After considerable discussion, they decided to run the picture large at the top of the front page.

Dozens of readers said they understood the paper's motives in printing the picture, but they did not think a picture of an injured child was the best way to highlight the problem. They thought the picture was insensitive, exploited the girl's pain, and violated the family's privacy.

Deputy Managing Editor Barbara Roessner told Papirno that she understood the emotional reactions the pictures prompted. "It often takes the brutal assault on a child who is indisputably innocent to affect people, to have an impact on their emotions," she said. "It's too bad that we in the media and the public stay brutally numb until that occurs."[12]

Sometimes ethical decisions about photographs become easier when journalists ask themselves what story they hope the picture tells. Editors at *The Tampa Tribune* decided not to use pictures of the bloody bodies of the sons of Saddam Hussein because the graphic photos were not essential to understanding the full impact of the story. They thought the pictures would do little more than shock readers and perhaps offend them. They reasoned that the real story for Americans was how Iraqis were reacting to the deaths and the release of the pictures. "That's why we went with a front-page photo showing Iraqis watching a television set that had the photos on the screen. From that distance, we also thought it was tasteful enough for the front page," an editor explained. Editors linked to the more graphic photos on their Web site.[13]

John Long, a former president of the National Press Photographers Association, suggests that the following questions can help separate images that need to be used from the merely sensational:

- Does the event have an impact on the community in general?
- Is there an overriding societal interest in the event?
- Does the photo further our understanding of some aspect of our community and help us make informed choices as a community?[14]

Should Journalists Help Victims?

Journalists – particularly photographers for print and television – frequently get into ethical difficulties at news events. Sometimes they are on the scene before or as emergency responders are arriving. Often there are people in need of help. The humane side of journalists encourages them to jump in and help. Yet, their professional responsibility is to provide the public with an understanding of the tragedy.

The clash of responsibilities is particularly burdensome for photographers. Reporters can put down a notepad for a few minutes and then go back to work. They have time to gather their thoughts and decide what to include and what to exclude from their stories. Photographers, however, may have only one opportunity to take the picture. They have to react now. If they miss the photo, it's gone. It's often even harder for television news crews. Print photographers can follow the axiom: "Get the pictures, let the editors decide what to do with them later." TV photographers may not have that luxury. Their images are often being broadcast live.

For many years, journalists defined objectivity to mean that they were fundamentally uninvolved observers of news events. During the Vietnam War in the 1960s, TV camera crews went to protests, many of which were staged for the Western media, and filmed Buddhist monks setting themselves on fire and burning to death. As horrible as the scene must have been to experience, none of the photographers made an effort to stop the suicides. Perhaps even more surprising – given the level of media criticism today – the photographers received little or no criticism from the American public. The sentiment of the day was that the photographer's job was to record the news, not to intervene.

Twenty years later, a man called a local TV station in Alabama and said he was going to set himself on fire in the town square to protest unemployment. Once the photographer had his equipment ready, the man doused himself with charcoal starter fluid and applied a lighted match. The photographer filmed the horror for several seconds before his partner rushed forward and tried to beat out the flames with his small reporter's notebook. The man survived but spent eight painful weeks in a hospital.[15]

As horrible as the events that day were, news accounts the next day focused on the question of the professional obligations of journalists. The public, scholars, and journalists agreed that the journalists' behavior and the underlying creed of emotional detachment were no longer acceptable. William Sanders, then president of the National Press Photographers Association, concluded he "would give up a picture to help somebody in trouble" because "you're a member of the human race first and a journalist second."[16]

That was also the thinking of Chris DeVitto, a young photographer for *The Lima* (Ohio) *News,* when he came upon a traffic accident in which a woman was trapped in her overturned car and was dangling upside down, being held in place by a seat belt. "My first instinct was to render aid to the victim," DeVitto said. He rushed to the car without his cameras. When he saw that the woman was not badly hurt and after being told that paramedics had been called, DeVitto got his camera and took some pictures (Figure 13.2).

Chris Merrifield of WWL-TV in New Orleans also put human life first. He waded into chest-deep water to pull a driver through the window of a sinking car. His boss told *USA Today*: "The kid just reacted.

Figure 13.2   Dangling by the seatbelt. Before taking the photo, the photographer ensured that the woman was not badly hurt and that paramedics were called. (*Photo courtesy of* The Lima *[Ohio]* News.)

We're proud of what he did. I would hope all of our people would do something like that rather than let someone drown."[17]

Journalist or rescue worker?

Often the decisions faced by journalists at tragedies are not as straightforward as those faced by Merrifield and DeVitto. Writing in *American Journalism Review*, Rachel Smolkin cited the experience of *The Washington Post's* Anne Hull, who interviewed a homeless woman and her hungry 6-year-old grandson trapped on an Interstate bypass after Katrina hit New Orleans. Hull said she followed her own ethical framework that while covering catastrophes, "we must try to remember that we are journalists trying to cover a story. That is our role in the world, and if we perform it well, it is an absolutely unique service: helping the world understand something as it happens."

But Hull was conflicted when the grandmother asked if Hull would take her and her grandson to Baton Rouge, where they could find help.

Hull knew that they had no place to sleep that night. "How can you explain that to somebody, why you can't take them to a shelter?" Hull asked. If Hull helped rescue the pair, it would change the story she planned to write about them. "I usually focus on an individual caught up in a situation," she explained, "and my role is to document how they figure their way out of it and the feelings that accompany them as they do it." Hull was torn. She wanted to help, but her journalistic principles told her not to. She called her editor for guidance. "I'm struggling here," she told him. She said her editor reminded her, "You're not an aid worker. You're not a rescue worker."

Hull continued to give water, PowerBars, and wet-naps to struggling survivors, according to Smolkin. She let countless people use her cell phone to call loved ones. But she concluded that when her notebook was still open and she was still gathering facts, she couldn't rescue someone by driving them out of New Orleans. "That seems to go beyond the line of duty for a journalist." Later, as Hull was sitting under an Interstate overpass writing her story on her laptop, a medic asked her if she was OK. She directed him to the grandmother and told him, "She needs your help." The medics took the pair to a shelter in Northern Louisiana. "If you can be of any help in giving assistance, by all means, do it," Hull advised.

Smolkin interviewed other reporters for her *AJR* article. The day after the storm, Brian Thevenot and photographer Ted Jackson of *The Times-Picayune* in New Orleans were in a boat in the hardest-hit area of the city. "We were doing our jobs," Thevenot explained. "We were chronicling what we were seeing. But if somebody needed a lift on the boat, we gave it to them. It didn't impede my job. I spent 98 percent of my time doing straight journalism and letting other people do the jobs they were there to do."

Smolkin advised journalists that if they are the only people around, they should do what they can to help:

> Remember, though, that your primary – and unique – role as a journalist is to bear witness. If you decide to act, do so quickly, then get out of the way. Leave the rescue work to first responders and relief workers whenever possible. The journalists covering Katrina showed compassion by offering water, rides and rescue, but their most enduring service was to expose the suffering of citizens trapped in hellish shelters and on sweltering Interstates, and to document the inexcusable government response. Without journalists fulfilling that essential role, the resources to help on a larger scale might never have arrived.[18]

Years ago, Martin Luther King gave similar advice to a photographer from *Life* magazine. When sheriff's deputies were shoving children to the ground during a civil-rights march in Selma, Ala., the photographer stopped taking pictures and went to the aid of the children. King heard about the incident and reminded him:

> The world doesn't know this happened, because you didn't photograph it. I'm not being cold-blooded about it, but it is so much more important for you to take a picture of us getting beaten up than for you to be another person joining in the fray.[19]

The public often does not understand this role of journalists. NPR's ombudsman said his network was swamped by calls from listeners who wanted to know why the network didn't just turn over its communication system to authorities whose systems had been knocked out by Katrina. Others wondered why if the TV networks could assemble the hundreds of employees to broadcast from New Orleans, they couldn't just airlift food and water to the Superdome. They apparently assumed the media could pull off a task that the National Guard couldn't. The Freedom Forum's Paul McMasters understands their questions. "Journalists step back from the fray to serve humanity on a different level," he said. "Yet journalists have been largely incapable of making that point to the American people."

Even when journalists do help, most believe they should not broadcast their own efforts because it appears to be "showboating." Fred Brown, former chair of the SPJ ethics committee, said, "It's more modest and thus nobler to help quietly and behind the scenes than to do it with cameras rolling."[20] NPR's Dvorkin agreed. He believed that when the news media broadcast their acts of kindness, it "ends up looking, sounding self-serving and manipulative." Bob Woodruff of ABC encouraged journalists to help people as much as the demands of their jobs allow. But he advised: "Never do it and roll on it with your cameras. By definition, if you need to do it, then your cameraman should need to do it as well... The real ones don't shoot it."[21]

Notes

1. Colleen Smith, "Pulitzer prize winners' exhibit a bracing photo album of historic moments," *The Denver Post*, August 30, 2004.
2. Quoted in Shaila Dewan, "How photos became icon of civil rights movement," *The New York Times*, August 28, 2005.

3. Peg Finucane, "The media can help us put a calamity like the recent tsunami in the right perspective without drowning us in violent imagery," *Newsday,* January 7, 2005.
4. Quoted in Smith, *op. cit.*
5. Joe Strupp, "AP polls journos, readers on sensitive shots," *Editor and Publisher,* March 1, 2005.
6. Gina Lubrano, "Choosing photos to tell the story," *The San Diego Union-Tribune,* March 25, 2002.
7. Richard Cunningham, "Child photos: Drawing the line," *Quill,* February 1988.
8. "Graphic excess," *Washington Journalism Review,* January 1986.
9. Richard Harwood, "Sometimes compassion," *The Washington Post,* April 28, 1991.
10. David House, "Practicing restraint and good news judgment," *Fort Worth Star-Telegram,* April 28, 2002.
11. Quoted in Richard Cunningham, "Seeking a time-out on prurience," *Quill,* March 1992.
12. Elissa Papirno, "A humanizing or dehumanizing photo?," *The Hartford Courant,* July 15, 2001.
13. "Media explain treatment of bodies' photos" *The Tampa Tribune,* August 2, 2003.
14. John Long, "Reflections by NPPA's Ethics and Standards Committee co-chairs," *News Photographer,* April 1998.
15. Nathan Kvinge, "Death on tape," *News Photographer,* April 1998.
16. Gannett News Service, *News Watch,* June 2, 1991.
17. Quoted from Fred Brown, "Getting involved is better than 'stony detachment,'" *Quill,* October/November 2005.
18. Rachel Smolkin, "Off the sidelines," *American Journalism Review,* December 2005/January 2006.
19. Gene Roberts and Hank Klibanoff, *The Race Beat: The Press, the Civil Rights Struggle, and the Awakening of a Nation,* New York: Random House, 2006.
20. Brown, *op. cit.*
21. Smolkin, *op. cit.*

Part 5 Conflicts of Interest

14 Journalists and Their Communities

More than 300,000 people crowded the streets of Washington, D.C., carrying pro-choice banners and singing protest songs. They were hoping to send a message to the U.S. Supreme Court that they disagreed with its ruling in *Webster* v. *Reproductive Health Services*, which many believed was a signal that the court was going to overturn its decision in *Roe* v. *Wade*, which legalized abortion.

A protest of this size was a major media event. Hundreds of journalists were on the scene. Among them was Linda Greenhouse, a *New York Times* reporter who covers the Supreme Court. But she wasn't there to report on the demonstration. She was there with the marchers who were protesting the decision. And she wasn't the only reporter who participated in the march: Dozens of journalists from papers all over the country were also among the protesters.

When these journalists returned to their newsrooms, many received a jolt. They got messages from their editors telling them that they had violated their newspapers' codes of ethics. The codes banned them from participating in any activities that may create or appear to create conflicts of interest.

Many of these journalists and some of their editors said they did not know that participating in the march would be considered unethical. When Greenhouse told the Washington bureau chief for the *Times* about her participation, his first reactions were that she had done nothing wrong. "People's private expressions are their own business," he told her. Then he checked the *Times'* guidelines on ethics and found a clause that seemed to ban such activities:

> The integrity of *The Times* requires that its staff members avoid employment or any other undertakings, obligations, relationships or investments

that create or appear to create a conflict of interest with their professional work for *The Times* or otherwise compromises *The Times'* independence and reputation.

But he still wasn't sure the rule would apply to Greenhouse's participation in the march. So he checked with *Times* editors in New York and learned that Max Frankel, then executive editor, was committed to the policy. He was told, "Max's view is that, as an example, you cannot cover the White House and wear a campaign button."[1]

Greenhouse and other *Times'* staffers were not punished by their paper for their participation in the march. She stayed on the Supreme Court beat because, her bureau chief said, "We have full faith and confidence in her professionalism. It's part of our profession that we try to discipline opinions, not that we're opinion-free."

But she was criticized by other journalists. "Most of my colleagues thought I was a jerk to be there," Greenhouse said, "and they let me know that, either politely or impolitely."[2] Some thought the *Times* let her off too easily. Eileen McNamara, who covered the abortion issue for *The Boston Globe* at the time of the march, said that Greenhouse had made "a terrible mistake" in marching and that the *Times* had "made a bad mistake in allowing her to continue to cover the issue." Greenhouse said she would follow the newspaper's policy and not participate in any more pro-choice rallies. "I don't intend to make a martyr of myself. I wouldn't want to do anything to undermine the credibility and objectivity of the profession," she told *Time* magazine.[3]

More than 15 years later, Greenhouse, whose coverage of the Supreme Court won a Pulitzer prize in 1998, was back in the hot seat. During a speech to 800 people at Harvard University, she was critical of the Bush administration and what she called "the hijacking of public policy by religious fundamentalism." The paper's public editor said the speech clearly stepped over the line set by the *Times* code of ethics, which limits reporters to stating in public factual statements what they could also write in news stories. Greenhouse said that she considered the statements factual and believed she "owed this audience the respect to speak from the heart."[4]

There's the problem in a nutshell. Many journalists want to be involved in their communities, yet they are aware that these involvements can lead to conflicts of interest – or the appearance of conflicts of interest. They may cause the public to wonder whether these journalists have given up their independence and ability to report truthfully. Such doubts are taken seriously by those in a profession in which being believed is everything.

Journalists and Free Speech

When Greenhouse's editor heard of her participation in the march, his first response was that she had done nothing wrong since she was expressing her opinions on her own time. Bosses in most businesses would probably say the same thing: "At work, you live by our rules; after work you are free to do pretty much what you want." But often that's not the way it works in journalism. Most newspapers and television stations have policies limiting what reporters and editors can say and do even when they are not at work.

Several newspapers and TV news departments have reminded their staffs not to participate in public demonstrations. In 2006 *The Morning Call* in Allentown, Pa., suspended for two days a feature writer for taking part in a local Gay Pride parade.[5] Many journalists were banned from attending concerts by Bruce Springsteen, Pearl Jam, and other rock groups that were fundraisers for the Democrats in the 2004 elections. One exception was the *Cleveland Plain Dealer,* where the editor said he considered the concert in his city an "entertainment thing" and that his staff could go.[6]

Many reporters have encountered problems in their professional lives for things they did in their private lives. Among them:

- A pro-choice reporter at a newspaper in South Florida was fired after she mailed miniature coat hangers, symbols of the procedures used when abortions were illegal, to every member of the Florida Legislature.
- *San Francisco Chronicle* suspended without pay technology columnist Henry Norr after he participated in a protest rally at the beginning of the U.S. invasion of Iraq.[7]
- Editors of *The New York Times* "made clear their disapproval" of reporter Michael Gordon for stating what he described as his "purely personal view" on a late-night talk show on PBS. Gordon defended President Bush's decision to send more troops to Iraq in 2007.[8]
- A reporter at *The Press Democrat* in Santa Rosa, Calif., was taken off coverage of the timber industry after a weekly paper quoted him as praising organizers of an anti-logging protest.[9]
- Some journalists criticized Nina Totenberg, National Public Radio's award-winning Supreme Court reporter, when she asked Supreme Court Justice Ruth Bader Ginsburg to officiate at her wedding. Totenberg countered: "I've known Ruth Ginsburg long before she

was on the Supreme Court. I'm delighted that she officiated at my wedding, and I do not consider it a conflict of interest."[10]

- Many news organizations have asked reporters not to join groups like the National Organization for Women or the National Rifle Association because these organizations become entangled in political issues.

Even expressing opinions in what they thought were private e-mails has caused problems for journalists. Farnaz Fassihi, a Middle East correspondent for *The Wall Street Journal*, wrote an e-mail to her friends describing the dangers of being a reporter in Iraq during the sectarian violence in 2006. She said:

> I avoid going to people's homes and never walk in the streets. I can't go grocery shopping any more, can't eat in restaurants, can't strike a conversation with strangers, can't look for stories, can't drive in any thing but a full armored car, can't go to scenes of breaking news stories, can't be stuck in traffic, can't speak English outside, can't take a road trip, can't say I'm an American, can't linger at checkpoints, can't be curious about what people are saying, doing, feeling. And can't and can't.

The e-mail was forwarded by her friends to their friends. Before long, it was being quoted in newspapers all over the world as part of stories about the role and abilities of journalists in Iraq. Fassihi also had to defend herself for violating conflict-of-interest policies:

> Here I was a reporter who had an opinion about the Iraq war, had voiced it privately to her friends and suddenly it was for public view. I was caught in between; one side praised me for speaking the truth about the mess Iraq had become and the other side accused me of showing bias and demanded I be reassigned.[11]

Personal blogs can also be troublesome. To head off problems, CBS News has a formal policy that requires all personal blogs to be approved by top-level managers. "We can't have people having personal blogs venting their opinions," a news executive said.[12]

Journalists and community service

Some believe that requiring journalists to avoid social issues is wrongheaded. *Rockford* (Ill.) *Register Star* executive editor Linda Grist Cunningham contends that the "we're-observers-only" tradition of journalism has hurt the news media "because we got real out of touch with the people for whom we were writing and about whom we were writing. We had a real superficial knowledge of things."[13] Yet journalists' efforts to be part of the real world sometimes draw them into the awkward position of being newsmakers themselves.

When Randy Hammer was the editor of the Marion, Ind., *Chronicle-Tribune,* he was asked to serve on the board of a workshop for disabled people. His employer, the Gannett chain, which often moves people from newspaper to newspaper, was making a push to get its people in touch with their communities. Hammer thought that a workshop for the disabled would be perfect. After all, he reasoned, helping the disabled is hardly a controversial cause.

It didn't work out that way for Hammer. The board voted to build a group home for people with disabilities in middle of a residential neighborhood, but the neighbors didn't want the home. When the paper editorialized that the home's opponents were narrow-minded, the neighborhood was angry. They believed that because Hammer was on the board, the newspaper was involved in making a decision and then criticizing those who disagreed. Hammer said. "They said the newspaper and I were part of a plot to destroy their neighborhood." Hammer's problems increased when the board worked out its strategy to respond to the neighborhood's challenge. As so often happens when journalists serve on such community panels, the board asked Hammer to keep the plans secret. At that point, he decided he had to resign from the board.[14]

Because journalists are good writers, groups often expect them to handle public relations chores like putting out brochures and alerting the media to the groups' events. Many papers forbid the practice because they can foresee conflicts of interest. But not all take that precautionary policy. At a Catholic church near Tampa, some female parishioners accused their priest of making sexual advances. Happening in the wake of a series of sex scandals involving priests, the allegations were big news. When reporters checked the church Web page to get the name of the person who handled media relations, they found that the phone numbers and e-mail addresses listed were for the Tampa bureau of the *St. Petersburg Times.* The church's volunteer public-relations liaison was a reporter there. As the investigation of the priest grew more involved, she dealt with media requests, counseled the priest on how to answer reporters' questions, and alerted at least one TV station to the breaking story.

Many journalists were surprised at her dual role. "If the reporter is advising the priest on significant matters that are newsworthy, the reporter clearly has competing loyalties," said Bob Steele, an ethicist at Poynter Institute, which owns the paper where the reporter worked. Editors at the *Times* said her conduct did not violate the paper's policies, although they wished she had not used her office phone number and e-mail address.

Many journalists said their papers would have taken tougher stands. Chris Chinlund, the ombudsman at *The Boston Globe*, said her conduct would violate her paper's rules. "I tend to take a pretty hard line on this stuff and say, 'We're journalists, and we can't afford even the appearance of a conflict.'" Gary Hill, a Minneapolis television journalist who was chair of the ethics committee of the Society of Professional Journalists at the time, said the reporter crossed a "shifting line" of what's ethical. "Most journalists would think it's OK to be involved in church, but I think you've got to draw a line at what role you play inside the church," Hill said.[15]

Many news organizations try to find a middle ground. The code of ethics at *The Virginian-Pilot* in Norfolk, Va., says it is fine for journalists to join civic organizations if they have no say in how those organizations are covered by the paper. Journalists, however, cannot "appear publicly on behalf of a civic group or themselves."[16]

Editors at *The Hartford* (Conn.) *Courant* were so suspicious of any appearance of conflict of interest that they once refused to run an Ann Landers column suggesting that readers give money to the Hereditary Disease Foundation. Landers was a longtime member of the group's board of directors. *Courant* editors noted that the paper had a policy against reporters writing about groups they were associated with, and they thought the rule ought to apply to Landers too.[17] On first glance, such conduct may seem hard to justify. No one suggested that the Hereditary Disease Foundation was not a fine charity. Yet, there are hundreds of fine charities. The question becomes: Is it right for a newspaper to endorse a charity because a columnist is on the board of directors and not to give similar support to the fundraising efforts of all the others?

Journalists and political parties

Many journalists have been embarrassed and criticized when they get too closely involved with political campaigns:

- A newspaper investigation named 17 journalists who contributed to a gubernatorial candidate in Massachusetts a total of $2,530, a small sum in a $1 million campaign. Most quickly asked for the return of their donations.

- A writer for *The Newton Tab*, a community paper owned by *The Boston Herald,* was heavily criticized for writing a flattering profile of a candidate after donating to his campaign.[18]
- Former CBS News anchor Dan Rather admitted he made an "embarrassing and regrettable error" when he was the star attraction at a Democratic Party fundraiser in Texas. CBS News was swamped by phone calls from people saying that Rather's action proved what they had thought all along: Rather was a Democrat masquerading as an objective reporter.[19]
- Rather was under attack again when his daughter donated $1,500 to the Kerry campaign in 2004.[20]
- A reporter in Knoxville wanted to make a "positive contribution" to her local schools by running in a nonpartisan race for election to a school board. Her paper's policy seemed to outlaw such behavior, and her editor gave her a choice: Keep the $25-a-month school board job or keep her job at the newspaper – but not both. Even though the race was nonpartisan, her editor pointed out the board spent hundreds of thousands of taxpayer dollars and was actively covered by the newspaper.
- Reporters from news organizations ranging from *The Miami Herald,* to the Duluth, Minn., newspapers, to WESH-TV in Orlando, Fla., have quit or been fired when they decided to become political candidates. Most newspaper codes specifically ban newsroom employees from running for or holding any elective office.

Why limit journalists' rights?

Many journalists believe there are several reasons that news people should not take part in public issues. They argue that as people participate in marches and organizations that promote causes, they become more deeply involved in these issues. The concern is not that reporters might deliberately slant their stories. Editors are supposed to keep that from happening. The fear is that while gathering information, they might unintentionally treat people who agree with them more favorably and unconsciously rely on these sources more heavily.

Many people have wondered whether this kind of unintentional bias may have affected media coverage of the abortion debate. "If you are a woman reporter under the age of about 50... you are writing about something that could happen to you," said Cynthia Gorney, who covered abortion for *The Washington Post*. She told *Los Angeles Times* media writer David Shaw:

> You're going to have a view on it... There's no way you can set that aside. The issue is whether you can, while holding that view, listen seriously to people of all stripes on this issue... and do what reporters are supposed to do... shed light and make clear why people hold the positions that they do.[21]

Some anti-abortion activists have argued that many reporters unconsciously ask tougher questions of anti-abortion leaders and seem less willing to take their opinions seriously. Shaw spent 18 months studying the media's coverage of the abortion issue and then wrote a four-part series in which he concluded:

> [W]hile responsible journalists do try hard to be fair, the culture in most big-city newsrooms automatically embraces the abortion rights side of the argument, and this results – however unwittingly – in scores of examples, large and small, that can only be characterized as unfair to the opponents of abortion, either in content, tone, choice or language or prominence of play.

Shaw cited a study of the *New York Times, Washington Post*, and the evening news on ABC, NBC, and CBS that found that women reporters quoted twice as many supporters of abortion rights as they quoted opponents of abortion. Among women newspaper reporters, the tilt was 3–1. At the same time, men reporters were evenly split on the use of supporters and opponents of abortion rights. News executives and reporters at these news organizations told Shaw that they thought their coverage was fair.

Leonard Downie, executive editor at *The Washington Post*, is so concerned that journalists may allow their personal opinions to unconsciously slant their coverage of political issues that he would prefer reporters not to vote. Going through the process of judging a candidate's fitness for office may subtly influence what reporters write, in Downie's view. That's why he has refrained from voting in any election in which he played a role in the paper's coverage. The *Post*, along with papers like *The Philadelphia Inquirer*, does not allow its staff to take part in any activity that might compromise the paper's credibility regardless of whether they are covering the issue.

Many reporters who joined the Washington abortion rights march were not only embarrassed by the criticism from their editors, but they were further chagrined when they learned that pro-life groups were using their participation in the march "to prove" their argument that the media were biased against them.

Too many restrictions?

Many journalists think the restrictions now in place at many newspapers intrude far too much into their private lives. They contend that they can express their opinions publicly and still do their jobs. Once the public sees that their stories are fair, there will be no loss of credibility.

A. Kent MacDougall, a former *Wall Street Journal* reporter and journalism professor, argued, "A well-trained reporter with pride in his craft won't allow his beliefs to distort his stories, any more than a Republican surgeon will botch an appendectomy on a Democrat."[22]

Many journalists would agree. They contend that placing limits on journalists' free speech is only a cosmetic effort to mask the fact that journalists have opinions. They argue that reporters' stories will be the same whether they keep quiet about their opinions or whether they express them openly. "There's a certain hypocrisy in trying to have the public think that just because a reporter doesn't march, he or she is somehow more objective than somebody who does march," *Newsday* columnist Gabriel Rotello told *American Journalism Review*.[23]

Some reporters contend that off duty, journalists should have the same rights as other Americans. Sandy Nelson of the *Tacoma* (Wash.) *Morning News Tribune* argued that newspapers treat journalists "like serfs." She said, "We have become the company's property 24 hours a day." When Nelson openly campaigned in support of the city's ban on discrimination because of sexual orientation, her editors moved her from a reporting position to the copy desk. Nelson sued to get her reporting job back. She cited a state law prohibiting employers from discriminating against employees because of their political activities. However, the state Supreme Court ruled against her. The court decided newspapers were an exception because they needed to prohibit political activism by reporters to protect their credibility. The U.S. Supreme Court let the ruling stand.[24]

Some believe that a blanket statement in a code of ethics banning any participation in public issues too sharply limits journalists' rights. But they also would acknowledge that when journalists feel very strongly about issues, they should not play a role in covering them. These writers, such as Deni Elliott of the University of South Florida, believe all reporters have at least one issue they feel so strongly about that they should not be allowed to write about it.[25]

When spouses, family, friends cause conflicts

After Rik Hayman decided to run for a seat on the Bay County Commission in Michigan, one of the first things he did was to put a large banner in his front yard. The wording wasn't very original, "Rik Hayman for County Commissioner," but the sign quickly became controversial.

Hayman's wife, Jalene Jameson, was the assistant metro editor for features at *The Bay City Times*. The paper has a strict policy against employees posting political signs in their yards or on the bumpers of their cars. Editor Tony Dearing told Jameson she had a choice: take the sign down or go on unpaid leave until the election was over. Dearing told the Associated Press:

> We think this is a pretty fundamental point, that journalists in the newsroom need to maintain objectivity and remain nonpolitical. We understand that Rik wants to put a sign up, but this is a case where Jalene is an editor in the newsroom, and we are asking her to comply with this policy.

Jameson decided to go on unpaid leave rather than remove her husband's campaign banner. When the company said she would not receive health insurance benefits while she was on leave, her husband decided to move the banner to a neighbor's yard.[26]

In Seattle, Elaine Bowers, the new bride of *Seattle Times* managing editor Michael R. Fancher, quit her job as press secretary to the mayor after only a day. Her job qualifications were not in doubt. She had been a reporter for *The Star* in Kansas City and the *Houston Chronicle* and had worked as press secretary to Missouri Gov. Kit Bond for two years. But if she stayed on in her new job in the mayor's office, her husband was going to lose his. *Seattle Times* management informed him that his wife's job put him in violation of the paper's ethics code. It states that staffers are not to make news judgments about individuals they are related to by blood or marriage. If she took the job, he would be transferred out of the newsroom. Bowers ended up taking a public relations job with the Seattle Public Health Hospital. Fancher was allowed to continue as managing editor, but had to remove himself from any news involving the hospital. Later he was promoted to executive editor.[27]

Other news organizations have taken less strident stands. CBS allowed Rita Braver to cover the Clinton White House even though her husband, Robert Barnett, was an old friend of the Clintons and worked for a while as a lawyer on the president's Whitewater defense team. According to Howard Kurtz of *The Washington Post*, Clinton thought Braver was unduly harsh on him just to prove her independence. He even joked to her, "You should get a divorce so you can go a little easier on me."[28]

A more common problem for journalists lies with friendships. Donald Smith, editor of the *Monticello* (Minn.) *Times*, recalled an incident in which a friend's son was caught stealing goods from parked cars. Shortly before deadline, the friend called him. "The grieving parent knows me well. I could feel her pain. Publication of the young man's name in our newspaper would make the situation worse, she hinted, raising even the possibility of suicide due to publication and pending court action." She asked if her son's name could be removed from the sheriff's report. Smith told the woman that since his paper prints every arrest, in fairness, he would have to run her son's name.[29]

Other editors in small cities have also felt peer pressure. In Port Angeles, Wash., a local doctor was suspected, but not charged, in the smothering death of a newborn baby. When the *Peninsula Daily News* printed the doctor's name, some of the doctor's friends tried to block editor John Brewer's nomination to the local Rotary Club.[30]

Reporters and Diverse Communities

In February 2004, San Francisco's decision to allow gays to wed prompted a national controversy. The issue quickly became even more controversial in the newsroom of the *San Francisco Chronicle*. The paper's city hall reporter and a photographer – both of whom had been covering the same-sex marriage issue – became one of the nearly 4,000 couples who took advantage of the change in the law.

Managing editor Robert Rosenthal promptly took them off the marriage story and assigned other staffers to it. Rosenthal told the Associated Press that the decision was not made because they were lesbians, but because they had crossed the line from observers to participants. "The real issue is the question of two people getting involved in the core story of the issue, which is getting married," he said. The photographer said she understood the argument, but she contended, "If people wanted to see bias before, they could have seen it because we were in a committed, long-term lesbian relationship and we wanted to get married."[31]

The ensuing debate quickly escalated into the larger question of whether gays should cover gay rights. It added another layer to the ongoing debate of how minority communities should be covered and who should be assigned to cover them. The concerns raised by gay reporters and gay communities echo those raised by African-Americans, Latinos, women, and other groups that the news media have not done a good job of covering their communities.

Three-fourths of African-Americans and about two-thirds of Hispanic and Asian-Americans believe news coverage of their communities would improve if they were covered by reporters of similar ethnicity.[32] Many journalists agree. Bob Lynch, a gay Native American who has worked at the *Houston Chronicle* and *Los Angeles Times*, believes diverse staffs give newsrooms "a great toolbox of reference." He says, "It would be unwise for any newspaper not to use its people in this way."

Putting that notion into practice has not been easy. Minority journalists say that they sometimes have to deal with unrealistic expectations from community members who expect them to provide only favorable coverage. "I've been accused several times of being an Uncle Tom because of my reporting of a story," said Don Hudson, managing editor at the *Jackson* (Tenn.) *Sun*. Other journalists say they too have been expected to do cheerleading instead of reporting. This troubles syndicated columnist Juan Williams, an African-American: "It seems some black readers want journalists to lie. My job is to pursue stories... not to ignore glaring needs in America's black communities."[33]

Another African-American reporter said he felt like he was caught in a vice. If his coverage of the black community was soft, he would be seen by some whites as unable or unwilling to be objective. But, he said, "If you come on too strong, black readers see you as a tool for whites." Another reporter put it this way: "You have to write a story that is palatable to whites and that may distort the truth of the story."[34]

Although the mainstream media are trying to improve the coverage of African-Americans, there are still incredible oversights. One paper wrote a glowing piece about the development of an area into an "ethnically diverse" community. But the pictures showed only white traditional families. When police asked a newspaper to run mug shots of felony suspects they suspected were living in the city, the paper agreed. All of the pictures were of black men even though there were also white fugitives, and no one at the paper thought to ask police about the discrepancy.

Perhaps these examples make it easy to understand why African-Americans are dissatisfied with media coverage. Nearly two out of three blacks asked in one poll said that at least once a week they saw something in the news media's coverage of black-oriented issues that offended them.[35] Nearly half thought news coverage worsened race relations. In another survey, 47 percent said newspaper coverage of crime news was unfair to their communities. TV news fared even worse, with more than half saying local and national television coverage was unfair.[36]

Many Hispanics, gays, and Asian-Americans have a different complaint. Héctor Ericksen-Mendoza, owner of the Hispanic Link News Service, said there's so little Hispanic news coverage that there's nothing to anger Latinos.[37] Studies have confirmed the so-called "brownout." Less than 1 percent of the stories on the evening CBS, NBC, ABC, and CNN newscasts were about Latinos or Latino-related uses.[38]

A survey of gay journalists found that they considered the media coverage of national gay issues to be adequate. But they complained that local coverage is weak and doesn't recognize their communities. "Editors forget that the community does more than hold a parade once a year," one said. Another noted that "gay issues don't make ratings" in Alabama:

> Even sensational crime stories involving gays do not sell. A guy had shot up his workplace... It came out his co-workers made fun of him because they thought he was gay. A reporter pitched it and it was turned down.[39]

Women in the newsroom

In 1971, nearly 80 percent of newspaper journalists were men. By 1982 about one in three was a woman. Curiously, that ratio was about the same more than 20 years later. Women make up about 40 percent of the TV news workforce. The number of women in news management is also holding steady. About a third of the top editors at the 30 largest papers are women, as are about 24 percent of TV news directors.

These numbers are not high enough, according to Jodi Enda, an experienced national correspondent. She has argued that the coverage of women's issues would improve if the news media had more women managers: "Without women decision-makers, it is tougher for women reporters to have their voices heard and get issues they see as important into print."[40]

Research suggests that the news media rely on men as experts in the fields of business, politics, and economics. Women in the news are more likely to be featured in stories about accidents, natural disasters, or domestic violence than in stories about their professional abilities or expertise. Other research has found that about 85 percent of the sources cited on the three network evening newscasts are men.[41]

Women in the sports community

Women have had trouble when they venture into the testosterone-dominated community of sports journalism. Only 14 of 435 newspapers surveyed had women in the top sports job, according to *Seattle Times* sports editor Cathy Henkel. "It's the hardest place in the newsroom to advance," she told the *San Jose Mercury News*. Henkel said there are many reasons for this, but she noted, "You're dealing with organizations that are primarily male-heavy at the top and all the way through. It's the good old boys' network times 10."[42] One survey found that a quarter to a third of sports editors believed women were "naturally" not interested in sports. Some used this as a justification not to hire women sportswriters or cover women's sports.[43]

Being taken seriously can be a problem for women. A coach once held up a football to sports journalist Jenn Hildreth and asked, "Do you know what this is?" When Jeanne Morris was assigned to cover a Minnesota Vikings football game in the 1970s, she was told women were not allowed in the press box. She had to sit outside – in a blizzard.[44] Women are no longer left out in the cold, but two out of three said they had experienced some form of sexual discrimination while on the job.[45]

The biggest battle for women journalists has been getting access to players. Stories in sports sections not only describe what happened during the game but emphasize the "whys." Therefore, sportswriters usually interview players immediately after games. In some individual sports like tennis, these interviews take place in pressrooms. However, for major professional team sports like football and baseball, they usually occur in the teams' locker rooms. Initially, this created problems. Some male athletes objected to allowing women into the room as they undressed and took showers. A few retaliated by flashing the women reporters, while others sent "gifts" of dead rats and phallic-shaped cakes. Some teams forced women sportswriters to wait outside the locker room while team officials brought players to them. Because of the delays, women sportswriters had much more trouble meeting deadlines than men did. In the late 1970s, syndicated columnist Elinor Kaine and *Sports Illustrated's* Melissa Ludtke sued professional football and baseball teams and won equal treatment.

But there are still ugly incidents. In 1990, three New England Patriots were fined by the league after they sexually harassed Lisa Olson of the *Boston Herald* in the locker room after a game. After her complaint became public, Olson was so heavily criticized by Patriot fans that she quit her job. In 1999, the Portland Trailblazers required guard Greg Anthony to apologize to Rachel Bachman of *The Oregonian* in Portland after he made inappropriate comments to her. Bachman did not write about the incident until it was included in a *Sports Illustrated* story about the "bad-boy Blazers."[46]

The "locker-room" question was renewed in 1997 with the start of the Women's National Basketball Association. Some wondered if the women would allow men into their locker rooms. The WNBA decided to follow the NBA's practice of opening locker rooms after the games. Unlike men in the NBA, however, the women wait to take showers until after the reporters leave.[47]

Women often have joined men in the broadcast booth at women's sports events. But in football, they were relegated to being what was derisively called "sideline chicks." Progress is being made, nevertheless, and in 2006 women were the main play-by-play announcers on ESPN coverage of some college football games.

Cases to Discuss

These scenarios are based on the experiences of reporters and editors. They have been modified for space and impact. In most of these situations, a reporter would seek advice from an editor – and the editors would make the final decision. But the initial input would come from the reporter, and good editors would listen carefully to the reporter before deciding. On some cases, you can check to see what the real editors did. That doesn't mean they did the right thing, but you can compare your thoughts with theirs.

Community case 1: Transplant group needs help

Although newer techniques are replacing the need for them, bone-marrow transplants have long been one option in the treatment of leukemia. The process had a couple of drawbacks. The donor's tissue had to be a good match. And donors had to be willing to undergo surgery to have some of their marrow removed, the recovery from which can sometimes be painful.

You're a reporter. A local group contacts you. They help find donors and serve as a support for donors and recipients. They plan to bring together a bone-marrow donor with a child who is recovering thanks to the transplant. They hope the resulting story will remind people of the importance of medical transplants.

You've done all the work. You've got the pictures. You got quotes from the donor. You have a feel-good story about a man doing a heroic deed to help a child.

Your paper has a policy of running background checks on the subjects of its stories. When you finally get around to doing that, you discover that the "hero" has a list of arrests for drugs and other things.

You mull your options. You could just forget about his record. But many readers are going to know the truth and think your paper hid or didn't discover his background. You could include them – but it certainly takes the edge off the man being such a hero. Or you could push the delete button and go in search of another story. **What do you decide to do?** (*The editors' decisions in this case are at the back of the book.*)

Community case 2: Help unite a family

Let's assume you're having a tough week ethically. Another feature you are working on is about a truck driver who has suffered what seems to be an amazing miscarriage of justice. One night when he is driving his rig on an Interstate highway, a car darts into his path. The accident severely injures his back and kills the driver and a child in the car. But it really wasn't an accident, the courts decide. The driver was trying to commit suicide and kill his children. What's the significance of that? The insurance company claims it covers accidents, not intentional acts, and this was the intentional act of a suicidal father. It refuses to pay the truck driver's health bills, and the courts agree that it is not required to do so under the terms of policy. To make matters even worse, his boss asks him if he is ready to return to work. He can't stand, let alone drive a truck. So the boss fires him.

The family is faced with amazingly huge medical bills. They are evicted from their home when they can't make the mortgage payment. The family is a large one and must split up because they can't find accommodation for all of them. Fortunately, a group plans fundraisers to try to reunite the family and hopes your stories will be the boost that their campaign needs.

When you do the background checks, you learn some disturbing information. At the time of the accident, the mother was facing charges of welfare fraud. The image of the big happy family before the accident fades. You find police records in which she has had restraining orders against the husband a few years ago and there are rumors of a divorce. **Do you include this information in your story?** *(This case is discussed at the back of the book.)*

Community case 3: Friendship call

Part One: You are a reporter in a small city. One of your best friends – a buddy since high school – has decided to run for City Council. You know she would be a good person for the job: honest, bright, and conscientious. Even in high school, she talked about a career in politics.

You friend plans a campaign kickoff party. She invites you to come: "It's going to be a big day in my life, and I'd like for you to be there."

What things would you consider before you decide? Would you go?

Part Two: Your friend gives you a campaign bumper sticker. **Would you put it on your car?**

Part Three: Assume that you decide to go to the kickoff party. During your friend's speech, she says she would like to thank some great friends who have supported her. With a flourish, she says, "And especially, I'd like to thank [your name goes here], the best reporter in town! [Looking at you, she continues.] Having the support of friends like you is vital to me." Her supporters clap enthusiastically. **What do you do?**

Part Four: Your friend's opponent calls your boss and says he doesn't think it's fair that the reporter who is covering the campaign openly supports his opponent. The boss turns to you and says, "We're shorthanded, and I really need you to cover the election. You're going to have to work your way out of the mess you created."

What do you say to the opponent? Put yourself in the opponent's shoes. Would you believe you?

Community case 4: It's my neighborhood

Part One: You work in a small newsroom and have the title "city editor." You are in charge of the local news. You've worked there for a while and have played a role in hiring most of the reporters who work for you. One local story that your reporters are covering is the city's plan to annex several areas. Annexation would mean that these areas would become part of the city and get all the city services. It also means that residents would pay city taxes, resulting in a considerably higher tax rate. It's likely to be a contentious idea.

A problem is that you live in one of the areas that may be annexed. Frankly, you don't think the benefits of being in the city are worth the additional cost in taxes. You neighbor has asked everyone in the neighborhood to come to his house for a pitch-in dinner and discussion of the proposed annexation. You expect it to be a heated conversation. You give it a lot of thought and decide to go because (1) you are a resident of the area, (2) your taxes, and in a sense your lifestyle, will be affected, and (3) you're curious about what will happen.

Shortly after the meeting begins, a neighbor you don't know well asks whether you are there as a journalist or as a resident. Will what is said at the meeting be in the newspaper? Another asks how you feel about it and asks if the newspaper plans to write editorials opposing or supporting annexation. **What would you consider before answering those questions?**

Part Two. After the meeting, the people opposed to the annexation decide to form an action committee. Sensing you agree with their side, they ask you to be a member. They don't know much about how things work around city hall and they are sure you could provide expert guidance. **Do you accept?**

Part Three: Despite the hard work by the committee, it looks as if the annexation is going to go through. One of your reporters is working on a story that, if confirmed, would probably stop the annexation from passing. But she hasn't confirmed enough of the details for your paper to run it. **Should you pass this information along to the committee members?**

Notes

1.   Eleanor Randolph, "The media and the march," *Messages: The Washington Post Media Companion*, Boston: Allyn and Bacon, 1991, pp. 341, 342.

2. David Shaw in "Can women reporters write objectively on abortion issues?" *Press Woman,* April 1991.
3. Laurence Zuckerman, "To march or not to march," *Time,* August 14, 1989.
4. Byron Calame, "Hazarding personal opinions in public can be hazardous for journalists," *The New York Times,* October 8, 2006.
5. Joe Strupp, "Reporter in 'gay pride parade' dispute claims civil rights violated," *Editor & Publisher,* June 22, 2006.
6. Joe Strupp, "Born to fund? Editors bar reporters from big election concerts," *Editor & Publisher,* September 17, 2004.
7. Dick Rogers, "Credibility at stake," *San Francisco Chronicle,* April 3, 2003.
8. Byron Calame, "Drawing the line," *The New York Times,* January 28, 2007.
9. "May reporters speak out on topics they cover?" *Quill,* March 1991.
10. Anthony Violanti, "Nina Totenberg's high-level insider's view," *The Buffalo News,* May 14, 2002.
11. Farnaz Fassihi, speech given as part of the Pringle Lecture series at the Columbia University Graduate School of Journalism, May 16, 2006.
12. "When journalists have opinions," *PublicEye* on CBSNews.com, October 10, 2006.
13. Kim Mills, "Taking it to the streets," *American Journalism Review,* July/August 1993.
14. Sandy Petykiewicz, "Many editors willing to join community groups," *ASNE Bulletin,* September 1992.
15. Brad Smith, "Journalist listed on site as church liaison," *The Tampa Tribune,* May 21, 2002.
16. Marvin Lake, "Report to readers. Ethics policy guides staff, informs public," *The Virginian-Pilot,* **April** 21, 2002.
17. Henry McNulty, "Let Landers be Landers every day," *The Hartford Courant,* May 24, 1992.
18. Bill Dedman, "Journalists' donations raise question of conflict," *The Boston Globe,* July 18, 2002.
19. Peter Johnson, "Rather apologizes for fundraiser speech," *USA Today,* April 5, 2001.
20. Allan Wolper, "Ethics corner," *Editor & Publisher,* October 26, 2004.
21. Shaw, *op. cit.* Subsequent references to Shaw in this section are to this article.
22. Zuckerman, *op. cit.*
23. Kim Mills, "Taking it to the streets," *American Journalism Review,* July/August 1993.
24. "No cheering in the press box," *Newsweek,* July 19, 1993; "Court lets newspaper curb reporter's activism," *Orlando Sentinel,* February 21, 1997, p. A 18; and "Court: Papers can bar reporter activism," *Orlando Sentinel,* October 7, 1997, p. A-7.

25. Cited in Zuckerman, *op. cit.*
26. Associated Press, "Bay City Times editor on unpaid leave after refusing to remove husband's campaign sign," *Detroit Free Press*, July 18, 2002, and Associated Press, "Bay City Times editor returns after disagreement over campaign sign," July 25, 2002.
27. "Can marriage and ethics mix?" 1983–84 report of SPJ-SDX Ethics Committee, Indianapolis: Society of Professional Journalists.
28. Howard Kurtz, *Spin Cycle*, New York: Basic Books, 1998, p. 44.
29. Donald Q. Smith, "Community role requires being part... and apart," *Newsworthy*, Fall 1995.
30. Susan Paterno, "I can explain," *American Journalism Review*, July/August 1998.
31. Lisa Leff, "Gay marriage presents thorny professional issues for journalists," Associated Press, March 25, 2004.
32. Mark Fitzgerald, "Blacks most upset by news coverage," *Editor & Publisher*, August 6, 1994, p. 15.
33. Sherri Owens, "Image problem," *Black Family Today*, December/January 1996.
34. "Report: Why blacks leave white media," *The Sun Reporter*, November 5, 2000.
35. Fitzgerald, *op. cit.*
36. *Ibid.*
37. Carolyn Terry, "Hispanic Links publisher gives Latinos a voice," *Presstime*, April 1995.
38. Serafín Méndez-Méndez and Diane Alverio, *Network Brownout 2001: The Portrayal of Latinos in Network Television News*, National Association of Hispanic Journalists, 2001, p. 3. The study was updated in Federico Subervi, "Network Brownout 2004," a report prepared for the National Association of Hispanic Journalists, 2004, available at www.unityjournalists.org.
39. Leroy Aarons and Sheila Murphy, "Lesbians and gays in the newsroom: 10 years later," Annenberg School for Communication report available on the Web site of the National Lesbian and Gay Journalists Association, www.nlgja.org.
40. Jodi Enda, "Women journalists see progress, but not nearly enough," *Nieman Reports*, Spring 2002.
41. Data compiled by Media Tenor Ltd. and reported on the FAIR Web site at www.fair.org.
42. Yomi Wronge, "M.N. names first female sports editor," *San Jose Mercury News*, June 2, 2006.
43. Marie Hardin, "Stopped at the gate: Women's sports, 'reader interest,' and decision making," *Journalism and Mass Communication Quarterly*, Spring 2005.

44. "If only they weren't all true," *AWSM Newsletter*, Spring 2002.
45. Marie Hardin and Stacie Shain, "Strength in numbers? The experiences and attitudes of women in sports media careers," *Journalism and Mass Communication Quarterly*, Winter 2005.
46. Paula Boivin, "Troubling issues in hard times," *AWSM Newsletter*, Winter 2002.
47. See Mary Schmitt, "Women sportswriters – Business as usual," *Media Studies Journal*, Spring 1997: Jennifer Frey, "A look inside the women's locker room," *The Washington Post*, July 27, 1977; and Virginia Watson-Rouslin, "The men's room," *Quill*, January 1987.

15 Freebies and Financial Concerns

Four out-of-towners are lounging on a corner mattress at B.E.D., one of the trendiest hot spots on Miami's South Beach. They watch the dancers and survey the posh surroundings as they slowly sip the *amuse-bouche* of lobster bisque while awaiting their selections from the French contemporary menu. "This is what you dream Miami would be like," one effuses. The foursome's experiences are like those of thousands of young adults who visit South Beach – with one major exception. When the check arrives, these guests didn't have to dig out credit cards. As *The Miami Herald* reported, the restaurant picked up the $650 tab, and a representative of the Greater Miami tourist bureau tossed down a $100 tip. They had not paid for their flights either. They stayed at a stylish Art Deco hotel on the beach, ate only at the best restaurants, and visited the most popular attractions – without spending a dime. These weren't your normal tourists. They were travel writers experiencing the best of South Florida.[1]

Journalists are offered all kinds of things by companies hoping for free publicity. Some of the gifts aren't very exciting. *St. Petersburg Times* columnist C. T. Bowen said it was easy to turn down freebies while covering small communities in Florida. He wrote:

> I must look cheap. A Land O'Lakes coffee shop owner once offered some gratis doughnut holes – not even legitimate strawberry-filled Krispy Kremes, mind you – when he learned that a trio of us worked for a daily newspaper. As he rang up our afternoon coffee purchases, he said, "Maybe you can write about my restaurant sometime." We declined and left the baked goods behind.
>
> A barber offered a free haircut if I would publicize the shop. Nope, not allowed.[2]

Other journalists – even those at college papers – are made offers that are considerably more tempting than doughnut holes. Daewoo, a Korean car company, flew college journalists to its plants in Korea to introduce them to its new line of cars, which it planned to market through college students. Entertainment companies also try to woo journalists. The arts and entertainment editor at San Diego State's *Daily Aztec* has been offered trips to New York for weekend interviews with Tom Cruise and director Cameron Crowe. Paramount once picked up the tab for college entertainment writers to travel to New York and spend a night in one of Manhattan's most expensive hotels. Sports editors at many college papers have received free Nikes.[3]

Some argue the best perks being offered today are given to writers who cover the electronic games market and review the new titles and hardware. When new games are in the works, the manufacturers fly them to California where they talk to designers and play prototype versions. For entertainment, the writers get to shoot guns, skydive, drive race cars, and engage in other activities related to the new game. "They take advantage of the stretch limos, five-star hotels and obscenely expensive restaurants," according to the UK's *The Independent*.[4]

Bloggers are also cashing in. Those who write about technology are so accustomed to receiving expensive free items that they started a campaign against Apple Computer, which they thought was too stingy with its gifts, according to *PR Week*. Other bloggers jumped at free trips to the Netherlands offered by Holland.com.[5]

Goodbye, Free Lunch

The freebie problem is a comparatively new one in American journalism. Although would-be seducers of the press have existed for years, they were hardly mentioned in early literature on journalism ethics. Press leaders did not perceive their efforts as a serious threat to journalistic integrity, perhaps because freebies were not all that common.

That changed with the growth of the public relations movement, which developed during the 1920s. Government, business, and other segments of society were advised to curry favor with the press. That often translated into gifts and free tickets, travel, and meals.

Journalists in those days did not see free tickets to the theater, circus, or baseball games as a problem. These perks went with the job; they made up for the notoriously low salaries. Many reporters assumed their news sources would pick up the tab for their drinks or meals. There was "a tradition in journalism of take what you could get," Richard B. Tuttle said when he was publisher and editor of the Elmira, N.Y., *Star-Gazette*.[6] Want to take the kids to an amusement park? Call the public relations office and tell them when you're coming. Can't afford a nice vacation? Promise travel agents and tour operators a flattering story in the Sunday travel section and go wherever you like. Occasionally the voracity of some journalists shocked even the public relations practitioners who arranged the freebies. A Disney World executive recalled a reporter from a Midwestern paper who rejected the free room arranged for him in one of Disney's nicest hotels. The reporter demanded a suite. She complied and, as a peace offering, suggested that the reporter and his wife have a complimentary dinner in the hotel's restaurant. The executive said, "They ordered from the right-hand side of the menu," picking only the most expensive items.

Christmas used to be a festival of freebies. In the mid-1900s, newsrooms often looked like the gift-wrap sections of department stores as the loot rolled in. Some, like baskets of apples from a well-known senator, would be for everybody; other gifts would be for specific writers or editors. Many older journalists can tell stories of newsrooms awash with fifths of whiskey and of journalists cheerfully trying to abide by early ethics rules that allowed them to keep as much as they could drink in one sitting.

Some newspapers placed their reporters in awkward positions. The newspapers were too cheap to pick up reporters' travel expenses, so sports reporters had to depend on the team's publicity staff to arrange travel to the games. Even political reporters were expected to accept free travel and hotel rooms from the candidates they were covering.

If you were to graph the history of freebies in America, there would be a line rising slowly through the 1930s and 1940s, reaching its highest point in the late 1950s and early 1960s, and then dropping slowly through the 1970s and 1980s and into the 1990s. The decline was prompted by the increase in professionalism among journalists.

Today, most American newspaper reporters insist on paying for their own meals and drinks, and most news organizations encourage them to pick up the check for their sources. Theater reviewers and restaurant critics pay full fare using the news organization's money. At some newspapers, gifts of food or flowers are given to homeless shelters and hospitals.

At others, like the *Herald and Review* in Decatur, Ill., when reviewers are finished with them the books and CDs are sold, often in silent auctions, with the money going to charities.[7] The news media spend thousands of dollars so that reporters can tag along with the president on his trips around the country and to cover sporting events.

Even in the most unregulated American newsrooms during the heyday of freebies, what American journalists received were small potatoes compared to what their counterparts in other countries still benefit from. German reporters often are given personal computers and large discounts on automobiles. Some even receive tax breaks from local governments.[8] Many Mexican journalists are on government or political party payrolls. Before the Gulf War of 1991, it was widely reported that Kuwait routinely offered reporters Mercedes automobiles and that many British and European journalists accepted them without hesitation. A columnist for *The Sunday Independent*, an influential British newspaper, was among UK journalists who bragged in a public-relations trade journal about some of the freebies he had received. His best free trip, he wrote, was to Australia, where he spent five days on a catamaran over the Great Barrier Reef followed by two weeks in plush resorts in a rainforest and the Outback.[9] Asian journalists told researchers that they see little wrong with accepting free trips, meals, etc. – but they balk at receiving gifts of money.[10]

The days of great freebies may be numbered for overseas journalists too. After editors at *The Sydney Morning Herald* in Australia placed limits on them, they printed a story listing all the gifts reporters had received during the previous week, including expensive meals and trips to Hong Kong, Amsterdam, France, and New York at the cost of the people who were the intended subjects of their stories.[11] Britain's *Financial Times*, a highly regarded national daily, created an ethics code for the first time in 2004. It joined *The Independent* and *The Guardian* among the handful of British newspapers to ban freebies.

Journalism, of course, is not the only profession worried about the undue influence of marketers. In the past, it was common for pharmaceutical companies to fly doctors to exotic resorts to introduce them to new drugs. One company even set up reward systems that promised free trips to Cannes on the French Riviera once the doctor had prescribed its drugs a certain number of times. After the news media ran stories questioning the junkets, the American Medical Association changed its code of ethics to limit such gifts.[12]

Government officials are also under increased scrutiny. State and federal governments are placing limits on the kinds of travel they can receive in an effort to keep the public from thinking that legislators are on the take. Gifts from lobbyists are limited by binding codes of ethics and, in some cases, laws. Even free tickets to sporting events can result in hefty fines in many communities.

What's Wrong with Freebies?

Nearly every media code of ethics bans freebies, for the following reasons.

The motives of the givers

Even the most naive reporters soon figure out that public-relations practitioners, politicians, and other newsmakers do not buy dinners or pay travel expenses because they think reporters are such nice people. They believe the gifts influence coverage. The tourist board of Broward County in Florida believed the $2,500 it spent paying the expenses of four writers from niche magazines was well spent when the first story appeared in a magazine that charged $5,000 for a full-page ad. Not only was it cheaper, the board knew that market research showed people put more trust in news stories than in advertising.[13]

Suspicions of the public

Imagine that a mayor accepts a vacation paid for by a local company. If, shortly after she returns, she proposes a law that would benefit that company, many voters are going to believe the company had bought her support. And therein lies another reason many news organizations do not allow journalists to accept freebies. Even if the journalists were not influenced by the freebies, the public may suspect they were. Keith Woods, a journalism ethics instructor at the Poynter Institute, said, "The public already thinks that advertisers have an undue influence on the news. If they see reporters acting like pigs at the trough, well, that doesn't help."[14] At the 2003 Environment Media Awards, scuffles reportedly broke out as media people tried to get free T-shirts.[15]

A privileged class?

Journalists used to accept all kinds of special privileges. Katharine Graham, publisher of *The Washington Post*, wrote in her autobiography, *Personal History*:

> Shortly after Russ Wiggins became managing editor of *The Post* in 1947, he summoned his police reporter. Wiggins asked if he was having parking tickets fixed. "Yes, sir," said the reporter, for people throughout the building. "I just take them to the station and give them to the chief."

Few, if any, news organizations today would allow their staff to fix parking tickets. First, they wouldn't like the idea of reporters being indebted to the police chief. Second, they know that getting such special treatment would be resented by the public, many of whom already distrust the media and believe journalists think they are above other citizens.

The appearance of hypocrisy

Although it is rarely stated in codes of ethics, many journalists avoid freebies and other financial relationships with people in power because of a fear of looking like hypocrites. For years, reporters have prided themselves on exposing politicians on the take. After all, it's news if the head of a congressional banking committee accepts a lavish vacation paid for by bankers, or if a candidate softens his position on gun control after receiving a campaign contribution from the NRA. Many journalists believe the media's moral stance on such matters is undermined if their colleagues are accepting gifts.

The real deal?

Reviewers and travel writers are often given special treatment. Service at restaurants and hotels is going to be first rate for them. Rooms will be spotless, and fruit baskets will be filled. Chefs may double-check the meals if they know the review will either encourage diners to come to the restaurant or cause them to stay away. Linsey McNeill, a travel writer for several British publications, says it's difficult to judge the relative value of some trips because everything is so carefully stage-managed. "You've had a great trip," she told a journalism review, "but it cost you nothing. I sometimes ask myself, 'Would I feel the same way if I'd paid £3,500 (about $6,500) for it?'"[16]

Direct pressure from gift givers

Some public-relations people pressure reporters to write favorable stories if they have accepted freebies. A few organizations are up front about what they expect when they give the media a freebie. Disneyland provides transportation for radio and television shows to do live remotes from the park in California. John McClintock, supervisor of publicity, said Disney expects a puff piece. "That will be a deal," he said. "No one is expecting objective reporting from that. That is a promotional relationship."[17] Some publicists play even harder ball. Sony made it very clear to Jeremy Horwitz that it was not happy with an article he wrote for *Intelligent Gamer* about a Sony video game called Crash Bandicoot. "I personally was yelled at over the phone by [a Sony public relations person] who made it clear to us we would not be receiving copies of Crash, and potentially other Sony products," he told *Columbia Journalism Review*.[18]

Privately, some writers admit that they shape their comments so they will keep getting freebies. One blogger who writes about high-tech gadgets told *Smart Money* magazine that he had received freebies worth thousands of dollars. "I'd never be able to afford the phone I'm talking on," he said, referring to a $600 Nokia model. The magazine writer asked if it was a good phone. "It's great as a music player, but it sucks as an actual phone." When his review appeared, however, he wrote that while "some features lack a little polish… it's worth its weight in gold."[19]

Bought for a Cup of Coffee?

"I can't be bought for a ham sandwich and a cup of coffee." That is the essence of one of the most common justifications for accepting freebies. Daniel Gilbert, a Harvard psychology professor, agrees that most people who say this are sincere. He wrote in a *New York Times* article:

> Legislators believe that campaign contributions don't influence their votes. Doctors scoff at the notion that gifts from a pharmaceutical company could motivate them to prescribe that company's drugs… Voters, citizens, patients and taxpayers can barely keep a straight face.

They have good reason to be doubtful. Gilbert cited psychological research suggesting that "decision-makers don't realize just how easily and often their objectivity is compromised. The human brain knows many tricks that allow it to consider evidence, weigh facts and still reach precisely the conclusion it favors." One study found that 84 percent of doctors suspected that their colleagues were swayed by gifts from drug companies, but only 14 percent thought the gifts affected their own decisions.[20] Writers may be just as vulnerable. Research done on game reviews suggests that reviewers who have taken free junkets gave the promoted games more favorable reviews than either the public or reviewers who had not received freebies. When asked about the effect of the freebies, however, writers thought they had maintained their objectivity.

Different Rules for Different Sections?

At many news organizations, the sports department is called the "toy shop." Perhaps because sports is not taken as serious journalism, sports writers often pay only lip service to codes of ethics that are strictly enforced in other departments in the same newsroom. When sports journalism professor Marie Hardin surveyed sports editors, she concluded that sports journalists were still living in the bad old days of freebies. Nearly half saw little wrong with accepting freebies. That sentiment was most prevalent among small-town editors, who tend to be younger journalists.[21] Long ago, the Associated Press Sports Editors organization wrote a code of ethics that banned both gifts and free and discounted tickets to events the sports writer was not covering – but the code is voluntary.

Some feature writers also believe the codes on freebies should be different for them. Kelly McBride, a former reporter for *The Spokesman-Review* in Spokane, Wash., was leading a discussion of freebies at a Poynter Institute ethics workshop for feature editors. One editor complained that codes on freebies were written with hard-news reporters in mind. McBride, writing on the Poynter Web site, described three ethical problems the editors had encountered:

- A pop music critic said that her boss had made it clear to her she should be constantly listening to different genres of music, hearing new releases, and exploring the cultural trends. But the newspaper would not buy any CDs. The critic was expected to get free ones.
- A wine critic wanted to do an independent test of every Cabernet manufactured in his home state. Paying for the wine was out of the question. Recognizing that the wineries might have an expectation

of favorable coverage if they gave the wine to the paper, he asked a distributor to provide the wine instead.

• A reporter wanted to do a consumer story on teeth whiteners. Some companies had sent out samples with their press releases. He bought other products to supplement the ones the paper had received. He included in the comparison the ones he got for free and the ones he bought.

McBride said her response was in keeping with most of the codes of ethics. The reviewer should buy the CDs or convince her editors to lower their expectation. The wine critic would need to buy the wine – or not do the stories. The newspaper should buy the teeth whiteners. The reactions from the feature writers and editors? Some of them found her approach "almost puritanical" and "impractical" because the newspapers would not pay out the money. McBride concluded:

> But if I learned anything from my close encounter with the feature editors it was that simply imposing a stringent policy might not get us very far. To do any good, a solid freebies policy must be workable and enforceable, too – an especially challenging combination in the day-to-day life of features sections.[22]

Freelancers face special problems

Beginning freelancers are particularly vulnerable to pressures from the givers of freebies. They cannot afford to pay up front the cost of an expensive trip in hopes of selling enough articles to come out ahead. A free trip makes their financial life much easier. The problem is that they have to make sure that they keep getting offered the junkets.

Some publicists recognize this and apply direct pressure. According to *Ryerson Review of Journalism,* a representative of the Japan National Tourist Organization told travel writers he would make no specific demands of writers except that they must write good things about Japan. "I don't want them to write about high prices in Japan," he said.[23]

More often, publicists see no need to tell travel writers that they must write positive features. They simply ask to see copies of the stories. Travel writers understand that if the publicists aren't happy with their work, they will stop getting free trips and their freelancing careers will likely end. "You don't want to get the reputation of being the negative guy," a former tourism director told *The Miami Herald,* "because that word gets around."

Many travel writers acknowledge that their stories are rarely critical. Established writers say they get enough offers that they can pick only the destination that they are sure they will enjoy. A few contend that they are not serious journalists but are adventure writers spinning yarns for armchair travelers. More commonly, travel writers contend that their stories are honest; they just leave out the unpleasant experiences like cockroaches in hotel rooms or bad food in a restaurant. One writer on a free junket to several South American cities was surprised when a hotel manager told him the hotel would provide an armed guard so he could safely visit some of the area's most famous tourist sites. The writer did not want to encourage his readers to visit such a dangerous city, so he omitted any reference to it in his feature describing the wonders of traveling in South America.[24]

Travel writers who pay their own way have been more forthcoming. A writer for the *Let's Go* travel guides was robbed and pistol-whipped outside his hotel in Caracas. In the guide, he warned readers about crime in the area. The publishers of travel books like *Let's Go* and *Lonely Planet* ban freebies altogether. *Frommer's* places limits on what its writers can accept.[25] Top travel magazines have similar rules. *Travel + Leisure*, *Playboy*, and other major publications won't buy from writers who accept freebies. Many large newspapers have a split personality on travel junkets: They do not allow their own staff members to accept them, but they do not hold freelancers to the same standard.

Freelance critics are placed in a similar untenable position. Newspapers and magazines want reviews that are timed to the opening of a movie or the release of a product. That means the freelancer must be on the list of people who are invited to pre-opening screenings or who receive products before they are on store shelves. Unfavorable reviews may mean their names are removed from the list. A staff writer can explain the situation to his editors, who will probably appreciate his independence. However, freelancers often discover that magazines prefer to purchase reviews from people who can deliver them on time.

Outside Jobs

Moonlighting, or holding down a second full- or part-time job, has become common in modern society. Other than possible damage to health, moonlighting seems to present few problems to most of its participants.

However, if you are a reporter, you need to be careful when selecting that second job. Writing a book is probably acceptable and, depending on the topic, may even be encouraged by your editors. It might make you some money and bring credit to you and your news organization. Before you write an article for a national magazine, you'd better get permission from your editor. But watch out if you want to write a promotional booklet for a local land developer – it could get you fired. Many news organizations have taken a dim view of outside jobs and activities that might cause the public to smell a conflict of interest.

Typical of their policies is the one at *The Boston Globe*. The *Globe* refused permission to a photographer who wanted to be the backup to the Boston Red Sox baseball team's official photographer. His role would have been to shoot pictures for the Red Sox yearbook, scorecards, and promotional materials.[26] A photographer at *The Washington Post* ran afoul of similar rules when he accepted the use of an RV to take pictures for a Web site called walmartingAcrossAmerica.com, sponsored by a group trying to improve Wal-Mart's image. The photos showed the RV parked at Wal-Marts to promote the company's policy of allowing campers to park overnight. The *Post* required the photographer to have his photos removed from the site and to refund the expense of the RV.[27]

Traditionally, most newspaper and news magazine journalists avoid anything to do with their own organizations' advertising departments in deference to long-standing rules about keeping news and advertising separate. But today it is becoming more common for journalists to produce special sections developed for advertisers. At small papers, reporters may even be asked to write puff pieces for yearly "progress" sections that highlight local businesses, and advertising departments may enlist copy editors to prepare sections with stories and photographs provided by advertisers. Often the journalists ask that their bylines not be used on such stories.

It's harder for broadcast journalists to hide their identities. At some local radio and television stations, making commercials, even testimonials, is sometimes part of news staffs' job. This may add to the income of newscasters and their stations, but it certainly detracts from their credibility as reporters and presenters of the news. Some TV news people get around this problem by having split personalities. During the 1980s, Glenn Rinker was recognizable throughout most of the nation as the happy shopper in TV ads for a furniture store chain. But not in Orlando, Fla., where he was the serious-minded news anchor for the CBS affiliate.

Rinker had a clause written in his contract with the advertising agency that prohibited it from showing his ads in Central Florida.

Of course, a great many broadcast journalists will not do advertisements. Carol Marin, a former anchor at then top-rated WMAQ in Chicago, declined to mix news and advertising. She was suspended for three days when she refused to read the names of two supermarkets that were passing out fire-prevention pamphlets. "I would not read the names of those stores so people could pick up a pamphlet and, maybe, buy a loaf of bread while they're there," she said.[28] Marin later quit the station when it hired Jerry Springer, host of the tabloid TV talk show, as a commentator.

Contests and News Judgment

Contests can be good ideas. An organization promotes a contest for reporting or editorial writing and lines up some respected editors and journalism professors as judges. Often the winners' work is reprinted and can serve as a model for other journalists, thus improving the craft. Many contests – the Pulitzers, SPJ Awards of Merit, the Society of Newspaper Design awards, and many regional contests sponsored by journalism groups – have achieved that goal.

However, some contests do not serve any altruistic purpose. The sponsors of these contests are trying to get their message to appear free in as many newspapers as possible. They hope that by announcing a contest for the best story that promotes whatever they want promoted and by promising a big cash prize, they can lure journalists into writing stories favorable to their causes. For example, the National Association of Realtors offered a cash prize for "articles dealing with real estate development, property tax relief, etc."[29] Other contests define themselves even more directly. South Carolina sponsored a contest "for articles promoting travel in South Carolina," and the Mexican National Tourist Council wanted articles "that promote travel to Mexico." But even if a contest isn't this blatant, it often isn't difficult to guess the kinds of articles that are likely to win. Paul Poorman, former editor of the Akron *Beacon Journal*, said he doubted that an exposé on the use of faulty concrete in interstate highway construction was likely to win a contest sponsored by the National Highway Contractors' Association and the Cement Institute.[30]

Many large newspapers now have written rules that limit the kinds of contests staff members can enter. And the Society of Professional Journalists has adopted guidelines for determining which contests fall within the society's code of ethics. Its rules are:

- No contests "should state or imply favorable treatment of a cause or subject."
- Approved contests should have judging panels that are "dominated by respected journalists or journalism educators."
- Cash awards should be accepted only if contests are wholly sponsored by professional journalism organizations, journalism foundations, or universities.[31]

Improving the Profession

Perhaps of all the ethical concerns raised in this book, the ban on free-bies seems the least fair. At many news outlets, publishers and station managers aren't bound by the rule. And upper-echelon editors and news directors usually make enough money that a ban on freebies is rarely a hardship for them.

That leaves two groups who are most tempted by freebies. One is the veteran moocher. We all know these people. They are always on the take. They never pick up the check; they never buy a round. If they are covering an event that offers freebies, they try to take two. And while we may be amused by their cheapness, it's a trait we don't respect; and neither does the public. They paint a tawdry picture of the profession.

The other group to whom freebies have appeal consists of young jour-nalists and journalists at news organizations with ridiculously low pay. A few tickets to an amusement park – let alone a free vacation – can become a big deal when your salary is at or below the poverty line. Media owners who place news professionals in this quandary are doing the profession a disservice.

Yet, all journalists must recognize that freebies aren't gifts. They are efforts to influence news decisions. The SPJ Code of Ethics says it very clearly: "Journalists should refuse gifts, favors, fees, free travel and spe-cial treatment, and shun secondary employment, political involvement, public office and service in community organizations if they compromise journalistic integrity." Turning down freebies is a small price to pay to help the profession regain the respect it must have.

Cases to Discuss

These scenarios are based on the experiences of reporters and editors. They have been modified for space and impact. In most of these situations, a reporter would seek advice from an editor – and the editors would make the final decision. But the initial input would come from the reporter, and good editors would listen carefully to the reporter before deciding. On some cases, you can check to see what the real editors did. That doesn't mean they did the right thing, but you can compare your thoughts with theirs.

Conflict of Interest case 1: The impoverished critic

It's your first job. You're a general-assignment reporter for a small rural daily. You're happy to have a job doing what you enjoy, and your editor lets you write pretty much what you like – as long as you produce the number of stories he wants. If your career goes as you hope, you want to be a feature writer for a large daily covering the arts: theater, movies, music. So you've started covering the arts and theater for your paper. There isn't a lot, and it's not great. But you would rather do that than cover council meetings.

People you've written about tell you of the summer theater series in a larger city about 50 miles away. Everyone in the arts world is terribly excited about it. The series is a combination of professional theater and local groups and runs throughout the summer. Lots of people from your town drive down, even though tickets are expensive (by rural standards). They say they've seen plays long before their New York debuts by some of the best young writers and directors. "It was surely something you would want to cover," they tell you.

You talk to your editor about your idea of writing reviews of the plays. He says the paper runs the schedules for the plays, and he thinks that's enough. Besides, the news budget and staff are limited. He'd rather you spend your time and the company's money working local stories. However, if you want to do it on your own time, he says the paper would be glad to run the stories. "As a matter of fact, I think it's a great idea. The New Play series has single-handedly put the state on the cultural map. Tell you what. If you're going to go anyway, I think we can pay you our regular mileage allowance. But we'll want some consistency. I don't expect you to review them all, but we can't review just one or two plays and then forget about the rest of the series."

You want to do it. It will be great experience and will provide good clips for your resumé when you go looking for a job as a feature writer.

You discover that the series is managed by three different agencies. One handles the touring companies of Broadway musicals. These often feature second-tier movie and television stars in oft-produced musicals aimed at middle America. A second agency produces well-known plays with local talent, both amateurs and professionals. It's been described as "very good community theater." The third agency is the one that is so famous. It produces new plays by young playwrights and stages dramatic new productions of classic plays. Critics consider it among the five or six most prestigious theater companies in the nation for new plays.

You contact the PR person for the Broadway series and tell her what you want to do. She immediately tells you that it will be no problem. She'll keep you informed of all press conferences and will make sure there are two tickets for you every opening night.

When you contact the community theater PR person, she tells you that she doesn't usually get requests from small papers 50 miles away. But she's willing to see if it might create more interest in the series. "We know we sell tickets up your way," she says. She says that she will alert you to a press conference with the stars and provide you with two tickets to the opening night of the first play. "You send me copies of what you write," she says. "If we did get more interest from up there, we'll consider working out something for the second play."

The PR person for the prestigious theater company says he'll gladly put you on the mailing list and make sure that all press releases are e-mailed to you. He says most opening-night tickets are $90, some are higher. "I know the local reporters all pay for their tickets," he says. "I'm sure you'll want to be treated the same way. Tell me when you want to come and we'll try to hold the best seats available for you. If you want, we can bill your paper directly." You thank him politely. You know that on your salary, there's no way you can pay $90 every month or so for tickets.

You wonder what to do. Do you write reviews only of the Broadway series that will let you attend free? Should you write a review of the first community-theater play and choose your words carefully in hopes of getting additional free tickets? Should you consider it an investment in your career, buy the tickets, and go back on the ramen-noodle diet that got you through college?

Conflict of Interest case 2: Burritos galore

You write one of those human-interest columns about things going on in town. You and a couple of other reporters decide to have lunch at a Mexican restaurant that is having its grand opening with lots of lunch discounts. The place is packed, so you have to wait. One opening-week lunch promotion is a drawing. Customers write their names on their business cards. If their card is drawn, the winner gets free lunch for 10 coworkers. You decide to do it.

Shortly after you are seated, the owner comes up with a big smile and tells you that you won the drawing! He hands you the prize, a coupon for 10 burritos lunches for you and your coworkers. Your lucky day! You go back to the newsroom and message some friends about your good fortune, asking if they want to go Friday. Good, free food is always appreciated. You figure this might even be a one-paragraph item for your column.

A friend on the copy desk bursts your bubble. Wasn't it odd that you won so quickly in such a crowded restaurant?

You begin to wonder, too. Accepting freebies, of course, is forbidden. If the owner had just handed you 10 burritos, you would have declined. However, your business card says who you are and where you work. Did the owner pick your card to curry favor with you and your paper?

Do you call it luck and have a good time with friends? Should you mention it in your column? Or is it best to not accept the prize? (*The newspaper's decisions are at the back of the book.*)

Notes

1. Douglas Hanks III, "Writers live it up; publicists get the tab," *The Miami Herald,* July 2, 2006.
2. C. T. Bowen, "We can't be bribed – not even with doughnut holes," *St. Petersburg Times,* August 18, 2002.
3. Jessica Yadegaran, "College papers struggle with ethics and freebies," Copley News Service, March 11, 2002 (www.copleynews.com).
4. See Steven Hill, "Geeks have all the fun," *The Independent,* February 28, 2005, and Justin Hall, "Ethics in video game journalism," *Online Journalism Review,* April 10, 2003.
5. "Freebies and the moral maze," *PR Week,* February 17, 2006.
6. Interview by Goodwin, October 14, 1981.

7. Dave Dawson, "Exploring the world of newsroom ethics," *Herald and Review,* October 20, 2006.
8. Tamara Jones, "Reporters in Germany open wallets for stories," *Los Angeles Times*, March 26, 1991.
9. "Freebies and the moral maze," *op. cit.*
10. Ven-Hwei Lo, Joseph Man Chan, and Zhongdang Pan, "Ethical attitudes and perceived practice: A comparative study of journalists in China, Hong Kong and Taiwan," *Asian Journal of Communication,* September 2005.
11. Robert Bolton, "Newspaper journalists and free travel, and the journalism of George Orwell," Australian Public Radio, July 29, 1999.
12. Jeffrey Seglin, "Just say no to gifts from drug makers," *The New York Times*, October 13, 2002.
13. Hanks, *op. cit.*
14. Rich McKay, "A race for freebies," *American Journalism Review,* April 2003.
15. David Weddle, "Swagland," *Los Angeles Times,* January 16, 2005.
16. Ian Gillespie, "The flip side of freebies," *Ryerson Review of Journalism,* Spring 1988.
17. Shawn Hubler, "Bottom Line: It's Not Just About The Bottom Line," *Los Angeles Times*, April 20, 2001.
18. Trudy Lieberman, "Gimme!" and "Perceived neutrality," *Columbia Journalism Review*, January/Februrary 1998, pp. 45–49.
19. Anne Kadet, "Romancing the bloggers," *Smart Money,* November 2006.
20. Daniel Gilbert, "I'm O.K., you're biased," *The New York Times,* April 16, 2006.
21. Marie Hardin, "Survey finds boosterism, freebies remain problem for newspaper sports departments," *Newspaper Research Journal*, Winter 2005.
22. Kelly McBride, "Help needed in freebie nation," Poynteronline.com, posted September 26, 2003. Also see Andrew Guy Jr., "The great American freebie debate," 2003 American Association of Sunday and Feature Editors Convention coverage on www.aasfe.org. Guy writes for the *Houston Chronicle.*
23. Ian Gillespie, "Travel writers may get a free ride – but it's often the readers who pay," *Ryerson Review of Journalism*, Spring 1988.
24. Interview by Smith, 2005.
25. Warren St. John, "A job with travel but no vacation," *The New York Times,* July 9, 2006.
26. "Columnist resigns after paper learns of his outside PR work," *Editor & Publisher*, November 9, 1985, p. 12.
27. Joe Strupp, " 'Wash Post' photog's Wal-Mart trip violates paper's policy," *Editor & Publisher,* October 11, 2006.

28. Bill Carter, "Chicago TV anchor quits after station hires talk-show host for commentary," *The New York Times*, May 4, 1997, p. A16.
29. "National and international journalism competitions," *Editor & Publisher*, December 28, 1985, p. 10.
30. Interview by Goodwin, April 8, 1981.
31. "Contests: Which programs qualify under codes of ethics?" 1984–85 report of SPJ Ethics Committee.

16   The Business of Journalism

The war in Vietnam had divided America. To hawks, the war was necessary to stop the spread of communism. Anti-war protesters were unpat-
riotic traitors who were giving aid to the enemy. To doves and many
young people, the war was senseless. They staged massive rallies and
sneered at President Lyndon Johnson with the chant: "Hey, hey, LBJ,
how many kids do you kill today?"

All the while, deep inside the Pentagon, officials were writing an
amazingly candid history of the war, documenting that American military and government leaders had misled and, in some cases, deceived
Congress and the American people in an effort to justify escalating the
conflict. This history, which became known as the Pentagon Papers, was
classified top secret. Yet a *New York Times* reporter obtained a copy.
When the *Times* began publishing his stories, the Nixon administration
got a court order forcing the *Times* to stop.

That's when reporters from *The Washington Post* got involved. They
tracked down their own copy of the Pentagon Papers. Working in seclu-
sion in executive editor Benjamin Bradlee's Georgetown home, they read
the lengthy documents, sized up their key findings, and prepared a series
of stories. Bradlee wanted it printed as quickly as possible, partly to
show unity with the *Times* and partly to help establish the *Post* as a
major player in American journalism.

However, many in the *Post* management wanted the paper to stay out of
this battle. The company's lawyers contended that Nixon would undoubtedly find out that the *Post* had copies of the Pentagon Papers and would
ask the courts for another restraining order. Once he did, the Post would
be embroiled in a lengthy – and very costly – legal battle. Further, the
lawyers argued, the Nixon administration might seek criminal charges

against the *Post* for violating espionage laws. They doubted that the First Amendment would protect reporters from those charges.

There were also business concerns. The Washington Post Co. was changing its status from a family-owned business to a publicly owned corporation. The company hoped to sell more than $1 million worth of stock. Frederick Beebe, chairman of the board of directors, worried that the stock offering would be canceled if the *Post* got involved in a messy lawsuit. Beebe also feared that Nixon might use the Federal Communications Commission to cause trouble for the Washington Post Co.'s television and radio stations. At that time, the FCC had considerable regulatory power over broadcasters.

In the middle of all these arguments was Katharine Graham, publisher of the *Post*. After lengthy telephone conversations with Beebe, Bradlee, and corporate attorneys, she told Bradlee to go ahead and publish the stories. David Rudenstine, a law professor who wrote the definitive history of the Pentagon Papers, described her decision like this:

> Graham assumed that publication would cause the government to sue the *Post* for an injunction; that there might be difficulties with the stock sale; and that there might also be repercussions for the company's electronic broadcasting stations. But she was deeply worried about the morale and commitment of her editors and reporters and about the reputation of the paper.[1]

The courts eventually allowed both the *Post* and the *Times* to print the Pentagon Papers. The information they contained changed many people's opinions of the war. The sale of Post stock went ahead, but the FCC did scrutinize the company's broadcast properties closely.

A quarter of a century later, managers of CBS faced a similar decision. *60 Minutes* had prepared a report charging that the top executives of tobacco companies lied to Congress when they testified that nicotine was not addictive. CBS found a former scientist for the Brown & Williamson tobacco company who said that the company's own research showed that nicotine was addictive. *60 Minutes* reporters also learned that tobacco companies knowingly added a cancer-causing substance to pipe tobacco.

Once Brown & Williamson heard that *60 Minutes* was preparing the report, it threatened to sue CBS. The suit would not claim that the reports were libelous or that they were false. Instead, B&W attorneys planned to accuse CBS of enticing the scientist to violate a clause in his contract that forbade him from talking about his work.

It was a novel way to sue the media. But media attorneys doubted the courts would allow it. James C. Goodale, who represented the *Times* in the Pentagon Papers affair, said it would be a "slam-dunk win" for CBS. Joseph B. Jamail, an attorney who won a $10.5 billion judgment for a similar claim by Pennzoil against Texaco, told *The New York Times*, "If you've got as much backbone as a banana, you go with that one. I just don't see the damages."

But other issues clouded CBS's decision. One was the relationship between the company's owners and the tobacco industry. At that time, CBS's parent company was the Tisch family's Loews Corporation. Loews also had an interest in Lorillard, a cigarette company. As CBS News was preparing the *60 Minutes* episode, Lorillard was negotiating with Brown & Williamson to buy six of its brands. Further, Lawrence Tisch, who was CBS chairman at the time, was the father of Andrew Tisch, the chairman of Lorillard and one of the tobacco executives who swore to Congress that nicotine in cigarettes was not addictive.

CBS executives had other things to consider. CBS and Westinghouse were negotiating a merger. An editorial in *The New York Times* suggested:

> With a $5.4 billion merger deal with the Westinghouse Electric Corporation in the works, a multibillion-dollar lawsuit would hardly have been welcome. Some of the executives... stand to gain millions of dollars themselves in stock options and other payments once the deal is approved.

CBS executives strongly denied that the prospect of monetary gain influenced them.

However, the story was killed. It was not until after *The Wall Street Journal* published a similar story that CBS managers allowed *60 Minutes* to broadcast the episode. The story's reporter, Mike Wallace, was blunt when he talked to reporters after the broadcast:

> [F]or the first time, CBS News and CBS management cared more about the sale to Westinghouse or the difficulties of perhaps defending a lawsuit than they cared about the news. As a result of which, it took us months to finally get a tobacco piece that we wanted, that was carefully reported and was worth putting on the air, to get it finally on the air.[2]

The issues and realities faced by executives at the Washington Post Co. and CBS were, of course, different. Yet one observation can be made: Management plays a key role in journalists' ability to practice their profession. Graham stood behind her journalists despite the threats to the financial health of the *Post*. CBS did not. As a *New York Times* editorial put it: "The most troubling part of CBS's decision is that it was made not by news executives but by corporate officers, who may have their minds on money rather than public service."[3]

Since the news media are big businesses, they are influenced by the same forces that bear on all American business enterprises. There is nothing intrinsically wrong or illegal about the media following the same economic Pied Pipers that motivate Wal-Mart, ExxonMobil, United Technologies, McDonald's, and Crazy Joe's Used Cars.

However, news businesses differ from other businesses in one important way: Their constitutionally protected freedom is interpreted by most people to mean that they are a semipublic service as well as private profit-seeking businesses. In a democracy, citizens must know what's going on. That job falls to the news media – in all its various forms. Most newspaper reporters take this role seriously, according to surveys. They see doing good journalism as their first role, and making profits for the corporation that owns the paper a distant second.

The clash between the professional values of journalists and the bottom-line concerns of owners is a major issue facing the news media. "Our democracy is far more fragile than we'd like to admit," said Frank Blethen, publisher of *The Seattle Times*, one of the largest remaining family-owned newspapers in the United States.[4]

The Changing Nature of Ownership

At the beginning of the 20th century more than 98 percent of American newspapers were independently owned, often by local families.[5] Some families owned newspapers to make money; others wanted the power and prestige that came with the ownership.

Many newspapers flourished under local publishers. Their roots in the community and their commitment to the family-owned business pushed them to produce quality papers. Often these families took such pride in their papers that they willingly poured a large part of their profits back into the newsroom to improve the newspaper. That's what happened to *The Washington Post*. Today it is considered one of America's best newspapers, but former *Post* publisher Donald Graham recalled a time when it was struggling. "In the early 1950s," he said, "the *Post* aspired to be a world-class newspaper; its heart was in the right place, but it just didn't have enough money. There's an old joke around the *Post* that in those days we could cover any international conference as long as it was in the first taxi zone." With owners who were willing to spend money to improve news coverage, the *Post* hired topnotch journalists and gave them the time and resources they needed to produce stories that were responsible and complete.[6] The papers in Louisville, St. Petersburg, Des Moines, and other cities gained national respect under family ownership.

Family ownership also had its downside. Some family-owned newspapers suffered under narrow-minded owners who pushed the papers toward one-sided reports and political favoritism. Journalism Professor John Hulteng cited several classic cases of activist publishers, such as conservatives Eugene Pulliam of *The Indianapolis Star* and William Loeb of *The Union Leader* in Manchester, N.H. When Loeb decided to back a candidate in one election, his paper began a crusade that included front-page editorials with misleading quotes from other papers. In one presidential primary, *The Union Leader* devoted twice as much space to Loeb's choice (who was not considered a serious candidate by most observers) as it did to all the front-runners combined. Similarly, when Robert Kennedy was running for president in the Indiana primary, Pulliam's *Indianapolis Star* heaped negative coverage on Kennedy while writing many favorable stories about a "favorite son" candidate who was running only to keep Kennedy from winning the Indiana primary.[7] A biography of Robert McCormick, legendary publisher of the *Chicago Tribune,* said that during his reign, the *Tribune* became "a megaphone to amplify the publisher's caprices." McCormick was so strongly against Franklin Roosevelt that 97 days before the 1936 election, a front-page headline in the *Tribune* read, "Only 97 Days Left to Save Your Country." McCormick liked the phrase so much he had the *Tribune's* switchboard answer all calls that way, each day counting down to election.[8]

While not all family-owned papers were used this blatantly to promote the owners' political philosophies, many were hopelessly co-opted by "sacred cows," a term journalists gave to the publisher's friends and favored institutions that were to receive preferential treatment. Others engaged in hometown boosterism that required reporters to paint rosy pictures of the city's economy and government.

Newspapers become a great investment

The number of family-owned newspapers has declined dramatically since the early 1900s when nearly all papers were owned by people who lived in the community. By the end of the 20th century, chains had gobbled up nearly all midsized and larger papers. These chains, like Gannett and McClatchy, are publicly traded corporations. That means they are not owned by individuals or families. Instead, the corporation issues stock. When investors buy stock, they, in effect, become a part owner of the corporation. Often they share in the company's profits and have a say in its management. Owners of corporate stock make money another way, too. If the chain's papers continue to be profitable, other people will want to own shares. Applying the law of supply and demand, the price of shares will increase, bringing additional wealth (at least on paper) to people who own stock.

For decades, that is exactly what happened. Newspapers had long "been able to generate rivers of cash decade after decade," as the national business magazine *Forbes* put it.[9] Corporations soon learned that, with a little effort, these rivers of cash could become torrents. In 1980 the profit margins of the *Chicago Tribune* were 8 percent; by 2000 they were 30 percent.[10] Between 1990 and 2000, industrywide, newspaper profits tripled.

Most investors were happy. They shared in the company's dividends and were receiving bigger checks year after year after year. Stock value also soared, giving investors another financial windfall. It would have cost about $2,400 to buy 100 shares of stock in one major media company in 1995. Five years later, the value of the stock had gone up and those 100 shares could be sold for around $5,800.[11] More than doubling your money in five years is an investor's happiest dream.

Because of this outstanding profit history, stock in media corporations was attractive to institutional investors like mutual funds, money managers, equity groups, pension funds, banks, insurance companies, and college endowment funds. Most of these investors had no interest in whether the newspapers were performing their public-service responsibilities. They were only interested in the profits. A Pulitzer Prize might be nice, but high annual yields were even nicer. These institutional investors owned more than half the shares in media giants like Gannett and Knight Ridder.

What happens when a corporation owns a paper?

Corporate ownership improved some newspapers. Often the corporations were only interested in the business side of the paper. Therefore, they gave journalists considerable editorial freedom. That was a welcome change in communities where newspapers had been tied to the ideologies and whims of local publishers. An even more positive development was that some corporate owners took pride in the journalism their papers produced. After the McClatchy chain bought the *The News & Observer* in Raleigh, the paper hired more reporters and began to emphasize hard-nosed coverage of the community.[12] The Tribune Co. improved the journalism at many of the papers it purchased, such as the *Orlando Sentinel*.

The Gannett chain, the nation's largest with about 90 daily papers including *USA Today*, has been credited with improving some small-city papers that it purchased. The chain brought in experienced editors and updated the papers' equipment and design. But the chain also is well known for its concern for the bottom line. In some cases, Gannett doubled the profits of newspapers it purchased by tighter management, volume buying, and much higher advertising rates. Robert H. Giles edited Gannett dailies in Rochester, N.Y., and Detroit. He contended that Gannett wants it both ways: "put out good newspapers and continue to make a lot of money, and you can't always do that."[13]

Some corporate owners are concerned only with the bottom line. These publishers keep the size of news staffs small so they can save money and keep their profit high. They require their staffs to work long hours churning out stories to fill the paper. To these reporters, some journalistic principles may seem like luxuries they can't afford. They don't have time to check several sources or provide social context to their stories. And to add insult to these injurious conditions, often these journalists are among the lowest paid in the business, barely making a living wage.

For many years, Thomson Newspapers Inc. was cited as a company that put profits far ahead of news. Some journalists who have worked for Thomson papers sarcastically quote a statement by the chain's founder, Roy Thomson: "The news is the stuff that separates the ads." At its peak in 1993, this Canadian company owned 156 dailies and 25 weeklies in the United States, more than 40 dailies and about 20 weeklies in Canada, and publications in Great Britain and Australia.

Thomson had a reputation for buying papers in small cities and turning them into cash cows.[14] Richard Harrington, president and CEO of Thomson, explained to *Presstime* how the company accomplished that feat: "We raised rates, cut costs, and made a lot more than 20 percent on margins." Harrington admitted Thomson was "known as a company that didn't put a lot of money into its papers."[15] The result was often a lot of second-rate journalism. One editor refused to label Thomson a newspaper chain, preferring to call it a "commercial printer."[16] A Canadian government commission that examined chain-owned papers in that country concluded that Thomson's "small-town monopoly papers are, almost without exception, a lacklustre aggregation of cash boxes."[17]

Thomson decided to leave the newspaper business and sold all its American papers in 2000.[18] Some contend the reason for Thomson's decline was that its papers contained so little news and were of such poor quality that readers abandoned them, causing advertisers to switch to less expensive media, often free shoppers.[19] "I think Thomson [Corp.] is a case where the marketplace eventually drove them out of the newspaper industry," said Jim Ottaway, chairman of Ottaway Newspapers Inc.

Corporate owners face problems

Early in the 21st century, newspapers faced stiff competition on many fronts. Newspaper circulations were falling. Of even greater concern was that many younger readers seemed to have no interest in the news. They didn't read newspapers, they didn't go to online news sites, and they didn't watch news on television.[20]

Advertising, which provides most of a newspaper's income, declined. In many communities, retailers like Wal-Mart, which is not a major print advertiser, replaced local department stories, which had been heavy advertisers. Auto dealers are a major advertiser in newspapers and on television. But recently, many began to switch to Internet ads, which were not only cheaper but allowed dealers to respond to people who viewed the ad. Manufacturers like Toyota introduced its Yaris and Rav-4 vehicles chiefly by using interactive Internet ads and downloadable video snippets for cell phones and iPods. "We don't just look for a page buy anymore," one executive said.[21]

Classified ads in newspapers also took a hit. For years, when people wanted to sell household goods, rent houses and find new jobs, they turned to the newspaper classified sections. Those small ads provided about 40 percent of a newspaper's income in 2000. Then Monster.com, Craigslist.org, eBay, and other Internet companies siphoned off much of the classified business. For newspaper owners and investors, the picture looked dreary. Papers were losing readers, advertisers, and classified ads.

None of this is to suggest that newspapers began to lose money. In fact, newspapers remained highly profitable by most standards.

Their profit margins were often twice that of the average for Fortune 500 companies. Yet, individual stockholders and institutional investors were not happy. They were used to receiving ever-higher dividend checks and to watching the stock price go up. When that was no longer happening, they demanded changes.

The sad tale of Knight Ridder

The saga of Knight Ridder exemplifies what can happen to corporate-owned chains with unhappy owners. Knight Ridder was once one of America's premier chains. It owned the highly regarded *Miami Herald*, *San Jose Mercury-News*, *Charlotte Observer*, and dozens of other respected papers. When a paper was purchased by Knight Ridder, good things usually happened. *The Philadelphia Inquirer* was a dismal paper when Knight Ridder bought it. Through infusions of cash and improved newsroom management, Knight Ridder turned it into the paper that won 17 Pulitzer prizes from 1972 to 1989 and attracted some of the nation's top reporters to its staff. Knight Ridder's *Akron Beacon Journal* won more Pulitzer prizes than any paper of its size.

However, faced with growing competition and a decline in advertising in the early part of the 21st century, the price of Knight Ridder stock began to decline. That meant that, on paper anyway, many investors were losing money. They didn't like that. Knight Ridder executives tried to satisfy them by increasing profits. They cut the size of the news staffs and reduced the money spent on gathering news. Newsroom morale sank. When ordered to lay off reporters, top executives at *The Philadelphia Inquirer* and the *San Jose Mercury News* resigned. The publisher in San Jose sent a letter to his staff saying that Knight Ridder's profit demands could risk "significant and lasting harm to the *Mercury News* – as a journalistic enterprise and as the special place to work that it is." The cutbacks continued. *The Miami Herald's* news staff was cut from more than 500 to 375, and *The Philadelphia Inquirer* lost 20 percent of its journalists.

Even these drastic cost-cutting efforts did not perk up profits quickly enough to satisfy investors. Soon the company ordered additional 10 percent across-the-board job reductions at its 32 newspapers.[22] Eventually, Knight Ridder's profit margins increased from 10 percent in 1995 to 20.8 percent in 2000. In 2005, the chain's chief executive Anthony Ridder told analysts, "The newspaper industry generally, and Knight Ridder specifically, are strong, healthy businesses with a bright future." Not everyone agreed. One very large investor believed his stock would be worth more money if the company were broken up. In 2006, he got his wish. Knight Ridder sold all of its papers and went out of business.[23]

If there was a bright spot in the disintegration of Knight Ridder, it may be that the papers were bought by the McClatchy chain, which has a reputation for solid journalism at papers like *The Sacramento Bee* and *The News & Observer* in Raleigh, N.C. Journalists and readers hoped that McClatchy would restore the quality of the former Knight Ridder papers. McClatchy, however, did not keep all of the Knight Ridder papers. When it sold the *Akron Beacon Journal* to a Canadian publisher, the news staff was told that the new owners really cared about journalism and that their jobs were safe. A few weeks later, 40 of the 160 newsroom employees were laid off. "You almost forget that we're actually profitable," one reporter said. The paper's profit margin was about 20 percent, which would be considered high in most industries.[24] McClatchy also sold the *Star Tribune* in Minneapolis to a private investment firm that had never owned a major news organization.

Other large newspaper companies were under similar strain. The Tribune Co. of Chicago bought the Times Mirror chain for $8 billion in 2000, creating a coast-to-coast media giant with papers like the *Los Angeles Times*, Long Island's *Newsday*, Baltimore's *The Sun*, *Hartford Courant*, *Chicago Tribune*, and *South Florida Sun-Sentinel*, as well as 22 television stations and the Chicago Cubs baseball team. Many experts predicted that the combination of these very profitable companies will create new synergies and opportunities for appealing to more advertisers and making more money for stockholders. That's not exactly what happened. A few years after the merger, under pressure to cut costs, the Tribune Co. began to reduce the number of employees throughout the chain. Much of what followed sounded like a repeat of Knight Ridder. A string of editors and publishers at the *Los Angeles Times* bucked upper management over the cuts. They were replaced. One editor received a standing ovation as he was escorted out of the building. By 2006, investors were encouraging Tribune to sell many of its newspapers and streamline its organization. In April 2007 Sam Zell, a Chicago real estate tycoon with no newspaper background, bought the Tribune Company in a complex financial deal. News staffs at several former Tribune papers were soon cut even further. Zell said he believes the Internet will become a major source of income for the company.[25]

Knight Ridder and Tribune Co., of course, were not the only media giants that were badgered into cutting costs. A survey by *Editor & Publisher* magazine found that 50 percent of publicly owned papers cut staff during the economic downturn of the early 2000s. The New York Times Co. laid off about 1,200 staffers at its newspapers, and CNN cut about 200 employees from its news operations. When NBC cut 700 jobs in 2006, *Broadcasting & Cable* magazine reported, "The reductions will be shouldered not so much by the struggling NBC entertainment division but by [NBC's] key profit center: news at its national broadcast and cable networks, and local owned-and-operated TV stations."[26]

Other forms of ownership

Some management experts now doubt that corporate ownership is in the best interests of the news media. Optimists among them hope that more newspapers can find ownership modeled after the one created by the Poynter family for the *St. Petersburg Times* in Florida. Nelson Poynter gave his majority share of the paper to an institute with two objectives: to keep the paper independent and to use its profits to fund programs to study journalism and train working journalists. The plan seems to be paying off. The Times Publishing Co. is a financially healthy, taxpaying, for-profit organization. *The St. Petersburg Times* is regularly listed among the most innovative papers in America. And the Poynter Institute is arguably the world's premier journalism think tank.[27]

Something similar happened in the UK. The family that owned *The Guardian,* one of Britain's premier papers, established a trust committed to continuing the paper's independence in perpetuity. A few small American dailies, such as *The Day* of New London, Conn., and the *Northeast Mississippi Daily Journal* of Tupelo, Miss., are also owned by charitable trusts or foundations. Whether this model of ownership spreads to other papers is yet to be seen. The Knight Foundation, a nonprofit set up by the Knight family, considered buying the Akron paper after the demise of Knight Ridder, but withdrew when bidding prices became too high.

Professor Joe Mathewson at Northwestern University believes American journalism would be in better hands if newspaper ownership followed the model of public television. He envisions changes in tax laws that might encourage corporate owners to give papers to nonprofit organizations. These organizations would behave like traditional media companies. They would pay their bills by selling papers and advertisements. And they would own property and pay wages (perhaps higher than profit-making newspapers do). But they would not be under pressure from stockholders to increase profits. They could concentrate on doing journalism.[28]

Many democracies allow their governments to help fund the news media. While British newspapers make profits much like American papers, the BBC is overseen by the government. Each year, Brits are required to pay a license fee of about $240 for each color television and about $75 for black-and-white models. These fees fund the BBC. Enforcement officers, using electronic surveillance devices and databases, catch about 1,000 people a day who are watching television without a license. Nonpayers can be fined as much as $2,000.[29] In Canada, more than half of the funding of the CBC comes from the government. And the French government paid subsidies to newspapers amounting to more than $500 million in 2007. It is considering setting up a foundation that would accept tax-deductible contributions to be distributed to newspapers. The French, whose papers cost about $2.50 a day, are among the least regular newspaper readers in Europe. Italian newspapers also receive government funding.

A return to local ownership?

Some communities have seen a return to local ownership of their newspapers. McClatchy sold *The Philadelphia Inquirer* to a group of Philadelphians. In 2006 local people expressed interest in buying *The Sun* in Baltimore, "not because it was the best business venture around" but because they believed news media ownership "is part civic responsibility." As this is written, local investors have expressed interest in the *Boston Globe, Hartford Courant*, and other papers.

Journalists and readers have one great wish: that new local ownership will be motivated by a sense of the importance of a paper in a community and allow journalists the freedom to practice their craft. That seems to be happening in some communities. Jay Grelen, a columnist at the *Arkansas Democrat-Gazette* in Little Rock, told *Editor & Publisher* that his paper's owner, Walter Hussman, has pushed for more education coverage, but "it has never resulted in any sort of interference." He also said the paper had a reporter and photographer in Iraq during October and has sent reporters to cover events ranging from combat in Afghanistan to Hurricane Katrina. "For a paper from Arkansas," he added, "that is pretty ambitious." Dale King, city editor of the privately owned *Boca*

Raton (Fla.) *News*, said he believed that problems are "a lot easier to deal with when your owner is upstairs rather than four or five states away."

However, local ownership worries some for two reasons. One is that it could mean a return to the days when publishers used their newspapers to push their own political dogmas and pet projects. A staff member at *The Greeneville* (Tenn.) *Sun* told *Editor & Publisher* that the family that owns his paper limits its coverage: "It is almost a throwback to the 1940s, a booster of everything local." The other worry is that some of the new owners will be no better than the worst of corporate owners and will suck the journalistic life out of papers in favor of quick profits. A criticism of many local owners is that while they may not unduly pressure managers to increase profit margins, they are also less willing to invest in expanding news coverage and modernizing equipment.[30]

After looking at the condition of newspaper ownership in the early 21st century, *The Christian Science Monitor* concluded, "Private, local ownership has its risks. But if it can give newspapers breathing room to find their way, it seems worth it – for the sake of journalism and an informed public."[31]

The Television News Business

People with enough money can start or buy as many newspapers as they want. Chains can own hundreds of newspapers. However, that's not the way things have worked in broadcasting. A government agency, the Federal Communications Commission, regulates the ownership of radio and television stations. Until the early 1980s, FCC rules limited a person or company to owning only seven television stations. Even with that limitation, there was lots of money to be made. Many equated having a license to own a television station with having a license to print money. A lazy owner could make a nice profit just from the fees the network paid for the station to carry its programming. Many stations scheduled only enough local programming to satisfy FCC requirements. In small communities, the required public-service news program was often just a man sitting behind a desk reading from the morning paper. However, with a little spunk and imagination, owners could turn their stations into fountains of money.

Then, in the early 1980s, the FCC decided to allow companies to own up to 12 television stations as long as they reached no more than 25 percent of the households in America. Many media companies jumped at the chance to buy more stations in bigger markets. They borrowed heavily and entered into bidding wars that pushed prices of stations to record levels. For example, just three years after WCVB, a Boston television station, was sold for $220 million, it was purchased by Hearst for $450 million.

The high profits being made by American broadcast stations caught the eye of Rupert Murdoch, an Australian press baron who owned media properties around the world. He became a naturalized U.S. citizen so he could meet FCC regulations that require owners to be Americans. Murdoch soon accumulated enough television stations to reach 21 percent of the nation's TV viewers, and later he started the Fox network with affiliates in most large markets and the Fox cable channels. In 1993 the FCC gave him special permission to own both a New York television station and the *New York Post*, despite its rules that one company can't own both a television station and a newspaper in the same town.

The 1996 Telecommunications Act added even more heat to the red-hot demand for broadcast stations. It abolished the limit on the number of stations one company could own and raised the coverage cap so that one company's stations could reach 35 percent of the nation's homes. The formula to determine the 35 percent limit was complicated. Some companies could reach more than 60 percent of homes and still comply with the act.

By the early part of the 21st century, the glory days of local station ownership were beginning to fade. Networks no longer paid local stations to carry their programming. In some cases, they expected local stations to chip in to cover the cost of some network programs. Even worse for local stations, networks began to experiment with ways to bypass them altogether, allowing viewers to download programs onto their computers and iPods. Meanwhile, viewers have been forsaking local news programs, a local station's biggest moneymaker. Particularly painful has been the loss of young adults, a favorite of advertisers.

Local stations are also losing some of their best advertisers. For years, American auto companies have been among their major advertisers. But serious financial problems have caused General Motors and Ford to cut back. Japanese and German companies have not traditionally advertised as heavily on television. Also, the ever-improving quality of video on the Internet has allowed Web sites to compete with television for video-based advertising. These factors combined to cause a 9 percent decline in advertising on local stations in 2006. A few strong stations in big-city markets were still incredibly profitable, with many posting 40 percent profit margins, according to *The Wall Street Journal*. Even in midsize cities, some local stations saw profit margins of 30 percent. But the majority of stations, particularly those owned by small companies and families, were not faring as well as they did a decade ago.[32]

Television finds profits in news

While newspaper companies sell primarily one product (the paper), broadcasters have two kinds of products: news and entertainment programming. In earlier days, station owners and network executives did not expect their news departments to make money. Some station owners neglected their news departments and scheduled only enough news and public affairs programming to satisfy FCC requirements. Other owners believed strong newscasts gave their stations prestige in the community and drew viewers to the moneymaking entertainment programs. They spent money willingly on their newsrooms. For these stations, news was a "loss leader," according to Ben Bagdikian, formerly of *The Washington Post*, who was referring to the grocery-store practice of advertising a few products at below-cost prices in hopes that buyers will fill their shopping carts with more profitable items.

The days of news-as-prestige began to fade when the networks discovered news could make money. Bagdikian places much of the blame on one program:

> *60 Minutes* was the best of times and the worst of times. It was the best of times in the sense that it did a lot of serious investigative reporting... But it was the worst in the sense that it was the first public affairs program that made money.

60 Minutes has been a Top 10 prime-time show for more than 20 straight seasons and has become one of the most profitable series ever on television. ABC and NBC chased in with *Primetime Live* and *Dataline NBC*. Network accountants liked these news magazines programs because they are relatively cheap, considerably less expensive than prime-time dramas.

In recent years, the number of people watching network evening news has plummeted. In 1996 about half of American homes tuned in to one of the evening network news broadcasts. By 2006, only a third did. Paradoxically, income from ads on news programs has not gone down significantly. The evening newscasts still account for about 20 percent of a network's revenue. That's because for many advertisers, network news is a great deal. Even the lowest-rated network newscast draws three times as many viewers as cable's highest rated newscasts, and the prestige of network news provides additional value. (Cable news ratings, of course, spike during crises and major events because of the cable networks' unmatched ability to cover breaking news.)[33]

The morning news shows are much more profitable than their evening counterparts. Before Katie Couric left NBC's *Today*, it was the biggest moneymaker on television. According to the *Sacramento Bee* newspaper, it earned an estimated $250 million annually in profits, more than the rest of NBC combined.[34] Mornings are so successful that the three networks keep expanding offerings. To cash in on the popularity of morning news programming, local stations now have news at 5 a.m. or 6 a.m., before the network programs start. Many stations with long-established news departments have found additional profits by providing news to less well-established stations that do not have news operations.

Growth of Ethnic Media

Newspapers produced by African-Americans have been around since 1827 when a group of black journalists established *Freedom's Journal*. The paper's first edition declared, "We wish to plead our own cause. Too long have others spoken for us." As journalism Professor Frankie Hutton points out, *Freedom's Journal* and other early black papers were more than anti-slavery tracts. *Freedom's Journal* emphasized news from black communities and told the stories of successful African-Americans. The paper, which directed its message toward both white and black readers, emphasized that blacks were Americans too.[35] By the time the Civil War began in 1861, more than 40 black-owned papers followed in the path of *Freedom's Journal*. The most famous was Frederick Douglass' *The North Star,* which rallied many in the fight against slavery.

After the Civil War, black-owned businesses sprang up and flourished, the ranks of the black middle class grew, and more than 1,000 black papers appeared. Some lasted only a few months, but others became major publications. The *Pittsburgh Courier* had a circulation of nearly 300,000. Other papers like the *Chicago Defender* and the *Amsterdam News* in New York City had circulations of more than 100,000. Editors of these papers championed the fight against color barriers throughout American society and encouraged black migration from the South to northern cities. These papers covered sports, particularly those of the historically black colleges, and heralded the integration of Major League baseball by Jackie Robinson. Most had lively pages devoted to society and entertainment news. Two black-operated wire services, patterned after the Associated Press, provided them with national and international news.[36]

The *Pittsburgh Courier* and *Chicago Defender* were circulated nationally. The papers were passed from family to family, and some ministers read them aloud to their congregations. Because the papers championed civil rights and migration by blacks to the North, some local governments in the South banned them. The papers had to be smuggled into cities, often by black porters on passenger trains. A former city editor of the *Courier* described the clandestine deliveries:

> Camouflaging its trucks, the *Courier* would smuggle small bundles of papers to the Pittsburgh railroad station, and porters would hide them aboard or under the trains... The papers were wrapped in a special weatherproof paper to prepare them for shipping. Once they arrived in the South, the porters would drop the papers off about two miles outside major cities such as Chattanooga, Tenn.; Mobile, Ala.; and Jacksonville, Fla. Black ministers would gather the papers and distribute them to the children in their congregations who served as newsboys and newsgirls.[37]

However, in the 1950s and 1960s, changing economic and social conditions weakened many of these papers. They were partly the victims of their own successful fight against segregation. Brent Staples of *The New York Times* wrote that "with the civil rights movement finally under way – and white papers belatedly interested in Negro news – black readers slipped steadily away." Also, with desegregation in housing, many African-Americans moved away from traditional black communities and stopped buying that community's newspaper. As these people left the community, many black-owned businesses lost customers and began to suffer financially. That left African-American newspapers in a bind. They were losing circulation, and many of their core advertisers were going out of business.

Today about 230 black papers are published. Most are weekly, although some, like the *Chicago Defender*, print daily. Most journalists at these publications believe their papers are heeding the *Freedom's Journal*'s call. Al-Nisa Banks, editor of the *Challenger* in Buffalo, N.Y., for more than two decades, contends that "The black press speaks to the specific needs of the African-American community; we want to provide a voice for those people who don't have a voice in the mainstream media."[38]

Although editors at African-American papers aim to fulfill the needs of their communities, they don't agree on how that's best done. Some, like the *Chicago Reporter*, practice hard-hitting investigative reporting. And some see their role as reporting the everyday events in the lives of their readers and promoting black leaders and organizations.[39]

For more than 50 years, two of the most successful magazines have been *Jet* and *Ebony*. Both magazines were founded by John H. Johnson, who also started the Black Entertainment Television cable network in the early 1980s. BET carried the first national news broadcast aimed at African-Americans. When Johnson sold the network to media giant Viacom in 2000, he reportedly became the nation's first black billionaire.[40]

The growing Latino and Asian media

Perhaps the fastest-growing ethnic media in America is Latino. In 1990 the circulation of Hispanic papers was 4.2 million; by 1995 it was 8.1 million. In 2002, there were more than 400 Hispanic newspapers, including about 20 dailies. In 2001, a bad year for the economy that saw advertising revenue in English-language papers drop nearly 10 percent, advertising review in Spanish papers was up 19 percent, according to the National Association of Hispanic Publications.[41] While circulation of mainstream newspapers is declining, Latino publications are averaging more than 3 percent annual growth. Spanish-language television stations are drawing many viewers to their newscasts. In Miami, Dallas, Los Angeles, and other cities, they score higher ratings than many English-language stations.

The Project for Excellence in Journalism included Spanish stations in its 2002 analysis of local television news. The researchers reported that Anglo and Spanish stations were essentially equal in quality in most cities and that Spanish stations edged out English-language stations in Miami. The report found differences in the nature of the news. Researchers determined that "Spanish-language local TV news is more populated by ordinary people, and filled with even more crime and victims than English-language TV. It is more interested in homelands far away, if not the world in general." The stations covered political news about South and Central American and Caribbean countries extensively. On the negative side, researchers found that stories were more often one-sided than stories on Anglo TV and were more likely to have unnamed sources.[42] Newspaper stories also often are written differently than in Anglo papers. At *Nuevo Herald* in Miami, an editor said the stories are shorter and more opinionated than in the parent newspaper, *The Miami Herald:* "It's just a different kind of style, and closer, I think, to what many Hispanics are used to."

Problems of the Under-Funded Newsroom

As bottom-line pressures continue, newsrooms are facing more budget cuts and at many papers and television stations, the quality of the news is suffering. One example is the predicament of newspaper copy editors. Until the late 20th century, copy editors checked news content for accuracy and grammar. Today, they also lay out the pages on computers. Meanwhile, budget cuts have reduced the number of copy editors at many papers. Trying to do more work in less time has resulted in more errors. As the number of reporters declines, papers are filled with stories from news services like the Associated Press. At smaller papers, copy editors hastily scan the first couple of paragraphs of stories from the AP or another news service. If the first few paragraphs look good and the story will fill the space, the story may appear in the paper without anyone in the newsroom ever reading it in its entirety. Stories aren't edited: They're shoveled into the paper.

Reporters are being put under increased pressure too. In many newsrooms, editors require reporters to produce a certain number of stories each week. If the newsroom is shorthanded, the editors increase the quota. To meet this new expectation, reporters may feel pressured to turn in stories before they have had time to gather all the information they need or to check additional sources to provide balance and ensure accuracy. They may produce stories with only one source, often a government official, and bypass important but time-consuming stories altogether. The papers are filled with "quick hits" that reporters can knock out in an afternoon.

News staffs at television stations often encounter the same problems. Although hiring by local stations is on the rise, the number of hours of news being broadcast is also increasing. "Cost-cutting, technology and tight-staffing and employment practices now dictate how TV stations cover the news," a veteran TV reporter said.

Typically, television stations often hire fewer than a tenth as many reporters as newspapers do in similar-sized cities. When Dan Rosenheim was managing editor of the *San Francisco Chronicle*, he oversaw a staff of 225 reporters. When he left that job to become news director at KPIX-TV in San Francisco, he had 16 full-time reporters. "Sixteen reporters to cover the same territory the newspaper covers with more than 200," Deborah Potter, a television journalist and consultant, emphasized in *American Journalism Review*. Philip Balboni, president of New England Cable News in Boston, told *American Journalism Review*, "No TV station in America has enough reporters."[43]

Trying to fill the local newscast with only a handful of reporters, assignment editors must choose carefully where to dispatch news crews. They must send them to stories that can be covered quickly and will provide good video. "We don't have time to do complex stories," one broadcast journalist in a Top 25 market said. "We have to do the quick stories, the easy stories. What's missing is the relevance."[44]

Some news directors say the problem is getting worse. In one survey, they said that by far the No. 1 obstacle to producing quality news was "not enough staff." The study found that reporters were required to produce an average of 1.8 packages a day. As one news director said, the sad truth is that "some editorial decisions have been based solely on saving money." Many stations turn to crime news. "It's the easiest, cheapest, laziest news to cover, because all they do is listen to the police radio, react to it, send out a mobile camera unit, spend an hour or two covering it and put it on the air," a former NBC News executive said.[45] At most stations, murders, convenience store holdups, and traffic accidents fill about a third of the evening newscast. At some stations, it's as high as 60 percent. As a reporter in a Top 25 market said, "We've become the police blotter."

Understaffed newsrooms are more likely to rely on public-relations people to help fill the news hole. At smaller newspapers, editors may glance at news releases and then cut and paste them into the paper with little or no editing. Because television news demands video, public-relations people and promoters know that they can get their message on the 6 o'clock news by staging media events that promise good pictures. One study suggests that as much as 70 percent of some TV newscasts are coverage of pseudo-events – events created by individuals or groups to draw attention to their activities or positions.[46]

Video news releases (VNRs) are also becoming a common way of filling time. Some call them "fake news" because they look and feel like part of a newscast, but they are produced by the companies or politicians mentioned. In some cases, the station's anchor introduces the story and leaves the impression that the reporter in the VNR works for the station. In other cases, a local reporter becomes part of the VNR by reading an accompanying script. Often the segment seems to be a buyer's guide – but only one company's products are mentioned.

More worrisome, the Bush administration produced a series of VNRs to promote controversial changes in Social Security, the invasion of Iraq, proposals for education, and other issues. Many local stations used them without mentioning the source. As *The New York Times* suggested, everyone benefits except viewers:

> Local affiliates are spared the expense of digging up original material. Public relations firms secure government contracts worth millions of dollars... The administration meanwhile gets out an unfiltered message, delivered in the guise of traditional reporting.[47]

Low salaries in under-funded newsrooms

Another downside of under-funded newsrooms is the low salaries paid to beginning broadcast and print reporters, often substantially below the average for recent college graduates. About 20 percent of new journalists begin their careers with organizations that do not provide basic benefits such as medical insurance.[48] An *American Journalism Review* article said that some small California dailies pay reporters about the same as people working in a Starbucks coffee shop.[49]

Unfortunately, low salaries have long been the norm for beginning journalists. In 1996, 22 percent of newspaper journalists under 25 earned salaries below the official poverty level of $15,141. Reporters at some small news organizations received pay raises in 1997– but only because the government raised the minimum wage. Worse, salaries at small papers often remain low despite the quality of work done by the journalist. When Betty Gray won a Pulitzer prize in 1989, her small-town paper, the *Washington Daily News* in North Carolina, gave her a $25-a-week raise.[50] After surveying salaries paid to entry-level journalists in Virginia, Steve Nash, a journalism professor, concluded that a beginner had better be prepared to drive a very used car and live on peanut-butter sandwiches.[51]

One reason beginners' salaries are so low is that people in journalism usually start at small newspapers and television stations. In the news business, salaries are almost directly proportional to the size of the paper's circulation or the television station's market. For example, at large papers like *The Boston Globe*, the minimum wage after five years with the paper was about $1,400 a week in 2006; at mid-sized papers like the *Canton Repository* in Ohio, $890; and at the *Norristown Times Herald* in Pennsylvania, $535. Starting salaries were about $1,600 a week at *The New York Times*. Journalists at all of these newspapers are members of The Newspaper Guild-CWA labor union. Salaries at non-union papers tend to be lower.

The salary spread is even wider in broadcast journalism. In the Top 25 markets, news directors make as much as $250,000. The average was $120,000 in 2006, according to surveys done at Ball State University. At small stations the median salary is about $65,000. Well-established anchors in big markets can make as much as $1 million a year. However, the median salary was $115,000 in 2006. The median salary for small-market anchors was $30,500. The spread for reporters is from $200,000 for a big-name reporter in a top market to $14,000 at the bottom of the heap. The median salaries were $51,000 in major markets and $20,000 at small stations. Despite television's reliance on visuals, broadcast photojournalists are paid a little less than reporters, with median salaries of $44,000 at top markets to $21,000 at small ones. Weathercasters are paid less than news anchors. Sports anchors and reporters are paid less than their news and weather counterparts.[53]

These low salaries contribute to the poor quality of journalism in many small cities and towns. G. Kelly Hawes, former president of the Society of Professional Journalists and an editor at *The Muncie (*Ind.*) Star*, asked, "Are news outlets attracting qualified applicants for poverty-level wages, or are they settling for what they can get?"

Beginning journalists who accept the low salaries often plan to stay at their first newspapers or television stations only long enough to get enough experience to move to better-paying jobs. At some smaller television stations, the turnover rate in the newsrooms is as high as 50 percent a year.[54] Rather than learn the needs of the community, reporters are looking for the story that might land them a job in a bigger market. Or they may leave the profession altogether. A study by journalism Professor Betty Medsger found that 43 percent of new journalists said they might seek jobs that paid better.

Lowering the wall

Underfunded newsrooms are chipping away at a long-established journalistic ideal. For most of the 20th century, editors and reporters envisioned an impregnable wall between news operations and business departments. The business side delivered the papers and sold the ads; the news side made all the decisions about the news content of the paper. Symbolic of this relationship, at one time elevators that carried advertising personnel to the *Chicago Tribune's* business offices could not stop on the floor where the newsroom was.

To many journalists, the wall between news content and advertising was as important as the separation of church and state in the U.S. Constitution. Of course, they recognized the importance of advertising in that it provides the bulk of a newspaper's income. "You've got to make money in order to produce good journalism," a former editor of the *Sacramento Bee* said. "It's just pretty axiomatic in my mind." He was worried, though, that newspapers may be moving down a slippery slope toward too much advertiser influence.

Staffs at larger newspapers have been able to fight off intrusions. John Cruickshank, who is now the publisher of the *Chicago Sun-Times*, told a *New York Times* reporter about conditions when his paper was controlled by Conrad Black's Hollinger Group: The paper's publisher "was constantly demanding that we write negative stories about non-advertisers and positive stories about advertisers – which, of course, we didn't do." Cruickshank added, "He wasn't averse to quality journalism; he just thought it should go on someplace else."[55]

Journalists at the *Los Angeles Times* were humiliated and readers surprised in the late 1990s when the paper's management, without telling top editors, the staff, or the public, entered into a profit-sharing agreement with the management of the Staples Center, the city's new sports arena. For its grand opening, the paper published a fawning special section. When the partnership was revealed, *Times* journalists wrote stories detailing this serious breach of the wall between advertising and news. When the Tribune Co. purchased the *Times*, it promised there would be no repeat of that misjudgment.

Unfortunately, at some smaller newspapers and television stations, the wall has been substantially lowered. Advertising salespeople promise potential advertisers that buying ads will result in a news story. A hardware supplier may be told it will be featured in a piece about lawn mowers. Restaurants may be told that if they buy an ad, the food critic will write a positive review.

At some newspapers and many television stations, the problem is not the lowering the wall between advertising and news: The problem is trying to keep advertisers from crashing through it. Advertisers constitute as much as 80 percent of a newspaper's revenue and nearly all of a television station's. Some advertisers use the clout of their advertising dollars to directly influence news coverage. A survey by professors at Marquette University found that more than 90 percent of newspapers had been pressured by advertisers to change or kill a story, and that about a third of the editors admitted that they had caved in and complied with advertisers' wishes.[56] In the early 21st century, some advertisers began to write into their contracts that publications must notify them before "objectionable content" is published so they can pull the ad or move it to another edition.[57]

More typically, advertisers threaten to stop advertising with the news outlet as punishment for running stories that are unfavorable. *The Washington Post* once ran a story about a Harvard University study predicting a decline in the prices of houses in the Washington area. To provide balance, the reporter included comments from experts who disagreed with the prediction. But the story still did not sit well with the real-estate community. Major builders withdrew an estimated $750,000 worth of advertising from the paper.[58] Some auto dealerships are so quick to wage war against negative coverage on local television stations that many stations avoid any coverage – except glowing reviews of new models. A consumer reporter at a Seattle television station wrote: "We don't even bother with most auto-related stories anymore. These days, even a simple consumer education story on how to buy a new car can draw the wrath of local car dealers."[59] When a sportswriter for the Carbondale, Ill., *Southern Illinoisan* compared the ineffective St. Louis Cardinal pitching staff to a bunch of used-car lemons polished up for quick sale by a shady seller, dealers complained. The paper printed an apology and suspended the sportswriter and his editor. The publisher said it was an "obsolete stereotype" of used-car dealers.[60]

Some newspapers bypass this kind of problem by creating special sections for automobiles, travel, and real estate that are produced by their advertising departments. Better papers label them "advertising" and some use distinct typefaces to further separate them from the news. The problem is that at some papers, journalists are required to produce these "advertorials," taking away time they could use to practice real journalism.

Advertising pressure is probably a greater problem in television newsrooms than at most newspapers. More than half of television news directors in one survey bemoaned the fact that advertisers have too much say in the news they present.[61] A news director in Detroit said the wall between news and business has completely disappeared at most local stations. "The business of television is not independent from the newsroom. It is absolutely a part of the newsroom," he said.[62] Surveys have found that viewers sense that the news content is not always controlled by journalistic instincts. A poll by the Radio–Television News Directors Association found that 80 percent of viewers thought advertisers had "undue influence" over news content.[63]

While editorial employees at many magazines fight to maintain a firm separation between ads and editorial content, the battle is all but lost at many consumer magazines. When advertisers buy space for their ads, they are promised entry into news stories much like the product placements in movies. An article on the value of walking might conclude, "So slip on your Reeboks and start walking." Readers apparently recognize this. Two out of three said they assumed product mentions in magazine stories were paid for by advertisers.

Equally obvious to readers is the practice at some publications of packaging stories with advertising. If a hospital buys lots of ads for its new heart center, the magazine might place a story between the ads about an upturn in the number of women having heart attacks. Even the prestigious *New Yorker* has fallen under the lure of advertising. The Target department store chain was the sole advertiser in one edition in 2005. The Target ads were even written in a type style similar to the *New Yorker's* and were not labeled "advertisement."[64]

One study compared recommendations in financial advice in newspapers to that in consumer business magazines like *Smart Money* and *Money*. Researchers reported that stories in the magazines were more likely to promote investments sold by advertisers. Unfortunately for trusting readers, those investments were less likely to pay off than the ones recommended by the newspapers or by *Consumer Reports,* a magazine that does not accept advertising.[65]

Advertising pressure has also found its way into Internet news sites and blogs. In an amazing irony, newspapers that have wrestled over whether to allow small ads on the front pages of news sections in their printed editions have few qualms about allowing all kinds of animated ads on the home page of their Web sites. Some news sites allow "sponsored content," meaning the advertiser has paid to have stories placed there.

Many Web sites and blogs try to help shoppers make purchasing decisions. They often allow readers to share their experiences with certain brands. Advertisers have found a clever way to get access even to blogs that pride themselves on providing unadulterated news and product reviews. One advertising firm pays $5 to freelance writers for each posting they make praising the products of the firm's clients.

Can Quality Journalism Make Money?

As might be expected, most journalists believe the answer to that question is obvious. In the long run, they believe, quality will pay off with higher circulations and ratings, more advertising, and growing profits. Much of the academic research says they're right.

One study found that when newspapers spent money on larger staffs, more and better local news, and in-depth coverage, their circulation figures increased.[66] Professor Philip Meyer, a former newspaper executive, believes he can explain why. In his book *The Vanishing Newspaper* and in several magazine articles, he argued that what the news media have to sell is their social influence and credibility. A quality product attracts readers. Having more readers makes the product more appealing to advertisers, who are willing to pay for the added value of having their ads surrounded by respected journalism.[67]

Some publishers have come to the same conclusion. Donald Graham, chairman and CEO of the Washington Post Co., told a group of stock analysts that he believed quality journalism "is going to pay in the long run." David Laventhol, another newspaper executive, argued that cutting the quality and size of the news product only gives readers more reasons not to buy a newspaper.

Perhaps the most surprising paper to benefit from an infusion of quality is *USA Today*. When the paper began, it was a thin publication that emphasized flashy design and quick-read stories with little depth or flair. Its own editor later joked that *USA Today* was "the newspaper that brought new depth to the meaning of the word shallow." For its first 10 years, it lost money for Gannett. In the 1990s, the paper posted its first profits and now is a moneymaker. Gannett executives think they know why things changed. "It has been the quality of journalism," said Tom Curley, *USA Today*'s publisher. "When the journalism improved, the advertising cascaded. It has been the improvement of the product that has brought in advertising." The paper hired more journalists and expected them to produce stories with depth, original reporting and enterprise.[68] The paper's front page is no longer dominated by celebrity news and lifestyle pieces. Its mix of hard and soft news is now about the same as the mix on the front page of *The New York Times*.

The circulation of the *Daily Herald* in suburban Chicago has grown faster than either of its more famous competitors, the *Chicago Tribune* and the *Chicago Sun-Times*. It is owned by Paddock Publications, a privately held family business. "There's a commitment to putting out a quality product, being of service to the community, making continual reinvestment in the product, and taking the long view of business," Dan Baumann, a retired publisher, said. The paper has twice as many journalists in its newsroom as the industry average for a paper its size and about 60 more editorial employees than the larger *Sun-Times*. Because of this blending of editorial excellence and business success, *Editor & Publisher* magazine named Doug Ray, the chain's current CEO, "Publisher of the year" in 2006.[69]

Quality news also seems to pay off for television stations. For several years a group called the Project for Excellence in Journalism, affiliated with the Columbia University Graduate School of Journalism, has studied local television news. After judging more than 30,000 news stories and analyzing more than 1,200 hours of local news, researchers determined that improving the quality of the journalism at the stations was "the most likely path to commercial success." Newscasts with quality journalism tended to get higher ratings and to draw the key the 18- to 54-year-old audience. "Quality seems to help across the board. While many factors influence viewership... quality journalism is not just incidental, it's actually good business." Newscasts were judged by the range of topics, number of enterprise stories, number of sources in the stories, number of viewpoints presented, and local relevance of the stories.

The organization provided a list of suggestions that it says would improve both the quality and ratings of local television stations. With a few alterations, the list could apply to all news organizations:

- *Do more enterprise reporting.* Original investigations and other locally sourced stories were shown to draw viewers and to hold them during the newscasts.
- *Cover more of the community.* Important local stories and national stories that are localized were found to draw and keep more viewers

than more sensational, "water cooler" stories obtained from national news agencies.

- *Air more long stories.* Although fast pacing is assumed to attract viewers, the research found that higher-rated stations were more likely to air longer stories. Viewers want stories they can sink their teeth into.
- *Source stories better.* Higher-rated stations were more likely to broadcast stories "with multiple sources and to feature sources with higher levels of expertise."
- *Hire more reporters and give them more time.* Stations with higher ratings put more of their budget toward staffing and less toward equipment. Reporters were expected to do fewer stories a day.

CNN's Christiane Amanpour, speaking at the 2000 Murrow Awards Ceremony, powerfully voiced the concerns of many journalists:

> The powers that be, the moneymen, have decided over the last several years to eviscerate us. It actually costs a bit of money to produce good journalism, to travel, to investigate, to put on compelling viewing.
>
> But God forbid they should spend money on quality… no, let's just cheapskate our way into the most demeaning, irrelevant, super-hyped sensationalism we can find. And then we wonder why people are tuning out in droves. It's not just the new competition, it's the drivel we spew into their living rooms… I believe that good journalism, good television, can make the world a better place. And yes, I believe good journalism is good business.[70]

Notes

1. David Rudenstine, *The Day the Presses Stopped: A History of the Pentagon Papers*, Berkeley, CA: University of California Press, 1996, p. 134. Details of the decision process at the *Post* are taken from this book.
2. "Wallace: Some investigative journalism is caricature," *WCCO Channel 4000 News*, May 17, 1996; a transcript of an interview between Wallace and Don Shelby.
3. Among the sources for the discussion of CBS were Lawrence K. Grossman, "Lessons of the *60 Minutes* cave-in," *Columbia Journalism Review*, January/February 1996, p. 39–51; Tom Wolzien, "The consequences of media empires in the United States," *Media Studies Journal*, Spring/Summer 1996; "With friends like these," *Mother Jones*, March 1996; "Up in smoke," *Frontline* documentary (lengthier versions of the interviews with Ben Bagdikian, James C. Goodale, and Lawrence Grossman were carried on PBS's Web site); and transcripts of *60 Minutes*, February 4, 1996.

4. Frank A. Blethen, "Only in variety is there freedom," presentation to a symposium at the University of Illinois at Urbana-Champaign, September 8, 2002.

5. Christopher H. Sterling and Timothy R. Haight, *The Mass Media: Aspen Institute to Communication Industry Trends,* New York: Praeger, 1978, p. 83.

6. Interview by Goodwin, June 4, 1981.

7. John L. Hulteng, *The Messenger's Motives: Ethical Problems of the News Media,* Englewood Cliffs, NJ: Prentice-Hall, 1976, pp. 214–220.

8. Richard Norton Smith, *The Colonel: The Life and Legend of Robert R. McCormick,* Boston: Houghton Miffin, 1997.

9. Alex Ben Block, "Communications media," *Forbes,* January 12, 1987, p. 99.

10. Paul Tash, in speech to Inland Press Association, September 12, 2002. Text of speech is available at www.poynter.org.

11. These figures are based roughly on Gannett stock prices. They take into account a 2-for-1 stock split but not any reinvestment of dividends.

12. Leonard Downie Jr. and Robert G. Kaiser, *The News About the News: American Journalism in Peril,* New York: Knopf, 2002.

13. Interview by Goodwin, October 15, 1981.

14. Kay Lazar, "Provincial profits," *News Inc.,* March 1990, p. 25.

15. Anne Lallande, "Alive and kicking," *Presstime,* p. 35.

16. Interview by Goodwin, October 21, 1981.

17. Quoted in Lazar, *op. cit.,* p. 23.

18. Thomson maintained ownership of its flagship paper in Canada, *The Globe and Mail.*

19. Stephen Lacy, "Newspapers confront a barrage of problems," *Nieman Reports,* Fall 2001.

20. Research indicates that young adults are less likely than older Americans to check Internet news sites or to read newspapers.

21. Michael Oneal, "A tidal shift for newspapers," *Chicago Tribune,* November 2, 2006.

22. *Fortune*; Felicity Barringer, "At Knight Ridder, good journalism vs. the bottom line," *The New York Times,* May 29, 2001; and Jim Naughton, "The Philadelphia Inquirer: Cuts jeopardize quality," *Nieman Reports,* Fall 2001. Also see David Shaw, "Papers' cuts put readership at risk," *Los Angeles Times,* July 3, 2001.

23. The decline of Knight Ridder was widely reported. Much of the information here came from Katharine Q. Seelye, "What-ifs of a media eclipse," *The New York Times,* August 27, 2006.

24. Denise Grollmus, "Beacon massacre," *New Times,* August 30, 2006, and Gloria Irwin, "Beacon to cut its news staffing," *Akron Beacon Journal,* August 23, 2006.

25. Phil Rosenthal, "On the future, dealmaking and bad press," *Chicago Tribune*, April 4, 2007.
26. "NBC U: More with less," *Broadcasting & Cable*, October 23, 2006.
27. For more about the St. Petersburg ownership arrangement, see Louis Hau, "Why newsrooms pray to St. Petersburg," *Forbes*, December 4, 2006.
28. Joe Mathewson, "Newspaper saved! Newspaper saved! Read all about it!" *Editor & Publisher*, December 8, 2005.
29. The price of licenses at www.tvlicensing.co.uk in 2007 is £135.50 a year for color and £44.50 for black and white. The fine is £1,000 plus court costs.
30. Joe Strupp, "New 'local' ownership raises new issues in newsrooms," *Editor & Publisher*, November 22, 2006.
31. "Giving newspapers breathing room," editorial, *Christian Science Monitor*, November 14, 2006.
32. Brooks Barnes, "Local stations struggle to adapt as Web grabs viewers," *The Wall Street Journal*, June 12, 2006.
33. John M. Higgins, "Big draw: Evening news can make money despite audience declines," *Broadcasting & Cable*, August 15, 2005; George Winslow, "News network's top story: Facing the future," *Multichannel News*, June 12, 2006; and Rachel Smolkin, "Hold that obit," *American Journalism Review*, August/September 2006.
34. Rick Kushman, "As Couric goes, so will all TV newscasts," *Sacramento Bee*, September 4, 2006.
35. Interview by Smith.
36. Roland Wolseley, *The Black Press, U.S.A.*, Ames: Iowa State University Press, 1990, pp. 68–69.
37. Ervin Dyer, "Porters' 'underground railroad' carried *Pittsburgh Courier* into the South," *Pittsburgh Post-Gazette*, February 24, 2002.
38. Anthony Violanti, "Black media prides itself on community service," *The Buffalo News*, February 22, 2002.
39. Discussions of the two papers can be found in Ashley Fantz, "The *Broward Times* delivers unconventional, often shrill journalism to an unsuspecting town," *New Times*, February 14, 2002, and Roger Williams, "Keith Clayborne in black and white," *New Times*, November 9, 2002. Also see Tammy Webber, "Investigative magazine probes race, poverty issues in Chicago," Associated Press report, February 15, 2002.
40. Eugene Kane, "BET's skimpy coverage no match for Jet magazine," *Milwaukee Journal Sentinel*, December 2, 2001.
41. Louis Aguilar, "Outlets for ethnic voices on rise," *The Denver Post*, March 31, 2002, p. K1.
42. Laurien Alexandre and Henrik Rehbinder, "Separate but equal" in *On The Road to Irrelevance*, Project for Excellence in Journalism, www.journalism.org, 2002.

43. Deborah Potter, "Body count," *American Journalism Review*, July/August 2002.
44. Comments made during a panel discussion on ethics at the Central Florida Press Club, April 10, 1997.
45. Lawrie Mifflin, "Crime falls, but not on TV," *The New York Times*, June 6, 1997.
46. Robert Rutherford Smith, "Mystical elements in television news," *Journal of Communication*, Fall 1979, pp. 75–82.
47. "The message machine: How the government makes news; Under Bush, a new age of prepackaged news," *The New York Times*, March 13, 2005.
48. "Salary, benefits dropping for J-grads," *Quill*, October/November 2002; Maria Mallory White, "Grads facing a decline in hiring," *The Atlanta Journal-Constitution*, September 8, 2002; and "Little increase in college graduates' starting salaries according to new ERI college graduate compensation study," College Press Wire, www.cpwire.com, November 13, 2002.
49. Tim Porter, "Vacancies in Vacaville," *American Journalism Review*, March 2003.
50. Heidi Evans, "Working for peanuts," *Quill*, April 1991, pp. 11–13.
51. Steve Nash, "With an efficiency, used car, peanut butter and byline, what more could one want," *Presstime*, April 1985.
52. Wages are taken from 2006 salary list on The Newspaper Guild Web page, www.newsguild.org.
53. RTNDA/Ball State University Radio and Television Salary Survey data is available at http://www.rtnda.org. Median salaries shown are from the 2006 survey. Also see Vernon Stone, "Paychecks and market baskets: Broadcast news salaries and inflation in the 1990s," St Louis: University of Missouri, 1997. Stone's research is posted on the University of Missouri School of Journalism's Web site.
54. Dow C. Smith, "Slowing the revolving door," *Communicator*, December 1996, p. 22.
55. Richard Siklos, "Lord Black's man preferred the ledger to the limelight," *The New York Times*, August 22, 2005.
56. Ann Marie Kerwin, "Advertiser pressure on newspapers is common: Survey," *Editor and Publisher*, January 16, 1993, pp. 28–29, 39.
57. Erica Iacono, "Advertisers' efforts to screen editorial tone grab media attention," *PR Week*, May 30, 2005.
58. Elizabeth Lesly, "Realtors and builders demand happy news and often get it," *Washington Journalism Review*, November 1991, p. 21.
59. *Ibid.*, p. 28.
60. "Darts and laurels," *Columbia Journalism Review*, July/August 1990, p. 14.
61. Survey by Bob Papper of Ball State University for Radio Television News Directors Foundation, posted on www.rtnda.org, 2003.

62. Sharyn Vane, "Taking care of business," *American Journalism Review*, March 2002 and John Lansing, "The pressure for ratings is hard to underestimate," remarks prepared for the "Journalism Values in an Era of Change" seminar, Poynter Institute for Media Studies, February 14–16, 1996.

63. Al Tompkins, "Balancing business pressure and journalism values," Poynter Online, April 9, 2002, www.poynter.org.

64 Lewis Lazare, "Target, New Yorker cross line," *Chicago Sun-Times*, August 19, 2005.

65. Jonathan Reuter and Eric Zitzewitz, "Do ads influence editors? Advertising and bias in the financial media," *Quarterly Journal of Economics*, February 2006.

66. Sooyoung Cho, Esther Thorson, and Stephen Lacy, "Increased circulation follows investments in newsroom," *Newspaper Research Journal*, Fall 2004.

67. Philip Meyer, *The Vanishing Newspaper: Saving Journalism in the Information Age*, St Louis: University of Missouri Press, 2004.

68. James McCartney, "*USA Today* grows up," *Columbia Journalism Review*, September 1997, pp. 18–25.

69. See Mark Fitzgerald, "Newspaper Publisher of the Year: The Daily Herald's Doug Ray," *Editor & Publisher*, April 3, 2006; Gregory Meyer, "E&P names Daily Herald's CEO 'publisher of the year,'" *Crain's*, March 27, 2006; Mark Fitzgerald, "Why one newspaper did not buy in to buyouts," *Editor & Publisher*, December 26, 2005; Mark Fitzgerald, "Some publishers believe in big newsrooms," *Editor & Publisher*, February 6, 2003.

70. Christiane Amanpour, speech to the 2000 Murrow Awards Ceremony. Transcript available at www.rtnda.org/news/2000/asera.shtml.

Discussion of Cases

Chapter 3: Truth and Objectivity

Truth case 2: Nobody's perfect

A weekly paper in Milwaukee uncovered the fact that the local daily paper was engaged in practices much like this. The weekly did criminal background checks and discover arrest records for the handyman, and the friendly guy was known as the "wheelchair pervert" to police. According to *Columbia Journalism Review*, editors at the weekly figured it was sloppy reporting and called the reporter to get her side of the story. Instead, the reporter and her editor defended the columns on the grounds that they were to arouse compassion. *CJR* was not convinced and awarded the newspaper a "dart" in its "Darts and laurels" column.[1]

Chapter 8: The Government Watch

Government Watch case 1: Sons die of drugs

In dealing with a case much like this, a newspaper decided enough was enough. It carried a lengthy story about the deaths, including interviews with neighbors and teachers and quoting public records. After describing the deaths, the story included this sentence: "A little more than a year after the brothers' deaths, police and prosecutors have taken no legal action. They say they're still conducting a criminal investigation. An assistant state attorney would say only that the case is complicated." About six weeks after the story appeared, the mother was charged in the children's deaths. Before trial, she pleaded no contest to child abuse, a felony.

Chapter 9: The Shady World of Unnamed Sources

Secret Sources case 1: Senator as rapist

When confronted with this situation, Michael Fancher, editor of *The Seattle Times,* decided to use the story about Sen. Brock Adams and to print a front-page message explaining his reasons for violating the paper's policy against printing anonymous charges. He said he decided to print the story while the campaign was under way because he believed the voters had a right to hear the allegations and because the story's development had reached "critical mass," meaning the paper had enough information from enough people to believe the story was true. "The bottom line is that we thought the basic choice we had was to withhold an important story we believed to be true or to tell the story without named sources, and it was a reluctant choice," the editor's note said.[2]

Once the story appeared, the paper's ombudsman said she received more than 200 phone calls, most of them against the paper's conduct.

Journalists are worried about the use of anonymous sources. Some would not have used the Adams story, even with the precautions the *Times* took. But a great many editors agreed with Fancher's decision. Andrew Barnes, then editor of *St. Petersburg Times,* said his editors argued about whether they would use the story if it had happened in Florida. "I came away thinking I would twitch a lot and then do it," he said.[3]

Secret Sources case 2: Musical inmates

A southwestern paper exposed the shuffling of prisoners around the county jail in stories that used anonymous sources. The guards also described "sardining," the practice of forcing prisoners into cells that were already full and giving them no mattresses. Jail officials denied that any inmates had been concealed from regulators or were forced to sleep on the concrete floor with no mattresses.

Chapter 10: Deception

Deceptions case 1: Nuclear terrorists on campus

ABC's *PrimeTime Live* did an investigation much like this in 2005. The program sent teams of graduate students to facilities on 25 college campuses including Ohio State, Kansas State, University of Florida, and Penn State. Many of these campus reactors are used in both science classes and nuclear medicine programs.

As ABC suspected, the students had no trouble getting into the facilities. They found unlocked doors, saw unmanned security booths, and, in some cases, were given guided tours that gave them access to control rooms and reactor pools.

Once the story was aired, the universities involved were not impressed with the discoveries. Some noted that even "dirty bombs" could not be made using the materials from their labs and, even if they could, labs had very small amounts of radioactive material. Florida said its reactor core is placed under massive shielding barriers, including about 50 tons of concrete. It's unlikely a bomb in a backpack would do much damage, it said.

Other universities said that reactors were guarded by elaborate security systems that were necessarily hidden. As for being able to tour the facilities, university spokespeople told *USA Today* that "as educational facilities, it's their job to spread the word about how nuclear energy is being used." One official said the network reporting that students were able to get close to the university reactor was no more surprising than reporting that students could get into a McDonald's. (A university spokesman dismissed a report of a sleeping guard, saying he was actually a parking lot attendant.)

Deceptions case 2: Undercover dead police officer

The reporter to whom this happened said it was tempting to listen to her comments, but ultimately he decided that he had worked too hard to get sources on the police beat to lose them for this dirty trick.

Chapter 11: Compassion, Privacy, and Ordinary Citizens

Privacy case 1: Intimate blogs

A North Carolina paper was confronted with many of these questions. The paper used information from all four blogs, including nearly all of the details in the case study.

The paper's public editor wrote, "Editors defended the use of the family's Web site information as valuable detail that helped readers better understand the tangled relationships of this strange family." The paper rejected the idea that it was violating anyone's privacy. One editor said, "We discussed it and concluded that people who are blogging don't have an expectation of privacy, because it's on the Internet. Anybody can find it." A journalism professor at the University of North Carolina agreed on both counts.

Readers were more critical. Many said the information in the stories from the blogs served no purpose and was purely sensationalism. Their most severe criticism was directed at taking information from the teens' blogs. They pointed out that the teens were not involved in the crime. They said blogs were the 21st century-equivalent of the private diaries that have long been part of growing up. Their privacy was invaded and little was learned. It's not big news that some teenage girls may not like their stepmoms or that teen bands play songs with socially incorrect lyrics.

The paper's public editor generally agreed with the paper's handling of the blogs. "But I have to wonder, as one who has parented two daughters through teenagehood, whether young people give due consideration to the consequences or... the permanence of their online soul-baring," he wrote. "It's a paradox. They are keeping diaries of their innermost feelings, but they're posting them for all to see."

Privacy case 2: Naming the professor

A college professor wrote in a national journalism magazine about this experience. The local paper ran a 13-paragraph story identifying both parents and listing their occupations. The paper reported that the man did not want to comment. The professor said that he was "dismayed to read my name and place of work" and "really stunned to read my wife's name and occupation." He said he planned to place more emphasis on compassion in his journalism classes. He acknowledged that the fact he was an op-ed writer made using his name more justifiable.

Privacy case 3: Riding the Raptor

While reporters and editors sympathized with his injuries, the young man has decided to sue a major local business for millions of dollars. The public should know about the functioning of its civil courts. This is probably a case where many in the public would apply a standard of compassion for the youth. For editors in this case, it was not a hard call. The public needs to know about the functioning of a civil suit – and the name of the person filing a suit is an important element.

Privacy case 4: Should these juveniles be named?

The media in the city where this happened were divided. One television station ran the story and used the boys' names. They had been charged as adults, so the names were public record. Another station used the story but did not name the boys. And the third television station decided not to use the story, as did the local paper.

Privacy case 5: Do you out this teen?

This case study is based on events outside Minneapolis. Although both major dailies and the television stations covered the disappearance, they all passed on the initial story of the missing neighbor and did not mention it in the stories about the father's press conference. The police report and the confession changed the story. One television station decided the relationship between the disappearance and the confession was too vague to justify naming the boy, who was in reality a rape victim. However, most of the Minneapolis media reported the confession. The Minneapolis *Star Tribune* included the detail from the confession about tying the boy's legs. As for the boy's visit to a gay-counseling center, the papers were debating it when they received reports that the car had been found. The *Star Tribune* included the detail in its stories. *The St. Paul Pioneer Press* used the picture.

Editors and news directors agreed these were "gut-wrenching" decisions, and they sought input from throughout the newsroom. They were in no hurry to expose the relationship between the boy and the man. Yet, they did not want people in the community to assume that some fiend was randomly kidnapping children. "Without that information [about the earlier molestation and the visit to the counseling center], readers were left with only half a picture," one editor said. "It is our job to enlighten readers, not to withhold information." Some thought the stories might make the community aware of the problems of gay teens.

Many people in Minneapolis were not happy with the coverage. Most wondered why newspapers and television stations had reported so many details of the teen's life and of the murder-suicide. They thought it was insensitive and sensational. Some staff members at the papers were also critical. They believed that the paper could have delayed some of the details and perhaps later examined how area high schools counsel youths.

Privacy case 6: Suicide downtown

Two papers were called on to make that decision. Both papers had policies that they did not cover suicides involving people who aren't public figures. Exceptions are made for murder-suicides or suicides in very prominent places. Each paper decided this attempted suicide was another exception. The man's exploits had caused traffic to be tied up in the downtown area. A crowd was present. Residents were not allowed to enter the building.

Yet, neither paper was completely happy with its decision. The larger paper put an eight-paragraph story in the zoned edition. It described the man's behavior and included the detail about the balloons, but did not name him. The smaller paper ran a 16-paragraph story and used the man's name. The story had an anecdotal lead: "Standing at roof's edge of the 16-story building in DeLand, [the man] bent his knees, looked down below at the concrete – and eventually thought otherwise. The sky above the College Arms Towers retirement apartment on North Amelia Avenue looked blue and calm, but management said 'a perfect storm' of factors Friday allowed a nonresident man on the roof of the city's tallest building…" The reporter interviewed residents who were angered at being kept out of their homes, and a minister who told of the suicide of a relative.

Chapter 12: Privacy for Political Leaders

Privacy of Public People case 1: The wayward president

The local newspaper decided that the university president was deceiving his superiors by denying the initial reports and engaging in risky behavior. It ran the stories about his activities but passed on the story about the "kinky behavior" for two reasons: The paper thought it was unseemly and by the time reporters had confirmed the stories, the president had resigned.

Privacy of Public People case 2: Politicians' pasts

The newspaper included both of them. Editors contended that being a prosecutor was a "position of significant public responsibility." The story was widely covered at the time, and they figured readers might recall the incident and wonder if it was the same person and, if so, why the omission. Editors defended running the man's previous record because the appointment "speaks to the stewardship of the elected officials who appointed him to a position that may weigh sensitive issues that go to the heart of the community's values."

Privacy of Public People case 3: School board president runs personal ad

The local newspaper decided to use the story. "Readers responded with a flurry of phone calls and e-mails. Some questioned whether legal, consenting, behavior between adults warranted the newspaper's attention. Others called for Johnson's immediate resignation," the paper's follow-up story reported. A ministerial association expressed its concerns.

The man decided to resign from the highly public position of school board president, but that he would stay on the board. The board accepted his decision, and those at the meeting gave him a sweeping standing ovation at the last school board meeting, which many took to be a show both of support for his sexual orientation and of anger that it had become an issue, according to a reporter at the meeting.

About two months later, when the man was going to a charter school meeting in California, he was stopped by airport security. Three marijuana joints were found in his luggage. He was not arrested, but when news of the event became public, he resigned from the school board.

Privacy of Public People case 4: A racist remark

The newspaper involved had to deal only with the second part: A city council member recounted the conversation at a press conference. After considerable debate over whether such an uncorroborated remark should even appear in the paper, editors decided to put the story in the state-local section (not on the paper's front page) and to emphasize the "he said–she said" aspect of the story. The same day, the paper ran an editorial saying that it was impossible to know if the council member's account was true. If the account were true, the editorial said, the man does not deserve to be mayor. But, if the account is a lie, then the other candidate does not deserve to be mayor for condoning the lie, and the council member should be forced to resign.

The candidate received endorsements from black friends and politicians and promised to hire a black city attorney. However, instead of the close race some expected, he lost in a landslide.

Chapter 14: Journalists and Their Communities

Community cases 1 and 2: Transplant group needs help and Help unite a family

One paper faced both decisions – although not in the same week.

The blood-marrow story was clearly a tough call. The paper didn't want to overlook the man's criminal problems. Yet, the story was about the heroics of people who undergo surgery to help others. In the end, the editors made a surprising decision. They decided to kill the story and wait for a similar one that did not present so many problems.

The plight of the truck driver had been widely reported, and the court ruling against him had been front-page news in some local papers. Editors decided to go ahead with the feature about the family. They included a reference to the welfare-fraud charges deep in the story. The abuse charges were from several years previously and were not mentioned. The divorce was a rumor, and no court action had been taken, so it was omitted.

Chapter 15: Freebies and Financial Concerns

Conflict of Interest case 2: Burritos galore

At a midsize Midwestern paper the reporter raised this question with the editor. The code of ethics was vague on the topic, but they agreed she could not accept the prize. The editor decided it was time to update the code – and to make sure everyone was better informed about the rules.

Notes

1. "Darts and laurels," *Columbia Journalism Review*, March/April 2006.
2. The case was widely reported. Details here were taken from Alex S. Jones, "Weighing the thorny issue of anonymous sources," *The New York Times*, March 3, 1992, p. A-14, and Frank Green, "Adams case spurs debate on use of unnamed sources," *The San Diego Union-Tribune*, March 4, 1992, p. A-2. Also see Cheryl Reid, "Anonymous sources bring down a Senator," *Washington Journalism Review*, April 1992, p. 10.
3. Quoted by Alex S. Jones, "Anonymity: A tool used and abused," *The New York Times*, June 25, 1991, p. A-20.

Index